To Her Credit

STUDIES IN EARLY AMERICAN ECONOMY AND SOCIETY
FROM THE LIBRARY COMPANY OF PHILADELPHIA
Cathy Matson, *Series Editor*

To Her Credit

*Women, Finance, and the Law in Eighteenth-Century
New England Cities*

SARA T. DAMIANO

Johns Hopkins University Press
Baltimore

This book has been brought to publication with the generous assistance of Darlene Bookoff.

Johns Hopkins University Press
2715 North Charles Street
Baltimore, Maryland 21218-4363
www.press.jhu.edu

Library of Congress Cataloging-in-Publication Data

Names: Damiano, Sara T., 1986– author.
Title: To her credit : women, finance, and the law in eighteenth-century New England cities / Sara T. Damiano.
Description: Baltimore : Johns Hopkins University Press, 2021. | Series: Studies in early American economy and society from the Library Company of Philadelphia | Includes bibliographical references and index.
Identifiers: LCCN 2020025877 | ISBN 9781421440552 (hardcover) | ISBN 9781421440569 (ebook)
Subjects: LCSH: Women—New England—Economic conditions—History—18th century. | Credit—New England—History—18th century. | Capitalism—New England—History—18th century. | Finance, Personal—New England—History—18th century. | Women—Employment—New England—History—18th century.
Classification: LCC HQ1438.N35 D36 2021 | DDC 330.90082/097409033—dc23
LC record available at https://lccn.loc.gov/2020025877

A catalog record for this book is available from the British Library.

Special discounts are available for bulk purchases of this book. For more information, please contact Special Sales at specialsales@jh.edu.

Johns Hopkins University Press uses environmentally friendly book materials, including recycled text paper that is composed of at least 30 percent post-consumer waste, whenever possible.

CONTENTS

The series Studies in Early American Economy and Society, a collaborative effort between Johns Hopkins University Press and the Library Company of Philadelphia's Program in Early American Economy and Society (PEAES), is honored to publish Sara Damiano's study, *To Her Credit: Women, Finance, and the Law in Eighteenth-Century New England Cities*. Based on a deep reading of over three thousand cases of creditors' suits to recover debts in Suffolk County, Massachusetts, and Newport County, Rhode Island, during the second half of the 1700s, Damiano has discovered stunning evidence of what she calls the "financial labor" of women who ubiquitously participated in shaping New England's economy. This occurred at a time and in a place that scholars typically characterize as divided between the household-centered, consumption-oriented, private lives of women and the public, production-directed, networked lives of men. In contrast, Damiano insists that women were deeply involved in the record keeping, written communications, daily negotiations, and courtroom proceedings that covered a wide scope of economic activities.

By the mid-eighteenth century, as households increasingly sought ways to increase incomes in order to participate in the consumer revolution afoot, women, argues Damiano, were active agents in the necessary activities of giving credit and settling debts, borrowing and lending (among men and women), deciding what to purchase and from whom, and making goods to sell over longer distances. While most transactions involving women continued to be face-to-face throughout the eighteenth century, and while their formal literacy remained less than that of men, women nevertheless employed the skills needed to bargain, keep their household and shop accounts, and interpret forms of written credit. Such records, as well as these women's in-person appearances and testimony, became a part of the debt litigation in county courts. In addition to the everyday personal exchanges that took place on village and urban streets, women's financial labor became a vital part of court proceedings in New England. While men were the ones who brought to court the overwhelming number of suits to recover debts, the extensive paperwork generated by these suits reveals that women played a central role in extending and receiving credit, determining what kinds of economic decisions were made in households, and participating in the continuous activities of market engagements. Women purchased goods in shops, sent female servants or went themselves to collect debts, made financial agreements with male producers and service providers, petitioned town councils and colonial legislatures regarding fiscal matters, and engaged in many other public economic transactions that are often seen by modern scholars as pertaining solely to the realms of men alone.

Although it is clear from the laws and pamphlet literature of the late eighteenth century that white New England society sought to clearly delineate the separation of men's and women's economic identities and bolster the restrictions on married women under the laws of coverture, this study shows that, to a surprising degree, widows and single women were borrowers and lenders, litigants, witnesses, and market participants. In addition, while kinship continued to play a central role in deciding how investments and businesses were structured, women—whether married or single—were sometimes equally as financially responsible as men for the well-being of family members and the transfer of wealth to relatives. Widows and single women ran businesses as laundresses, retailers, tavern keepers, and owners of boardinghouses, all of which required ongoing decisions about using credit. When contests over debts arose, they became actors in courtroom litigation. When they became clients, women directed their attorneys and submitted bonds, promissory notes, account books, and receipts that often were written in their own hand. When they were called as witnesses, their testimony about economic agreements carried weight.

In all, Damiano gives us an array of compelling stories about women participating in an economic environment steeped in credit and debt that were drawn from court and probate records, as well as the era's private correspondence and newspapers. We have not known much about such instances until recently.

Cathy Matson, Series Editor
Richards Professor of American History Emerita, University of Delaware
Director, Program in Early American Economy and Society,
Library Company of Philadelphia

This study is born from an insistence that, when we break down an act into its component practices, the essential contributions of previously unseen individuals come into view. That insight is even more true with the publication of my book, which would not have been possible without the generous help of numerous individuals and institutions throughout my years of research and writing. Drafting these acknowledgments amid the COVID-19 pandemic, I am especially appreciative of the support of mentors, colleagues, friends, and family, and of the power of that support to transcend physical distance. It is a privilege to express my gratitude here.

I made my first foray into the records of the Newport County Courts as an undergraduate at Brown University. There, Seth Rockman introduced me to early American social history, and Mike Vorenberg patiently and attentively advised my senior thesis. I was fortunate to continue my studies at Johns Hopkins University, where, under the expert mentorship of Toby Ditz and Philip Morgan, I completed the dissertation from which this book was developed. Toby's scholarship on gender and commerce remains a model for my own, and I am grateful for her discerning editorial eye and steady confidence in my abilities. I am equally grateful for Phil's probing questions and intellectual curiosity. Other Johns Hopkins faculty, especially Mary Fissell, François Furstenberg, John Marshall, Mary Ryan, and Judith Walkowitz, expanded my thinking and offered valuable insights from a range of perspectives.

Cathy Matson has been a key supporter of this project since its early stages, when I first held a short-term fellowship in the Program in Early American Economy and Society (PEAES) at the Library Company of Philadelphia. I have benefited greatly from her deep knowledge, incisive critiques, and ongoing encouragement. Perceptive feedback from the anonymous reader for Johns Hopkins University Press guided my revisions, and Laura Davulis and Esther Rodriguez efficiently steered my manuscript through the publication process. I am also grateful to graphic artist Kate Blackmer for her extraordinary attention to detail as she prepared my book's maps, and to Kathleen Capels and Melissa Johnson for their care in copyediting and indexing the manuscript.

Community is vital amid the often-solitary work of research and writing. At Johns Hopkins, the participants in the Atlantic History Workshop and the Gender History Workshop pushed me to ask and answer tough questions. My scholarship has been sustained by the camaraderie of friends and colleagues whom I first met in graduate school: Joseph Adelman, Sarah Adelman, Zara Anishanslin, James Ashton, William Brown, Claire Cage, Jessica Clark, Robert Gamble, Stephanie Gamble, Norah Gharala, Claire Gherini, Jonathan Gienapp, Katie Hemphill, Amanda Herbert, Katie Hindmarch-Watson, Cole Jones, Katie Jorgenson-Gray, Ren Pepitone, Katherine Smoak Radburn, Nicholas Radburn, James Roberts, Jessica Roney, David Schley, Joshua Segal, Joshua Specht, Sarah Templier, Christopher Tozzi, Jessica Valdez, Molly Warsh, and Rachel Calvin Whitehead. Joe Adelman, my academic "older sibling," deserves special thanks for fielding so many questions and commenting on multiple drafts.

I joined several other scholarly communities during crucial stages of this writing process. In 2013–2014, my colleagues at the McNeil Center for Early American Studies helped me clarify my arguments and explore connections across academic disciplines. Daniel Richter, director of the McNeil Center, offered a model of scholarly generosity and good humor that continues to define 3355 Woodland Walk. A PEAES postdoctoral fellowship provided much-needed time to reflect on my project, and Lindsay Schakenbach Regele was the ideal office mate and sounding board. During that fellowship, a manuscript workshop sponsored by PEAES and convened by Cathy Matson guided the transition from dissertation to book. Thanks to the participants—Jessica Blake, Holly Brewer, Kathleen Brown, Elizabeth Jones-Minsinger, Cathy Matson, Lindsay Schakenbach Regele, Daniel Richter, and Jessica Roney—for their perceptive readings and for brainstorming this work's title. My time at the Omohundro Institute's Scholars Workshop further clarified this book's direction. I am indebted to my fellow participants—Steffi Dippold, Julie Fisher, John Garcia, Ebony Jones, Alison Madar, and Julia Mansfield—for their insights and solidarity, and to Catherine Kelly, Joshua Piker, Nicholas Popper, Karin Wulf, and Nadine Zimmerli for their mentorship.

I arrived at Texas State University in 2016, and I am grateful to all of my colleagues and students for creating such a stimulating and supportive environment in which to write and teach. Thanks to department chairs Mary Brennan and Angela Murphy for their guidance, and to the participants in the Swinney Faculty Writing Group, coordinated by Shannon Duffy, for their feedback on several chapters. Geneva Gano, Jeffrey Helgeson, Margaret Menninger, Jessica Pliley, José Carlos de la Puente, Caroline Ritter, and Ana Romo provided helpful critiques at crucial moments in the writing process. Special thanks to Ana for her mentorship, and to Carrie for her friendship over countless mugs of bottomless coffee, as well as for reading the entire manuscript prior to peer review. Conversations in my graduate seminars helped clarify my aims for this book, and I thank my students for their insights. Beyond the perimeters of San Marcos, Evan Haefeli, April Hatfield, Robert Olwell, and participants in the Early Americanists in Texas Seminar welcomed me into their fold and commented on several chapters. Conversations with Julie Hardwick have proven to be one of the joys of moving to Texas; my book is far richer, thanks to Julie's insights and deep historiographical knowledge.

This volume also reflects the generosity of the broader scholarly community. I was fortunate to meet Ellen Hartigan-O'Connor and Karin Wulf early on in my graduate studies. Ellen and Karin have both commented on significant portions of my work, and their advice and encouragement have animated my research and revisions. Along the way, many others provided valuable insights and suggestions. While this list undoubtedly contains omissions, I am especially grateful for the collegiality of Mary Bilder, Caylin Carbonell, Jonathan Chu, Deborah Cohen, Laurel Daen, Cornelia Dayton, Carolyn Eastman, Amy Froide, Sally Hadden, Jared Hardesty, C. Dallet Hemphill, Rachel Herrmann, Donald Johnson, Marjoleine Kars, Lindsay Keiter, Sarah Knott, Philippa Koch, Bruce Mann, Simon Middleton, Mary Beth Norton, Mairin Odle, Caitlin Rosenthal, Samantha Seeley, Alexandra Shepard, Jordan Smith, Lindsay Van Tine, and Serena Zabin. I presented drafts of chapters at the McNeil Center for Early American Studies and the Omohundro Institute colloquium. At conferences, Cornelia Dayton, Margaret Hunt, Sarah Knott, Cathy Matson, Alexandra Shepard, and Mary Beth Sievens commented on papers that became portions of this volume. Jessica Roney provided helpful feedback on a chapter as I approached publication. Julie Fisher has proven to be an invaluable interlocutor and editor during our regular long-distance workshops. While Julie has (thus far) read this book only in two-page selections, her passion and insights have shaped virtually every page.

Librarians and archivists provided access to crucial sources and offered helpful advice. Thanks especially to Andrew Smith at the Rhode Island Supreme Court Judicial Records Center, as well as to Elizabeth Bouvier and John Hannigan at the Massachusetts State Archives, for entertaining my countless requests for case files. At the Rhode Island State Archives, Kenneth Carlson and Gwen Stern oriented me in searching among Rhode Island's legislative records. Martha Clark offered similar assistance at the Massachusetts State Archives. James Green and Connie King at the Library Company of Philadelphia, Bert Lippincott at the Newport Historical Society, Kathy Ludwig at the David Library of the American Revolution, and Peter Drummey and Conrad Wright at the Massachusetts Historical Society introduced me to documents and collections that I would not have found otherwise. At Texas State University's Alkek Library, Margaret Vavarek helpfully responded to my queries, and the staffs of the acquisitions department and interlibrary loan office swiftly tracked down materials.

Many institutions provided financial support for the research and writing of this book. Thanks to the American Historical Association, the American Society for Legal History, the David Library of the American Revolution, the History Department and the Research Enhancement Program at Texas State University, Johns Hopkins University, the Massachusetts Historical Society, the McNeil Center for Early American Studies, and the Program in Early American Economy and Society at the Library Company of Philadelphia. Megan Zeller at Johns Hopkins University, Amy Baxter-Bellamy and Barbara Natello at the McNeil Center, and Roberta Ruiz and Madelyn Patlan at Texas State University helped me navigate the bureaucracies at these institutions.

Earlier versions of portions of this work appeared in several journals. Material from chapter 5 appeared in "'To Well and Truly Administer': Female Administrators and Estate Settlement in Newport, Rhode Island, 1730–1776," *New England Quarterly* 86, no. 1 (Mar. 2013): 89–124, reprinted by permission of the *New England Quarterly*. Material from chapter 6 appeared in "Writing Women's History through the Revolution: Family Finances, Letter Writing, and Conceptions of Marriage," *William and Mary Quarterly*, ser. 3, 74, no. 4 (Oct. 2017): 697–728, and in "Agents at Home: Wives, Lawyers, and Financial Competence in Eighteenth-Century New England Port Cities," *Early American Studies* 13, no. 4 (Fall 2015): 808–35. Permissions for their use have been granted by the Omohundro Institute for Early American History and Culture and by Penn Press.

Friends and running partners scattered across the United States helped me maintain a sense of balance amid the enormous undertaking of writing a book. For making me laugh, for listening, for celebrating my good writing days and not caring about my bad ones, I especially thank Allie Brown, Bryn Burkholder, Carly Dillen, Barry Lewis, Kim Machnik, Dustin Meeker, Lillian Pinault, Joshua Reiter, Mandie Samuels, Melissa Tanner, Stacy Ward, Kate Warnell, Kelly West, and Amy Voiland. Marianne Elliott and Lauren Fleshman helped me see the writing process in new ways.

I reserve my deepest gratitude for the Damiano, Tabak, and Miranda families. Love and support from my parents, David Damiano and Barbara Tabak, has made this book, and my every endeavor, possible. Writing about New England happily facilitated many trips home. On long research days, I was buoyed by my parents' companionship and hospitality—and the endless supplies of farm-fresh berries and garden tomatoes during the summer months. I admire the strong moral compass and intellect of my brother, Steven Damiano; I'm looking forward to his questions about this book. My paternal grandmother, Grace Damiano, is our family's best archivist and historian. I am glad that all of those graduate school trips along the I-95 corridor allowed us to spend so much time together. I cherish our conversations and eagerly await sharing this work with her. My late grandparents—Robert Damiano, Morton Tabak, and Clara Tabak—likewise expressed keen interest in my studies. In their own distinctive ways, each would have been overjoyed to see this book come to fruition. I also appreciate Harry, Valerie, and Paul Miranda's warm welcome into their family and their interest in my work.

Although in very different ways than during the eighteenth century, the household still remains a central institution in daily life. I am exceptionally fortunate to share my household with Daniel Miranda, whom I met when this project was in its relative infancy. I wrote in my dissertation's acknowledgments that Dan always provides the right blend of encouragement and distraction, and that remains true to this day. He has made the writing of this book possible through his commitment to an equitable partnership and his countless small, daily acts of kindness. Our conversations and adventures have immeasurably enriched my life, and I can't wait to journey onward together.

To Her Credit

Introduction

A copy of an eighteenth-century handbook, *The American Instructor: or, Young Man's Best Companion*, bears an intriguing inscription. Eight years after the text's publication, an unmarried Quaker woman from Pennsylvania wrote on the inside cover, "Deborah Morris, her book, 1756."[1] Morris was not among the book's intended audience. The volume's author, George Fisher, concerned with the "tradesman" and a "Man's Credit," touted advice for the "young Man" seeking to become "dexterous in Business."[2] While British colonists routinely labeled the holdings of their private libraries, Morris's ownership and marking of this particular book confounds our expectations of eighteenth-century commerce as a masculine realm.[3]

Yet much of *The American Instructor* would have been useful to Morris in her myriad economic roles. Morris was a landlady, retailer, and investor, as well as the guardian and financial supporter of her nieces and nephews.[4] The handbook in which she inscribed her name, depicting a world awash in financial transactions, contained guidance for drafting myriad documents. Morris perhaps consulted the text's sample bonds, promissory notes, or receipts in order to complete her own versions of these documents.[5] As she entered transactions into her numerous daybooks and ledgers, she may have referenced Fisher's guidance on "the Ingenious Art of book-keeping" or recalled his caution against trusting an inexperienced accounting instructor who, "for want of the Practical Part, knows hardly any Thing of the Matter."[6] In apportioning her time, she quite possibly recollected Fisher's instruction to appear industrious: "the most trifling actions" affected one's image and could make a creditor "easy Six Months longer."[7] Although we can only guess at how Deborah Morris used *The American Instructor*, even briefly perusing the volume would have reminded her that written transactions, daily practices, and social reputation were inextricably linked within her economic world.

Philadelphia printers Benjamin Franklin and David Hall produced *The American Instructor*, a revised version of a British handbook, with the stated goal of meeting colonists' unique informational needs.[8] In so doing, they acknowledged the accelerated economic and legal developments that occurred throughout British North America during the final two-thirds of the eighteenth century. From roughly the 1730s onward, the pace of economic exchange quickened. Households increasingly prioritized market-oriented transactions, with the goal of accumulating sufficient income to purchase the period's widening array of consumer goods.[9] In port cities, which were important hubs of overseas trading, commercial sectors became more sophisticated.[10] Written systems of personal credit and debt, or borrowing and lending between individuals, undergirded these economic transformations. Credit offered an alternative to transporting specie over long distances and facilitated exchanges when individuals lacked payment at the time of purchase.[11] Such an increased reliance on written credit, in turn, spurred changes in the law. In the absence of modern financial institutions, like banks, debt litigation in county courts offered one of the few means by which creditors could enforce financial obligations. Rates of debt litigation spiked, and the courts increasingly prioritized procedural adherence, rather than substantive considerations of justice. Lawyering became a well-defined profession, as attorneys built businesses serving this growing cadre of litigants.[12] Moreover, colonists' changed use of credit, debt, and the courts was saturated with social and gendered meaning, because understandings of creditworthiness encompassed both one's character and financial standing.[13]

As encapsulated by the apparent disjunction between Deborah Morris's ownership of *The American Instructor* and the text's stated audience, such sweeping economic and legal transformations forced British Americans to confront crucial questions surrounding gendered financial labor and the social order. To what extent would women be eligible to extend and receive credit? Which members of households and families would undertake the everyday labor required to establish and manage economic relationships? What roles would laypeople, both women and men, play in the increasingly technical proceedings taking place in colonial courtrooms? How would communities and their courts balance considerations of individuals' circumstances, including those of women, against the desire to establish a predictable financial and legal system? And, most significantly, how would women's and men's involvement in everyday practices surrounding credit constitute or complicate gendered social hierarchies?

These issues were, at the core, considerations of political economy. "Political economy" refers to the interrelationship between government and the economy. The term insists that what is economic is fundamentally political, as well as that a major task of government is determining how to intervene in the economy and, by extension, society writ large.[14] Questions surrounding women's place in economic and legal life engaged key arms of the state: county courts and colony law. They also possessed implications for social order and hierarchy. Participants in these debates included not only governing men, such as judges and colony legislators, but also lawyers and laypeople who collectively delineated acceptable practices through their daily dealings, routine debt litigation, and occasional appeals.

This study interrogates the gendered political economy of British America by tracking the practices through which colonists managed relationships of personal credit and debt, a core component of the eighteenth-century financial system. As a work of gender history, the book analyzes the gendered dimensions of credit transactions and debt litigation by locating women as economic and legal actors and comparing their activities with those of men.[15] As a social history of economic life and the law, it simultaneously reconstructs, in granular detail, the often-overlooked actors, spaces, skills, and strategies that facilitated the workings of eighteenth-century financial networks, including the legal proceedings that enforced them.[16] These endeavors are necessarily intertwined. Women, families, and households preserved webs of credit and debt. At the same time, prosaic financial and legal activities shaped not only social relations between and among men and women, but also understandings of masculinity and femininity. This project largely focuses on those free white women who are most visible in county court records, but it also includes lower-class, Native, and black women when possible.[17]

My investigation is grounded in Boston, Massachusetts, and Newport, Rhode Island, during the final two-thirds of the eighteenth century. Puritans founded Boston as a "city upon a hill" in 1630, while religious dissenters cast off from Massachusetts Bay established Newport as a haven of religious toleration in 1639. These settlements grew into New England's two largest ports. They also ranked as the third and fifth most populous cities in British North America. Colonial Boston's population peaked at roughly 17,000, while Newport numbered 9,200 residents by the eve of the Revolution.[18] Questions of political economy, historians suggest, possessed distinctive weight in these New England cities, given their colonies' religiously motivated foundings. Bostonians contested and forged new political economies as the city and its hinterlands became increasingly enmeshed in the Atlantic World, supplying foodstuffs and raw materials to the Caribbean and purchasing imported goods from Britain. Newport underwent a parallel transition, one marked by the emergence of a wealthy merchant class who flouted imperial regulations. Market integration led Boston and Newport residents to increasingly prioritize secular rather than religious values and, through a series of debates, to insist that their governments' obligation was facilitating rather than regulating economic activity.[19]

In this study I argue that, from 1730 to the Revolution, white urban women's financial and legal work was an essential component of New England's political economy. Although studies of women's work typically focus on productive and reproductive labor, managing financial ties required just as much time, skill, and resources.[20] Women's labor, capital, and connections undergirded the positions of Boston and Newport as nodes linking New England's hinterlands to other Atlantic places. While access to credit and debt was most extensive for free white women of middling or elite socioeconomic status, everyday practices and the centrality of households to economic life demanded that married and unmarried women of all ages and social classes participate in commerce and legal proceedings. Acting as borrowers and lenders, litigants, witnesses, and financial agents, women engaged in skilled practices similar to those of men. In so doing, women brought stability to Boston's and Newport's economies in two important regards. First, amid men's frequent absences, arising from seafaring and military service, female labor preserved household and family resources in the face of economic uncertainty. Second, women's skilled use of credit provided an element of predictability in financial relationships, helping to buffer them against volatile markets. Ultimately, everyday practices surrounding credit and debt contributed to the malleability of colonial social hierarchies: indebtedness intensified women's vulnerability, while status as a creditor enabled women to exercise power over men.

This study also finds that, during the mid-eighteenth century and accelerating during the Revolutionary era, legal and cultural changes began to circumscribe women's authority in financial matters. As the courts increasingly privileged predictable debt collection, they enhanced the financial precariousness of widows, as such women's livelihoods often hinged on the same assets claimed by creditors. Massachusetts and Rhode Island each carved out limited exceptions to this favoring of creditors, yet common dispensations affirmed the legitimacy of the masculine legal profession and men's business pursuits. At the same time, elites asserted gendered class identities that likewise marked finance and the law as masculine realms, foreshadowing the more extensive cultural redefinition of practices surrounding credit that would occur during the nineteenth century.

Investigating women's involvement in financial practices reshapes understandings of the development of Atlantic capitalism and the social relations that undergirded it. Recent scholarship has significantly broadened our narratives of the development of commerce and early modern empires. Elite male merchants initially received the bulk of historians' attention, but we are uncovering increasing evidence to suggest that women and men of all classes took part in forging both financial networks and the state.[21] With family and kinship ties structuring businesses and investing practices well into the nineteenth century, women were necessarily key conduits, especially in facilitating the transfer of wealth and the consolidation of alliances through marriage. As investors and lenders themselves, women provided the credit that made systems of deferred payment possible, and their funds contributed to various institutions, including the Virginia Company, the Bank of England, and the US Treasury. Other women helped support family enterprises and, especially in port cities, ran businesses, such as shops and taverns.[22] Despite these findings, historians still struggle to incorporate gendered power and women's contributions into broad narratives of capitalism and economic development.[23] Close attention to everyday practices offers a remedy for these persistent challenges.

Uncovering women's use of credit and debt and their involvement in associated debt litigation underscores that eighteenth-century financial infrastructures were at once heterosocial and profoundly gendered. In Boston and Newport, and throughout the British Atlantic World, marriage conditioned both men's and women's access to credit. Matrimony shaped spouses' legal statuses and facilitated the intergenerational and interfamilial transfer of assets that, in turn, enabled families to extend and receive credit. Through marriage, men lay claim to others' wealth and labor, resources that enhanced their ability to position themselves as seemingly autonomous economic actors. Meanwhile, marriage dictated the terms by which women accessed credit and the visibility of their labor within the historical record. Even though married, single, and widowed women often used credit in similar manners, only unmarried women could independently form contracts and engage in litigation. Men's and women's uses of credit also diverged in other key ways. Boston and Newport men engaged in both local and long-distance transactions, and they appeared in debt litigation as creditors and debtors in roughly equal proportions. In contrast, women's credit networks were predominantly local, and female litigants in debt suits were overwhelmingly creditors rather than debtors. Yet women and men also engaged in shared patterns of activity, because they recognized that specific powers inhered to the roles of creditors, debtors, plaintiffs, defendants, and witnesses. Such acceptance of women's financial labor buttressed households and businesses against the ongoing shocks of economic turmoil and men's mobility.

These two fundamental features of eighteenth-century credit networks—their gendered contours and the common repertoires of behavior that were accepted for all participants—sat in productive tension with one another, helping to give meaning to cultural understandings of credit during the same period. Moreover, as Boston and Newport residents took part in daily borrowing and lending, printed texts circulating throughout the Atlantic World mobilized and inscribed categories of masculinity and femininity in their appraisals of credit. Essays and pamphlets used the allegorical "Lady Credit" to discuss the merits and hazards of lending. Credit's femininity could positively connote women's supposed moral constancy and fruitfulness, or it could negatively personify financial risks through the figure of the changeable seductress.[24] Novels, advice manuals, and certain common insults intertwined women's sexual reputations and credit, contending that promiscuity and falling prey to "seduction" were akin to losses of credit. Within this same framework, men who experienced financial failures were weak and feminized; orderly records and sound finances signified proper manhood.[25] Gender offered a rich vocabulary for interpreting economic life. Precisely because both women and men so routinely used credit, cultural arguments could be mapped onto women's everyday practices.

Broadening our understandings of labor to encompass activities surrounding credit transforms how we conceptualize early modern women's authority. While some scholars have suggested that divisions between the "masculine public" and the "feminine private" were firmly entrenched by the middle of the eighteenth century, urban spaces defied such characterizations throughout the colonial period.[26] This becomes apparent, first of all, when we examine financial practices occurring with a crucial legal and economic unit, the household. During this era, households were simultaneously dwelling places and places of business. They also became sites of legal consequence, in which parties negotiated binding agreements, sheriffs summoned debtors to court, and bystanders observed activities and signed documents that could later provide the basis for formal witness testimony. As members of households, women took part in all of these activities, both through happenstance and established divisions of responsibility. In eighteenth-century British America, as in early modern Europe, households were necessarily public and heterosocial places, and women acquired significant knowledge and power by virtue of their presence within them.[27]

Following women as they managed credit and debt also underscores their visibility in urban places beyond the household that we might otherwise have characterized as forming the "masculine public." Both in their own right and as agents, women called on others in houses and shops to purchase goods, initiate agreements, deliver payments, and collect from debtors. Women appeared before town councils, attended regular sessions of the county courts, and visited the offices of attorneys, justices of the peace, and court clerks. In order to complete all of these activities, women moved about. They walked crowded city streets and narrow alleys, rented horses and carriages, and hired boatmen. Women's visibility extended to the world of print, which they mobilized as they searched for missing items, settled debts, and pressured opponents in financial disputes. Attention to financial activities both recasts the household as a public and heterosocial space, and allows us to locate women within virtually every extra-household and governmental setting within their communities.

When conceptualizing patriarchal authority in the British Atlantic World, we often take as our starting point the British common law principle of coverture, which stipulated that wives' legal identities were subsumed under those of their husbands. Within this framework, widows and single women possessed all of the same legal powers as men, so we tend to characterize unmarried women's market participation as more extensive than that of married women.[28] To the extent that we do uncover evidence of married women's economic activities, we portray them as "deputy husbands," emphasizing the wives' services as agents or stand-ins for their husbands.[29] The present study of financial practices yields a different picture. Coverture did limit women's ability to own and transmit property. Its consequences for female engagement with credit and debt, however, were more limited.[30] Although colonists occasionally invoked coverture strategically in debt suits, married and unmarried women's use of credit encompassed common skills, practices, and responsibilities. To illustrate that point, this volume brings together examples of wives, widows, and single women undertaking similar activities during each phase of credit relationships.

Women's participation in the credit economy required a variety of legal and economic skills, only two of which were literacy and numeracy. As of 1710, roughly 45 percent of white women and 70 percent of white men in New England could sign their names, and New Englanders' rates of signature literacy continued to increase throughout the eighteenth century.[31] Shaped by the region's religious origins and its emphasis on personal engagement with the Bible, such literacy rates are higher than those in other places in British America. At the same time, such figures underscore that in New England, as elsewhere in the Atlantic World, women received less education in reading, writing, and mathematics than men.[32] Yet financial and legal competence demanded other, more specific skills. These included knowing how to pressure debtors and rebuff creditors, use and store financial records, hire and direct attorneys, and interact with local law enforcement. Observers of financial activities noted the parties' gestures, remarks, and ways of handling papers, in order to interpret and testify to financial relationships. Even literate men and women enlisted others to draft financial instruments, letters, and court filings, in order to ensure that their form and content matched their formal purposes. By recognizing literacy and numeracy as two tools among many, we can see abundant evidence of women strategically shaping financial negotiations and lawsuits. More broadly, sensitivity to these skills helps us better understand eighteenth-century laypeople's dynamic engagement with print, manuscripts, and the law, and it offers a model for analyzing other professional arenas, including science and medicine.[33]

In its attention to the contours of financial activity, including the spaces in which they occurred, the involvement of married and unmarried women, and women's skills and strategies, this study reveals the malleability of social hierarchies in early America. We are accustomed to thinking about colonial gender relations using the framework of patriarchy, and eighteenth-century Boston and Newport were indeed patriarchal societies.[34] At the same time, financial networks and the courts were heterosocial arenas. Women routinely transacted business with men, and female engagement with credit and debt litigation was commonplace and highly visible. As women navigated credit transactions and deployed associated skills, they entered scenarios governed as much by status and financial relationships between the parties as by abstract notions of gender differences. For men as well as women, indebtedness was a form of vulnerability. Debtors possessed limited abilities to challenge creditors' demands, and their property and persons were subject to seizure. Meanwhile, female creditors used the assertive tactics common to all creditors; female clients, like men, directed their attorneys; and female witnesses possessed the power to ratify transactions and shape case outcomes, just as men did. Through credit transactions and associated legal activities, many women thus cultivated an authority available to them in only a few other forums. Given the ubiquity of credit transactions and debt litigation, such moments of situational authority were highly significant elements of social relations.

The following chapters also intervene in debates concerning the changing status of women during the early modern period and the long eighteenth century. Some historians have suggested that the development of formal institutions during the colonial period, including an increasingly proceduralist court system and long-distance economic networks that relied on written instruments, was necessarily detrimental to women, whose authority remained rooted in informal economies and the household.[35] This book challenges such characterizations of the eighteenth century, both by arguing that women's funds and labor were vital components of legal and economic developments, and by recasting the household as a public site of mixed-sex financial activity. It also disputes such narratives' structuralist models of decline. Aligning with studies illuminating the contingent cultural and political processes that marked economic institutions as the domains of skilled men, this volume identifies the late eighteenth century as a period in which men and women gradually and unevenly recast financial and legal labors as masculine activities. In so doing, it highlights an additional way in which Americans, like their counterparts elsewhere in the Atlantic World, reconstituted the body politic as increasingly white and masculine during the Age of Revolutions.[36]

By the early decades of the eighteenth century, Boston and Newport shared similar relationships to Atlantic capitalism. As commercial entrepôts, Boston and Newport connected New England's interior with locales throughout the Atlantic World. Raw materials from the region, especially fish, timber, and agricultural products, passed through Boston and Newport en route to the Caribbean and Western Europe. In turn, profits from the sale of such exports enabled New Englanders to purchase Caribbean molasses and finished goods from Britain. In Newport, a major slave-trading port, transactions in these commodities were inseparable from the transport and sale of enslaved Africans. Relying on the same infrastructures that supported their other activities, Newport merchants sent slaving vessels to the African coast and transported their captive cargos to destinations in the Americas, mostly in the Caribbean.[37]

The labors and livelihoods of all Boston and Newport residents were enmeshed with Atlantic trading. The cities' mercantile orientations relied on auxiliary industries and services, ranging from building ships and barrels to transport goods, to keeping taverns and boardinghouses that offered respite to visiting sailors. Virtually all of Boston's and Newport's industries and businesses, ranging from transatlantic merchant firms to small artisanal shops, were family ventures. Within them, women forged interfamilial alliances and wealth transfers through marriage, and they dictated their households' consumer choices, decisions that were inseparable from the success of family businesses. In many trades, women managed the finances and kept records, whether temporarily or as part of established divisions of responsibility. Still other women were servants, laundresses, retailers, landlords, and keepers of taverns and boardinghouses, providing city residents and visitors alike with necessary goods and services.[38]

In Boston and Newport, women's financial labor stabilized New England's political economy against the upheavals of demographic imbalances and economic volatility. Like other eighteenth-century ports, the two cities housed more women than men. These communities' sex ratios became increasingly skewed over time, due to the hazards of men's maritime work and, as the region became drawn into imperial warfare from 1739 onward, military service. By the conclusion of the Seven Years' War, women headed 20 percent of the households in both cities. In practice, the number of female heads of household at any given moment was even higher, because so many men were at sea or engaged in war.[39] In addition to depleting cities of their men, maritime labor and military service posed financial problems, since mariners and soldiers only received their pay following the completion of their voyages or tours. Women limited the social and economic upheaval of men's enlistments by managing households in their absence, both temporarily and, given the high mortality rates of seafaring and military service, permanently as widows. Moreover, as tavernkeepers, landlords, and shopkeepers, women enabled the prevailing systems of deferred payment through their willingness to extend credit to sailors, soldiers, and their families against future income.[40]

Urban women's financial strategies also buttressed households, families, and businesses against economic upheaval. Beginning with the War of Jenkins' Ear in 1739 and continuing with King George's War (1744–1748) and the Seven Years' War (1756–1763), imperial conflict brought periodic shocks to Boston's and Newport's economies. War temporarily stimulated industries, including shipbuilding. At the same time, disruptions to merchants' trading networks caused contractions of credit and chains of failure that extended to other urban residents. Inflation, coupled with shortages, led to rising prices for necessities, including food and firewood. Brief interludes of peace, on the other hand, plunged cities into depression as the economic stimulus of war was removed. While both Newport and Boston experienced these boom and bust cycles arising from war, the cities' overall trajectories differed. The shocks of war aside, Newport experienced an overall trend of increasing prosperity as the city strengthened its trade connections with the West Indies and deepened its involvement in the transatlantic slave trade. Boston, in contrast, plunged further into economic decline. Despite the periodic stimulus of war, the city struggled to compete with other rising New England ports, including Newport and Providence, and with mid-Atlantic ports that possessed more-productive hinterlands. Such challenges swelled the ranks of the city's lower sorts and increased their financial hardship.[41]

Contested currency policies exacerbated economic uncertainty and depression. Each colony's government emitted its own currency for use in local and regional trade, and such monies circulated freely throughout New England. With residents of Massachusetts and Rhode Island each accepting the other's currency as legal tender, one colony's currency policies equally affected the other. Positioned at the center of debates about New England's political economy and possessing a strong tradition of acting as an independent polity, Massachusetts and its capital of Boston harbored the region's most intense debates about currency policy. In 1690, Massachusetts began printing paper money, in order to address shortages of coin and finance war with neighboring French colonies. Such fiat currency, which was not backed by gold or silver, rapidly depreciated in value and caused dramatic price inflation. For the next sixty years, Massachusetts periodically emitted large quantities of paper money, with the colony's leadership all the while intensely debating currency policies, including whether to print new paper money and how to remove deflated currency from circulation. Meanwhile, although Rhode Island was smaller and less populous than Massachusetts, that colony printed significantly more paper money. When imperial regulations led the Bay Colony to begin shrinking its money supply in 1741, Rhode Island frustrated these efforts by continuing to print large quantities of its own money, much of which circulated in Massachusetts. Then, in 1751, the British Parliament passed the Currency Act, which curtailed the printing of money by the New England colonies and gradually reduced the amount of paper money circulating in the region.[42]

In the course of their everyday dealings, New Englanders coped with these fluctuations in the money supply and the uncertainty created by ongoing debates about currency policy. Regardless of whether individuals exchanged local currency or simply used it as a unit of value when recording transactions, shifts in the availability of paper money affected prices and consumers' purchasing power. Women, who were frequently responsible for the day-to-day work of managing their households' finances and buying provisions, were on the front lines of responding to such challenges. Large emissions of paper money decreased the relative value of wages, causing hardship for Boston's and Newport's laboring families as they lost purchasing power. Contractions in the money supply disrupted market exchanges by causing shortages in the amount of currency, especially small bills, in circulation.[43]

The region's monetary policies also shaped creditors' and debtors' choices, including those of women managed credit relationships. Periods of actual or anticipated inflation favored debtors over creditors. Debtors attempted to delay payments in order to benefit from the declining value of their debts, while creditors, to the extent that they received payment, obtained devalued paper money worth less than the original debts. During recessions and financial crises, chains of creditors called in their debts, triggering domino effects of financial failures as debtors struggled to pay. The British financial crises of 1762 and 1772 intensified these challenges. Merchants in the metropole (Britain) sought payment from colonial artisans, who in turn called in the debts of their local clientele. Local and transatlantic financial climates shaped litigation practices, as well as creditors' and debtors' strategies outside of court. Amid the general trend of widespread litigiousness, creditors initiated the greatest quantities of lawsuits during periods of pronounced recession or dramatic inflation.[44] Boston and Newport women—as creditors and debtors in their own right; as witnesses; and as representatives of their households in front of lawyers, local officials, and the court—both drove and responded to these trends in litigation.

The commercial development of New England's leading ports reinforced their status as hubs of legal activity and vanguards of legal change. Boston and Newport, as the county seats, were the respective meeting places of the Suffolk and Newport County Courts, both of which also serviced the smaller surrounding towns (fig. I.1). Four times per year in Boston and twice a year in Newport, residents watched as locals and out-of-towners alike flocked to court sessions. Boston and Newport residents contributed the majority of cases heard in their county courts, and professional coteries of lawyers developed in both cities.[45] As cosmopolitan centers of print culture, Boston and Newport each possessed their own newspapers, with pages regularly containing legal news and notices, and residents could purchase legal treatises and commercial handbooks in booksellers' shops.[46] All of these factors made city residents especially conversant in the workings of the law and meant that legal activities inside and outside of court were closely intertwined.

Compact urban geographies and crowded living arrangements further shaped Boston and Newport residents' commercial activities and encounters with the

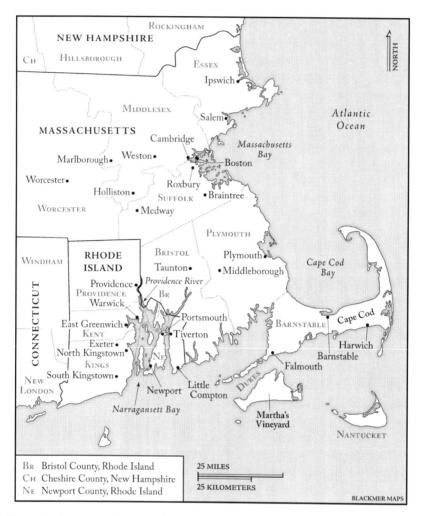

Figure I.1. Counties and towns of southeastern New England, c. 1775. Map by Kate Blackmer

law. Men and women transacted much of their business on foot and face-to-face. Eighteenth-century Boston was only two miles long, and no point in the city was more than half a mile from its waterfront (fig. I.2). Newport extended for roughly one mile along Narragansett Bay (fig. I.3). At the level of the household as well as the city block, individuals lived in close proximity to one another.[47] Urban dwellings sheltered what Ellen Hartigan-O'Connor and others have termed "housefuls," or combinations of family members and unrelated individuals, including tenants, apprentices, servants, and enslaved men and women. In pre-Revolutionary Newport, the average household size was seven people, while in Boston, it was more than nine. Although such household sizes were smaller than those in agrarian communities, where families relied on their children as laborers, port households were especially likely to contain temporary configurations of individuals beyond the nuclear family. An estimated 80 percent of adult residents rented rather than owned their living quarters, and mobile populations of sailors and laborers likewise sought short-term housing. Not only did such rental arrangements constitute credit relationships in themselves, but the shifting, intimate nature of urban housefuls also drew women and men into others' financial and legal affairs.[48]

Even as Boston and Newport occupied distinctive niches within the Atlantic economy, this study's methodologies and insights also apply to places throughout the Americas and Europe during the early modern period. I occasionally incorporate examples from other Massachusetts and Rhode Island towns, especially those in Suffolk and Newport Counties, in order to suggest practices shared by New England's port and agrarian communities.[49] As British colonies, Massachusetts and Rhode Island employed a legal framework derived from their metropole's legal system. Boston's and Newport's financial networks were also part of a larger Atlantic system, and the two cities' economic and demographic structures resemble those of other midsized ports. The flourishing scholarship on early modern women and gender, of which this study is a part, increasingly points to commonalities across empires, including the centrality of households and women's extensive, skilled involvement in the microlevel power negotiations surrounding finance and law.[50]

Because credit transactions and debt litigation were omnipresent in the eighteenth-century, records of such activities abound. This book relies most heavily on court records. I have examined the more than 800 extant petitions to the Massachusetts and Rhode Island legislatures concerning debt suits, as well as more than 3,600 debt cases heard in the courts of Suffolk and Newport Counties, of which Boston and Newport were the respective county seats. In order to provide a multifaceted analysis of credit and debt, this study also uses numerous other sources, including probate records, family correspondence and financial documents, attorneys' business records and correspondence with their clients, newspapers, and legal and commercial handbooks.

In its extensive use of court records, this volume harnesses the potential that such sources offer for a holistic analysis of early modern economic life and its gendered dimensions. Debt suits provide obvious evidence of patterns of litigation, including gendered participation in lawsuits. Scholars of colonial British America, including several gender historians, have fruitfully analyzed county court records from this vantage point.[51] But this study is the first to systematically mine this exceptionally vast archive for evidence of everyday financial and

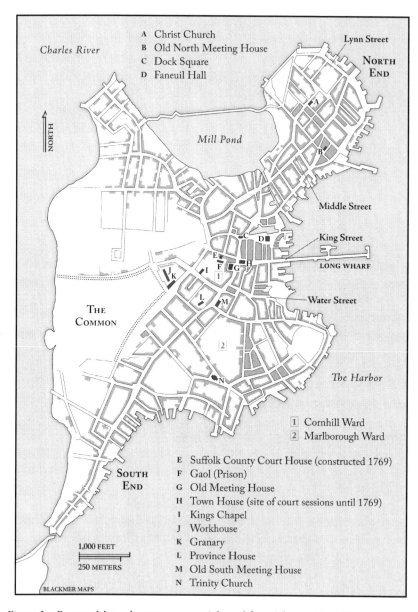

Figure I.2. Boston, Massachusetts, c. 1775. Adapted from Thomas Hyde Page, *A plan of the town of Boston, with the intrenchments &c. of His Majestys forces in 1775: from the observations of Lieut. Page of His Majesty's Corps of Engineers, and from the plans of other gentlemen* (London: Wm. Faden, 1777). Map by Kate Blackmer

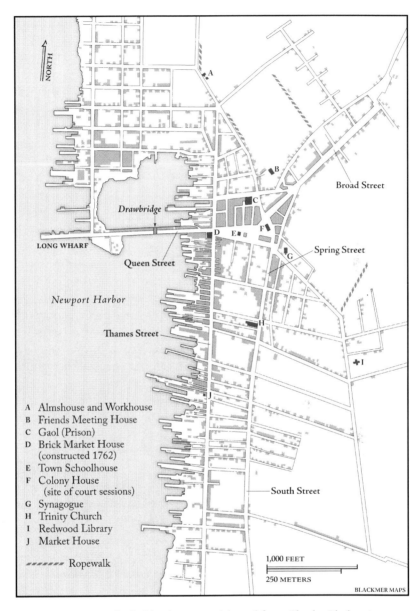

Figure I.3. Newport, Rhode Island, c. 1777. Adapted from Charles Blaskowitz, *A Plan of the town of Newport in Rhode Island* (London: Wm. Faden, 1777). Map by Kate Blackmer

legal practices, especially those outside of court. When creditors initiated debt suits, they submitted the relevant bonds, promissory notes, and accounts to the courts as evidence; such sources collectively attest to the broad spectrum of British Americans who used credit and debt. Litigants' arguments recounted the parties' prior agreements or attempts to settle. Witnesses' testimony interpreted the mechanics of financial negotiations and the individuals who participated in them. The small details of these documents' content and form—a sheriff's scrawl that a debtor's court summons was "served on his wife," a witness's or agent's signature on a promissory note, or multiple handwritings on a bond—shed light on the wide circle of individuals who engaged with credit and the skills that they exercised.[52] Legal conflicts represent only a slice of the larger universe of credit transactions, most of which never reached the courts. Nonetheless, court cases provide invaluable evidence of practices and norms that colonists otherwise had little reason to document, preserve, or articulate.

This book interweaves three methods for analyzing legal sources. First, quantitative analysis facilitates comparisons between women's and men's activities, establishing the broad backdrop that is necessary for interpreting specific examples. Second, readers will meet individual women whose stories are recounted in as much detail as the sources permit. Several of these women, especially Temperance Grant, Abigail Hewes, Ann Maylem, and Sarah Peirse, waged protracted legal battles, generating voluminous documentation, and their disputes illustrate the practices and stakes surrounding eighteenth-century credit and debt. Third, this study culls small details from sources in order excavate financial and legal practices that would otherwise remain opaque, such as drafting bonds or hiring attorneys. Doing so opens up a little-known world of women's financial and legal labor, and it is particularly useful for highlighting activities of married women, whom sources often mention only in passing. In generating the extensive records associated with debt litigation in the county courts, lawyers and clerks were not merely creating an archive of legal disputes, but also a compendium of everyday practices that women and men otherwise had little occasion to document.

When sifting through sources in this way, it is important to also attend to the power relations embedded within the archive (i.e., the historical record), what Marisa Fuentes describes as the ways in which "documents shape the meaning produced about them in their own time and our current historical practices."[53] One important consideration is how the record-keeping practices emerging from coverture subordinated, or even obscured, wives' activities. Whereas married women seldom appeared in financial and court records apart from their husbands, these same sources positioned men as independent, self-determining legal and economic actors, only occasionally noting when their wives' labor or financial resources had contributed to a transaction. By both recovering married women's economic contributions and drawing attention to the reading strategies required to do so, this study highlights the ways in which documentary practices helped constitute the institution of marriage, a cornerstone of early modern patriarchy.

Intersections between social hierarchies and the construction of the archive also lead free white women of at least moderate means to appear far more prominently in colonial records than poor women and women of color. At mid-century, roughly 12 percent of Newport's population, and 8 percent of Boston's, was enslaved.[54] These laborers lacked the power to establish legally binding contracts, a necessary first step in credit transactions. In addition, port cities were places of growing inequality and widespread poverty, especially during the economic downturns suffered by Boston from the 1740s onward and by Newport during the Seven Years' War.[55] Amid such social stratification, the majority of female creditors and debtors were probably of midding or elite status, as their wealth, social connections, and business activities all facilitated their involvement in borrowing and lending.

Boston's and Newport's small populations of free blacks and Natives, including Wampanoags and Narragansetts, possessed the legal capacity to form contracts, but not necessarily the means to do so.[56] Urban free blacks and Natives tended to live in relative poverty, and, increasingly demarcated by white residents as outsiders, they largely lacked the social connections necessary to participate in formal credit transactions. As historians have documented, cash and in-kind trading were especially important to such marginalized individuals. They made frequent, small purchases rather then enter into standing credit relationships. They were also active participants in the informal economy, a sector consisting of unregulated and sometimes illegal activities, including pawning, peddling and huckstering, the keeping of unlicensed taverns, and prostitution.[57]

Shards of evidence suggest that blacks and Natives, including women, occasionally used credit in their own names. In 1745, for example, two black women, described only as "Negro Dina" and "Negro Sue," were among the creditors of Newport widow Ann Kees. After Kees's death, Dina and Sue each received a few shillings from her estate in payment of debts, probably for labor rendered or goods delivered. We learn about of such transactions only because the estate administrator enumerated them in an account, but we do not know the precise circumstances that led Kees to become indebted to these two women.[58] That same year, a Native woman, Mercy Freeman, loaned £21 to fellow Newport resident Hannah Easton. This transaction entered the official record when Freeman later sued Easton for the debt, yet surviving records describe Freeman only as a "spinster" and "Indian woman" and do not detail the nature of her relationship with Easton.[59] At the same time as the examples of Dina, Sue, and Mercy Freeman highlight the inclusion of women of color in economic networks, the rarity and brevity of such mentions manifest and reproduce eighteenth-century power relations.

Credit and debt also reinforced British colonialism and systems of bound labor. By encouraging Natives to purchase British goods and run themselves into debt, colonists used indebtedness as the first step in compelling Native men and women to both forfeit their lands and enter the systems of indentured servitude and debt peonage that became increasingly prevalent during the first half of the eighteenth century. Financial pressures led some free blacks to sign indentures in which the imposed conditions closely resembled slavery, and masters could exploit the overlap between these systems of bound labor by claiming their indentured servants as their slaves. In moments that manifested these enslaved people's status as property, white residents sold, auctioned, and seized such bound men and women, in order to facilitate the payment of debts.[60] As Boston and Newport residents used the forms of personal credit that are the focus of this study, they participated in one arena of a much larger system in which financial ties undergirded social hierarchies.

Because recovering information on women's financial labor demands assembling shards of evidence from across multiple decades, and because everyday practices surrounding credit evolved slowly, a strictly chronological structure does not serve this book's purposes. In analyzing eighteenth-century British America, it is important not to overstate ordinary men's and women's awareness of macroeconomic factors, or the extent to which such knowledge guided daily practices. It is telling that in the vast archives of the county courts, which were a particularly important arena for enforcing financial obligations, litigants and witnesses alike seldom referred to monetary policy or economic conditions. Instead, regardless of whether litigation occurred amid periods of recession or prosperity, or of monetary surplus or scarcity, court cases attested to an enduring set of practices and expectations governing financial activity. Through the repetition of such patterns of conduct inside and outside of court, Boston and Newport women were among those who brought a measure of regularity to their communities amid an era of turmoil.

This volume therefore adopts a multileveled approach, moving simultaneously through the lifespan of credit relationships and the cascading problems of political economy confronted by New Englanders during the eighteenth century. Chapters 1 through 5 consider the period spanning from roughly 1730 to 1775, when the pace of credit-based market exchanges quickened and debt litigation became ever more central to the enforcement of financial obligations. Chapter 6 then charts continuities and changes during the final decades of the eighteenth century.

Chapter 1 examines the contours and stakes of urban women's fiscal practices, showing that their financial dealings sustained their households and communities in the face of high rates of male mortality and mobility. In chapter 2, I look more closely at the question of who would engage in the everyday work of borrowing and lending. Women's skilled labor was paramount to all stages of credit transactions outside of court, beginning with parties haggling over the terms of loans, and ending with payment. As urban residents used written credit more frequently, they also turned to the courts when they could not collect their due. Chapter 3 finds that women's financial and legal savvy extended to the process of debt litigation, including their interactions with lawyers and local officials. Chapter 4 uncovers the role of female witnesses within the period's increasingly formal economy and courts, illustrating that witnessing provided an important arena of learning and a source of social and legal authority. In chapter 5, I turn to the final stages of acrimonious disputes: hearings before the highest courts of Massachusetts and Rhode Island. Here, colonists grappled with the legal system's privileging of creditors' claims. Officials and laypeople evaluated cases within a framework premised on men's and women's similar capabilities. Over time, however, court outcomes elevated male lawyers and businessmen and narrowed the legal defenses available to indebted widows, the women who most often used petitioning. Finally, chapter 6 charts intertwined discourses of gender and class during the Revolutionary era. Following the temporary upheaval of war, middling and lower-class women largely resumed their prior uses of credit. Meanwhile, elite families increasingly cast the messiness of credit transactions as a male domain and positioned women's distancing from finance as a marker of class privilege.

As lawsuits concerning debt advanced through the courts of colonial Boston and Newport, they generated extensive documentation. These included complaints, summonses, responses, and verdicts, as well as accounts, financial instruments, and witness testimony. Once a case was concluded, the court clerk stacked all of these irregularly sized sheets, folding the larger ones in an attempt to create uniformity. He folded another piece of paper around the documents' exterior, to create a sheath, and bound the pages together, either by inserting a straight pin through them or by tying a string around the parcel. He wrote the parties' names on the outside of the packet, then filed it away for safekeeping. Thousands of such eighteenth-century cases now rest in the archives of Boston's and Newport's courts, with some remaining unopened since the clerk finished his handiwork. Upon removing the rusted pin or slipping off the hardened string from one of these case files, the unruly pile of documents springs to life, shedding light on a dynamic world of financial relationships, one in which women and men alike were integral and skilled contributors.

CHAPTER I

"To the advantage of herself & the honorable support of her Family"

Women and the Urban Credit Economy

In March 1746 in Newport, Rhode Island, ship captain Simeon Potter excoriated Temperance Grant, a prosperous female shopkeeper. At a dinner attended by Rhode Island and Philadelphia traders at a leading merchant's house, an irate Potter proclaimed that Grant's actions were "wrong." He condemned Grant again at the shop of David Moore, "before severall people," and lambasted her once more in front of a crowd in "the street before the Coffee House." Although verbal attacks on early modern women often concerned their supposed promiscuity, Grant's alleged misdeeds were unrelated to sex. In Potter's eyes, Grant had committed another equally serious transgression: inappropriate use of credit.[1]

Potter's choice to criticize Grant in multiple venues underscores that she was fully integrated into Newport's economy. In what appears to have been a calculated smear campaign, Potter denounced Grant before mostly male audiences, ranging from elite merchants to chance bystanders. He criticized her both indoors and outdoors, including in a quintessentially public site: the street in front of the coffeehouse. Grant was not personally present to defend herself in these moments.[2] Potter's criticism of Grant's commercial practices, however, could only injure her reputation to the extent to which she already moved within these urban spaces and social circles. Grant sued Potter for slander in

May of that same year, indicating that she indeed found his words to be damaging.[3]

Temperance Grant was a widow, but to focus only on this fact misses an opportunity to more fully situate Grant and her female contemporaries, wedded as well as single or widowed, within the economies of eighteenth-century Boston and Newport. Married women of that period lacked independent legal identities, but Grant's widowhood enabled her to run a shop and engage in legal disputes in ways that are readily visible to historians.[4] Yet residents of New England ports, both male and female, married and unmarried, collectively faced intertwined economic and social challenges. The stories of four women in the 1740s—Temperance Grant, Mary Prince, Bathiah MacDaniel, and Abigail Hewes—offer a window into these urban economic cultures where personal credit was ubiquitous for white men and women alike, undergirding countless transactions that ranged from small and local to large and transatlantic. For these four women, as well as for their contemporaries, credit was bound up with one's character and reputation, and this elevated the importance of financial dealings and disputes.

By 1740 Boston's and Newport's economies were firmly centered on their status as commercial entrepôts linking New England's hinterlands with the Atlantic World. The cities' merchants exported raw materials to the Caribbean and imported finished goods from Britain, and a host of auxiliary businesses, ranging from barrel-making to tavern-keeping, developed to support the ports' commercial orientations and serve their labor forces. Turning on borrowing and lending, all of these market-oriented activities led residents to engage in written credit transactions and assume the associated economic risks with greater frequency. At the same time, Boston's and Newport's maritime orientations yielding pressing questions of which individuals could access credit and perform the crucial labor of managing its relationships. When men accepted posts as sailors and ship captains, they entered into systems of deferred payment that placed distinctive demands on urban credit networks, and they left behind families who needed to provide for themselves in the absence of male household heads.[5] Once Britain resumed imperial warfare against Spain in 1739 and France in 1744, new opportunities for men to enter military service and join privateering ventures intensified these economic and demographic strains.[6]

Amid high rates of male mobility and mortality, free white women's financial activities anchored and preserved family units, commercial networks, and urban economies. Women such as Temperance Grant, Mary Prince, Bathiah MacDaniel, and Abigail Hewes sought ways in which to support themselves and their families, maintain profitable businesses, and obtain necessary goods and services. As they did so, they figured out how to use credit to their advantage, and they managed their reputations within frameworks that linked financial standing and personal character. Although considerable attention has been paid to economic ties among women, much of their labor surrounding credit involved interactions with men.[7] Through their everyday activities, as well as their legally recognized involvement in transactions, women defined the urban economy as a heterosocial realm. For their part, other urban residents, both male and female, widely accepted free white women's use of credit. Although gender differences structured countless aspects of men's and women's lives, and gendered language offered a potent register for policing women's activities, Boston and Newport residents seldom curtailed or critiqued women's economic practices.[8] They did so only in limited ways and in retrospect, either when it was to their immediate financial advantage to do so, or when women had dramatically deviated from established norms.

Bathiah MacDaniel and Mary Prince: Marriage Law and Women's Economic Powers

In Newport and Boston during the 1740s, two married women engaged in seemingly ordinary credit transactions that would later spark lawsuits. For five weeks in 1740, Bathiah MacDaniel, the wife of mariner Bryan MacDaniel, boarded with widow Abigail Fry in Newport. MacDaniel pawned her family's household goods to Fry as security for the rent. By the following year, Fry still had possession of the pawned goods, so Bryan MacDaniel sued her. Five years later, in 1746, Mary Prince, the wife of Boston ship captain and shopkeeper Joseph Prince, settled a debt with merchant Nathaniel Wheelwright. She paid him £96 for tea her family had purchased. Joseph Prince sued Wheelwright in 1748, arguing that his wife had overpaid for the tea and that Wheelwright refused to return the excess amount.[9] Taken together, these two episodes clarify both the extent and the limits of married women's economic powers in colonial British American port cities.

Descriptions of women's access to credit often foreground the significance of their marital status and, to an extent, this emphasis on marriage is useful. Common law, the body of metropolitan British precedents that provided the starting point for law in British North American colonies, distinguished between unmarried women (*femes sole*) and married women (*femes covert*) such as Bathiah MacDaniel and Mary Prince. Whereas widows and single women possessed the same rights and powers as men, including in economic matters, coverture technically subsumed wives' legal identities under those of their husbands. Coverture thus shaped the terms on which married women accessed credit and debt, and, equally significantly, how the archive documented these transactions.[10]

We should also be careful not to interpret coverture as a descriptive account of the economic activities of colonial *femes covert*. One of the most potent articulations of this legal principle did not appear until the eve of the American

Revolution, well after our two case studies. In 1765, William Blackstone, in his *Commentaries on the Laws of England*, famously declared that a married woman's legal identity "is incorporated and consolidated into that of the husband: under whose wing, protection, and *cover*, she performs everything."[11] Blackstone's words have been cited as an encapsulation of colonial women's legal status ever since. Yet Blackstone departed from prior leading treatises, which neither completely subordinated wives to their husbands nor offered unified theories of patriarchs' authority over wives, children, and servants. A Philadelphia printer published the first North American edition of *Commentaries* in 1771, and it was not until the Early Republic that its ideas significantly took hold.[12] While divergences between technicalities and practice exist in countless areas of the law, we must be particularly attentive to such gaps regarding eighteenth-century marriage law, where Blackstone's words cast such a long shadow, and where legal and financial documentation actively positioned married men as autonomous actors, obscuring their wives' economic contributions.

Examining disputes surrounding married women's financial transactions highlights the dynamic interplay between economic exigency, law, and documentary practices. The examples of Bathiah MacDaniel and Mary Prince underscore the point that—despite recording practices attributing financial transactions to male household heads—credit was a family-based system. Especially in port cities, including Boston and Newport, where commerce and war increasingly pulled men away from home, residents permitted wives' use of credit and debt, because such women's labor and resources helped preserve households and commercial networks. At the same time, men and women were sufficiently familiar with coverture that they mobilized it in attempts to retroactively invalidate transactions by *femes covert* when it was in their monetary interest to do so. Because married women's financial activities were vital to the workings of urban economies, coverture offered accessible but only partially effective lines of legal argument.

Systems of family credit yoked together the fortunes of husbands and wives, including Joseph and Mary Prince and Bathiah and Bryan MacDaniel. Given that eighteenth-century people possessed limited means by which to reliably assess one another's credit, reputations were collective as well as individual. Men and women assessed the wealth and esteem of potential trading partners' families and households when evaluating creditworthiness. A married man's financial worth certainly shaped his family's access to credit, but so did the resources of his wife, who likewise brought her own assets to the marriage. Whether or not they had read advice books for tradesmen, Bryan MacDaniel and Joseph Prince would have been familiar with such texts' position. A man's choice of spouse was "a point, on which your whole happiness and prosperity depend," in part because "a fair wife with empty pockets, is a noble house without furniture:

showy, but useless."[13] Casual conversation between MacDaniel's and Prince's contemporaries likewise acknowledged that wives added value to their new households. In 1738, when discussing a debt owed by William Bennet, one Newport man asked another whether "the woomman which William Bennet married made him good pay." The other replied that "she had." Bennet's wife's assets brought him a newfound ability to pay his creditors, and the community took note.[14]

In addition to contributing to their households' wealth, wives—including Bathiah MacDaniel and Mary Prince—bolstered married couples' shared connections and reputations. Because it was difficult to obtain accurate intelligence about potential trading partners and secure agents' loyalty, membership in a trusted family could signal one's creditworthiness. Long-distance merchants were among those who preferred to do business with their own kin, and marriages strengthened alliances between trading partners and within firms.[15] As part of its defense of marriage, a 1735 essay in the *Philadelphia Gazette* accordingly noted that a man does not "*lose Friends* but gain them, by prudently marrying; for there are all the Woman's Relations added to his own, ready to assist the new-married couple." The essay further remarked that a married man "is sooner trusted in Business, and can have credit longer and for larger sums than if he was single," because his contemporaries would view him as "more firmly settled" and "under greater Obligations to behave honestly, for his Family's Sake."[16] Married women's choices also contributed to their households' creditworthiness, as handbooks acknowledged when they urged men to select "frugal" spouses and enjoined wives to modulate their spending based on their families' assets.[17] Even Benjamin Franklin, whose autobiography stressed his self-made rise to prominence, noted that his wife, Deborah Read Franklin, "assisted me much by attending the shop and we throve together."[18] Couples' economic standing hinged on the social resources, financial decisions, and labor of wives as well as husbands.

At the same time as husbands and wives jointly shaped their families' credit, understandings of legal responsibility and practices of financial record-keeping obscured women's contributions. Coverture stipulated that married women could not contract debts or extend credit in their own names during marriage. In keeping with this fact, eighteenth-century financial documents consistently attached legal responsibility to men, even when their wives conducted the transactions in question. Accounts named men as the titular and financially liable parties, even as individual entries included purchases or cash outlays delivered to wives, or payments received from them. Even when married women's labor or financial resources undergirded the agreements crystallized through bonds and promissory notes, these documents named their husbands as the debtors or creditors. Despite colonists' recognition that husbands' and wives' credit was intertwined, financial records positioned men as autonomous economic actors, while depicting wives as subordinates "drawing on" their husbands' credit.[19]

These tensions between social and legal understandings of spouses' credit played out in the examples of both Bathiah MacDaniel and Mary Prince. Landlady Abigail Fry explained that Bathiah MacDaniel sought lodging from her in 1740 because Bryan MacDaniel had left his family "turned out of doors and unprovided of habitation." Perhaps the sailor simply had gone to sea without adequately providing for his family, a plausible circumstance, given the straits of maritime work. Sailors were among port cities' poorest and most economically precarious free laborers. Because they typically only received their pay following the completion of voyages, they and their families often counted on their communities to extend them credit against their future wages.[20] Or, as the evocative phrase "turned out" suggests, perhaps Bathiah and Bryan had informally separated. Doing so was common in an era in which divorce was available only in exceptional circumstances that involved adultery, desertion, or extreme cruelty.[21] Although the "law of necessaries" allowed wives facing such marital difficulties to purchase basic necessities without their husbands' direct approval, courts and communities wavered on when this common law principle applied. Either way, Bathiah MacDaniel's precarious circumstances led Abigail Fry to fear that the MacDaniel family might not pay their rent. Fry took the rare step of demanding security from her prospective tenant. Bathiah MacDaniel pawned numerous household goods, including a feather bed, probably her family's most valuable possession, in order to obtain housing.[22]

Joseph and Mary Prince's actions, meanwhile, exemplify the conjoining of spouses' credit under their husbands' names. In 1745, Mary Prince's husband, Joseph, bought green tea from merchant Nathaniel Wheelwright, promising to pay for his purchase at a later date. Wheelwright's assessment that the Prince family was creditworthy most likely encompassed Mary's actions and resources. With Joseph's work as a ship captain taking him to sea for long periods, Mary provided stability in the family business by managing the Princes' retail shop while Joseph was away. She may also have run the shop at other times and contributed financial resources to the couple's enterprise. Despite these considerations, Wheelwright documented the sale as occurring between him and Joseph alone. The following year, while Joseph was away, Wheelwright dunned the Prince family at their shop. He showed Mary Prince an account stating that the Princes had purchased two chests of tea, and she paid him the amount supposedly owed, £96. When Wheelwright credited Joseph Prince's account accordingly, the merchant's record-keeping reinforced Mary's position as her husband's agent.[23]

Bathiah MacDaniel's rental arrangement and Mary Prince's payment for goods fit within a larger pattern of extensive financial activity by *femes covert* throughout the colonial period, especially in port cities. The absences of men such as mariner Bryan MacDaniel and ship captain Joseph Prince posed interrelated social and economic problems for these cities. Months, or even years, could elapse without word from a ship's crew, creating uncertainty about whether a *feme covert* had become a *feme sole*. If seafarers' wives could not transact business in their husbands' absences, credit networks would grind to a halt. Lacking the ability to provide for themselves, families could become dependent on the towns' limited systems of relief for the poor.

New Englanders responded to these problems when they used legal channels to expand the powers of sailors' wives. In 1711, the Rhode Island General Assembly noted that "many Merchants and Mariners, going to Sea on Voyages, are often absent many years and unheard of," leading "their wives and families" to "suffer" financially until word of such men's deaths reached Rhode Island. It authorized wives whose husbands had been "absent and unheard of for three years" to receive the powers of administration required to sue for debts owed to their missing spouses' estates. By 1717, the legislature enlarged such women's powers to collect debts and control family property, explaining that the previous law was not "so full and extensive as hath since been found necessary." Nonetheless, the revised law proved to be insufficient. Assemblies in Rhode Island and elsewhere faced a continual stream of petitions from mariners' wives seeking to appear in court or sell real estate, and they overwhelmingly granted these requests.[24] These laws and petitions, however, offered relief only in exceptional circumstances. They did not assist those women whose husbands simply went to sea for several months and then returned, as was the case for Mary Prince and Bathiah MacDaniel.

Beginning in the 1740s, imperial warfare brought new urgency to the questions surrounding married women's legal powers and their associated economic precariousness in Boston and Newport. Following the conclusion of Queen Anne's War in 1713, the British colonies entered a quarter-century of relative calm. Then, in 1739, conflict with Spain over commercial trading rights erupted into the War of Jenkins' Ear. That war, in turn, intersected with broader conflicts between European empires, and the War of Austrian Succession lasted until 1748. While merchant vessels had long drained Boston and Newport of able-bodied adult men, war compounded these problems. Port cities contributed a disproportionate share of New Englanders who manned the sudden uptick in privateering vessels or who enrolled in naval and military service. In 1740, roughly a thousand men from the Boston area enlisted in the British naval campaign to the Spanish port of Cartagena. Hundreds more joined subsequent campaigns between 1741 and 1744. In 1745, an additional three thousand Massachusetts residents, many from Boston, joined the British military's assault on Louisbourg, a major French holding at the mouth of the St. Lawrence River.

The following decade, the resumption of conflict in the Seven Years' War again led to widespread enlistments by urban men, this time from Newport as well as Boston.[25]

Military and naval service and privateering posed two intersecting challenges to New England's largest ports. First, like the sailors on merchant ships, soldiers and crews on privateering and naval vessels only received their pay following the completion of their tours. This structure left unresolved the question of how such men's families would support themselves in the interim. Second, war exacted a severe death toll. Several of the period's campaigns had high mortality rates—it is estimated that only one-fifth of those in the Cartagena campaign survived—and this exacerbated Boston's and Newport's already skewed sex ratios. By 1742, 1,200 Boston women, or an estimated 30 percent of the city's adult female population, were widows. By 1764, Boston had 122 adult white women for every 100 men. Newport, which had nearly equal numbers of women and men prior to the Seven Years' War, had 125 adult women for every 100 men in 1775.[26] Together, deferred payment systems and high male mortality rates compounded women's economic struggles. By the 1740s, the wives and widows of merchant seafarers—women like Bathiah MacDaniel and Mary Prince—were part of a larger cohort that also included the wives and widows of soldiers and naval and privateering crew members, as well as single women unable to marry, due to their cities' demographic imbalances.

Boston and Newport entertained a variety of solutions for supporting women amid men's absences and deaths. At the same time as city leaders contemplated organized solutions—including workhouses, mutual aid societies, and textile manufacturing—ordinary residents developed equally important informal remedies through their willingness to transact business with married women.[27] Allowing *femes covert* to engage with credit and money ultimately furthered many people's economic interests. By settling the account with Wheelwright, Mary Prince buttressed her family's reputation for prompt payment. She also prevented that merchant from repeatedly dunning her household or suing to collect the debt. By pawning her belongings, Bathiah MacDaniel obtained housing for herself and her children. The two creditors, Nathaniel Wheelwright and Abigail Fry, likewise benefited. Wheelwright obtained £96 that he could then use elsewhere in his business; Fry obtained both a paying tenant and security if that tenant defaulted on her rent. In these and countless other instances, economic exigencies led city dwellers to accept married women as partners in financial transactions.

Although Bathiah MacDaniel and Mary Prince initially used credit and debt without incident, coverture subsequently came into play through litigation, as both women's husbands sought to retroactively undermine their wives' transactions. When Joseph Prince returned home and learned of his wife's payment of

£96 for two chests of tea, he insisted that he had purchased and received one chest, and not two. He demanded Wheelwright return the overpayment. When Wheelwright refused, Joseph Prince sued him.[28] Similarly, at some point in the year following Bathiah MacDaniel's stay with Abigail Fry, Bryan MacDaniel discovered that the landlady held his family's belongings. Fry maintained that the MacDaniels remained indebted to her and refused to relinquish the goods, so Bryan MacDaniel sued for the items' return.[29] Both lawsuits engaged the gap between the letter of the law regarding coverture and married women's accepted roles within urban economies. As Joseph Prince and Bryan MacDaniel clumsily matched legal categories with the realities of their wives' activities, they produced narratives that opposing parties could easily deconstruct.

In the case of the Newport wife who pawned goods to obtain housing, Bryan MacDaniel bypassed direct engagement with coverture and instead focused on Fry's refusal to relinquish his property. In his May 1741 lawsuit, he demanded that Abigail Fry either return the bed and household goods or compensate him for their value. MacDaniel sued Fry using the legal actions of detinue and trover, both of which concerned defendants' unlawful detaining of property, rather than the circumstances under which they had acquired such property. How Fry had acquired those possessions was irrelevant to Bryan MacDaniel's suit. Thus his filings strategically omitted his wife's transactions with Fry, and even the existence of his wife. Although MacDaniel did not cite the principle of coverture by name, it informed his implicit denial that a married woman could establish accounts and pawn family possessions.[30] In her response, however, landlady Abigail Fry called attention to a married woman's discretionary power apart from her husband. She explained that Bathiah MacDaniel's need for housing arose from her difficult circumstances, that the tenant had pawned her household goods as security, and that she had left her rented quarters without paying up.[31]

In the Boston lawsuit, Mary Prince's status as a *feme covert* was one of numerous elements of Joseph Prince's claim. His initial 1748 complaint cast his wife's supposed overpayment as simply a loan to John Wheelwright.[32] While Prince's declaration did not mention that it was Mary who had given the funds to Wheelwright, its substance implicitly acknowledged the validity of the transaction. Joseph Prince's strategies evolved during the case's appeals. In 1749, Prince requested that the Massachusetts legislature grant a re-hearing of the case, and the genre of the petition allowed him to fully recount the events in question. Prince's petition began by describing accounting errors surrounding the purchase of the tea and then explained that, when Wheelwright called on Mary Prince for payment, she was unfamiliar with this backstory. In Joseph Prince's telling, "the Petitioner's wife incautiously paid Mr. Wheelwright his account wherein two chests were expressed." Mary's marital status appeared as a passing description, but the petition did not argue that her position as a *feme co-*

vert necessarily invalidated her economic activity. Mary's payment, moreover, appeared as just one detail in Joseph's litany of misfortunes and injustices, beginning with shoddy record-keeping and ending with absent witnesses and biased referees. Joseph Prince appeared less concerned with curtailing his wife's financial authority than with regaining £48 through whatever argument might stick.[33]

As in the Newport lawsuit, Joseph Prince's strategy led his opponents to highlight married women's essential economic contributions. In his response to Joseph Prince's petition, Wheelwright portrayed Mary Prince as a competent shopkeeper who acted independently during her husband's absence, including by storing and selling the tea in question. Insisting that Mary would have "best known of the mistake if any there was," Wheelwright sardonically observed that Prince demanded a refund on the spurious grounds that he was "better knowing what his wife did in his absence than she did herself." With "their memories assisted by length of time," Wheelwright quipped, the Princes had "acquired the faculty of remembering they never had but one chest of tea."[34] Within the adversarial context of litigation, Wheelwright, like Fry, situated the transactions at issue within the routine economic activities of married women in port cities.

In the controversies surrounding Mary Prince and Bathiah MacDaniel, questions of married women's legal capabilities were intertwined with issues of patriarchal authority, but this was not always the case. Through their refusal to acknowledge their wives as savvy economic actors, both Joseph Prince and Bryan MacDaniel asserted their command over their households. In other circumstances, however, opposing parties, and even women themselves, strategically invoked marriage law. In one Newport lawsuit in 1733, a male defendant persuaded the court to throw out a debt suit brought by a married woman, even though she lived apart from her husband. The defendant successfully argued that a woman could not claim the legal powers associated with widowhood before her husband was dead.[35] In 1735 and again in 1739, a mariner's wife, Bethiah Hedge, persuaded the Newport court to dismiss two men's lawsuits concerning unpaid debts, arguing that her opponents had erroneously labeled her a widow. Hedge maintained that she was married and thus was unable to contract debts or be sued. While some reported that Hedge's husband, a mariner, had died in Jamaica in 1731, such news remained uncertain, so Hedge once more used her marriage as a legal shield several years later.[36] Coverture provided a useful lexicon for financial disputes, and, depending on a case's circumstances, it might be either men or women, married individuals or their opponents, and plaintiffs or defendants who incorporated the principle into their claims.

Just as litigants' arguments surrounding coverture proved to be situational, the courts' verdicts also varied within and across cases. Referees appointed by the Newport court ordered Abigail Fry to either return the furniture and goods to Bryan MacDaniel or pay him £15.5.[37] In Boston, Prince won his case in the Court of Common Pleas and again in the Superior Court when Wheelwright appealed. Wheelwright then appealed once more, and this time the court ruled in his favor. That outcome led Prince to petition the Massachusetts legislature, who submitted the case to a new group of referees, although the record does not contain their decision.[38] These two disputes suggest the larger issue of the courts' inconsistent responses to questions of married women's legal capabilities. At times the courts aligned themselves with husbands seeking to retroactively curtail their wives' powers, while in other instances, they endorsed established community practices that accepted married women as economic actors.

The controversies surrounding Bathiah MacDaniel and Mary Prince provide a multilayered view of married women's economic activities. Because a family's reputation and resources shaped an individual's creditworthiness, all members of households and kinship networks were necessarily interdependent. This was particularly the case in port cities, including Boston and Newport. Especially amid the toll of imperial warfare, the absences of mariners and ship captains such as Bryan MacDaniel and Joseph Prince disrupted family units and credit networks, thereby heightening the importance of married women's labor.

At the same time, men's and women's economic activities occurred within different legal parameters. Whereas marital status was irrelevant to men's capabilities at law, colonists could invoke the distinction between *femes sole* and *femes covert* in order to circumscribe married women's powers. One historian has described coverture as existing in "suspended animation" in early modern Britain, and this phrase aptly describes the contemporaneous functioning of coverture in colonial port cities.[39] Under ordinary circumstances, married women's involvement in financial matters stabilized their families and credit networks, and urban residents such as Nathaniel Wheelwright and Abigail Fry accepted such activities. Occasionally, however, one party in a dispute invoked coverture, because it was to their direct advantage to do so, as it was for Bryan MacDaniel and Joseph Prince. Here the disjuncture between law and practice yielded strained and flimsy arguments.

This interplay between everyday practice and marriage law structured the archive and has important methodological implications for historians. As long as married women's labor and decisions remained uncontroversial, financial and legal records obscured *femes covert* or subordinated them to their husbands. In this way, routine documents perpetuated cultural constructs of masculine self-determination and feminine dependence. Paradoxically, it was precisely during those moments when disputants reanimated the principle of coverture that married women's economic contributions became most visible. Conflicts such as those surrounding Bathiah MacDaniel and Mary Prince reveal the exceptional circumstances in which coverture gained power within courts of law, but they also expose the workings of port economies, in which married women's financial labor was both common and necessary.

Temperance Grant's Slander Suit: Widows' Financial Practices and the Meanings of Credit

During the same decade in which Bathiah MacDaniel and Mary Prince managed their households while their husbands were at sea, Newport resident Temperance Grant became a widow. Grant's husband, Sueton, was a quite prominent and affluent merchant. The family lived in a large two-story home just off Thames Street in the center of Newport, near the location where the Brick Market would later be constructed.[40] Prior to his death, Sueton Grant's business was seemingly on the upswing. Imperial warfare offered novel opportunities for profit, as the British government demonstrated renewed willingness to issue letters of marque to private vessels. Like many of his contemporaries, Grant purchased a privateering vessel in partnership with other elites. In September 1744, Grant, his partners, and a visiting official were inventorying a recent voyage's bounty in a gunpowder-filled Newport warehouse when a pistol discharged, sparking a massive explosion. Badly burned, Grant and three other men succumbed to their injuries within the week. Newspapers as far south as Philadelphia described the "sorrowful accident," explaining that "the loss of such Men," whose lineage and character they described in depth, and the "awful manner and occasion of their death" rendered the disaster "a heavy Blow" to Newport. Sueton Grant, such reports added, left behind "a disconsolate widow with a numerous Family of children."[41]

As a married woman and then as a widow, Temperance Grant was a vital contributor to Newport's economy. During Sueton Grant's lifetime, she helped run the family's retail business. After his sudden death, she administered his estate and became the independent proprietor of the family's shop, where her conduct brought her into conflict with Simeon Potter. Following Temperance Grant's affairs allows us to see connections that bridge the economic activities of *femes covert* and *femes sole*. During all stages of women's lives, their use of credit was bound up with family interests, and their financial activities helped uphold economic networks that were transatlantic as well as local. At the same time, Grant's widowhood afforded her legal independence and enhanced notoriety, preconditions for what became her extremely public dispute with Simeon Potter, one in which she and Potter articulated understandings of credit that governed men's and women's economic activities.

In the fall of 1744, Temperance Grant, then thirty-six years old, assumed control over her late husband's affairs. Sueton Grant had not written a will, and so had not named executors to settle his affairs and distribute his assets. Therefore, as was its role in such circumstances, Newport's probate court appointed administrators of his estate. That body named Temperance Grant as a co-administrator, along with a male relative, Patrick Grant. The duo faced a daunting task. At the time of his death, Sueton Grant owned a sizeable estate, valued at over £3,050.[42] The prominent merchant also left behind a tangled network of credit relationships arising from his commercial trading and involvement in privateering ventures, the most complicated and costly variant of merchant partnerships. As administrators, Temperance and Patrick Grant assumed legal responsibility for paying debts owed by the deceased and collecting debts owed to him. Their positions led them to interact with many creditors and debtors within a compressed time frame, and only after completing this task could they legally distribute the estate's assets to heirs.

At this moment, Temperance Grant joined a larger cohort of Newport women who became executors and administrators. Battles, shipwrecks, and illness claimed the lives of many New England men during the 1740s, and families and local governments regularly relied on such men's wives to settle their affairs. Husbands routinely appointed their wives as executors of their wills. In commercial regions throughout the Northeast, more than half of the husbands who wrote wills appointed their wives to serve as their executors.[43] Colony laws likewise required that probate courts first seek to assign administration to "the widow or next of kin of the deceased person."[44] In Newport, women composed 40 percent of administrators and executors throughout the mid-eighteenth century.[45] As was true of Temperance Grant, more than 80 percent of female administrators and executors were widows responsible for their husbands' estates. The vast majority of such women acted on their own, without a co-administrator or co-executor.[46] While the record does not specify the reason for the joint appointment of Temperance and Patrick Grant, it is likely that the complexity of Sueton's affairs or the suddenness of his death shaped the probate court's decision. Or these circumstances may have led Temperance to request a co-administrator.

The selection of female administrators and executors, including Temperance Grant, fit within a broader eighteenth-century framework that presumed a unity of interests between spouses. Beginning shortly after her marriage in 1734, Temperance Grant ran her family's drygoods shop. Her responsibilities included tending to customers and taking inventories. In a letter she wrote to Sueton when he was away in 1735, she noted that she had much "to doo Be twene the Shop and the hous."[47] Although her family's business structure would have provided her with little consolation following her husband's tragic death, it would have earned praise from Daniel Defoe, who, like some other handbook authors, argued that "every Tradesman" should "make his wife so much acquainted with his trade . . . that she might be able to carry it on if she pleased," because such knowledge would enable her to successfully serve as his administrator or executor.[48] As Defoe articulated, eighteenth-century men and women accepted women's economic engagement insofar as their labor preserved family wealth, credit networks, and community interests. Just as Mary Prince's and Bathiah MacDaniel's transactions limited the consequences of their husbands' absences, Temperance Grant's activities helped sustain her household and minimized disruptions to Newport's economy following the sudden death of a commercial magnate.

The Grant family's large business meant that Temperance Grant's activities as estate administrator were extensive. Temperance and Patrick Grant initiated numerous lawsuits against Sueton Grant's creditors, especially during the years immediately following his death. Temperance Grant also spent an unusually long time, twenty years, administering her husband's estate. In 1764, as the law required, she finally presented an accounting of her activities to the Newport Town Council. According to this document, Sueton Grant's debts totaled £10,051, exceeding his assets by £864. (The merchant's estate was never legally designated as insolvent, so Temperance and Patrick Grant presumably used their own incomes to make up this difference.) Only the second page of the account survives, yet it displays the magnitude of Temperance Grant's tasks: the £2,213 worth of debts itemized on that page included payments to twenty-two different individuals.[49]

Although co-administrators assumed identical responsibilities, estate administration possessed a different significance for Temperance Grant than for Patrick Grant. For women, unlike for men, estate administration marked a transitional stage, one that amplified their involvement in the credit-based economy. Women's service as administrators and executors, most commonly arising from their husbands' deaths, often marked the end of their status as *femes covert* and their new designation as *femes sole*. Even for women who were extensively involved in credit transactions during marriage, as was Temperance Grant, estate administration imbued familiar activities with new significance: women were now conducting transactions as the legally responsible parties. Their labors foreshadowed a life stage in which women would contract and settle debts in their own names. Moreover, estate administration most significantly enhanced women's visible involvement in the economy. Because men could independently contract and sue throughout their adult lifetimes, cases arising from estate administration composed only a small slice of their debt litigation: just 4 percent in Newport County.[50] In comparison, roughly one-third of the women who participated in debt litigation in the Suffolk and Newport courts did so as administrators or executors.[51] With coverture obscuring a large segment of the female population's economic activities, administrators and executors made up a sizeable proportion of those women eligible to independently participate in credit transactions and litigation.

Aside from its distinctive emotional toll, wrapping up the affairs of one's husband also carried different stakes than other forms of administration and executorship. Men like Patrick Grant certainly possessed a financial interest in the estates they administered. As heirs or creditors, they stood to obtain a portion of those assets that remained after all debts were settled. For widows administering their husbands' estates, this personal investment was magnified. The resources at issue were the primary ones on which women, including Temperance Grant, relied for their comfort and livelihood. Payments to creditors or difficulties collecting from debtors meant that there was less money available to support their families. Household goods sold to pay debts were the same ones on which widows relied for their everyday comfort and survival.[52] During estate administration, as during marriage, a woman's financial activities were uniquely bound up with those of her husband.

Amid her transition to widowhood and her activities as an administrator, Temperance Grant continued her family's retail activities. By keeping the family shop open, Grant was again representative of a larger category of urban women, in this case, entrepreneurs, including shopkeepers and tavernkeepers. In addition to serving city dwellers, such women played an important role in the Atlantic economy by catering to itinerant mariners who routinely disembarked in major ports in search of food, lodging, and provisions. By the 1740s, such seafarers included not only the crews of merchant vessels, but also, increasingly, privateers.

It was in selling to one such privateering crew where Grant made the business decision that ultimately attracted Simeon Potter's criticism. In March 1745, six months after Sueton Grant's death, the *Prince Charles of Lorraine* stopped in Newport. The ship was captained by Simeon Potter and was bound for the Caribbean, a major arena of war, trade, and privateering. Sailors from the crew, some of whom were Dutch, visited Temperance Grant's shop.[53]

Selling to privateers involved a distinctive risk. Visitors to Boston and Newport shops routinely lacked ready cash, so retailers sold them goods on credit, tracking their purchases in running accounts that the customers pledged to pay at a later date. Such arrangements were especially common, and they were decidedly necessary when selling to sailors, as seafaring's structures of deferred payment meant that such men were usually short on cash. While collecting payment from one's clientele was never a sure bet, loaning to sailors carried a unique form of uncertainty. In addition to being relative unknowns, mariners were poor and highly mobile. If they purchased goods on credit and then skipped town without paying, shopkeepers like Grant could not chase them down or extract their due through debt litigation. Retailers assumed the most intense version of such risks when selling to privateering crews, as opposed to those on merchant vessels. As Temperance Grant almost certainly knew, given her husband's prior investments in privateering, whereas sailors on commercial ventures received wages upon the end of the voyage, privateering crews were paid only from shares of any eventual prizes. Such men sometimes returned home without receiving any bounty. Even payouts from successful tours could be significantly delayed as ships awaited admiralty court proceedings. This was perhaps the case when Sueton Grant, his partners, and the visiting official engaged in their fateful inventory of the Newport warehouse's contents.[54]

Temperance Grant opted to sell to the Dutch sailors on credit, but she bent established practices in her attempts to lessen the financial uncertainty arising from this decision. In port cities throughout the Atlantic World, other shopkeepers, including women, sold to sailors on credit in exchange for powers of attorney—that is, legal documents empowering one individual to act in another's stead in specified matters. When used in this way, powers of attorney allowed authorized retailers to garner sailors' future income in payment of their debts, an option that offered much more security than simply allowing sailors to run up accounts.[55] Had Grant used powers of attorney, they would have authorized her to collect just the debts owed to her, and only if the sailors refused to pay. But Grant deviated from this standard usage. She persuaded the ship's crew to sign bills of sale of their individual shares of the vessel's profits as payment for their purchases. The value of these shares might considerably exceed the original debts. The bills of sale offered Grant the highest possible leverage over her debtors, essentially allowing her to speculate on the potentially lucrative privateering voyage.[56]

While Temperance Grant's use of bills of sale was unconventional, the fact of her business dealings with men as a shopkeeper and widowed administrator was commonplace. The law required administrators and executors to file accounts of administration upon completion of their duties. Such probate records are an excellent place to turn to when situating Grant's activities within the broader milieu of urban credit transactions. Accounts of administration offer snapshots of individuals' financial relationships at the times of their deaths. They enumerate all creditors who collected payments from estates and all debtors who delivered them, as well as the sum paid or collected in each settlement.[57] While such accounts do not capture the total universe of credit transactions, they do illuminate the rough outlines of urban credit networks.[58]

Probate records from mid-century Newport underscore that men and women routinely interacted with one another within the urban economy. Among those men whose estates entered probate, 12 percent of all credit relationships were with women, while the remaining 88 percent were with other men.[59] Accounts for women's estates indicate that 78 percent of their credit relationships were with men, while 22 percent were with other women.[60] Because administration accounts attribute credit transactions to the legally responsible parties, rather than to married women or other female intermediaries, we can safely assume that, in practice, women participated in a higher percentage of transactions than these figures suggest. Yet, even taken at face value, these snapshots of Newport residents' estates make it clear that women's activities within the credit economy were routine and familiar to most contemporaries.

When placed within this context, Temperance Grant's dealings with the privateering vessel's crew are less remarkable than two commonplace understandings of the eighteenth-century economy might lead us to believe. Some historians of the colonial period have described only men's business activities, either intentionally or unintentionally suggesting that credit networks lacked female participants. Others have reconstructed the vibrant networks in which women traded goods and services among themselves. Based on these two approaches, we might expect that the majority of the transactions by Newport's women were with other women.[61] That city's probate records do suggest the importance of female networks, since women made up a larger share of creditors and debtors in administration accounts for women's estates than for men's. Nonetheless, the overall figures from Newport probate records underscore the prevalence of mixed-gender financial ties. Women, including Temperance Grant, participated in credit transactions, and they almost necessarily interacted with men. For men like the visiting mariners, involvement in the urban economy entailed routinely transacting business with women.

Although the mere fact that Temperance Grant sold goods to men was not controversial, her boundary-pushing strategies made her the target of Simeon Potter's criticism. Potter, as we have seen earlier in this chapter, verbally attacked her business dealings in numerous venues in Newport. Over and above any protective impulse toward his crew, Potter had a vested interest in discrediting Grant at that time, as he had several lawsuits in progress against her as co-administrator of her late husband's estate.[62] Potter repeatedly declared that Grant "had taken bills of sale for the shares of several men" from the privateering vessel, and that she "had made the men sign [these instruments] instead of Powers of Attorney." Potter depicted this as the desperate strategy of one who was financially overextended and excessively litigious, noting that Grant had filed nineteen cases at the upcoming court session, which "would give her her hands full."[63]

Potter called attention to Grant's use of an unconventional financial instrument and the power dynamics of her transactions with the sailors. By insisting that Grant "made" the sailors sign the bills of sale, Potter insinuated that she had either coerced her customers or taken advantage of their relative ignorance. (In apparent support of Potter's narrative, some sailors testified in the resulting lawsuit that they believed they were signing powers of attorney.[64]) Potter also played into conventional understandings of class and nationality and the associated inversion of gender hierarchies. Potter implied that Grant, a prosperous female shopkeeper and Newport local, had used her superior commercial savvy to trick the Dutch sailors, men who were outsiders and non-native English speakers of limited means. In at least some circles, listeners were shocked by Potter's narrative of Grant's misdeeds. At the merchants' dinner (mentioned at the beginning of this chapter), one of the leading men in attendance proclaimed that "he should not have thought such a thing" possible, and that "if it was so it was wrong."[65]

Potter's insults presumed that Grant maneuvered within a world in which similar norms governed men's and women's economic behavior. *The complete English Tradesman*, the same manual that urged husbands to make their wives familiar with family businesses, defined an "honest tradesman" as one who would "neither cheat or defraud, over-reach or circumvent his neighbor, or indeed any body he deals with." Within this framework, creditors could legitimately vary the mode and length of loans and interest rates on them, depending on their assessments of the reliability of potential debtors. Yet they were also expected to charge fair prices and show forbearance toward well-intentioned debtors by pursuing debt litigation only as a last resort.[66] Insofar as women adhered to these standard practices, their business decisions attracted little attention from contemporaries. In her use of bills of sale and her possible trickery, however, Grant deviated too far from accepted protocols. Once she did so, Potter criticized her in ways that closely resembled the offending words in slander suits between men, which likewise centered on honesty and creditworthiness in business dealings.[67] In claiming that Temperance Grant had cheated the sailors and rushed into debt litigation, Potter recognized that the powerful connections between financial activity, character, and reputation pertained to women as well as to men.

Even as Temperance Grant refuted Potter's allegations, she shared his understanding of creditworthiness. In her May 1746 lawsuit, Grant accused Potter of "contriving to destroy [her] reputation and credit." As was common in colonial slander suits, this paired reference to "reputation and credit" underscores that Temperance Grant, like other British Americans, saw these two terms as inseparable. One's financial standing reflected on one's character, and, in the absence of modern institutions and centralized sources of financial information, reputation and character were proxies for financial creditworthiness.[68] Far from downplaying her retail activities, Grant characterized her business as "a large share of Trade & Merchandize." By adopting the same lexicon found in male merchants' letters and in handbooks for tradesmen, she depicted herself as a person of "good Fame and Repute" who "governed herself by the Principles of Virtue and Honesty." Grant insisted that she had "ever been well esteemed" for her "just & honest dealing among mankind with whom she transacted business."[69]

When defending herself as an honest trader, Grant also noted that she conducted her business "to the advantage of her self & the honorable support of her

Family." Such words painted Grant as conforming to the counsel of Defoe and others that averred, "one great end of an honest tradesman's diligence is the support of his family."[70] At the same time, by alluding to her husband's passing less than two years previously, these lines functioned as a supplemental gendered strategy. Colonial culture often considered widows to be deserving of charity and stressed that they were obligated to support their families following their husbands' deaths. In light of the Grant family's prestige and the attention that the gunpowder explosion received, Temperance Grant's words implied that her business strategies were a necessary response to her unanticipated widowhood.[71] Overall, Grant's insistence on her honorable business practices served two functions in her lawsuit: it resuscitated her reputation within the public forum of the courtroom, and, as was required by the legal definition of slander, marked what Potter said as untrue.

In order to be slanderous, statements needed to be damaging as well as false, and this aspect of Grant's claims likewise linked financial credit and personal character. Grant explained that Potter's words had brought her into "shame and disgrace" by intimating that she had "deceived sundry Persons . . . under a pretense of serving them." This caused "hurt in her business & trade," depriving her of the customers and long-distance trading partners whom she "justly deserved."[72] Grant's language of damaged reputation and its links to economic misfortune made sense within a world in which parties scrutinized others' conduct and profitability as evidence of their creditworthiness. Vilifying Potter for acting "wickedly and maliciously," the female shopkeeper's complaint mirrored the rhetoric of men's correspondence and slander suits, which similarly coupled considerations of reputation and economic loss.[73]

Temperance Grant ultimately lost her suit. In her initial filing, she demanded £10,000, an exorbitant sum symbolic of the intense damage Potter allegedly caused to her reputation. In the lower court, a sixteen-member jury ruled in Grant's favor but awarded her only £10. This outcome satisfied neither Grant, who viewed the sum as insufficient, nor Potter, who protested the jury's siding with the female shopkeeper. Both parties appealed to the Superior Court, where another jury ruled in Potter's favor, finding that he had not engaged in defamation.[74] Yet Grant's defense of her reputation within the public theater of the courtroom may have been just as important in preserving her business standing as any monetary award. Despite Simeon Potter's efforts to ruin her, Temperance Grant lived in Newport until her death in 1791, and she remained an affluent and visible participant in Newport's economy and legal system for many years. She owned slaves, continued to run her shop, sued delinquent debtors, and testified as a witness in others' lawsuits.[75]

Although Temperance Grant's dealings as an administrator and litigant were exceptionally complex and prolonged, in other respects her conduct is representative of broader patterns of female economic contributions. As did countless other Newport women, Grant took part in a family business. She became the administrator of her husband's estate following his death. As a widow, she extended credit and retailed needed goods in her own name to her customers, many of whom were men. Even as Grant's activities thus exemplify women's centrality to credit networks, there are other aspects of her story, including her elite standing, her husband's tragic death, and her protracted conflict with Simeon Potter shortly thereafter, that set her apart.

Temperance Grant's tribulations illuminate the parameters of women's use of credit, even though most women never found themselves embroiled in slander suits. Grant's shopkeeping business was not, in itself, controversial. Rather, she became the target of Potter's vitriol when she deviated too far from established norms, and this suggests that women's use of credit was an ordinary, accepted component of urban life. Moreover, even as Grant and Potter engaged in a bitter dispute, their actions emerged from a shared understanding of credit that pertained to both women and men. In port cities, including Newport, residents participated in a heterosocial world of credit transactions in which assessments of personal reputation shaped one's standing in the marketplace, and one's economic conduct reflected on his or her character.

The Hewes Family's Tannery: Bodies, Space, and Financial Practices

At the same time as Joseph Prince and Bryan MacDaniel struggled to regain their assets and Temperance Grant attempted to restore her reputation against Simeon Potter's insults, the Hewes family of Boston engaged in a protracted credit dispute with Nathaniel Cunningham. Although the immediate legal issues in the case were between men with a formal standing at law, the heated controversy spilled over into household settings. In so doing, it involved numerous women, most notably Abigail Hewes, the wife of George Hewes. Because urban properties were mixed-gender spaces used for both residential and commercial activities, high-stakes financial conflicts encompassed individuals beyond the named creditors and debtors. Moreover, in exceptional circumstances, gendered understandings of bodies and household space could intersect with financial practices, alternately empowering and constraining women as economic actors.

For twelve long years, the fledgling artisans of the Hewes family battled with their former business associate, wealthy Boston merchant Nathaniel Cunningham. Brothers George and Robert Hewes were men of relatively limited means. Their father had not provided them with an inheritance, and George Hewes spent his teenage years as an apprentice.[76] In 1734, the Hewes brothers partnered with Cunningham, borrowing thousands of pounds from him in order to establish a tannery. In return, George and Robert Hewes promised Cunningham half of the tannery's eventual profits. Tanners were among the highest-status artisans in colonial cities, so, for the Hewes family, joining with Cunningham offered the prospect of upward social mobility. Entering the tanning business necessitated purchasing land, supplies, and labor, and these start-up costs would have been beyond the Hewes' means without Cunningham's investment. The trio's business arrangement thus typified the transatlantic flows of credit and capital that linked Boston to the Atlantic World. Metropolitan merchants extended credit to Boston peers such as Cunningham, who, in turn, made advances to local artisans like the Hewes.[77] By 1738, the once-promising partnership had dissolved, giving rise to an unusually long and bitter dispute. The Hewes brothers and Cunningham each scrambled to recover debts allegedly owed by the opposing side.[78] This led to twenty-five or more lawsuits, testimony by at least thirty-two witnesses, and numerous appeals that reached the highest Massachusetts courts.[79]

Both the nature of the conflict and its setting in 1740s Boston contributed to the deep acrimony between the Heweses and Cunningham. The large amount of money at issue and the complex entanglement of the parties' finances meant that both sides doggedly fought to come out ahead. The social implications of credit amid a worsening economic climate further elevated the stakes of the dispute. In the late 1730s and 1740s—the timespan of the conflict involving the tannery—Boston entered a period of economic depression. Possessing less-productive hinterlands than mid-Atlantic ports like New York and Philadelphia, Boston struggled to compete favorably with these major ports. Laborers and artisans were among those hardest hit by their city's decline, and the Hewes family probably feared that it would be impossible to rebound if the partnership's disintegration favored their opponent. In attempts to highlight their predicament and garner sympathy for their plight, the Hewes brothers described themselves as "poor laborers lain under great disadvantages" as they fought against "a man of great wealth & interest."[80] Meanwhile, for Cunningham, the partnership's termination occurred at a time when Boston merchants were increasingly unable to maintain a favorable balance of trade with the metropole. Losing the tannery's revenue threatened to compromise Cunningham's ability to pay his British merchant creditors and, within that period's understandings of credit, defaulting would have reflected poorly on his character.[81] Ultimately, both the Hewes family and Cunningham sought not only to recoup their losses, but to also preserve their reputations for honest dealing, much like Temperance Grant had done in her slander suit.

The Hewes property, centrally located in Boston, was an early epicenter of the dispute with Cunningham. In spite of the Hewes family's claims that they were poor laborers, their holdings were considerable. Touted in tannery advertisements as "the most convenient and commodious place for Business in Boston," the family's land was on Water Street, one block south of the city's major commercial artery, King Street.[82] It contained the two-story house of George and Abigail Hewes and several outbuildings for the production and retail sides of the tanning business. The Heweses maintained their records in a "counting house"; tanned and stored their leather in several small shops and warehouses; and sold leather, meat, and soap from their retail shop.[83] The site and its environs were bustling places. Servants and boarders lived with the Hewes family in their residence; apprentices, hired hands, and slaves worked at the tannery; and customers and other Bostonians walked along Water Street. Events on the Hewes property were broadly visible to Bostonians, and this escalated the tensions between the Hewes family and Cunningham.

Just as Simeon Potter sought to tarnish Temperance Grant's reputation by criticizing her in public spaces throughout Newport, Cunningham used guerilla tactics outside of the court to mark the Hewes brothers as dishonest. In 1739, the conflict reached a head as Cunningham and his associates kept watch and patrolled around the perimeter of the Water Street property. Both day and night they yelled, brandished clubs, threw stones at the windows, and rattled sticks along the fence. They also tried to cart leather, soap, and commercial records away from the tannery. Cunningham maintained that the court had authorized him to seize the Hewes family's property as payments for their debts, and claimed he was preventing his opponents from moving their leather beyond the sheriff's reach.[84] Equally, Cunningham's actions attempted to sway public opinion against the Hewes brothers, since the tannery's workers and customers, neighbors, pedestrians, and those inside the family's house inevitably saw and heard the chaos. Cunningham's unconventional methods underscored the intensity of the controversy and drew others into the fray.

It was during this time that George's twenty-eight-year-old wife, Abigail, entered into the disagreement with Cunningham. Whereas the transactions of Mary Prince, Bathia MacDaniel, and Temperance Grant precipitated their involvement in the resulting disputes, family relationships and urban geography drew Abigail Hewes into a falling-out between men. Because her possessions and assets were bound up with those of her husband, Abigail Hewes had a direct stake in the conflict with Cunningham. And, with her family's living quarters located on the same property as the tannery, she could not help but notice Cunningham's disturbances. When George Hewes was imprisoned as a result of one of Cunningham's many lawsuits, it fell to his spouse to protect her interests and act as her husband's agent.

Abigail Hewes confronted Nathaniel Cunningham inside and outside her residence four times in the spring and fall of 1739. In April, as Cunningham and his men tried to seize the tannery's supplies, Hewes, then approaching her third trimester of pregnancy, came out into the yard to stop them.[85] Twice in June, during the ten days prior to the birth of her child, she spoke to Cunningham inside her house.[86] The fourth and final episode occurred in September. A bedridden Abigail Hewes again tried to stop Cunningham and his associates from seizing the family's property, this time by relaying a message through a servant she sent out into the yard.[87] Her four exchanges with Cunningham exemplify the range of sites in which discussions of credit occurred.

During these encounters, Abigail Hewes alternately presented herself as an innocent bystander and as an involved party in the dispute. During the April incident, she firmly sided with her family. Positioning herself as her husband's agent, Hewes demonstrated in-depth knowledge of the controversy as she asked Cunningham, "You have sued my Husband for ten thousand pounds, and by what authority now do you take all this leather?" When Cunningham continued to root through the tannery's stores, she ordered, "My Husband charges you upon your perill not to remove one hide."[88] In June, Hewes again criticized Cunningham for his use of tactics beyond formal legal channels, saying that she "hoped when he got all he could by the Law he would be contented."[89]

Abigail Hewes employed a second tactic in June, accusing Cunningham of causing *her* undue suffering, when his dispute actually concerned the tannery. Characterizing his actions as "Barbarous," she complained that there was "no body to help her," because he had imprisoned George and Robert Hewes and seized the family's slaves. Moreover, she protested that Cunningham and his men "made so much noise that she could not sleep night nor day" and that it was impossible for "she and her children" to "subsist when they were so hemm'd in and in such Danger by his peoples throwing stones."[90] Cunningham's reply carried Abigail Hewes's remarks to their logical conclusion. He proposed that, since she was troubled by an affair that arguably did not concern her, she and her children should relocate to her father's home in nearby Roxbury. Such a move would have transferred Abigail Hewes from the care of one patriarch, her imprisoned and indebted husband, to another, her father. She swiftly rejected this proposal. Claiming the Hewes family property as her own, she refused to "go out of her own house to please him or any one else."[91] The multiple grounds on which Abigail Hewes protested against Cunningham's conduct attest to her complex positioning as a married woman drawn into a protracted familial dispute.

Atypical elements of Abigail Hewes's conversations with Cunningham in June suggest that she may have manipulated the gender dynamics of household spaces to her advantage. Negotiations surrounding credit routinely occurred in homes, so the mere fact that Hewes conversed with Cunningham inside her residence was not unusual. Cunningham, however, spoke with her in a second-floor bedroom, rather than in one of the first-floor rooms that the family would have typically used with visitors. With Hewes clearly in the late stages of her pregnancy, that chamber, moreover, resembled a birthing room. During what historians have termed "social childbirth," expectant mothers withdrew to the company of other women. In keeping with these practices, female relatives, friends, boarders, and servants were all present in Abigail Hewes's quarters when she spoke with Cunningham. As the time for the birth approached, female attendants drew curtains, blocked keyholes, stoked fires, and lit candles. Men's presence in such spaces was, as historian Laura Gowing explained, "lewd, disorderly, and uncivilized."[92] When Hewes conversed with Cunningham, her chamber was not yet shut off from the outside world, but her numerous female onlookers signaled that she was in the early stages of preparing for labor.

Knowing that Cunningham most likely would be uncomfortable in such a feminine space, and that his presence could be construed as inappropriate, Abigail Hewes may well have spoken to Cunningham in her chamber to maintain the upper hand in the conversation. Several bystanders reported that Hewes had invited Cunningham upstairs. Hewes's mother, Abigail Sever, explained that her daughter, "who was then sick," "got off of her Bed and looked out of the Window and called to Mr Cunningham and desired him to step up Chamber to her."[93] Boarder Ruth Loring likewise recounted that "Mrs Hewes called to the Maid to desire Mr Cunningham to Come up chamber to her." Loring further suggested that, upon entering the room, Cunningham had attempted to remain "as calm and as mild as possible," and that Mrs. Hewes had provoked him. Hewes, Loring explained, "said several things which moved [Cunningham]," but he remained resolved that "she would not make him angry." It was only when she expressed her hope that Cunningham "would be contented when got all he could by the Law" that he got up from his chair and "seemed surprised."[94] No witnesses explicitly stated that Cunningham had entered the room uninvited, or that Abigail Hewes had at any point ordered him to leave.[95] Regardless of whether she invited Cunningham upstairs or simply exploited a favorable situation as it unfolded, the June conversations offered a prime setup for her husband's lawsuit.

The conversations between Abigail Hewes and Nathaniel Cunningham yielded one of the many legal cases between the Hewes brothers and Cunningham. In January 1740, George Hewes sued Cunningham for acts of trespass committed the previous June. He alleged that Cunningham had disturbed his then-pregnant wife by overseeing a raucous watch outside the family's house and had "threatened" her, so that she was "much terrifyed, could not rest, & was cast into a dangerous Fever." As a result, George contended, Abigail had given birth prematurely and was unable to nurse. He was put to "great Expense" caring for his wife and their sickly infant. He sought £500 in damages.[96]

George Hewes's claims aligned with prevailing views of childbirth. While George did not assert outright that Cunningham had entered a birthing room, he played on understandings of gendered space when he implied that Cunningham's conversations with Abigail were inappropriate. His lawsuit also reflected understandings of the female body as a porous vessel. Within this view, any external force exerted upon women, including emotion, could disrupt the flow of bodily fluids and cause illness. Pregnant women were especially vulnerable to such shocks. Anger could cause a sudden influx of blood into the womb, leading to a miscarriage or premature labor, while fright could cause a contraction of bodily fluids and thus cause trouble when a woman was nursing.[97] George implied that Cunningham had brought on these difficulties by maintaining the watch on the Hewes' property and speaking harshly with Abigail.

Abigail Hewes appeared within her husband's lawsuit as his possession and as the passive recipient of Cunningham's offenses. Within the larger context of the twenty-five or more lawsuits between the Hewes brothers and Cunningham, the hotly contested January 1740 case was part of each side's efforts to emerge as the net creditor following the breakup of their partnership. Other simultaneous cases concerned individual debts supposedly owed by the Heweses or Cunningham, and property that Cunningham allegedly seized from the Hewes family. In one such suit, the Hewes accused Cunningham of taking four enslaved men who worked at the tannery and sought £500 from him as damages.[98] By seeking damages for harm allegedly committed against Abigail, George Hewes positioned his wife as yet another object in this ongoing accounting.

This line of argument silenced Abigail Hewes, overlooking her active confrontation of Cunningham. Much like the claims by Joseph Prince and Bryan MacDaniel, George Hewes's legal filings hinged on understandings of coverture, where he was the protector, or even the owner, of his wife's body. Moreover, George's claims invited scrutiny of Abigail's body by women as well as men. Women's intimate work in caring for other women authorized them to become witnesses in lawsuits concerning the female body, such as rape and fornication cases, and George Hewes's unconventional allegations meant that women's words played an important role in the case.[99] Yet Abigail herself could not testify, as the law barred wives from bearing witness for cases in which their husbands were parties.[100]

As the trial unfolded, Abigail Hewes's four female attendants, a female midwife, and a male doctor assessed her conversations with Cunningham and their effects on her emotions and health. Recounting the exchanges between Abigail Hewes and Cunningham in depth, these witnesses evaluated whether she was "very much Surprized" by Cunningham's remarks or remained "well composed and free from any surprise or concern." They disputed whether "Cunningham's frighting" had led Abigail Hewes enter "such a Weak & Low Condition" that her life was in danger, or whether she was inherently "a weak woman inclining to a Consumption," whose labor proceeded "well and better" than expected. And they debated whether Hewes delivered her daughter early, "in as miserable a Condition as any . . . Delivered Alive," or on time, as well as whether she had her milk "frightned away from her," or had experienced similar difficulty nursing her previous infants. The proceedings gave voice to medical professionals and to laywomen's knowledge of financial disputes and the female body. Abigail Hewes herself, despite being present as some of the witnesses testified, did not speak to her own emotions, health, or medical history.[101]

In the case concerning Cunningham's alleged harm to Abigail Hewes, the Boston merchant ultimately came out ahead. The Court of Common Pleas initially awarded George Hewes £100, one-fifth of the sum he had sought. Cunningham appealed to the Superior Court, where the judges overturned the original decision and ordered Hewes to pay Cunningham's court costs.[102] Even within a framework that stressed emotions' powerful effects on the body, it was difficult to link Abigail Hewes's conversations with Cunningham with the complications she experienced several days and weeks later. A ruling in favor of George Hewes, moreover, would have required the court to accept his claim that the second-floor chamber was a feminine space when Cunningham intruded into it. As the events of the controversy powerfully demonstrated, and the court's judgment seemingly affirmed, urban residences and their environs were, under ordinary circumstances, heterosocial spaces that were put to multiple simultaneous uses.

Although George Hewes lost the case concerning Abigail's body, the Hewes family emerged as the ultimate victor within its larger conflict with Cunningham. The final stages of the contest attested to its high stakes. The penultimate act occurred in 1748, when the parties agreed to submit their many outstanding disputes to referees. These court-appointed arbitrators reversed all of the court's prior judgments in favor of Nathaniel Cunningham and determined that Cunningham owed the Hewes brothers a net balance of £2,234. The legal battle then reached its final détente in 1750, more than a decade after the former partners first severed their relationship. By this point, two of the key parties, Nathaniel Cunningham and George Hewes, had died, and Nathaniel Cunningham Jr. had taken up his late father's cause. In his last failed appeal, a petition that the Massachusetts legislature dismissed, Cunningham Jr. contended that he lacked sufficient background knowledge to effectively combat the Hewes family. While such pleas of ignorance were, in part, a strategy to win the legislators' sympathies, they equally reflected the protracted affair's intensity.

Cunningham Jr.'s petition characterized the matter as consisting of "sundry disputes and controversies" and "a number of cross actions."[103] Such restrained language hardly did justice to the conflict's complexity and scale, including the locations it spanned and the numerous women and men it involved.

The protracted legal affair between the Hewes family and Cunningham is exceptional not only for its magnitude, but also for the unconventional nature of George Hewes's claims. As we will continue to see, overt references to femininity are notably absent from the overwhelming majority of eighteenth-century financial disputes. In contrast, gendered understandings of bodies and urban space were central to the 1740 case. The battle between the tanners and the merchant escalated as Abigail Hewes entered the third trimester of her pregnancy and reached its apex as she prepared for labor. This was a perfect storm that drew maximal attention to gender relations, since the intensely embodied experience of childbirth was strongly associated with gendered work patterns, uses of space, and forms of knowledge. The second-floor chamber's multiple uses and Abigail Hewes's dual roles as pregnant mother and interested economic actor created circumstances that she quite possibly used to her advantage at the time of her conversations with Cunningham. After the fact, these same dynamics led others to scrutinize Abigail's body within the context of a larger credit dispute. The conflict between the Hewes family and Cunningham brought to the forefront understandings of the female body and the gendering of household spaces that more often remained in the background of eighteenth-century economic life.

Conclusion

In eighteenth-century Boston and Newport, virtually all residents' labors and economic pursuits supported the cities' involvement in Atlantic commercial networks. Market-oriented transactions involving credit were routine, and quite frequently they occurred between women and men, with women of varied social classes doing business with a variety of men, ranging from commercial elites to those of limited means. As estate administrators penned accounts that offered snapshots of the deceased's financial networks, they captured this fundamentally heterosocial character of New England's port economies. The dealings of Bathiah MacDaniel, Mary Prince, Temperance Grant, and Abigail Hewes reinforce this picture. The Princes and Grants, as middling and elite families engaged in retail trades, purchased imported goods from major wholesalers. Mary Prince settled with supplier Nathaniel Wheelwright, and news of Temperance Grant's business strategies piqued the interest of the Newport and Philadelphia merchants gathered for dinner. Abigail Hewes, who was part of a family of artisans, tangled with a prominent merchant and investor, Nathaniel Cunningham. Women also found clienteles among lower-class men, as is most vividly illustrated through Temperance Grant's sales of goods to Dutch sailors. Given the extent to which economic activity bound women and men together, it is fitting that only one of our four women, Bathiah MacDaniel, found herself in a dispute arising from a credit relationship with another woman.

Women's contemporaries widely accepted their involvement in financial dealings. The circumstances of the four figures depicted here—MacDaniel, Prince, Grant, and Hewes—exemplify the factors that facilitated free white women's vibrant and vital roles within urban economies. Far from existing as private or purely domestic realms, households functioned both as centers of financial activity and as economic units, and this facilitated the extensive use of credit by women as well as men. Boston and Newport residents readily involved women in actions of economic and legal importance. These included borrowing from and lending to women, seeking payment from them, and wrangling with them inside and outside of court over financial matters. Only after the fact did third parties, whether husbands or interested observers (such as Simeon Potter), attempt to curtail or discipline women's conduct. As New Englanders widely recognized during that period, these women's use of credit was especially necessary because, after 1740, women increasingly outnumbered men in both Boston and Newport. Bryan MacDaniel, Joseph Prince, and Sueton Grant were part of a larger cohort of sailors, ship captains, merchants, and soldiers who routinely went abroad for long periods, leaving their wives behind to preserve households and family businesses. As a result of the continued tolls of seafaring and war, Boston and Newport also contained growing populations of widows, many of whom, Temperance Grant included, supported themselves by supplying goods and services to residents and visitors.

The ordeals of Bathiah MacDaniel, Mary Prince, Temperance Grant, and Abigail Hewes all emerged from the ubiquity and high stakes of credit transactions in New England's largest ports. Matters of credit and debt permeated Boston and Newport. While households were centers of financial activity, so were docks, warehouses, shops, yards, streets, and coffeehouses. Women's economic involvement took them to each of these places, both as direct participants and as subjects of intrigues. In all of these settings, financial standings and practices were bound up with considerations of character and reputation that, in their broad outlines, pertained to all. The intertwined financial and social meanings of credit motivated Simeon Potter to persistently criticize Temperance Grant, and they led Grant to sue him for £10,000 in damages. Similar concerns spurred Cunningham to harass the Hewes family and induced the two parties to engage in twelve years of suits and countersuits. Although many routine transactions occurred without incident, the social significance of credit created a potential for explosive conflicts involving women and men alike.

At the same time, some significant differences marked women's and men's engagements with credit and debt. Credit was often collective. Households survived through the pooling of labor and resources, and individuals' reputations remained tied to those of their households and families. Yet, during marriage, women were positioned differently within systems of household and family credit than were men. For married women like Bathiah MacDaniel and Mary Prince, their daily financial responsibilities were extensive, but coverture both obscured such activities within the documentary record and provided a vocabulary through which men could retroactively constrain the economic powers of *femes covert*. The social and legal significance of marriage also meant that estate administration occupied a distinctive place in the lives of women, including Temperance Grant. Women primarily settled the affairs of their late spouses, as opposed to doing so for other relatives and friends, as men often did. The probate process thus served as a bridge between their status as *femes covert* and *femes sole*, and their own future livelihoods were uniquely bound up with the finances of the deceased. Family ties differently mediated men's and women's relationships to the urban economy.

Gendered understandings of space, bodies, and social hierarchies could surface in financial disputes and, in rare circumstances, shape their courses. In three of our four conflicts, gendered understandings of feminine comportment and patriarchal households were not emphasized. Simeon Potter did not state outright that Temperance Grant had violated norms of proper womanly deference to men, but he hinted at this when implying that she had tricked the sailors. Grant chiefly stressed her standing as an honest trader, but she also suggested that Potter, a powerful man, had prevented a widow from fulfilling her obligation to provide for her family. Joseph Prince's and Bryan MacDaniel's lawsuits both concerned their wives' economic power, yet neither man explicitly framed his case in these terms. In contrast, spatial and embodied understandings of gender directly shaped the dispute between the Hewes family and Cunningham. Abigail Hewes's impending labor and the temporary construct of the birthing room made Nathaniel Cunningham an outsider when he entered her second-floor chamber. Hewes perhaps used these considerations to her advantage when she conversed with Cunningham, and her husband certainly did so when he sued Cunningham for causing bodily harm to mother and child. Here, pregnancy brought gender issues to the forefront, to a degree that was atypical for urban credit transactions.

In eighteenth-century Boston and Newport, men and women routinely interacted in matters of credit and debt. Because understandings of credit linked considerations of personal character and financial probity, relationships of indebtedness shaped gendered power relations. Nonetheless, surveying the ways in which free white women gained access to credit, as well as the meanings of their transactions as revealed through explosive conflicts, is only the first step in analyzing the extent of their power and influence. To more fully appreciate the ways in which economic life helped constitute eighteenth-century social relations, we must look more closely at the lifespan of credit relationships, beginning with the everyday work surrounding borrowing and lending.

CHAPTER 2

"She Hath Often Requested the Sum"
Credit Relations Outside of Court

As Boston and Newport developed into bustling ports, their residents relied on credit and debt to structure a wide range of market-oriented transactions. In the absence of sufficient quantities of ready cash, borrowing and lending undergirded myriad business and labor relationships. Bostonians and Newporters also increasingly used credit to purchase the widening array of imported consumer goods touted by their cities' shopkeepers.[1] While credit and debt often fade into the background as invisible conduits of exchange rather than as objects of study, every stage of these credit relationships required time, attention, and skill, beginning when parties initially formed agreements. Urban residents engaged in additional activities when they sought or provided payment, contested financial claims in lower-level courts, or appealed to higher authorities.

With maritime labor and military service leading many Boston and Newport men to travel abroad or die young, women assumed much of this financial labor, beginning with the phases of credit relationships that transpired outside of court. Amid the largely anodyne language of the period's financial and legal records, men and women occasionally used evocative verbs that acknowledged this reality. One man recalled that an artisan's wife "carried on and managed" all her husband's business. Female creditors stressed having "often requested" payment from debtors. A Newport widow, awarding herself compensation for her work administering an estate, cited her "Time & Trouble In Runing after People to Settle Accompts Collect Debts & in Paying Money."[2] Taking such suggestive phrases as its point of departure, this chapter analyzes free women's financial labor outside of court. By mining legal records for shards of evidence concerning the routine practices that preceded debt litigation, we can establish a kaleidoscopic portrait of the centrality of women's skilled work to Boston's and Newport's credit economies.

Women in these two cities handled the full complement of financial records and, in so doing, drew on a set of well-established practices that were common to women and men. In practice, a household's activities situated all of its members as creditors or debtors, enabling or even requiring them to engage in the telltale practices associated with these roles. At the same time as some women engaged with credit and debt as *femes sole*, many others did so as a result of their positions within households. Wives, daughters, and female servants could pay or collect debts on behalf of the household heads named in written records. Furthermore, while reading, writing, and arithmetical skill were certainly components of financial activity, other competencies were equally required in managing credit. These included tracking down or evading one's trading partners, striking the desired posture of assertiveness or deference, handling documents, and enlisting allies for assistance. Although women typically possessed more-limited literacy and access to formal schooling than did men of a similar class standing, all city dwellers exercised significant financial and legal savvy as they moved through their communities and regions as borrowers and lenders.

Acting as a creditor or debtor shaped men's and women's social positioning in Boston and Newport. Male and female creditors manifested their authority over debtors through their use of discretionary power and assertiveness. Creditors dictated the terms on which they extended loans, tracked down and confronted debtors, and enjoyed the final say in determining whether debtors had discharged their obligations. Debtors, whether men or women, responded to creditors' collection efforts through their own patterns of movement and the use of written records. As long as creditors possessed documented proof of loans, however, debtors only had limited abilities to push back against demands. Attending to the labor associated with borrowing and lending, then, underscores the contingent nature of social hierarchies within New England cities. A woman or a man could exercise authority over one acquaintance as a creditor, while, at the same time, deferring to another in his or her capacity as a debtor.

Women's Uses of Credit: Forms and Frequency

Two major factors determined the ways in which New Englanders engaged with credit. First, positioning oneself as a creditor or debtor shaped an individual's behaviors and goals within a given relationship. Second, written records of financial obligations structured the mechanics of settlements and the relative power of creditors and debtors within their interactions. Before delving more deeply into women's financial practices, then, it is necessary to examine the forms of credit that they employed and the frequency with which they did so.

Boston and Newport residents used four kinds of financial records to track and establish their credit relationships: accounts, promissory notes, bonds, and bills of exchange. Accounts tallied debits or credits and recorded one person's ongoing dealings with another. These took a variety of forms, ranging from rudimentary jottings on scraps of paper to the highly technical products of double-entry bookkeeping. All such records shared certain fundamental features. Because one party in a two-sided financial transaction could draw up an account without the involvement or approval of the other, accounts did not represent debtors' formal promises to pay. They specified neither interest rates nor the dates by which debtors would pay off their balances, and rewritten accounts carried the same weight as originals in courts of law. These features meant that accounts created significant room for negotiation between creditors and debtors during settlements.

Bonds and promissory notes, in contrast, were binding legal documents. Through promissory notes, debtors pledged to pay certain sums, without predetermined penalties if they failed to do so. Bonds established not only debtors' promises to pay the specified sums, but also the relevant penalties, typically twice the amount of the original debts, if they failed to do so. Beyond these differences, the original bonds and promissory notes had similar legal value. Because they contained debtors' signatures, they constituted legally binding promises. Creditors could assign them to third parties, who then possessed full standing to collect on them. In comparison with accounts, bonds and promissory notes allowed for much less pushback by debtors.

Boston and Newport residents chiefly used a fourth instrument, bills of exchange, in overseas trading. These bills functioned similarly to present-day checks. When an individual writes a check, he or she instructs a bank to withdraw a specified amount from his or her account and pay it to the bearer of the check. In the case of bills of exchange, individuals or commercial firms replaced the role of a bank. When a person wished to "draw on" a distant debtor, he or she drafted a bill of exchange, or instructions requiring a debtor to pay a specified sum to that instrument's holder within a stipulated time period. The bill's creator then sold it into circulation locally, with the bill's price reflecting assessments of the debtor's creditworthiness. In so doing, the bill's author received satisfaction for his or her debt relatively quickly. Ultimately, after the bill was sold from person to person, some purchaser would send it across the Atlantic Ocean. There it continued to be sold until someone presented it to the named debtor, who was then legally required to adhere to the bill's terms of payment.

The legal properties of each of these document types suited them to particular kinds of relationships, reflecting a range of distances, durations, and levels of trust between parties. Bills of exchange, bonds, and notes all signified one-time obligations, whereas individuals primarily used bills of exchange in conjunction with transatlantic trade. Bonds and promissory notes typically facilitated local and regional transactions. Accounts captured ongoing trade relations that spanned varying distances. Some accounts were between neighbors, while others bridged the Atlantic Ocean, such as when a British merchant maintained an account listing goods sold to a shopkeeper in North America. Creditors assessed debtors' trustworthiness when determining which forms of financial papers to use. They opted for accounts when dealing with trusted ongoing trading partners, while they often preferred bonds and notes when transacting business with relative strangers or less creditworthy individuals.[3]

These features meant that the relative prevalence of the various kinds of financial records changed over time. In the seventeenth century, the ubiquity of ongoing, neighborly exchanges meant that New Englanders chiefly recorded debts within accounts. By the early eighteenth century, ordinary people, especially those living in cities and towns, more routinely engaged in market-oriented transactions. As they did so, they conducted an increasing number of their dealings using bonds and promissory notes, while also continuing their widespread use of accounts.[4]

Because accounts, bonds, promissory notes, and bills of exchange demanded different skills and variously structured transactions, comparing women's and men's use of these forms of credit is an important starting point for discussions of financial practices. Debt cases offer the largest archive of financial documents from individuals across the class spectrum, so they provide a rough indicator of the relative frequency with which women and men used accounts, promissory notes, and bonds. (Lawsuits in county courts tended not to concern bills of exchange.) County court records demonstrate that similar overall patterns characterized women's and men's use of credit during the four decades prior to the Revolution. In both Suffolk and Newport Counties, cases concerning formal financial instruments (bonds and promissory notes) made up the largest share of women's and men's debt cases, with men engaging in suits concerning bonds and promissory notes only slightly more often than women (tables 2.1 and 2.2). Cases concerning accounts, meanwhile, made up slightly less than half of both women's and men's debt cases in both counties.

Such similarities suggest that, contrary to historians' speculations, patterns of use did not mark particular assets or records as "feminine" or "masculine." Some historians have contended that eighteenth-century women preferred to invest in credit instruments rather than land, because they were liquid and portable. By this logic, we might expect to see a higher proportion of women's

TABLE 2.1.

Types of debt cases in the Newport County Court of Common Pleas, 1731–1771

	Debt cases (N)[a]	Accounts (%)	Bonds and promissory notes (%)	Other debts (%)[b]
Men	1,078	43.7	48.7	7.6
Women[c]	252	42.8	44.0	13.9
Female non-administrators	145	47.6	42.1	11.7
Female administrators	110	36.3	47.2	16.4

Source: Record Books and Case Files, Newport County Court of Common Pleas, Rhode Island Supreme Court Judicial Records Center.

[a] On sampling, see the appendix. In order to create a sufficiently large sample of women's cases, this table includes data from more court terms for women than for men. This table therefore should not be read for evidence of the overall ratio of male and female litigants in debt cases, a topic discussed in chapter 3. Because some cases concerned multiple kinds of debt, percentages may not total 100.

[b] Includes cases concerning rent, bills of exchange, oral promises, and those of unknown type.

[c] Some cases included both female administrators and female non-administrators. Therefore the total number of women's cases is smaller than the sum of these subcategories.

TABLE 2.2.

Types of debt cases in the Suffolk County Court of Common Pleas, 1730–1770

	Debt cases (N)[a]	Accounts (%)	Bonds and promissory notes (%)	Other debts (%)[b]
Men	875	36.7	52.9	10.0
Women	134	32.1	44.8	23.1
Female non-administrators	84	28.3	40.5	25.0
Female administrators	50	34.5	50.1	20.1

Source: Record Books and Case Files, Suffolk County Court of Common Pleas, Massachusetts State Archives.

[a] On sampling, see the appendix. In order to create a sufficiently large sample of women's cases, this table includes data from more court terms for women than for men. This table therefore should not be read for evidence of the overall ratio of male and female litigants in debt cases, a topic discussed in chapter 3. Because some cases concerned multiple kinds of debt, percentages may not total 100.

[b] Includes cases concerning rent, bills of exchange, oral promises, and those of unknown type.

than men's cases concerning bonds and promissory notes. Others have argued that the sophisticated financial acumen associated with bonds, promissory notes, and bills of exchange limited their use primarily to men.[5] The essential similarities between men's and women's debt litigation challenge both of these hypotheses, demonstrating that all New Englanders saw fit to use whatever modes of credit were available to them.

Deeper comparisons reveal that women encountered bonds and promissory notes in slightly different ways than men (tables 2.1 and 2.2). Women were more likely to use these instruments as administrators and executors, rather than as debtors or creditors in their own right. The percentage of female administrators' and executors' cases concerning formal instruments is similar to that of male litigants, a population overwhelmingly comprised of non-administrators. Such findings reflect the fact that female administrators and executors overwhelmingly settled men's estates, so men's transactions determined the forms of credit that they encountered. In contrast, suits concerning accounts that were brought by female non-administrators in Newport County formed a slightly larger share of women's own cases than of men's or female administrators' cases, probably because this mode of record-keeping predominated in the retail and service sectors in which women routinely participated. Even though women were less likely than men to establish obligations using bonds and notes, female administrators' extensive use of these instruments attests to women's familiarity with them.

Judging from the transactions that reached the county courts, women were also more likely to encounter bonds and promissory notes as creditors than as debtors. In Newport County, women were plaintiffs and creditors in 68 percent of the cases concerning promissory notes and 65 percent of the cases concerning bonds.[6] Similarly, women in Suffolk County were plaintiffs and creditors in 73 percent of the cases concerning promissory notes and 79 percent of those concerning bonds.[7] In contrast, women in both Newport and Boston were plaintiffs in approximately half of the cases concerning book debt, and creditors and debtors made up a roughly even split of male users of all forms of credit.[8] Several factors may have contributed to women's distinctive and lopsided use of bonds and promissory notes. Widows and single women, often possessing more-limited assets and sources of income than men, may have encountered difficulty obtaining credit using formal instruments. Alternatively, female debtors may have strategically avoided the inflexible terms associated with bonds or notes. Or, since they tended to primarily receive credit from others in their capacity as laborers and consumers, they may have had a limited need to borrow using these instruments.

While court records provide insight into the relative frequency with which women encountered various modes of credit, probate records suggest a relationship between the wealth of *femes sole* and the extensiveness of their credit networks. Unsurprisingly, widows and single women with larger estates tended to use credit more extensively than those of limited means. Newport's Ann Kay, the sixty-six-year-old widow of a wealthy colony official and landholder, was sufficiently prominent that a Boston newspaper published word of her death in 1740. At that time, she possessed a considerable estate, valued at £5,933. Of the total sum, £3,883 consisted of upward of ten bonds and promissory notes, most for several hundred pounds. Such instruments constituted almost two-thirds of Kay's estate. Thus they were not only an important component of her wealth, but also attested to her role in infusing capital into her community.[9] Similarly,

Ann Chaloner, the widow of Newport merchant Walter Chaloner, held bonds and notes totaling £1,116, or more than one-quarter of the value of her estate, when she died in 1770.[10]

Prominent women of means also persuaded other Newport residents to loan them money. Such women's debts were small, relative to the value of their estates. Ann Kay, in 1740, owed debts totaling £91 to six individuals. Given that the men who inventoried Kay's residence found £162 in cash, she could have paid such debts whenever she chose to do so.[11] In 1745, Patience Redwood, a member of a leading Newport merchant family, likewise owed a total of only £30 to seven individuals, while her estate was valued at £4,689.[12] Such women used borrowing not as a significant source of cash, but rather as a pragmatic arrangement in the course of their ongoing financial relationships.

Women of moderate means used credit in more circumscribed ways. In 1740, Barbara Trott of Newport died in possession of a modest estate, valued at £51. She owned a limited amount of furniture—only a feather bed, chest of drawers, chairs, and a table, each of which was "old" or "small." She had a mere £4 in cash, a fraction of the sums kept on hand by wealthier women, including Ann Kay.[13] Yet Trott nonetheless used credit in small quantities in the course of her everyday dealings. Upon her death, she owed four Newport residents amounts ranging from a few shillings to several pounds, and one man, Peter Easton, owed her £3.[14] Sylvia Woodman, whose estate was valued at £149 in 1746, was indebted to four individuals and was the creditor to one. Each sum in question was less than £20.[15] Women who were not among the top echelons of the elite also participated in larger transactions. When Elizabeth Duploise died in 1747, she held only one credit instrument. Yet this bond was worth £85, more than one-third of the total value of her estate.[16] While Duploise's bond probably held greater importance for her than did one for a similar amount held by Ann Kay or Ann Chaloner, all of these women's credit instruments testified to their involvement in Newport's economy.

Female entrepreneurs, such as tavernkeepers and shopkeepers, used credit much more extensively than their wealth alone would suggest. One Boston shopkeeper, Rebecca Amory, who advertised having "choice" imported goods to be "sold reasonably," made an increasing number of purchases on credit as her business grew. She went from making 39 payments totaling £825 in 1732 to 122 payments totaling over £3,000 in 1736.[17] Another Boston shopkeeper, Martha Salisbury, stocked her shelves with goods bought on credit from the London merchants Lane, Son, and Fraser. Salisbury purchased bills of exchange in Boston and shipped them across the Atlantic to pay her suppliers. She extended credit to a wide circle of Bostonians as she sold her wares, maintaining accounts for eighty individuals between 1753 and 1773.[18] Given that such women's businesses involved continually establishing and settling debts, their financial lives required even more transactions and interactions than would be visible within snapshots from probate records.

Accounts, promissory notes, bonds, and bills of exchange collectively structured credit relationships throughout New England's ports and the larger British Atlantic world. Overall, the same patterns characterized women's and men's use of credit, with city dwellers spreading their activities across all available forms of credit, doing so in roughly similar proportions. For women as well as for men, wealth and economic pursuits shaped their patterns of financial activity. While even women of limited means extended and received credit, affluent women and entrepreneurs did so most extensively. Yet certain patterns also distinguished women's financial activities from men's. Widows and single women availed themselves of formal credit instruments primarily to borrow rather than to lend money, and their economic pursuits led them to use accounts slightly more often than men. In addition, estate administration marked a more significant departure from daily life for women than it did for men. Settling estates increased women's contact with bonds and promissory notes, such that their patterns of financial activity even more closely resembled those of men. As we continue to investigate everyday practices, we will frequently encounter women keeping and settling accounts, loaning funds using bonds and promissory notes, and acting as administrators and executors.

Contracting Debts

When debts were contracted, a spirit of negotiation authorized all interested parties to systematically evaluate potential agreements. The terms of contracts were vital to all subsequent stages in the lifespans of credit transactions. Before they formalized their agreements, prospective borrowers and purchasers could push back against undesirable terms in ways that were not possible later. Creditors, meanwhile, were equally invested in the form and content of written agreements, because such considerations shaped their subsequent abilities to collect debts. Like men who engaged in similar activities, women demonstrated financial savvy, numeracy, and familiarity with a wide range of records during these early stages of financial relationships.

As women took part in transactions, they mobilized their knowledge of finance and value to shape the terms of agreements. Some of these financial activities arose from women's roles as consumers. During the rise of a consumer economy in the mid-eighteenth century, Boston and Newport merchants imported increasing quantities of luxury goods, and ordinary families, in turn, purchased such goods—often on credit—as markers of their social status and refinement. Women, who were responsible for much of the work in provisioning their households, routinely shopped for both these imported fineries and everyday necessities.[19]

One such woman, Eunice Rhodes, visited cabinetmaker John Goddard's shop in 1761 and 1762 and carefully appraised potential purchases. Mid-century Newport possessed a thriving cabinetmaking industry, and the ample choices afforded to residents meant that they could demonstrate their discerning taste as they shopped for furniture.[20] Rhodes repeatedly called on Goddard to inquire about prices and place orders. In 1761, Rhodes, then a single woman, expressed interest in purchasing a dining table and a bookshelf. When Goddard told her that they cost £120 and £700, respectively, she replied that she found these prices "very deer" and that she would not order the furniture without first seeing if someone else could make it more cheaply. Once she had asked around and determined that Goddard's price was the going rate, she returned to the shop and commissioned the furniture.[21]

Eunice Rhodes continued to patronize Goddard's shop the following year, after her marriage to Thomas Hazard. Early in 1762, she ordered a chest of drawers costing £250. Goddard agreed to make the chest out of mahogany, a fashionable and exotic hardwood imported from the Caribbean and Central America that symbolized Newport's connections to Atlantic commerce. Several months later, Rhodes returned to Goddard's shop to see if her order was ready. At this point Goddard and Eunice Rhodes Hazard discussed the chest's design, and Goddard upped his price to £300. Hazard agreed to pay the higher price but cancelled her earlier order for the dining table and commissioned a smaller tea table in its place.[22] During her conversations with Goddard, Hazard emerged as a discerning consumer, one with a keen sense both of value and of how much debt she was willing to incur as she furnished her household.

Other urban women negotiated with men and assessed value when engaging in commercial ventures. During the mid-1750s, Katherine Bristow of Newport managed her family's partial ownership of a sloop, the *Willing Maid*, used in coastal trading. Bristow possessed a capacious power of attorney from her husband, mariner John Bristow. In recognition of the fact that his shipboard work generated extended absences from Newport, John had authorized Katherine to act "fully" for him in "all matters and things whatsoever," even if they required "specialized authority" beyond the powers enumerated in the document. Accordingly, when Peter Phillips purchased, on credit, the Bristow family's share of the *Willing Maid*, Katherine Bristow negotiated the sale. Phillips directed his agent to "ask M^rs. Bristow" at what price she would be willing to sell. Katherine informed the agent that her asking price was £850. After consulting with Phillips, the agent counteroffered £750. Katherine accepted, and the parties finalized the sale.[23] Phillips's choice to seek out Bristow indicates that he recognized her decision-making power. Indeed, Phillips later recounted to other Newport residents that he had "bought one quarter of [the] sloop of M^rs. Bristow," and John Bristow echoed that Phillips had purchased the share "of his wife."[24]

Women also shaped agreements within the collective decision making of households and family businesses. In 1739, Newport innkeepers Elisha Card and his wife jointly evaluated potential business opportunities. Militia captain John Freeborn recognized the couple's shared control of their establishment. When Freeborn wanted the Cards to prepare a dinner for his company's training day, he came to the door of the inn and specifically called for both Elisha Card and his wife. The couple initially "objected" to preparing the dinner, presumably because they had not been fully compensated for similar work in the past. After taking part in "considerable conference," they acquiesced only when Freeborn promised to personally pay for the dinner if no one else would do so. Witnesses who later recounted these negotiations consistently linked the husband and wife, at no point suggesting that Card made decisions apart from his spouse.[25]

The activities of Eunice Rhodes Hazard, Katherine Bristow, and Elisha Card's wife demonstrate unmarried and married women's central roles in forging credit-based agreements. British Americans ordinarily had little reason to document in depth the mechanics of their financial activities, and women's involvement in these three episodes entered the historical record only because all of them eventually resulted in contested lawsuits in which witnesses testified. Cabinetmaker John Goddard sued Eunice Rhodes Hazard's husband for the cost of the furniture she purchased; mariner John Bristow sued Peter Phillips when he failed to pay for his share of the *Willing Maid*; and Elisha Card sued John Freeborn when, as the Cards had feared, Freeborn never paid for the militia dinner. While the plaintiffs' and defendants' court filings in these cases contain no mention of women's involvement, the witnesses who testified exposed the back-and-forths that preceded the agreements.[26] In each instance, the parties involved took stock of the intersecting considerations of personal reputation, risk, economic necessity, and the values of goods and services. Such negotiations were a critical first step, because the power dynamics tipped dramatically in favor of creditors once the parties formalized their agreements. Female creditors and debtors alike mobilized financial savvy and cutting speech in their attempts to achieve favorable terms.

Once a potential creditor and debtor reached an agreement, they inscribed it in the appropriate record. Accurately committing agreements to paper was of great legal and social importance. Documents' legal properties shaped the terms on which creditors could ultimately collect their due, and written records served as vital evidence when transactions became the subject of lawsuits. In arrangements between men, participants and observers consistently described the drafting of documents as a distinct step following the oral negotiations, one that the parties might either undertake themselves or enlist others to complete.[27]

As did others throughout the early modern Atlantic World, New Englanders associated proper records with men's honest business dealings. Commercial handbooks and bookkeeping manuals stressed that well-kept accounts afforded their owners both the "Satisfaction" of tracking their gains and the advantage of knowing "the true state of [their] Affairs and Circumstances" when making business decisions.[28] Merchants, who possessed some of the most fully elaborated views of the relationship between record-keeping and credit, prided themselves on maintaining meticulous records, because their absence indicated "moral laxness or slovenliness, as well as technical incompetence."[29] In practice, eighteenth-century people seldom kept fully accurate accounts and ledgers, nor did they balance their books at the recommended regular intervals.[30] Yet prescriptive literature elided this reality, instead contrasting men's formal accounting practices with women's supposed lack of record-keeping. "Many an Oyster-woman drives a continual Trade and keeps no Books at all," cautioned one author, quickly going on to counsel his male readership that "If you will be a Merchant, you must act as a Merchant."[31] A failure to keep proper records was depicted as feminized and unacceptable for men engaging in trade.

Even as commercial handbooks disparagingly linked insufficient record-keeping with femininity, women adeptly employed the appropriate documents to establish credit relationships. Women's use of promissory notes, bonds, and account books all involved financial and legal skill, but each kind of record also demanded forms of knowledge specific to its structure and production. The vast archive of financial documents naming women as creditors and debtors collectively attests to their proficiency in managing this range of records. Dissecting individual episodes offers an additional vantage point by elucidating the specific competencies that women mobilized in translating their economic activities into writing.

Promissory notes were always handwritten, and women who took part in creating them required both access to the necessary writing supplies and a familiarity with the form's key elements.[32] Drafting a promissory note first required locating a quill, ink, and paper. This paper could be any available full or partial sheet, sometimes even one that had previously served other purposes. One promissory note given to Newport tavern keeper Abigail Stoneman was drafted inside a hand-drawn and split open nine of clubs, suggesting its production amid card playing at her establishment (figs. 2.1 and 2.2).[33] Surrounded by the date at the top of the document and the debtor's signature at the bottom, a promissory note's core was a single first-person sentence in which a debtor pledged to pay a sum, either by a specified date or "on demand." When Sarah Underwood accepted a promissory note from Archibald Campbell in 1752, she would have verified that it contained the following constitutive elements: Campbell "promised to pay" to Underwood "on order the sum of forty eight pounds eleven shillings & three pence old tenor three months after date with interest until paid for value received." When Esther Kean gave Joseph Anthony

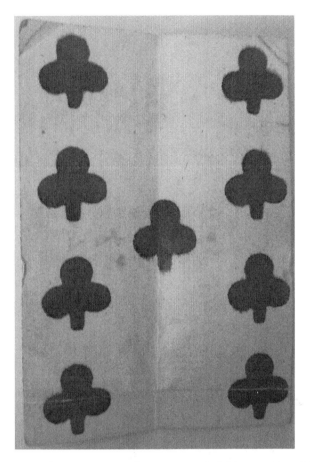

Figure 2.1. Exterior of promissory note from Benjamin Wickham to Abigail Stoneman. *Stoneman v. Wickham,* Newport County Court of Common Pleas, November 1770, #97, Rhode Island Supreme Court Judicial Records Center. Photo by the author

a promissory note in 1761, it likewise stated that "I promise to pay or cause to be paid to Joseph Anthony on order the sum of eighty six pound eight shillings old tenor on demand for value received."[34] It was common practice for parties to read completed promissory notes aloud, and this most likely facilitated such women's involvement in these transactions, while also underscoring their obligation to ensure the notes' accuracy and completeness.[35] Even women who possessed limited writing abilities used promissory notes, as indicated by the numerous ones in which female debtors signed in different hands than the main text or, less frequently, with their marks (fig. 2.3).[36] Women's use of promissory notes suggests their familiarity with this form and the financial relationship it embodied.

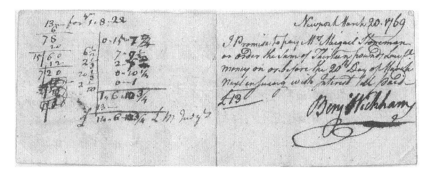

Figure 2.2. Interior of promissory note from Benjamin Wickham to Abigail Stoneman. *Stoneman v. Wickham*, Newport County Court of Common Pleas, November 1770, #97, Rhode Island Supreme Court Judicial Records Center. Courtesy of the Rhode Island Supreme Court Judicial Records Center

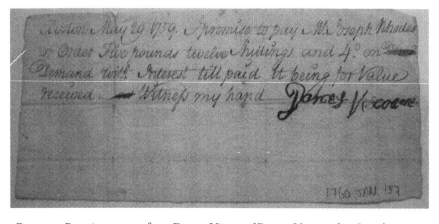

Figure 2.3. Promissory note from Dorces Viscoun [Dorcas Viscount] to Joseph Rhodes. *Rhodes v. Viscount*, Suffolk County Court of Common Pleas, January 1760, #157, Massachusetts State Archives. Photo by the author

Women who used bonds, on the other hand, demonstrated skill in purchasing and accurately completing technical forms. Individuals could hire notaries to handwrite bonds or purchase blanks from printers or booksellers and complete the relevant portions. The latter practice became more frequent as the availability of printed materials increased.[37] By 1767, the work of filling in printed bonds was so commonplace that a newspaper columnist referenced it when mocking stylized and hyperbolic obituaries. Announcing that a set of "copper plates" had been made containing the standard text of death notices, with "void spaces in them wherein to insert the *Station, Occupation,* and *Age* of the Persons deceased, and the *Time of their Death*," the satirist remarked that the work of drafting obituaries was akin to filling out "our blank bonds."[38]

Although bonds became familiar and were widely available, their use required significant knowledge. Two Newport residents, widow Sarah Lancaster and landowner John Mumford, filled out one such printed bond in 1731 (figs. 2.4 and 2.5). Through this instrument, Mumford promised to pay Lancaster £132.17 within one year, or else be liable for £265.14. As was the case on all bonds, the printed text for the obligation from Mumford to Lancaster was skeletal and legalistic. For those unfamiliar with these instruments, such language would not have provided sufficient contextual clues about either the text to be inserted

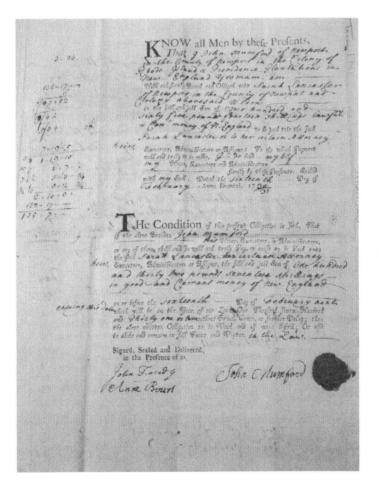

Figure 2.4. Bond from John Mumford to Sarah Lancaster. *Bourse v. Mumford,* Newport County Court of Common Pleas, May 1741, #97, Rhode Island Supreme Court Judicial Records Center. Photo by the author

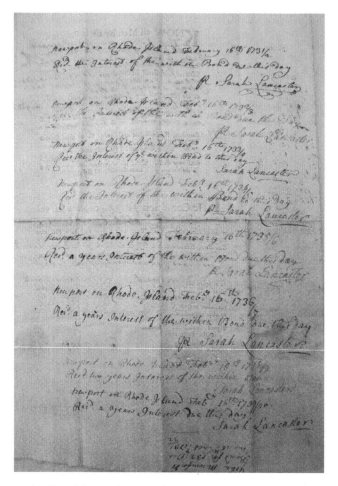

Figure 2.5. Back of bond from John Mumford to Sarah Lancaster. *Bourse v. Mumford,* Newport County Court of Common Pleas, May 1741, #97, Rhode Island Supreme Court Judicial Records Center. Photo by the author

into the blanks or the relationship constructed by the document. Instead, whoever completed the bond knew what to insert in each blank. Mumford's full name, place of residence, and occupation followed the introductory phrase "Know all Men by these Presents." The amount of the original debt, £132.17, was inserted in the second paragraph, following "the full and just sum of," while the amount of the bond's penalty—double the original debt, as was standard—appeared after the same phrase in the first paragraph.[39] These and numerous other details transformed the blank bond into a legally enforceable instrument. Whether or not women filled out bonds themselves, their involvement in the creation of such instruments demonstrates their willingness to engage with technical forms.

Whereas bonds and promissory notes attested to women's skill in establishing a single financial obligation in writing, accounts reflected their ability to track exchanges over longer time periods and record them in a standard format. At its most basic, an account contained three key elements: the creditor's and debtor's names at the top of the page, a listing of transactions and their amounts, and a balance at the bottom of the account. Newport shopkeeper Sarah Rumreil demonstrated familiarity with these elements in her account with shipbuilder William Carr from 1748 to 1749, which tracked thirty-eight purchases of cloth, thread, pins, and paper made on sixteen separate days and summed his balance due, £55.14.5 (fig. 2.6).[40] Women could also adopt the form of an account for single transactions, such as when Boston shopkeeper Lydia Barnard drafted John Lyddiard's account in 1751, indicating that he owed her £4.3.6 for "sundries d[e-livere]d him in my shop" (fig. 2.7). Barnard's written account suggested a second layer of her competencies. It noted that the value of the "tea, sugar, bread, pork, and rum" purchased by Lyddiard had been "tacken from chalk score," indicating that Barnard had engaged in a more rudimentary form of record-keeping prior to drafting the account.[41]

A small number of female entrepreneurs used double-entry bookkeeping, a more sophisticated and technical form of accounting. This was a hierarchical organizational system, involving three separately bound volumes. Transactions were recorded in a waste book when they initially occurred, and then were transferred to a journal, where they were sorted into two categories, debits and credits. In the final stage, they were entered into the most authoritative record of transactions, the ledger, which contained a separate page for each person with whom the book's author conducted business.[42] As part of her double-entry book-keeping practices, Boston shopkeeper Martha Salisbury maintained a ledger tracking her relationships with each of her customers from 1753 to 1773. Individual entries within each account meticulously noted the date, amount, and nature of each purchase made on credit. The account of Mr. Goldsmith, for instance, specified that he purchased half an ounce of silk on May 1, 1758, for twelve shillings and six pence, then returned three days later to purchase nineteen shillings' worth of ribbon and silk. Salisbury also used her account book to keep track of monies received and debts outstanding. Entries documented the dates and amounts of payments she collected, specifying whether they were "by cash" or "in a note of hand." Accounts that were fully paid were struck through, while occasional tabulations noted amounts "left to pay" on open accounts.[43] Salisbury's ledger offered a detailed record of her long-term business relationships, one that she could readily consult to determine the standing of individual customers.

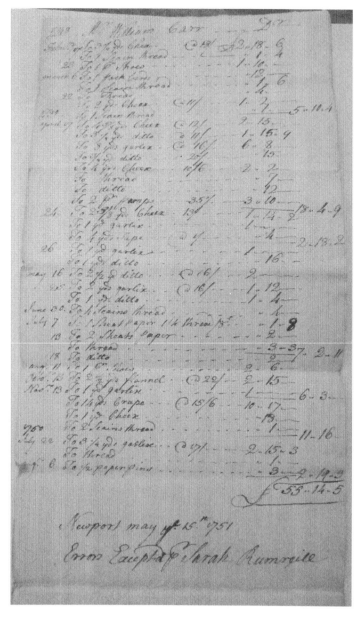

Figure 2.6. Account of William Carr with Sarah Rumreil. *Rumreil v. Carr*, Newport County Court of Common Pleas, May 1751, #207, Rhode Island Supreme Court Judicial Records Center. Photo by the author

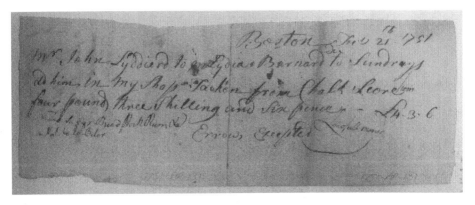

Figure 2.7. Account of John Lyddiard with Lydia Barnard. *Barnard v. Lydiard,*
Suffolk County Court of Common Pleas, April 1751, #131, Massachusetts State
Archives. Photo by the author

While we do not know whether Salisbury was the one who maintained her
own ledger, the mere fact of its existence attests to her engagement with sophisticated accounting practices of the kind detailed in handbooks for merchants
engaged in transatlantic trade. Some female shopkeepers did complete their own
bookkeeping. Boston retailer Elizabeth Murray stressed the importance of this
skill. Noting that many families were "ruined by the woman not understanding accounts," she persuaded her brothers to send their daughters to Boston to
learn shopkeeping and bookkeeping under her tutelage.[44] Yet delegating book-
keeping to others was common at the time, and it is certainly possible that Salisbury relied on a hired clerk or one of her two sons to maintain her ledger.[45]
Even if she did so, her business activities would necessarily have led her to
collaborate with this individual, including by providing the basic information
that eventually was entered in the ledger. Women's engagement with accounts,
then, involved varying levels of skill, from the basic numeracy and literacy
demonstrated by Lydia Barnard's "chalk score" and rudimentary paper account
to the sophisticated commercial knowledge evinced by Salisbury's records.

Married women and *femes sole* engaged in similar recordkeeping. While the
historical record tends to attribute accounts exclusively to household heads, telling
statements within legal disputes expose bookkeeping by married women. In
1741, a dispute between two Bostonians, shipjoiner Daniel Ballard and victual-
ler Nicholas Williams, led the courts to capture the bookkeeping responsibilities of Ballard's wife within the legal record. Daniel Ballard sued Williams for
payment of a debt, and Williams insisted that the amount sought was too
high. He maintained that he had delivered groceries to Ballard's household and
that Ballard had not credited him appropriately. Ballard countered Williams's

claims by recounting their prior dealings. As Ballard did so, he noted that his wife "kept the account for what was delivered" to their household, and that, during their earlier efforts to settle outside of court, he and Williams had consulted her records together as the authoritative record of their trading. Her accounting never would have entered the historical record but for two preconditions: the protracted conflict between the two men, which eventually reached the colony's highest court, and inadequate record-keeping by Williams, who admitted that he "had no other acco[un]t in his book for what was delivered." Ballard embedded these details within the overall narrative of his prior dealings with Williams, and officials appear never to have remarked upon the involvement of Ballard's wife. This case, and others like it, suggest that bookkeeping by wives was more prevalent and accepted than its frequency in the historical record would suggest.[46]

After producing financial documents, women further demonstrated their understanding of such records' significance by carefully storing them. Female creditors retained the bonds and promissory notes that they obtained from their debtors, while women who authored accounts preserved them, so they could be referenced when it came time for settlement. Women's choices about where to store their papers reflected the varying roles that credit played in their daily lives. While female entrepreneurs housed commercial records in their places of business, other women kept their records in their homes or on their persons. When court-appointed assessors inventoried deceased women's belongings, they documented this range of locations where women safeguarded their records.[47] Some women placed their papers inside purses or pocketbooks, receptacles suitable for carrying documents with them as they went about their business.[48] Other inventories listed women's bonds and promissory notes immediately following the entries for trunks, chests, or boxes, strongly suggesting that women stowed their financial papers inside these containers for safekeeping.[49] Since many areas of eighteenth-century residences were mixed-use spaces, some women kept their boxes and papers in rooms used for dining and entertaining visitors. Other women stored documents in bedrooms, indicating that they viewed such instruments as long-term investments, to be sheltered away from the fray of household activity.[50]

Through their sustained handling of financial documents, women became deeply familiar with their contents. A Bostonian, Margaret Hazly, called on such knowledge in 1763 when she lost a bundle of papers. Hazly placed an advertisement in the *Boston News-Letter* seeking the return of her "Sundry Papers" (fig. 2.8). As did men who placed advertisements concerning lost documents, Hazly carefully enumerated the individual papers she had misplaced. These included "a Deed of Lands," "four Receipts of House-Rent," and "a Paper consisting of two Articles, signed by John Ruddock, Esq." Hazly also recalled the

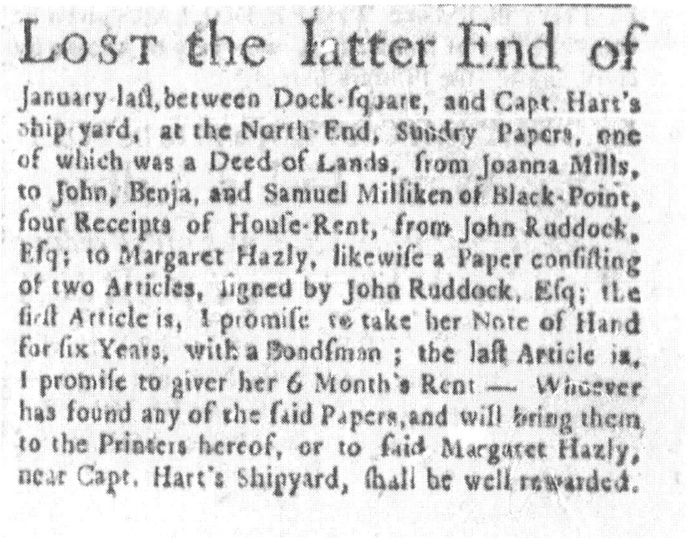

> **LOST** the latter End of January laſt, between Dock-fquare, and Capt. Hart's ſhip yard, at the North-End, Sundry Papers, one of which was a Deed of Lands, from Joanna Mills, to John, Benja, and Samuel Milliken of Black-Point, four Receipts of Houſe-Rent, from John Ruddock, Eſq; to Margaret Hazly, likewiſe a Paper confiſting of two Articles, ſigned by John Ruddock, Eſq; the firſt Article is, I promiſe to take her Note of Hand for fix Years, with a Bondſman ; the laſt Article is, I promiſe to giver her 6 Month's Rent — Whoever has found any of the ſaid Papers, and will bring them to the Printers hereof, or to ſaid Margaret Hazly, near Capt. Hart's Shipyard, ſhall be well rewarded.

Figure 2.8. Advertisement, *Boston News-Letter,* March 17, 1763, [3]. America's Historical Newspapers and the American Antiquarian Society

text of the Ruddock's promises, noting that "The first Article is, I promise to take her Note of Hand for six Years, with a Bondsman; the last Article is, I promise to give her 6 Month's Rent." Either Hazly was so familiar with her documents that she had memorized them, or she kept duplicates elsewhere, as a precaution. As did men, Hazly concluded her advertisement by pledging that any individual who returned the papers would be "well rewarded."[51] Hazly's promise of a reward, and, even more fundamentally, her decision to publish a newspaper advertisement, indicate the high value she attached to her papers.

Women removed documents from their storage places in the course of their daily activities, and, in contrast with the static snapshots of probate inventories, Hazly's advertisement captures women's dynamic use of financial documents. Hazly specified that she had lost her papers "between Dock-Square and Capt. Hart's ship yard, at the North-End." Hazly's description, demarcating a swath of Boston roughly two-thirds of a mile long, mapped her travels through the city as an economic actor. Hart's shipyard, the landmark closest to Hazly's residence, was located off Lynn Street, while Dock Square was one block north of King Street, in Boston's commercial center.[52] Losing one's papers while out in the town was not a mistake that was exclusive to women. Men placed newspaper advertisements concerning lost documents, including the kinds that Hazly listed, much more frequently than women.[53] Circulating through the city with documents in hand was a routine feature of economic life for both men and women.

Accounts and some bonds and promissory notes, containing entries spanning many years, provide direct evidence of women preserving and retrieving them. The bond that John Mumford gave Sarah Lancaster became the site of additional record-keeping by Lancaster (fig. 2.5). For eight years following the bond's creation, Mumford paid annual interest to Lancaster. Each year, Lancaster pulled out the bond from its resting place and meticulously recorded Mumford's interest payment on the reverse. Indicative of the importance she attached to the bond as a legal record, she consistently noted the place of payment, "Newport on Rhode Island," and signed with a flourish, underlining her last name. The bond itself thus attests not only to Lancaster's repeated interactions with Mumford, but also her conservation of it during the remaining days of each year. Given that written records played a crucial role in settlements between creditors and debtors, the ability to store and retrieve financial documents—and, in rare instances, to secure the safe return of lost papers—undergirded women's exercise of other financial and legal expertise.

Overall, women's entry into credit relationships required two layers of skill. First, obtaining favorable terms when contracting debts involved bargaining. This was particularly important, because the contracting of debts allowed potential creditors and debtors to haggle on a relatively equal footing, which subsequent stages of their relationships would not permit. Second, translating such debts into writing demanded familiarity with the appropriate records, whether promissory notes, bonds, or accounts. Women negotiated forcefully and displayed keen understandings of value as they became borrowers and lenders, and they demonstrated financial, legal, and numerical acumen as they took part in producing and storing the records that solidified their transactions.

Dunning and Reckoning

Once parties had established agreements, the next major phase in their credit relationships was the settling of debts. Creditors and debtors sometimes sought to settle simply because a significant amount of time had elapsed, or because the payment date specified on their bonds or promissory notes had passed. In other cases, external events spurred this phase. Individuals became concerned about debtors' financial difficulties, or they sought to resolve their affairs prior to dissolving businesses, traveling, or relocating. Death and the appointment of estate administrators likewise brought new urgency to wrapping up outstanding obligations.

Collecting and paying local debts were intensely personal, face-to-face acts. Eighteenth-century women and men repeatedly used two words in their descriptions of this process. They referred to "dunning," as in Daniel Defoe's discussion of merchants who must "go about, *a dunning* among their dealers."[54] They also mentioned "reckoning," or meeting to review the papers associated with a transaction and determine the amount that one party owed the other. These evocative terms highlight crucial elements of settlement: movement and interpersonal negotiation. Women engaged in these well-established practices associated with collecting and paying debts, and they demonstrated financial and legal knowledge as they did so. Whereas establishing obligations allowed for pushback by both parties, the power dynamics of settlements, including in its spatial dimensions and conversations, favored creditors. Attending to debt collection and payment, in other words, underscores that positioning within individual transactions significantly shaped the ways in which men and women interacted with one another in economic realms.

Credit relationships had a distinctive choreography. Telltale movements signaled the individuals' status as creditors or debtors and their desire to either settle promptly or prolong financial relationships. Creditors tracked down and confronted their debtors in attempts to obtain payment. Debtors, meanwhile, could facilitate or forestall creditors' collection efforts. Debtors who were willing to pay voluntarily sought out their creditors, while reluctant debtors either waited until the creditors called on them, or made themselves unavailable in order to avoid paying. Numerous debt cases between men suggest their use of such patterns of travel or avoidance.[55] These practices were so well established, moreover, that legal and commercial handbooks assimilated them into their overall framework, linking credit and reputation. Unlike the well-intentioned but distressed debtor who willingly "called upon" his creditors, the dishonest debtor who intended to "defraud" was likely to either run away, "departing from his own house, with the intent to secrete himself and avoid his creditors," or hide himself "by keeping in his own house, privately, so as not to be seen or spoken with by his creditors."[56] The ways in which creditors and debtors did—or did not—move through their streets and communities announced their intentions.

Women engaged in behaviors common to all creditors when they traveled throughout their cities and regions in attempts to collect from their debtors. Elizabeth Murray Campbell, the Boston shopkeeper who encouraged her nieces to learn bookkeeping (see earlier in this chapter), described her dunning practices in unusual detail in a 1760 debt suit concerning purchases by a young woman, Mehitable Bayard. In the lawsuit, Campbell nominally acted as the administrator of her late husband's estate, yet she had almost certainly sold the goods in question and produced the resulting account. From July 1757 to November 1758, Bayard repeatedly visited Campbell's shop, running up an account totaling £34.2.2¾ as she purchased lace, thread, ribbons, and other dressmaking supplies. The account listed her father as the legally responsible party but specified that the goods purchased were "For Miss Hitty."[57]

In support of her claim that neither father nor daughter had discharged their account, "'tho requested," Campbell recounted her movements through Boston.

On October 19, 1759, she set out to collect the debt. Campbell, who resided in the centrally located Cornhill Ward, first walked to the residence of Bayard's father in the adjacent Marlborough Ward, only a few blocks away.[58] Bayard's father refused to pay unless he first received a written order from his daughter, who was now married. (Perhaps he wanted his daughter to acknowledge that the account was correct, or perhaps he saw his daughter's new household as being liable for the debt.) Campbell accordingly spoke with Mehitable Bayard Porter that same day. In order to visit her former customer at her new residence in the neighboring town of Roxbury, Campbell travelled roughly two-and-a-half miles each way, a distance that would have required significant time to traverse on foot, or considerable funds if she rode in a hired carriage. After speaking with Mehitable, Campbell returned to Bayard's father's Marlborough Ward residence and again demanded payment of the debt.[59] Campbell's time-consuming trips and conversations underscore that travel was a constitutive element of debt collection, and that systems of family credit could complicate this work.

Women also journeyed between farther-distant towns as they pursued their debtors. In 1730, Providence resident Margaret Fuller, a single woman who was also known as "Irish Pegg," travelled to Newport and spent several days there to collect £6.16 due on a bond from Newport mason Thomas Howes. While Fuller's agreement with Howes was, on its surface, a bilateral one, her collection efforts led her to converse with numerous men and women, all of whom became aware of her status as a creditor. Fuller first employed a boatman to transport her down the Providence River and across Narragansett Bay, chatting with him along the way and explaining the purpose of her trip.[60] Once in Newport, Fuller spoke with Thomas Howes, agreeing to accept a barrel of sugar from him as in-kind payment of the debt. Fuller next visited the residence of a second mason, whom she persuaded to front the sugar for Howes and to deliver it to a tavern. Fuller and her boatman went to the tavern and picked up the barrel the following day. Fuller also called at the residence of a Newport cooper and his wife. While this stop was seemingly a social one, she recounted her agreement with Howes as she discoursed with the couple.[61] In comparison with essentially local collection efforts, such as those of Elizabeth Murray Campbell, trips such as Fuller's involved greater planning and led to additional layers of economic activity, including hiring the boatman and most likely renting a room during her overnight stay. Female creditors, regardless of the distances that they travelled, engaged in practices common to all moneylenders. Using elements of surprise and intrusion to their advantage, they made concrete their legal and economic authority over others as they appeared at debtors' residences unannounced.[62]

Women's patterns of movement as administrators and executors differed slightly from those settling debts in their own right. Female administrators and executors did engage in the standard practice of dunning their debtors, as

Elizabeth Murray Campbell's pursuit of the Bayard family suggests. Indeed, as part of his argument that tradesmen should equip their wives to administer their estates, Daniel Defoe insisted that a married woman should know not only the names of her husband's debtors, but also "where they dwell," so she could call on them for payment.[63] Yet, because estate administration demanded that women settle many debts within a compressed time period, their houses became centers of heightened financial activity, with creditors and debtors alike calling to wrap up affairs with estates.[64]

As credit networks widened and port cities became home to an increasing number of weekly newspapers, women and men alike turned to print as a technology to facilitate estate settlement. Through their advertisements in newspapers, administrators and executors urged creditors and debtors to settle, without seeking to track them down individually. In 1745, Boston widow and administrator Jane Carter announced that she could be found "on Wentworth's Wharffe," while in 1755 widow Jane Hunting informed readers that she would be settling her husband's estate "at her House in Middle-Street the North End of said Boston" (fig. 2.9).[65] In 1764, Newport widow Jane Brown and her co-administrators settled her late husband's accounts daily "at the store formerly occupy'd by the deceased, from 10 to 12 o'clock in the afternoon." Newport widow Rebecca Briggs administered her late husband's estate in her "dwelling house" on "the third and fourth day of the first week of every month" in 1773.[66] Capturing the geography of estate administration, the text of such announcements closely resembled that of men working to settle estates.[67] Thus female administrators' and executors' activities, including their recourse to print, paralleled those of men.

Both male and female creditors made use of assertive speech in their efforts to collect debts. When creditors confronted debtors, their words contained threats, whether implicit or explicit, that they would sue for payment. Eighteenth-century New Englanders consistently used the verbs "asked" and "demanded" to describe creditors' attempts to obtain payment. In a 1748 slander case in Massachusetts, male and female witnesses used similar language to describe their efforts to collect debts. In that suit, a Boston shipbuilder, Richard Tucker,

ALL Perfons having any Demands on the Eftate of Capt. Jofeph Hunting, late of Bofton, deceafed, are defired to apply to Jane Hunting, fole Execu/rix of the Will of faid deceafed, at her Houfe in Middle-Street the North End of faid Bofton, in order for a Settlement. And all thofe who are indebted to the fame Eftate, are required to make fpeedy Payment to faid Executrix.

Figure 2.9. Advertisement, *Boston Evening Post*, September 22, 1755, [3]. America's Historical Newspapers and the American Antiquarian Society

claimed that another man had slanderously labeled him as a delinquent debtor. (Because the law held that only untrue statements were slander, the creditors' experiences went to the case's key issues.) On the defendant's side, male and female creditors described their own dealings with Tucker. A woman stated that she "demanded" money from him and that "he often promised to pay it but never did," while several men recalled that they had "often asked" Tucker for money owed, but he never made good on his debt.[68] All the witnesses suggested that Tucker had failed to pay them despite their recourse to the standard practices of creditors, and their parallel vocabularies underscore that assertive speech was a recognized element of both male and female creditors' conduct.

Widow Mary Sheffield, displaying the forcefulness authorized by her status as a creditor, was among those who engaged in these common practices of "asking" and "demanding" as she pressed a male debtor for payment. In August 1732, Sheffield, acting as administrator of her late husband's estate, sought to collect £21.5 on a bond from Peter Weast. While both the Sheffields and Weast owned land, the Sheffields were of higher social standing than Weast.[69] Mary Sheffield's activities as a creditor reinforced the authority she possessed by virtue of her class status. Sheffield traveled from her home in South Kingstown to the adjacent town of North Kingstown, where Weast lived. There she confronted him inside another family's residence, as several men and women looked on. According to these witnesses, Sheffield showed Weast the bond, and Weast denied that it was his. Sheffield accordingly asked Weast "whether that was not his hand writing which signed that bond." This line of questioning reminded Weast of his weak legal position, since one of the few legal defenses available to debtors in cases concerning bonds was proving that they had not signed the instruments in question. Moreover, Sheffield was cleverly pressuring Weast to acknowledge his signature on the bond in the presence of observers, as such an admission would strengthen her case if she later sued. Weast squirmed in response to Sheffield's question. Two witnesses recalled that he "answered yes" but insisted that the debt in question was only £3, while a third simply "said it was like his hand." Sheffield refused the £3 offered by Weast, instead choosing to sue him.[70] Sheffield never demonstrated the deference that we might otherwise expect a woman to show to a man. Instead, she repeatedly pressured Weast and used her knowledge of the law to her advantage, exemplifying the ways in which female creditors used tools of direct confrontation to collect debts.[71]

Female creditors also exercised their power as they evaluated settlements proposed by their debtors. While creditors sometimes received cash, they also accepted in-kind payments (as did Margaret Fuller when she obtained a barrel of sugar from Thomas Howes, discussed earlier in this chapter) or allowed debtors to transfer outstanding debts to more-secure forms, such as from an account to a promissory note. Amid the economic uncertainty created by the imperial wars and paper money debates of the mid-eighteenth century, navigating these multiple types of payment required female creditors to assess price, market fluctuations, and risk. When provisions were scarce at the start of the Seven Years' War, Boston widow and shopkeeper Grace Gardner allowed customers to pay their accounts using fish or lumber. By April 1758, however, Gardner was experiencing economic hardship and needed cash. In the same newspaper advertisement in which she put her house and shop up for rent and threatened to sue delinquent debtors, she announced a change in her payment policies, explaining that "Where she has agreed to take Fish or Lumber, and the Time of Payment is elapsed . . . after August next, she will take nothing but Money." As her economic circumstances changed, so, too, did Gardner's practices, which was well within her prerogative as a creditor.[72]

Female creditors also assessed whether to accept debtors' offers or hold out in hopes of obtaining a more favorable outcome in court. Mary Sheffield, the widow who grilled Peter Weast about a bond, was among the numerous female creditors who declined a debtor's partial payment, opting instead to sue for the full amount. Because creditors who won their cases sometimes obtained debtors' property as satisfaction for their debts, women also sized up debtors' possessions as they assessed whether to sue. In 1766, Thomas Rogers proposed to settle an account with Newport widow and estate administrator Sarah Lewis, but she declined the £21.6.3 offered by him. As Rogers jotted down at the time, Lewis "would not receive it," declaring instead that she would "sue for both the slaves," whose ownership was also at stake in this financial dispute.[73] When female creditors, such as Sarah Lewis, refused debtors' in-person offers and opted to instead take their chances in court, they manifested their possession of the upper hand during settlements. Moreover, in a rare direct reference to slavery within the Newport and Suffolk court records concerning debt, Lewis's decision stands as a reminder that enslaved people were property that could be seized for the payment of debts in eighteenth-century New England, and that women as well as men attached value to such individuals' bodies.

The same system that empowered female creditors placed female debtors in positions of economic vulnerability, and even fear. As debtors, women became the targets of all the weapons they used as creditors, including surprise, intrusion, assertive speech, and the power to accept or reject proposed settlements.[74] In addition, when women borrowed from men, systems of gendered power intersected with creditor-debtor relations, compounding male creditors' authority over their female debtors in ways that did not occur between creditors and debtors of the same gender. Rachel Clark most likely encountered such power differentials when she met to settle her accounts with another Medway, Massachusetts, resident, weaver Hugh Brown, in April 1740. Clark was an unmarried woman of limited means, and her only possession of value was her bed. She was unable to write and probably could not read, which placed her at a disadvantage relative to Brown. When parties settled accounts, they typically examined one another's records in order to ensure the documents' accuracy. In this case, however, Brown read Clark's account aloud to her. Compromising Clark's ability to scrutinize each line, this altered procedure required her to trust that Brown was faithfully relating the account's contents.[75]

After Brown rattled off what was written down, Clark agreed to give him a promissory note for £15, the supposed amount of her debt. A bystander drafted the note and read it aloud, and she signed it with her mark. By doing so, she gave herself additional time to pay the debt, while also placating Brown by acknowledging in writing her indebtedness to him. When the debt later became the subject of litigation, several male witnesses claimed that Clark signed the note voluntarily and that it was therefore valid. In contrast, the only female witness, Mary Clark, either perceived the events differently or saw an opportunity to advance a plausible narrative that was more advantageous to her kinswoman's cause. Mary Clark maintained that Rachel Clark had only signed the note when Brown insisted he would "carry her to gaill [jail] . . . right away" if she did not do so.[76] Mary Clark's recollections called attention to creditors' power to imprison debtors who owed amounts greater than the value of their assets. Yet they equally suggested the especially imbalanced power dynamics of an interaction between a poor and probably illiterate female debtor and a male creditor. While face-to-face settlements required all debtors to make on-the-spot decisions, often under threat of legal action, such strains could be particularly acute for female debtors.[77]

Urban men's mobility and frequent absences from home required women to carefully evaluate demands from their families' creditors. During unexpected visits by creditors, women faced pressure to make legally binding decisions, regardless of their familiarity with the debts in question. In 1764, Boston creditor Jeremiah Condy attempted to use to his advantage the power dynamics of a man calling on a woman during her husband's absence. He instructed his male agent to collect a debt from "Mrs Fales, when the squire is absent." Condy even specified that the agent should delay his visit, "rather than that the gentleman should be acquainted with it," as "otherwise the intention of it, viz. to get the money paid which has been so long since due, may be defeated." Condy may have believed that Mrs. Fales and her husband held different opinions regarding the debt in question or that, of the pair, she was less familiar with the specifics of the claim. Regardless of his precise reasoning, Condy strategically played on the limits of unity between husband and wife. Mrs. Fales possessed the legal authority to act as her husband's representative, but her actions could differ from his.[78]

While in many cases wives and daughters paid debts without incident, some women actively resisted settling with creditors in the absence of male household heads. In 1732, a married woman wrote in reply to a creditor's request for payment. She professed that she was "[inclined] to let the matter rest" and allow "you and my husband to setel things Between you when he comes from Carolina." Another refused to pay a debt on a promissory note during her husband's absence because she "had no orders about the note, nor [had] she anything to pay with if she had."[79] Such statements sit uneasily with other evidence demonstrating married women's extensive, skilled involvement in their households' finances. While some wives may have been genuinely reluctant to act without direct instruction from their husbands, women may well have strategically invoked the absence of household heads in order to obtain additional time to pay debts. One Newport landlord suspected as much, complaining in 1774 that his male tenant, who was then away from home, had gone eighteen months without paying rent. "It seems his wife is determined to tarry in the house till her husband shall return," he lamented to his lawyer, adding that "his being absent cannot be a good reason for the rent not to be paid."[80] By interacting with creditors who visited their households during men's absences, women played a vital role in the functioning of the credit economy, and their involvement created opportunities for strategy and even coercion by all involved parties.

As men and women took part in the settling of debts, financial documents were a central component of their interactions. Well-established procedures, emerging from the documents' legal significance and evidentiary value, dictated when and how relevant papers should pass between creditors and debtors. Under ordinary circumstances, account books never left the possession of their owners and authors. Once signed into effect, bonds and promissory notes remained the creditors' property until the debtors satisfied their obligations. At that point, creditors returned the cancelled documents to debtors, thus renouncing any further claims by surrendering the very evidence that would have allowed them to sue. Creditors also issued receipts to debtors, either entering them into receipt books, or drafting them either on small slips of paper or on the reverse side of bonds and promissory notes. New Englanders carefully preserved their receipts, because they offered protection against having to pay the same debt twice.

As creditors and debtors, women demonstrated familiarity with these largely unspoken and unwritten practices. Under ordinary circumstances, women's handling of financial documents received minimal commentary, which attests to their mastery of this constitutive element of transactions. In exceptional instances, however, women co-opted standard practices to their advantage, and here we can more clearly see their skill and knowledge in action. One such woman (mentioned earlier in this chapter) was Margaret Fuller, the Providence widow who travelled to Newport and arranged for Thomas Howes to give her a barrel of sugar as payment on a bond. After picking up the sugar from the tavern, Fuller left for Providence with the bond still in her possession. In the weeks that followed, Howes requested Fuller to return the bond, but she refused to do so, preferring instead to have him wait and suffer indefinitely. As she told one messenger, "she would not send the bond down but would make the old dog smoke for it." Other remarks by Fuller suggest that she retained the bond because she was unable to sell the sugar for as much as she had expected, as well as because Howes had not returned a "ring, and hair Pegg & clasp" belonging to her.[81] Regardless of Fuller's motivations for keeping the bond, she benefited from having the uncanceled instrument remain in her possession. She later sued Howes for the debt and won her case in the Court of Common Pleas.[82]

Women also displayed their knowledge of financial documents during settlements, when they examined the records of those with whom they had transacted business. Careful review was an especially important component of transactions involving book debt, and individuals scrutinized line items in each other's accounts to verify their accuracy. In 1731, Newport widow Joanna Chapman walked to a neighbor's house to settle an account with him. Although Chapman was capable of signing only with her mark, she reviewed her neighbor's records and agreed to pay him for some items but not others. She offered him a twenty-shilling paper money bill as payment for foodstuffs but refused to compensate him for acting as a night watchman, insisting that he had done so as a public service.[83] In 1758, widow Bethiah Norton, a resident of Martha's Vineyard, similarly refused to give her creditor a promissory note for the amount of her debt to him. She protested that he had sent two versions of her account that "[differed] in the sum" she supposedly owed and insisted that he send a new, accurate account.[84] Ten years later, a widow likewise refused to pay a debt until she received a "more particular account," because "she and her sons had overlook'd all [their] accounts" and could find "nothing" in their own records to substantiate the creditor's claims.[85] Women held their trading partners to high standards of accuracy and consistency, and their attention to small details enabled them to push back against creditors' claims.

After obtaining payment from debtors, creditors issued them receipts. Much like promissory notes, the most straightforward receipts were single, concise sentences. While receipts were less complex than other instruments, drafting them nonetheless required familiarity with their form. The first line of a typical receipt stated the place and date of payment. The document then specified the amount of money received, the person who delivered it, and whether it constituted payment "in full" or "in part." The person receiving the payment signed at the bottom. Both male and female creditors demonstrated discernment as they assessed whether debtors had satisfied their agreements, as well as a facility with receipts when they opted to issue these documents.

Receipts bearing women's signatures indicate that those with many different levels of literacy and financial skill engaged in the production of such records.

Property-owning Bostonian Elizabeth Barnes, for example, drafted and signed a flawless receipt in which she acknowledged that she "Rec[iev]ed of Mrs Reb. Amory fifty Pounds in part for a Cask of Cocoa" (fig. 2.10).[86] Other receipts drafted in women's own hands incorporated these documents' key elements but contained minor errors of spelling or phrasing, underscoring that even women with a limited formal education were nonetheless well versed in the form of receipts. Bostonians Hannah Willard and Mary Faneuil, for instance, issued receipts for "twenty tow pounds" and "fivety pounds" respectively, while Mary Hill noted that she received "18" but omitted the unit of currency.[87] Other women's receipts bore their signatures in different hands than those of the main text. For

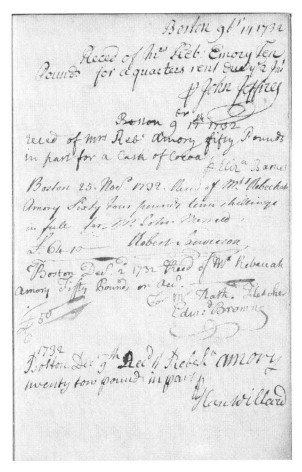

Figure 2.10. Page containing receipt of Elizabeth Barnes to Rebecca Amory, September 17, 1732. Rebecca Amory Receipt Book, Amory Family Papers, Massachusetts Historical Society. Collection of the Massachusetts Historical Society

some, this simply may have been a result of the circumstances of the receipt's production or the parties' desire for formality. Newport widow Ann Drake possessed sufficient writing and accounting skills to keep her own account of clothes made and altered for another Newport resident. Yet an individual with more ornate penmanship drafted the associated receipt, and Drake affixed her name at the bottom.[88] Other women obtained assistance in penning receipts because they lacked the ability to do so themselves, as in the case of a woman who signed her name as "Elesabth Noel" and included an alternate phonetic spelling of her surname on the same document (fig. 2.11).[89] Female creditors' wide-ranging involvement in drafting receipts underscores that women with varying levels of literacy

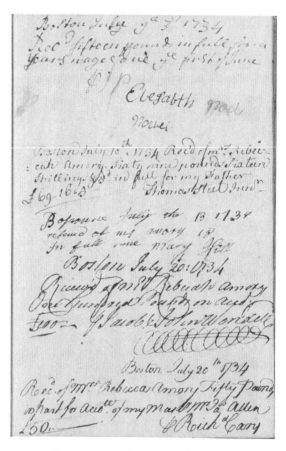

Figure 2.11. Page containing receipt of Elesabth Noel [Elizabeth Noel] to Rebecca Amory, July 3, 1734. Rebecca Amory Receipt Book, Amory Family Papers, Massachusetts Historical Society. Collection of the Massachusetts Historical Society

and writing ability became lenders and, in so doing, assumed responsibility for producing the associated documents.

Collecting payments and issuing receipts constituted a phase of credit transactions that was especially likely to involve women acting on behalf of their families and households. Men and women who were not nominally creditors could issue receipts, as long as they noted the individuals for whom they collected payments.[90] Women were often present when debtors called at households and family businesses, and thus they were frequently the ones who drafted receipts. Mary Carr of Newport received £20 that the local butcher owed to her husband in 1730, while Bostonian Magdalene Wroe issued a receipt for £19 in 1733 on behalf of her husband.[91] In some of these instances, married women entered particular transactions for the first time. In others, it is likely that they issued receipts for debts that they had taken part in contracting. Women also drafted receipts as representatives of other family members. Deborah Eustice wrote and signed a receipt on behalf of her sister in 1735, while Sarah Newton did so as her mother's representative in 1742.[92] Because the format of receipts privileged capturing precise moments of payment, including the specific individuals who were involved, such documents offer an unusually direct window into women's involvement in settling debts. Even women who were not creditors in their own right issued legally binding discharges by generating the appropriate records.

For their part, female debtors took pains to ensure that their creditors created the necessary papers. In 1741 and 1742, Deborah Johnson, a widow from East Greenwich, Rhode Island, made sure that John Walton thoroughly documented her payments to him. Johnson had purchased cloth and assorted sewing supplies on credit from Walton. Johnson, who was later described in a petition as "a person that can neither read nor write," enlisted several witnesses to "see the said John [Walton] give her credit . . . in his book" when she paid him. Aware of the importance of written records, Johnson used her social connections to compensate for her limited literacy.[93]

Women carefully stored records of payment so they could consult them during times of need. Within collections of family papers, receipts given to women are by far the most abundant form of women's financial documents. In addition, women sometimes had all their creditors enter their receipts into a single receipt book, as did Boston shopkeeper Rebecca Amory. Her receipt book, spanning from 1732 to 1737, contains six hundred entries documenting her payments. Such large quantities of receipts, whether loose or bound, suggest both the female debtors' commitment to obtaining them at the time of payment, and their concern for storing them thereafter.[94] These records, in turn, facilitated women's rebuttals in the rare circumstances when creditors dunned them for the same debt twice. Elizabeth

Aborn, the widow and administrator of Newport shopkeeper Joseph Aborn, cited her inspection of financial documents in a letter to prominent Philadelphia merchants Thomas Wharton and William Pollard. When Wharton and Pollard wrote to Aborn to request settlement of a "large balance" they were supposedly owed, she categorically refused to pay, replying that "You will find by the enclosed copy of a receipt that the account was settled above two years since."[95] Aborn's interaction with Wharton and Pollard alludes to the role that receipts could likewise play in face-to-face interactions with debtors, with women appealing to written evidence to lend credence to their assertions.

Both in their own right and as members of households, women contributed to the functioning of the economy by settling debts. Here, much like what occurred during the creation of agreements, men and women engaged in shared practices and demonstrated similar skills. During this concluding stage in the lifespan of a transaction, however, the power dynamics of credit relationships shifted firmly to the creditors' favor, regardless of gender. In some instances, debtors voluntarily delivered payments to creditors, an act that was, in itself, a form of deference. When debtors declined to do so, creditors had multiple tools at their disposal. They tracked down debtors, spoke forcefully to them, scrutinized proposed settlements, rejected those that were undesirable, and exercised control over financial documents. Debtors, meanwhile, could cite errors or inconsistencies in records, but otherwise they only had a limited ability to push back against creditors. As they undertook these standard practices surrounding debt collection and payment, women and men shaped their social positions relative to others, underscoring the highly situational nature of authority within economic networks.

Conclusion

Within the documentary record, women tend to appear in fleeting, fragmentary ways as participants in credit transactions. Bonds, promissory notes, and receipts contain their signatures. Headings and line entries in account books list their names, and court records identify them as plaintiffs and creditors, or debtors and defendants. While the sheer quantity of such evidence underscores how female borrowers and lenders helped build the increasingly commercialized economies of Boston and Newport, such brief mentions of women provide comparatively little insight into the practices through which they engaged with credit. Nonetheless, by attending to well-documented disputes, revisiting formulaic instruments from new perspectives, and mining surviving records for telling details, a composite picture of women's financial labor emerges. As free white women engaged in the various phases of credit relationships, beginning with forming agreements and ending with dunning and settlements, they undertook practices common to all creditors and debtors. These included calculated travel, assertive speech, and the careful handling of financial documents. Assembling these details casts all of the brief mentions of women as creditors and debtors in a new light. When we recognize that each such reference is representative of countless small actions in cities where men were frequently absent, it becomes even more apparent that women were crucial and active participants in urban credit networks.

In Boston and Newport, functional skills were the gateway to involvement in the credit economy. A wide range of women used credit, from entrepreneurs running long-term businesses, to widows and single women engaging in one-time borrowing and lending, to wives and daughters acting on behalf of their households. In the process, they demonstrated proficiency in traveling through their cities and regions, navigating questions of price and value, drafting and handling financial documents, and mobilizing assertive language during negotiations and settlements.

While literacy certainly facilitated women's ability to engage in such activities, limited reading and writing skills did not preclude their participation. As we have seen, women who could not read enlisted allies to accompany them to settlements. Those who could sign only with their marks engaged in deliberations about the terms of notes and bonds, listened carefully as the resulting documents were read aloud, and scrupulously saved them for years afterward. Women who had shaky handwriting or used phonetic spellings still drafted accounts and receipts accurately containing these documents' standard elements. Even among New Englanders with flawless penmanship, routine practices included purchasing forms and hiring notaries or clerks to complete them. During a period characterized by the proliferation of written records, credit relationships retained significant oral and face-to-face components, and women navigated this economic world in ways similar to those of their male contemporaries.

By allowing us to locate women moving through their communities and transacting business in a variety of settings, attention to practices surrounding credit also revises our understanding of the gendering of urban space. When they settled debts, women as well as men hired boats and carriages, trudged through city streets, and knocked on doors, sometimes triangulating between several people and locales in a single day. They transacted business in a variety of places, including houses, shops, and taverns. Moreover, all this activity arising from women's credit relationships was highly visible to their contemporaries. Contrary to eighteenth-century periodical literature's emerging distinction between the "masculine public" and the "feminine private," port cities and their streets remained heterosocial spaces in which women's out-of-doors presence was routine and unremarkable.[96]

Finally, debt collection practices highlight the extent to which direct interactions shaped power relations between women and men. As we saw in chapter 1, more than four-fifths of women's credit relationships were with men, and more than one-tenth of men's credit relationships were with women. Financial ties intersected with patriarchal social structures. During the initial stage in forming agreements, standard practices enabled all involved parties to negotiate forcefully with one another, regardless of gender. Thereafter, creditors possessed legal as well as social authority over their debtors. They manifested such authority by tracking down debtors, demanding payment, evaluating proposed settlements, and controlling the possession of financial documents. When female creditors dunned male debtors, financial practices and female skill complicated and even temporarily undercut gendered hierarchies. On the other hand, when male creditors pursued female debtors, patriarchal authority reinforced such financial relationships, intensifying the vulnerability that women experienced by virtue of their status as debtors. The ubiquity of credit and the everyday activities it generated contributed to the malleable, contingent nature of social relations in eighteenth-century New England cities, as well as throughout the early modern Atlantic World.

CHAPTER 3

"And Thereon She Sues"

Debt Litigation, Lawyers, and Legal Practices

As colonial New Englanders engaged in market-oriented transactions and written credit relationships with increasing frequency, they spurred transformations in their legal institutions. Once intrapersonal measures to collect debts failed, lawsuits offered the only institutional mechanism by which colonial creditors could obtain their full due. Beginning in the early 1700s, New Englanders, including Bostonians and Newporters, therefore resorted to debt litigation with increasing frequency. Every county's court system experienced surges in caseloads that dramatically outpaced population growth. Periods of economic uncertainty further intensified residents' reliance on the courts. In Boston and Newport, the volume of debt cases peaked amid the currency crises of the 1740s and early 1750s and then remained elevated until the Revolution. Such suits stoked the businesses of the region's emerging class of full-time professional lawyers, who, in turn, further reshaped the courts' handling of debt litigation as they based their courtroom arguments on narrow questions of law.[1]

In June 1765, an elite Newport widow, Penelope Stelle, alluded to this changed relationship between credit transactions and the courts when she purchased a run of advertisements in the *Newport Mercury*. Attempting to settle the accounts of her deceased husband, a merchant and ship captain, she admonished that his debtors were "requested to make immediate payment, to prevent their being sued to November Court."[2] Stelle's threats echoed those of other female estate administrators, who likewise demanded that debtors pay promptly in order to "prevent further trouble," cautioning that "they may expect to be sued to next Court," "without any exception of persons."[3] Such language was not an empty threat. Five months after issuing her printed warning, Stelle availed herself of the courts' heightened role in debt collection. She hired a lawyer and, initiating a process that began with the sheriff summoning her opponents to court, launched a spate of lawsuits against her husband's debtors.[4]

Some have argued that it was in this arena, the county court system, that women lost visibility and influence in economic and legal life during the eighteenth century. Women who proceeded to court, like Penelope Stelle, have been portrayed as aberrations, their lawsuits "drowned out" by the much larger quantity of debt suits between men. The eighteenth's century's transformations in debt litigation, so the standard story goes, occurred to the detriment of women. Had Stelle's grandmother sued a debtor in the early 1700s, she would have spoken to the court directly, and officials would have decided her case based on a substantive consideration of its issues. In contrast, when Stelle sued her late husband's debtors following the publication of her threatening advertisements in 1765, she hired a prominent attorney, Henry Marchant. He shepherded her cases through the court, where legal technicalities largely determined their outcomes. In other words, women's power in the courts seemingly eroded, both because they found it harder to bring suits, and because the courts began to displace a concern for substantive justice with an emphasis on procedural justice, which favored male litigants.[5]

Even as procedures for litigation in the county courts became more streamlined during the eighteenth century, the skilled labor of female litigants and other women drawn into lawsuits remained essential to the functioning of the courts and the rise of the legal profession. Activities outside of court profoundly defined the legal system in ways that cannot be seen if our view of the law remains bounded within the courtroom, so this chapter treats debt litigation as three concentric circles of activity.[6] It first surveys the overall contours of women's involvement in debt cases, then turns to the gender dynamics of two key components of civil suits—attorney-client interactions and court-ordered seizures of persons and property—that involved successively wider networks of individuals beyond the cases' named litigants. Just as examining financial activities outside of court reveals free women's extensive and skilled involvement in the credit economy, attending to litigation as a process likewise allows us to see women as essential actors in debt suits who demonstrated numerous competencies in the course of protecting their and their families' assets.

Female participants in debt litigation included not only the widows and single women who became plaintiffs and defendants in their own right, but also the wider circle of women—particularly wives, landlords, and tenants—who gained familiarity with the law through their interactions with attorneys and sheriffs. For female litigants in debt cases, the courts generally served as a tool of empowerment. Women, as plaintiffs and creditors in the majority of their cases, benefited from a legal system in which most plaintiffs won their debt cases without challenges from their opponents. Even such uncontested cases, however, required significant coordination between attorneys and their clients. Free white women were a key component of eighteenth-century lawyers' growing businesses. Whether as independent litigants or as representatives of their households, such women demonstrated their familiarity with finance and the law as they supervised their attorneys in the same ways as men. The ubiquity of debt litigation, moreover, meant that residents routinely encountered sheriffs and their deputies carrying out court orders. As these officers attempted to guarantee the defendants' appearances at the next court session, women were among those who protected their households' property and legal interests. During a period characterized by the courts' increasing emphasis on legal procedure and the rise of the all-male legal profession, activities surrounding debt litigation nonetheless extended well beyond the courtroom, and women cultivated and mobilized significant financial and legal skill through their interactions with lawyers and local officials.

In a continuation of the power dynamics that characterized face-to-face financial dealings, one's status as a creditor or debtor intersected with other forms of social hierarchy, including gender, when those transactions became the subject of litigation. While women on both sides of debt cases demonstrated their familiarity with finance and legal procedure, their status as creditors or debtors shaped their interactions with lawyers and sheriffs. Both male and female creditors authoritatively directed their attorneys, and they publicly demonstrated their power as they lay claim to debtors' property and persons. In contrast, female debtors played on the complementarity between their gender and indebtedness in interactions with their attorneys, and hierarchies of gender and financial obligation reinforced one another when male sheriffs seized female debtors' persons and property, often at the direction of male creditors. Debt litigation, a routine element of eighteenth-century life for women as well as for men, both shaped and was shaped by social relations outside of court.

Female Litigants in the County Courts
As New Englanders initiated debt suits with growing frequency, the Boston and Newport courts became extremely busy institutions. In Massachusetts and Rhode Island, county-based inferior courts, called Courts of Common Pleas, possessed original jurisdiction for all civil matters concerning more than forty shillings. Newport County's Court of Common Pleas met biannually, while

Suffolk County's court sat in Boston four times per year, in order to handle the greater number of lawsuits generated by that region's larger population. Each court convened for as many days as was necessary to handle that session's caseload. By 1730, Suffolk County's court heard over four hundred cases per term. In Newport County, the court's work increased from 153 cases in its May 1731 term to 430 cases in a single term just twenty years later. In both Suffolk and Newport Counties, upward of three-quarters of all cases concerned debts.[7] This prevalence of debt suits reflected both the proliferation of credit transactions and the court's important function in holding debtors accountable when personal promises broke down.

Female litigants in debt cases were among those who contributed to the busy sessions of the Suffolk and Newport courts. Female creditors used these venues to pursue their debtors, and creditors sued delinquent female debtors. Overall, between 1730 and the Revolution, debt cases involving women made up 9 percent of such cases in the Suffolk County Court of Common Pleas, and 12 percent in the Newport County Court of Common Pleas.[8] Upward of 95 percent of women's cases in both courts were against male opponents.[9] Even though the number of female litigants and the percentage of debt cases involving women were small, their continuing involvement in litigation marked the courts as a heterosocial institution throughout the colonial period. Furthermore, rather than steadily declining, the number of cases with female litigants fluctuated across court terms.[10] While the number of cases involving women in a given term was easily skewed by personal choices and economic circumstances, the proceedings of every single court session reminded Boston and Newport residents of women's roles as borrowers and lenders.

The circumstances under which women became litigants differed from those of men. Male litigants appeared in court as plaintiffs and defendants in debt suits in roughly equal proportions. In contrast, women were much more likely to appear in debt cases as plaintiffs, rather than defendants. In Suffolk County, women were creditors and plaintiffs in 69 percent of their cases, and in Newport County, 65 percent.[11] Such patterns of female involvement parallel those in other counties throughout New England, where women likewise overwhelmingly participated in debt litigation as plaintiffs.[12]

Several possibilities may explain the disproportionate involvement of female litigants as creditors, rather than debtors. Patterns of borrowing and lending may have produced these courtroom trends. Women might have possessed few reasons to incur considerable debts, or they perhaps avoided indebtedness as a matter of strategy, or potential creditors may have hesitated to lend to women. Alternatively, New Englanders' choices surrounding litigation may have led women to appear in court primarily as creditors, either because female creditors were especially likely to sue their debtors, or because female debtors were unlikely to be sued. Women may have tended to pay their debts promptly, to prevent their creditors from suing them, or perhaps creditors showed particular forbearance toward female debtors, declining to sue them and effectively treating their loans as charity.

Creditors occasionally considered their debtors' genders when deciding whether to sue. In 1774, for instance, one elite Newport man indicated his willingness to accept partial payment from a widow and forgive her remaining balance. Priscilla Card paid her male creditor £20 out of the £30 she owed him. Although the creditor stated that he believed he "richly earned" the full sum, he concluded that he would accept the lesser amount, rather than "distress a woman or child."[13] Examples such as this are anomalies, however, and one would expect much more commentary to this effect if creditors overwhelmingly forgave women's debts. Gendered patterns of lending and litigiousness remain an important area for future research, one that will probably need to be pursued through individual case studies, as opposed to aggregate analysis.

Regardless of the reasons for women's disproportionate involvement in debt suits as plaintiffs, female litigants tended to be well positioned within a legal system that increasingly favored plaintiffs and creditors. In Suffolk and Newport Counties, male and female plaintiffs alike won more than 80 percent of their debt cases. They prevailed in the overwhelming majority of these by default, meaning that their debtors failed to appear in court or declined to contest the creditors' claims.[14] Defendants responded infrequently in debt suits, in part because few pleas were available to them. Whereas seventeenth-century courts entertained a wide range of arguments, by the 1730s the courts generally viewed written records as offering inconvertible evidence of debts. Defendants could point out technical deficiencies in the plaintiffs' filings, but they possessed few grounds on which to challenge the substance of their opponents' claims. Combined with the fact that women overwhelmingly participated in debt cases as plaintiffs, the culture of uncontested debt suits led female litigants to win the overall majority of such cases.[15]

Sarah Burrington of Tiverton, Rhode Island, was one widow who benefited from this transformed legal context when she filed a slew of lawsuits. In 1769, Burrington became the administrator of the estate of her late husband, a wealthy landowner and major creditor. In the four years that followed, she filed thirty suits to collect debts owed to his estate, and she won all but one of these cases by default. This strong track record in part reflected Burrington's skill in navigating the legal system. Although she possessed limited writing abilities and signed legal documents with her mark, she knew how to initiate lawsuits by hiring and directing an attorney. Rhode Island's legal climate, favoring creditors, equally contributed to Burrington's twenty-nine successes. As long as she and her attorney submitted the requisite documents to the court and drafted them properly, her late husband's debtors lacked any grounds on which to challenge the lawsuits. Burrington's one unfavorable outcome underscores this point. In that single unsuccessful book debt case, her opponent's attorney protested that her court filing left the sum in question blank. It also lacked an account as supporting evidence, as was required "by law." Burrington and her lawyer withdrew their suit, acknowledging that these lapses had fatally weakened their claims. Compliance with legal procedure and evidentiary standards facilitated her victories all of her other cases. Debtors may have stood poised to combat creditors' demands, but opportunities to do so were rare by the middle third of the eighteenth century.[16]

Whether or not women were physically present in court, each session drew public attention to their involvement as creditors and plaintiffs. Court proceedings opened with the calling of cases, which occurred before a crowded courtroom. In 1785, one lawyer described the scene as "pell-mell, helter-skelter," and "thronged with publicans, sinners, innholders, retailers, and justices."[17] The court clerk read aloud the names of the parties in each of the hundreds of cases that had been filed for that court term, pausing after each one to confirm that the relevant parties or their attorneys were in attendance. This process, which could last for several days, forced those present to note the involvement of female litigants. While some litigants, including women, relied on attorneys to act in their stead, others personally responded to the clerk's call. Catherine Cunningham, for instance, recounted that, as a party in a case in 1740, she "was in court & answered as often as called."[18] After the clerk finished announcing the list of cases, contested suits continued on to trial, a stage that drew further attention to women's economic activities when they became the substance of disputes.

For those female litigants who personally attended court, lawsuits were significant, not only because of the mixed-gender audiences before whom they occurred, but also because of the spaces they led women to enter. The courts' meeting places buttressed their official nature. Newport's Court of Common Pleas convened in the Colony House, while Suffolk County's court met in Boston's Town House until 1768 and then took place in a purpose-built courthouse thereafter. All three buildings were located at prominent sites near the top of their cities' main commercial thoroughfares. At a time when most buildings were squat, wood-framed houses, the courts stood out as taller brick structures. Other activities occurring in these same buildings further associated the court sessions with commerce and governance. The first floors of both Newport's Colony House and Boston's Town House were merchants' exchanges—open spaces for conversing and transacting business. Newport's court convened in the same second-floor room used by the legislature, while Boston's Town House also contained the probate office, register of deeds, and meeting rooms for the governor, the council, and the legislature. Whereas men appeared in governmental buildings in numerous capacities, court sessions were one of only a handful of instances in which women did so. By giving rise to debt litigation, women's everyday uses of credit facilitated their visible participation in state institutions.

Just as debt collection outside of court temporarily reconfigured social hierarchies, so, too, did women's most common role in litigation—that of unchallenged creditors—enhance their authority over their former trading partners. Initiating and winning debt cases enabled female creditors to lay claim to others' property and, in some instances, their bodies, through imprisonment. When women opted to initiate lawsuits against debtors, sheriffs summoned them to court. The law required debtors to guarantee their appearance in court by surrendering property equal to the value of their debts or by giving a bond. Defendants who could not satisfy these demands faced imprisonment until their court dates. Moreover, women who won their debt cases acquired additional discretion and power. They claimed their due by obtaining court orders (called writs of execution) and filing those documents with sheriffs. This could be done immediately following a court term, many months later, or, if creditors ultimately settled with their debtors outside of court, not at all. Once women obtained executions, sheriffs carried out court judgments by attempting to collect payment from the debtors. When debtors could not pay in cash or with property, the sheriffs confined them to jail. The wheels of debt collection turned only with concerted action from creditors, and this led to debtors' apprehension about whether and when creditors might lay claim to their assets.[19]

As creditors, women not only ordered sheriffs to apprehend debtors' property, but also, at times, directly participated in the seizure of it. Elizabeth Swinnerton, a widow, had loaned the considerable sum of £136 to fellow Newport resident and clockmaker Thomas Harris, accepting his promissory note as a guarantee of future payment. When Harris did not make good on his debt with Swinnerton, she sued him in the May 1751 court session. The month before the court sat, Swinnerton and the sheriff sought to notify Harris of the suit. Timing their visit carefully, in an attempt to surprise Harris, they arrived at "45 minutes after seven" in the morning. Harris was not at home, so, with Swinnerton pointing out his possessions, the sheriff claimed the raw materials and tools of Harris's clockmaking trade as security for the debt. The items seized (including five sawhorses and eleven chisels) were so cumbersome that carting them away would have been a labor-intensive process for the sheriff and any others who assisted him. But by laying claim to such significant quantities of Harris's property, Swinnerton compromised the clockmaker's ability to continue his business and demonstrated her standing as a creditor in a way that almost certainly attracted the neighbors' attention.[20]

Female creditors exercised additional authority by dictating the conditions of their debtors' release from prison. Boston and Newport each housed all imprisoned individuals within a single jail, but, unlike those convicted of criminal offenses, colonial debtors were not wards of the state. By law, debtors, once confined, remained in jail either until they paid their debts, or until creditors acquiesced to their release. Individuals had a limited ability to earn money once they were in jail, and presumably they would have paid their debts earlier if they possessed sufficient assets. Creditors therefore imprisoned their debtors primarily in order to encourage the debtors' allies to make loans or give bonds on their behalf. As long as creditors paid the associated jail fees, they could keep their debtors in prison indefinitely, whether as a pressure tactic or out of spite.[21] While *femes sole* determined when to imprison and release debtors in the course of their own lawsuits, such decision-making power also extended to wives acting on behalf of their households. In 1761, a married woman, Hannah Brayton, dictated the terms of laborer Joseph Seaby's discharge from Newport's jail. Imprisoned because he could not pay his debt to Hannah Brayton and her husband Benjamin, Seaby found an employer who would transmit his earnings directly to the Braytons. Although naming conventions in court records emphasized Benjamin Brayton's involvement, a witness noted that Hannah Brayton personally negotiated with Seaby and agreed to his release.[22] Imprisonment extended the importance of interpersonal negotiations surrounding credit, providing an additional arena in which female creditors wielded power over their debtors, who most commonly were men.

The same legal structures that empowered female creditors caused hardship for the much smaller number of women sued for debts. Female debtors possessed limited grounds on which to challenge lawsuits filed against them. As did many male debtors, more than two-thirds of female debtors lost their cases, and the great majority did so by default.[23] Moreover, like the men who were the targets of women's lawsuits, female defendants faced a loss of property or imprisonment when they could not pay their debts. When Rachel Clark, a single woman from Medway, Massachusetts, was sued for a debt in 1741, the sheriff seized her bed as security, despite her protest that "she has no other bed."[24] In 1771, Abigail Simon, the widow of a Newport merchant, faced numerous debt suits. Her creditors had noticed her precarious financial circumstances and rushed to seize her assets. They laid claim to her furniture and, once no furniture was left, her home. Simon's right to her dower (a third of her husband's estate) offered limited protection. Her creditors permitted her to remain in one-third of her house but mandated that she rent out the remaining two-thirds and deliver that rent to them.[25]

Women who lacked sufficient assets to satisfy their creditors faced imprisonment for debt. Relative to the hundreds of debt suits heard by the courts in a single term, the number of debtors who were confined at any given time was small. In practice, most debtors remained in prison for only a few weeks.[26]

Women were among those who were occasionally imprisoned for debt, and even the fear of imprisonment shaped their actions. In her 1757 petition to the Massachusetts legislature, Boston widow Sarah Hunt recounted her efforts to escape debt's shadow. Shortly after her husband's death in 1740, Hunt formalized a commercial partnership, selling imported wholesale and retail drygoods with her son-in-law. The pair struggled to prosper amid Boston's worsening economic depression and contractions in transatlantic credit. When Hunt's son-in-law died, the firm was insolvent, its debts exceeding its assets. Hunt, who was then age sixty and described herself as "in her declining years without any possibility of retrieving her affairs," attempted to avoid imprisonment for debt. She signed all of the firm's assets over to its creditors for proportional distribution; in exchange, they pledged not to seek additional payment at law. But one creditor persisted in suing Hunt, leading her to petition the legislature. Hunt lamented that without that body's intervention, she would "be committed to gaol" and "for ought she knows perish there she having parted with all she has in the world to satisfy the creditors."[27]

Sarah Hunt's narrative, and others like it, referenced several intertwined cultural archetypes and social problems that were familiar to New England legislators. Hunt's petition positioned her opponent as a conspiring creditor bent on harming his well-intentioned debtor. Meanwhile, Hunt herself appeared as a vulnerable widow, an image that aligned with Boston's growing population of impoverished widows. Hunt's predicament further reflected the plight of female debtors within a system that privileged creditors' claims and made minimal allowances for financial failure. Insolvency befell elite women, such Sarah Hunt, as well as poor ones.[28] Traders such as Hunt, engaged in large-scale commercial transactions, were particularly likely to face numerous creditors who would be reluctant to forgive sizeable debts. Once they were insolvent, female debtors had few ways in which protect their assets and bodies, and even a single persistent creditor could threaten a woman's independence and comfort. Hunt's fear of imprisonment led her to invest time and money in petitioning, and she successfully persuaded the legislature to permanently extinguish that one creditor's claim. In ruling in Hunt's favor, as well as in granting similar requests by men, this body acknowledged the limited redress available to debtors within existing legal structures.[29]

As New England's judicial system coped with a surge in debt cases in the early eighteenth century, and as caseloads then stabilized at new, higher levels, regular court sessions made visible the economic activities of Boston and Newport women in their own right and as estate administrators. No court attendee could overlook the clerk's shouting of female litigants' names during the calling of cases, or the presence of women waiting in the gallery for their cases to be tried. Court cases structured relations of power at the same time as they conferred public visibility. For the majority of female litigants who were creditors and plaintiffs, the court's growing emphasis on legal technicalities worked to their advantage, leading to their winning most cases by default and facilitating their claims to the property and bodies of their debtors, most of whom were men. This same system made the small number of women who were debtors and defendants tremendously vulnerable, particularly when they were insolvent. Female defendants, possessing few viable strategies for challenging their opponents' claims, faced the seizure of their belongings, houses, and persons. Yet this focus on legal procedure and case outcomes encompasses only a portion of women's involvement in the transformed world of debt litigation. The road to court began much earlier, with their decisions to hire attorneys.

Attorney-Client Relationships

By the mid-eighteenth century, the practice of law had become a recognizable profession in Boston and Newport. All litigants who wished to make substantive legal arguments hired attorneys. These lawyers were men, so the development of New England's legal system, on its face, fits a narrative that is familiar for the medieval and early modern periods. In fields ranging from medicine to the clothing trades, formally educated men displaced informally trained laypeople, ostensibly silencing women and excluding them from the work in which they had previously engaged.[30] Yet, when we attend to attorney-client interactions in Boston and Newport, it becomes clear that the legal profession grew through and alongside continued female involvement. Women were a constitutive element of attorneys' urban clienteles, in part because cities possessed large populations of *femes sole*, many of whom engaged in the sorts of business and investment activities that could yield litigation. In addition, especially in port cities with highly mobile male populations, all residents were expected to advance the collective interests of their households, interests that sometimes necessitated dealing with lawyers. Success in debt litigation demanded not only attorneys' technical competencies, but also labor and acumen on the part of the women who oversaw their and their households' lawyers. Examining the use of attorneys thus not only revises our understanding the rise of New England's bar, but also recasts professionalization as a dynamic process, rather than a set of top-down changes imposed by men. The example of the law encourages us to look for other moments when professionals and laypeople jointly redefined categories of expertise through their interactions, as well as to recognize ways in which women mobilized significant and often novel forms of skill and influence as they collaborated with emerging male professionals.

Whereas lawyers were uncommon figures in seventeenth-century New England, a recognizable legal profession cohered during the second half of the eighteenth century. In seventeenth-century Massachusetts and Rhode Island, the practice of law was not yet a well-defined vocation. Many litigants hired laypeople with informal expertise to draft their court filings, or they simply opted to speak for themselves in court. Massachusetts outlawed lawyers between 1641 and 1648, because the colony's Puritan leadership believed attorneys bred excessive litigiousness. The few men who called themselves lawyers lacked a formal legal education, and they simultaneously engaged in other occupations.[31] During the mid-eighteenth century, professional attorneys supplanted informally trained practitioners. This new cohort shared common educational backgrounds and derived their incomes exclusively from the practice of law. Although a successful legal career could ultimately be highly profitable, most would-be lawyers were young men who came from middling families and aspired to upward mobility. They typically attended Harvard or Yale, an experience that groomed them to become men of letters, and then undertook apprenticeships with senior attorneys to learn the law and internalize the profession's norms. Over the course of their careers, leading colonial lawyers gained significant wealth and notoriety, becoming some of the most affluent members of their communities and holding high-level political offices.[32] By the eve of the Revolution, roughly ten and fifteen professional attorneys, respectively, practiced in Newport and Boston.[33]

Lawyers' efforts and litigants' choices jointly fueled the legal profession's growth during the first half of the eighteenth century. In Suffolk County, attorneys founded a bar association in 1758. That body both fostered sociability among legal practitioners and worked to establish professional norms. In 1745, Newport lawyers signed an agreement to regulate their business practices, an act that served as the precursor to the founding of the city's bar association after the Revolution. Increasingly united, attorneys successfully lobbied courts and legislatures to reduce competition from outsiders and the untrained. Both Massachusetts and Rhode Island instituted rules restricting who could argue cases in court, and Massachusetts stipulated that only lawyers could draft writs, the legal documents through which plaintiffs summoned their opponents to court.[34] These regulations positioned attorneys to reshape courtroom proceedings. Basing their arguments on legal technicalities, lawyers won cases by calling attention to their opponents' procedural irregularities and improperly drafted documents. As attorneys made themselves increasingly valuable in litigation, men and women alike more consistently chose to engage their services, which, in turn, further reinforced the emerging bar's strength. By the mid-eighteenth century, plaintiffs, regardless of gender, always hired lawyers when initiating lawsuits, as did defendants seeking to respond to cases filed against them.[35]

The practice of law during the eighteenth century was a business based on volume. Thus women were a vital component of attorneys' clienteles. Lawyers charged for individual services, such as drafting documents or attending court.

The standard fees for each activity were low, generally less than £1, and many were stipulated by statute. Attorneys maximized their profits by riding circuit (traveling to the staggered court sessions of several counties) and by taking on as many cases as possible. Even for a well-known practitioner like John Adams—whom we tend to associate with his work in notable trials, such as that of the British soldiers implicated in the Boston Massacre—routine cases accounted for much of a lawyer's time and income. One year after his admission to the bar, Adams proposed bolstering his professional reputation, both by making "frequent visits to the Neighborhood" to "converse familiarly with Men, Women and Children," and by insinuating himself with "Merchants, Shop keepers, Tradesmen, &c." At the height of his law career, Adams's practice had grown to become the largest of any colonial Massachusetts lawyer. In a single year, he drafted 262 writs for the Suffolk Inferior Court and represented thirty-eight defendants, while also taking cases in the Superior Court and courts in other counties. As Adams's early musings on building his practice had acknowledged, women contributed to lawyers' businesses both by hiring their own legal counsel and by initiating cases that, in turn, spurred others to seek representation.[36]

Hiring and interacting with lawyers carried different meanings for women of various social classes. Elite women moved within the same social milieus as their lawyers, and legal fees proved to be manageable for them. During the decade prior to the Revolution, Abigail Stoneman operated a series of teahouses and coffeehouses in Boston and Newport, and she hired lawyers in order to sue customers with outstanding tabs. Described in newspapers as being "of very polite and genteel address," Stoneman was wealthy enough to sit for her portrait. Her coffeehouse, which she advertised as serving "gentlemen," was a center of colonial *belles lettres* culture, and Stoneman herself occupied a position of social authority as its proprietor. Eager to participate in networks of elite sociability, Newport's leading lawyers were among those who patronized Stoneman's establishment and held club meetings there.[37] When it came time for Stoneman to sue her customers, she was thus turning to lawyers with whom she had already interacted regularly. Such attorneys' fees were also small, relative to Stoneman's business income. In the early 1770s, lawyer William Ellery charged Stoneman twelve shillings for each writ he filed on her behalf. During these same years, Stoneman sold large bowls of punch for twenty shillings, and boarders paid eighteen shillings per week to rent her rooms. Overall, Ellery's fees to represent Stoneman in seven lawsuits totaled £12.6, far less than the accounts many customers accumulated at her coffeehouse.[38]

In contrast, hiring an attorney was considerably more financially burdensome and momentous for middling and lower-class women. During the same years when he worked for Stoneman, Ellery also represented Newport widow Mary Searing. Searing cobbled together a living through several small business ventures, including taking in boarders, grinding chocolate, and selling drygoods. Searing employed Ellery to file answers (at six shillings apiece) for her in two lawsuits in which she was a defendant, as well as to obtain a copy of a court judgment (at eight pence) in a third case. While Searing's overall account with Ellery was quite small, relative to Stoneman's, it would nonetheless have been consequential for a woman struggling to get by. Moreover, for Searing, collaborating with Ellery meant interacting with a man who was very much her social better.[39]

For women of all social classes, knowing how to interact with attorneys was a skill, one that was vital in navigating the economy and the legal system. The first step in a woman's partnership with a lawyer was knowing where and how to employ one. Women used the information gained from their social networks in choosing among the many lawyers who were available for hire. When Bostonian Sarah Perkins was sued in the Providence, Rhode Island, court in 1771, she asked around to find a lawyer. Regular attendees of that court reported seeing Newport-based lawyer Henry Marchant there often, so Perkins wrote to him and asked him to take her case.[40] Other women demonstrated their preferences when they hurried to hire a particular attorney before their opponents did so. When she was about to be sued, Elizabeth Thomas wrote to James Otis in 1746, requesting his "assistance as my attorney" and instructing him not to represent her opponent "on any account."[41] Women also exercised consumer power when they switched from one lawyer to another. Widow Ann Maylem, whose legal disputes will be discussed more extensively in chapter 5, hired a new attorney in 1744 when, contrary to her instructions, her first pick withdrew an important case.[42]

Men and women engaged local lawyers by visiting their offices, often run out of the attorneys' homes, and hired distant ones by corresponding with them.[43] Whether in person or through letters, laypeople persuaded lawyers to represent them by describing their cases' content and working out terms of payment. The attorney-client partnership was itself a credit relationship, with lawyers maintaining accounts of services rendered to clients and, when necessary, suing for payment on those accounts. Laypeople's creditworthiness and assurances of prompt payment helped persuade attorneys to take their cases. Prospective clients also solidified their lawyers' assistance by providing them with the financial records—such as bonds, promissory notes, accounts, or receipts—that surrounded the debts in question. These documents both served as legal evidence and contained the information that attorneys used to draft their legal filings, so clients indicated their commitment to use a particular lawyer when they delivered the originals to him.

By the eve of the Revolution, a powerful set of usually unspoken rules governed attorney-client interactions. Newport lawyer Henry Marchant articulated these norms in an acrid letter to Francina Muir, a widow from Virginia's Eastern Shore, in 1774. Muir, who was the administrator of her late husband's estate, wrote to Marchant and asked him to collect a debt owed by a Rhode Islander. Muir's letter and enclosures lacked the requisite details, and such omissions were especially problematic, given that Marchant claimed to have "no knowledge" of Muir or her husband. Marchant remarked that it was "surprising" that Muir had provided "no evidence" of the debt in question, despite the fact that the debtor had supposedly written a letter in which he acknowledged the debt. Marchant instructed Muir to "send that letter by a safe hand," along with "other papers tending to prove that matter." Muir's second error was writing "nothing" about how she would compensate her lawyer for his labor and any court fees. Marchant insisted that "before I begin suit it would be necessary I should know how I am to be satisfied." He refused to blindly extend credit to a prospective client of uncertain reputation.[44]

Muir faced multiple layers of difficulty in hiring Marchant. Residing far away from Rhode Island, she was probably unfamiliar with that colony's legal protocols. Marchant also viewed Muir as an outsider. While he routinely took on the cases for distant letter-writers, these were typically male merchants who were part of the same network as his current clients. When these men contacted Marchant, they presented letters of introduction or referenced their mutual acquaintances. Muir's failings led Marchant to conclude his letter to her on an ambivalent note. Having enumerated the steps that she needed to take to secure his assistance, he then wrote, "That done, I shall endeavor to render you every service in the power of your humble servant."[45] During the same period in which Marchant expressed skepticism about Francina Muir's request, many other women hired Massachusetts and Rhode Island attorneys without incident. As they did so, they mobilized the skills and social connections that Francina Muir lacked.

In 1754 and 1755, Newport lawyer Augustus Johnston kept a detailed account of the work he performed for one Newport widow, Margaret Holmes. The account captures the three broad categories of services that attorneys rendered to their male and female clients: providing legal expertise outside of court, drafting legal documents, and arguing litigants' cases. First, attorneys offered guidance and looked into cases during the months between court sessions. For example, Johnston billed Holmes for "advice & directions about settling her affair with Peter Phillips & Oliver White." He also visited the residence of Joseph Fox, a notary who kept copies of documents on file after drafting them, and charged Holmes for "perusing papers" there. Together, these services cost £10, less than one-eighth of the £81 that Holmes owed Johnston.[46]

In the remainder of his work for Holmes, Johnston directly advanced his client's cases through the courts. He drafted and obtained numerous legal documents, and such labors composed the single largest category of entries on Holmes's tab. He also initiated lawsuits by completing writs (printed forms instructing the sheriff to summon Holmes's opponents to court) and filing declarations (formal statements of complaint). When Holmes's opponents contested her suits, Johnston submitted written pleas in response. As Holmes's cases moved through the system, they accumulated court fees, and these, too, were associated with particular documents. Each time Johnston appealed a case, he filed an appeal bond and paid the associated fee. Successfully arguing an appellate case required access to the lower court records, so Johnston also purchased copies of them. He fronted these costs, then charged them to Holmes's account. The final component of Johnston's work for Holmes was personally representing her in court. For this, he assessed a flat fee per Court of Common Pleas case, as well as additional sums for arguing her cases in the appellate court.[47]

Johnston's account of services provided to Holmes illustrates the ongoing nature of attorney-client partnerships. A case's progress through the courts hinged on numerous small actions that laypeople entrusted to their lawyers, including timely filings of documents and punctual appearances in court. Given that litigants might, at any stage, opt to withdraw their suits or cease to challenge their opponents' claims, lawyers did not push matters forward without instructions from their clients. Furthermore, because most lawyers' businesses spanned multiple counties, they might not attend a particular court session without specific instructions to do so. Even after hiring a lawyer, women needed to demonstrate vigilance throughout the course of their lawsuits.

Margaret Elliott, a widow, recognized the importance of such ongoing communication in her repeated efforts to direct attorney William Brattle. In 1753, a man sued Elliot regarding a book debt. Elliott, however, remained convinced, as she later explained, that she "did not then . . . owe him one farthing." Joining the numerous other women who journeyed through their regions in order to manage credit relationships, Elliott rented a horse. She intended to travel twenty miles east from her Massachusetts hometown of Holliston to Cambridge to hire Brattle as her lawyer. Elliott never reached Cambridge, however. Thrown from her horse, she broke several bones and was forced to return home. Unable to speak personally with Brattle, Elliott relayed a message instead. At Elliott's direction, Brattle represented her in the August court session and had her case postponed to the December term. When winter came, Elliott's injuries still had not healed. She again sent word to Brattle, asking him to act for her in the case.[48]

Through her two messages, Elliott demonstrated her resourcefulness in hiring a lawyer, and a specific one at that. When Elliott later detailed the affair in a petition to the Massachusetts legislature, she signed it with her mark. It is therefore almost certain that she did not pen her own letters to Brattle. Instead, her actions demonstrate a different skill: the ability to enlist a trusted local ally who could either relay her instructions orally or draft letters for her. Within Elliott's strategy, direct and indirect communications with her attorney served different functions. She possessed enough financial intelligence and familiarity with her affairs that she was confident she owed nothing to her opponent, and she sought to meet with Brattle to share information that was crucial to her case. Seeking its postponement, Elliott's two messages were stopgap measures.[49] But Brattle never received the second missive. Lacking directions from his client in advance of the December court term, he did not assume that Elliott wished to continue challenging her creditor's demands. No one appeared in court to represent Elliott, and she lost her case by default. A successful outcome in court depended on ongoing instructions from a client to her attorney. In this case, the chains of communication broke down.[50]

While most of the evidence regarding women who hired attorneys pertains to *femes sole*, married women also collaborated with lawyers. In fact, attorneys' papers contain a small number of letters from *femes covert* writing in depth about the handling of legal matters. In 1757, Martha Parker, a married woman, wrote to her family's attorney, James Otis, because a debtor who was sued by her husband desired to be released from jail. Parker informed Otis that she had "made inquire [inquiry] concerning his estate" and was reluctant to agree to this request, because she discovered that the debtor had sheltered his house from creditors' claims by transferring the deed to another individual. Parker's letter contained no mention of her husband being away from home, but instead portrayed her as acting within an ongoing collaboration with Otis.[51]

Married women and other female dependents also facilitated lawyers' work on behalf of their households. Women served as intermediaries between men and their attorneys, such as when one man relied on his daughter to obtain documents from lawyer James Otis in 1754. Urging Otis to send the documents "by his daughter," the client insisted that "I am afraid you will forgit them & it is best to send them by her & then you won't be troubled by them."[52] When men were away from home, their wives also notified attorneys of pending lawsuits and provided funds to secure their continued services. In 1763, a lawyer instructed his messenger to "call upon Mrs. White of Taunton Nathaniel White's wife" and obtain "four dollars for the jury and a fee to myself," or else he would not argue the case at the next court session.[53] In port cities, such coordination between married women and attorneys was particularly commonplace. Residents expected mariners' wives would seek legal counsel while their husbands were at sea, since that was in keeping with such women's overall responsibility for managing their households' finances and assets. When the wife of Newport mariner Richard Jones informed the sheriff that her husband was away on a voyage in 1740 and could not respond to a lawsuit described in a legal notice, the sheriff "advised her immediately to deliver the copy I gave her to her husband's attorney." Recording his actions in the case file, this official saw his directive not only as benevolent counsel, but also as part of his legal obligation to exercise due diligence when notifying parties of lawsuits.[54] Much like other practices surrounding credit, collaborations with attorneys could involve all the members of households, including dependents.

Examining correspondence between lawyers and clients further elucidates the nature of their relationships. Many laypeople worked with attorneys entirely through face-to-face conversations, and such meetings generated minimal written records. Thus letters to and from lawyers are useful, not only because they provide insight into one common variant of attorney-client relationships—those which included correspondence—but also because they provide suggestive evidence of the dynamics of such partnerships, writ large.

As they wrote back and forth to each other, clients and attorneys shaped their respective positions as principals and agents. Principal-agent relationships, a vital component of economic networks during a period in which people and news traveled slowly, pervaded the eighteenth-century Atlantic World. These included collaborations between masters and apprentices; merchants and factors or ship captains; and even, as we have seen, husbands and wives. As modeled in letter-writing manuals and carried out in practice, such relationships were hierarchical, but they also contained inherent tensions. Principals, possessing supervisory authority, expected their agents to both comply with instructions and exercise discretion in time-sensitive matters. Yet reliance on agents was equally a form of dependence.[55] Litigants, as principals hiring agents, not only expected their attorneys to adhere to directives, but also to employ their legal judgment and professional expertise. Within the intersecting social hierarchies that characterized the eighteenth-century Atlantic World, men's and women's relationships with their lawyers were broadly similar, defined by the same range of situational possibilities. A woman's ability to skillfully adopt the position of a principal, as well as her gender, shaped her dealings with her attorney.

Male and female clients alike instructed their lawyers, while also authorizing them to exercise discretion. The letters of Martha Parker, a resident of the Cape Cod town of Falmouth, to James Otis exemplify the polite tone used by clients as they gave orders to their attorneys. Parker, who appears to have been administering an estate, forwarded financial documents to Otis and instructed him to sue the named debtors. As she did so, she managed multiple financial conflicts and demonstrated her in-depth knowledge of legal procedures, including filing writs. In a 1757 letter, she rattled off directives to launch four lawsuits. With reference to one debtor, Parker wrote that "I can't get him to setel" and "I think it best to sue him to an account." Regarding another, she stated, "I have enclosed two notes of David Fowler of the vineyard pilets [pilots] and desire you would file writs for them."[56] Parker also asked Otis to represent her in suits in which she was a defendant, writing in 1761, "I shall have some actions next court if I don't make up before court. Desiar you to answer if my name should be cold [called] in court."[57] As did other clients, Parker urged Otis to carry out her instructions with speed, admonishing him to act in one case "as soon as you can" and in another "as soon as may be." Although couched as requests for favors, such instructions by Parker—as well as those by other women and men—made it clear that lawyers were agents hired to carry out their principals' wishes.[58]

Clients, including Parker, also afforded their attorneys discretion in other matters. Just as agents responded to shifting local conditions without the principals' express approval, so, too, could attorneys' legal expertise and up-to-date knowledge of disputes authorize their choices. Men and women alike urged their lawyers to act "if you think it be best" or "as you see fit," or to do what "your honour thinks most proper." They used these phrases both in a general sense, often at the conclusion of their letters, and in reference to particular matters.[59] Martha Parker, for instance, directed Otis "see how the matter is" in one suit in which a debtor supposedly possessed evidence of payment. She deferred to him on whether to persist in suing the debtor, noting that "if you think it best to let fall the action I shall be satisfied with it."[60] Attesting to the situational nature of attorney-client relationships, such statements routinely appeared in the same letters in which laypeople also provided precise instructions.

Lawyers, meanwhile, displayed deference to principals through the timely sharing of information and pledges of future service. As they did when writing to their male clients, attorneys sent their female clients detailed updates that assumed an understanding of legal terminology and procedures. In 1766, Connecticut lawyer William Samuel Johnson informed Bostonian Rebecca Gibbons that he was waiting for her debt case to come to trial, as "the note is in suit and the counsel concerned for the defendant tell me that they shall plead full payment of it." He promised that "you may depend upon my making the best defense I can against their objections." In 1769, Henry Marchant similarly reported to Anne Devisme of New York that "I have sued and got judgments ag[ains]t Whipple & Chace," and that he expected she would have her money by June of that year. Apologizing that "my hurry of business prevents me from writing so often as I would," he pledged, "I never neglect writing when anything turns up necessary to be communicated to my clients."[61] As Marchant's broad assurances to Devisme about the treatment of "my clients" underscores, lawyers viewed all paying clients as entitled to updates about their affairs.

At the same time as they demonstrated deference and loyalty toward their clients, attorneys asserted their professional authority, arising from their legal knowledge and specialized skills. They routinely instructed clients in how to prepare documents for court in ways that complied with the tightened evidentiary standards that were well established by mid-century. When Rebecca Gibbons suggested that she might have additional documents to prove her case, in his 1766 letter William Johnson replied that she should "send me sworn copies of them and all the evidence you can furnish in the case." In a case in 1771 concerning book debt, Henry Marchant likewise instructed Sarah Perkins that "it will be necessary that a justice in Boston examine and compare your account with the original entries and ledger & certifie that it agrees therewith." He advised Francina Muir in 1774 to "procure an attested copy of your husband's will & probate thereof and letters testamentary . . . all proved under the hand and seal of the Gov'r or at least a notary public."[62] Such detailed instructions and occasional didactic tones were not reserved only for female clients. Lawyers similarly asserted their expertise as they schooled even elite men in aspects of legal procedure.[63] A degree of malleability thus characterized both men's and women's written interactions with their attorneys. At some moments, litigants authoritatively issued directions and lawyers dutifully provided detailed reports. In others, attorneys' firsthand knowledge and legal expertise authorized them to exercise discretion and even instruct their clients.

Because the attorney-client partnership was inherently malleable, multiple intersecting variables shaped the tenor of any one such relationship. While gender dynamics were certainly one important consideration, social class and status as a creditor or debtor intersected with gender and shaped how laypeople collaborated with their lawyers. Women's letters display a spectrum of possibilities in how they interacted with their attorneys.

Some men and women, including Newport widow and shopkeeper Sarah Rumreil, issued crisp instructions to their lawyers. In 1746, attorney James Otis received a letter from Rumreil as part of his ongoing work on her behalf. While this is the only surviving letter from Rumreil to Otis, its high level of assumed knowledge and its lack of introductory greetings make clear that it was part of a well-established relationship between an entrepreneur and her lawyer. The note moved through three matters involving Ridington, West, and Williams with succinctness, indicating her mastery of finance and legal procedure:

> Sir
>
>   Inclosed you have the deed of Ridington and also the credit that must be given to wests account £11.9. As to William's affair I must acquaint you that as he is a shuffling chap you will do well to take care how to manage him and likewise give the same caution at present to the officer [That] is all at present from
>
>   Sir your very Hum[ble] Servt
>
>   Sarah Rumreill.[64]

Twice using the imperative "must" and once instructing Otis to "take care," the text unambiguously positioned Otis as an agent obligated to follow Rumreil's orders. Through its conciseness, the letter evinced confidence that Otis would continue to act for Rumreil.

Regardless of whether Rumreil penned this letter herself, her authoritative tone was made possible and appropriate by her status as a creditor, her social class, and her business activities. As a creditor to both West and Williams, whom the letter condemned as a "shuffling chap," Rumreil interacted with Otis from a position of economic power and moral superiority. At the time, she was becoming one of Newport's most visible and affluent female entrepreneurs. Rumreil continued her family's shopkeeping business for several decades following her husband's death in 1743, purchasing luxury goods from leading merchants and retailing them to Newport residents. She was regularly a plaintiff in the Newport courts and, when Rhode Island conducted a tax assessment in 1767, she owned "1½ buildings," held £228 in money and stock, and owned taxable goods valued at £234.[65] As a result of the success and longevity of her enterprise, Rumreil, like other men and women who regularly moved within the same social and economic circles as the lawyers they hired, directed Otis from a position of relative parity.

Other women positioned their attorneys as possessing the unique capability to save them from distress by virtue of their legal expertise. Whereas Rumreil's letter issued commands to Otis, these prospective clients adopted a tone of supplication, writing to "intreat," "pray," or "beg" for the lawyers' assistance. Lacking Rumreil's emotional restraint, they insisted that they had been "wronged," "troubled," or "ill treated" by their opponents, and that losing their cases would not be "just," would be "hard," or would leave them "absolutely ruined."[66] Phebe Hinckly, who appears to have written to James Otis herself, sought the attorney's services when she was sued for a debt in 1762. She began by explaining, "These [lines] are to enliten you in this cas I think it would be as just to pay for my bring up ever cinc I was two years old as to pay this bill." Lacking the specific directives and legal terminology of Rumreil's letter, the entirety of Hinckly's letter outlined her plight, and she concluded with the vague request that "I think it very hard and trust that you will see that things are rited."[67] Hinckly's letter, and others like it, cast lawyers as benevolent protectors.

Men as well as women sometimes assumed a posture of supplication when seeking the assistance of attorneys. For example, Isaac Doane of Harwich, Massachusetts, adopted a tone that was similar to Phebe Hinckly's when he wrote to James Otis about two lawsuits in 1739. In one, a creditor persisted in suing Doane for the full amount of a debt, even though Isaac claimed to have already paid the majority of it. In another, a debtor was attempting to "misprove" that Doane had already received the sum in question. Doane begged Otis to "Pray take care of my busines for I leave it to you as I am wronged in this affare," and, just one line later, "Pray don't do me injustice."[68] Contrasting sharply with Rumreil's polished correspondence, the phonetic spellings and breathless syntax of Hinckley's and Doane's letters suggest that neither occupied a position within New England's learned commercial elites.

While pleading for a lawyer's assistance was not an exclusively feminine posture, the attorney-client relationship took on additional gendered significance in the letters of some female debtors. Linking their plight to their femininity, they appealed to their lawyers as chivalrous patrons who aided them in times of distress. References to poverty and either youth or advanced age often reinforced such women's descriptions. In letters to James Otis authored between the 1740s and 1760s, Hannah Norton, Elesabeth Hammond, and Anne Johnson, respectively, identified themselves as a "poor girl," a "humble and obedient hand maiden" in a "distrest condition" in her "declining years," and "a poor old widow that is left distetut [destitute]." These women narrated their circumstances in ways that agreed with these characterizations. Hannah Norton cast her opponents as mythical, uncontrollable beasts: Otis had previously saved her from "harpies who would have made a morsel of her to their devouring jaws had you not interposed," and her "necessity" led her to again "flie to [Otis] for assistance." Hammond lamented that her creditors and her two adult sons threatened to seize all of her assets, and "to be stript of all ye labor I have dun in forty five years . . . is hard." When she "[prayed]" that Otis would "take a ceare [care] & to [act] for me," she invited him to restore the patriarchal protection no longer provided by her late husband or sons.[69] In sharp contrast with Sarah Rumreil, these women juxtaposed feminine vulnerability with masculine legal skill and protection. While their language certainly reflected their precarious circumstances and need for representation, it attested equally to their savvy in navigating the growing professionalization of the legal system. These women, familiar with the procedure for hiring lawyers, used emotional registers that increased their odds of securing the attorneys' assistance.

Even as lawyers defined themselves as increasingly central to legal proceedings during the middle decades of the eighteenth century, ordinary men and women remained engaged in the work of litigation. Laypeople contributed to the growth of the legal profession, as the debt cases generated by all New Englanders, including women, fed the attorneys' growing businesses. As form of principal-agent relationship, collaborations between laypeople and their hired lawyers were necessarily malleable. Some clients stressed their reliance on attorneys and begged for their assistance. For women, this posture could be explicitly gendered. Other clients, including affluent female creditors, authoritatively directed their lawyers from a position of relative parity. All litigants actively managed their attorneys, including by enlisting their assistance, establishing credit relationships, providing payment, supplying the necessary information and legal documents, and supervising the lawyers' ongoing labor.

Debt Litigation beyond the Courtroom

Much of the legalistic activity associated with debt litigation occurred outside of the courtroom. This included not only ongoing coordination between attorneys and clients, but also the actions of local officials carrying out court orders before and after debt suits. While many historians have noted the large volume of debt cases in the eighteenth-century, they have devoted much less attention to the serving of writs as a site where ordinary people, including women, engaged with the law.[70] With New Englanders initiating hundreds of new cases each term in the Courts of Common Pleas, serving their opponents with writs was a common and highly visible occurrence within colonial communities, all the more so because of its seasonality. Attending to the seizure of property and persons occurring in the course of debt litigation expands the circle of women participating in it and exercising legal skill.

On February 17, 1766, constable Joseph Foy arrived at the Boston residence of Edward Peirse well after dark. Peirse was not at home, so it was his wife, Sarah, who answered the door when Foy knocked. As the constable explained to her, he visited because a Boston cordwainer, Benjamin Starr, had sued her husband regarding a debt. Foy's actions that evening became the basis for a lawsuit by Starr, in which Sarah Peirse testified, in the Suffolk County Court of Common Pleas in April of that year. Although Peirse was unable to write and signed her deposition with an *X*, she possessed a strong understanding of the legal importance of that February evening's events and a detailed memory of them. When she testified before a justice of the peace, the resulting statement was nearly two full pages long, much more extensive than a typical deposition. With Sarah Peirse as our guide, we can see debt litigation's capacity to ensnare many individuals, far beyond those named in a lawsuit.[71]

Benjamin Starr began his lawsuit in the same way as all other creditors: he purchased a writ. This legal document instructed the sheriff or his deputy to summon Edward Peirse to court and take sufficient security to guarantee Peirse's appearance. Constable Joseph Foy went to Peirse's residence on February 17 with this writ in hand. In addition to informing this debtor of the lawsuit against him, Foy aimed to take control of enough of Peirse's property to equal the value of the debt. Officials typically seized household goods, including furniture and tools, but in a move that manifested enslaved people's status as chattel, they sometimes also apprehended such laborers as security.[72] In the absence of sufficient property, Foy would force Peirce to either enlist bondsmen or face imprisonment. Foy was obligated by law to carry out the writ's instructions to seize Peirse's property or person, and sheriffs and constables who failed to carry out their duties risked lawsuits from disgruntled plaintiffs. While not all creditors personally were present when writs were served, Starr was. He either accompanied Foy or arrived partway through the evening's events.[73]

Foy's visit to the Peirse family's residence occurred within the cyclical ebb and flow of activity surrounding the quarterly sessions of the Suffolk Court of Common Pleas. Each court session was preceded by a series of deadlines, including those for plaintiffs to purchase writs, for sheriffs to serve writs on defendants, and for defendants to file answers. Litigants were very familiar with these deadlines and attempted to use them to their advantage.[74] This yielded a flurry of activity on certain key days. Holding out hope that debtors would settle outside of court and thus avoid the time and expense of litigation, many creditors delayed filing writs until the last possible day. Many debtors likewise waited until the deadline to file answers, either because they were availing themselves of all possible dilatory tactics, or they were attempting to reach a settlement outside of court. On important deadlines, clerks' offices became, according to one Rhode Islander's description, "full of people," and were characterized by the "hurry of business."[75] Each influx of lawsuits prior to a court session sent sheriffs and their deputies fanning out to serve large numbers of writs during a concentrated time frame. Foy's visit to the Peirses' residence, occurring in February when the next court session was not until April, took place outside of these usual patterns. It appears that Starr was so intent on suing that he saw no point in waiting, perhaps because doing so would allow other creditors the have first claim to Peirse's assets. Regardless of Starr's motivations, the resulting episode offers a window into a process that was repeated hundreds of times per year in Boston and Newport.

According to Sarah Peirse's testimony, Foy spoke with three residents in her household while serving the writ that February evening. First, he spoke with Peirse herself. This was common, as the law allowed sheriffs and constables to serve writs on the wives of male defendants. Especially in port cities, local officials routinely found married women, but not their husbands, at home when they came bearing legal notices. While some wives simply accepted writs on behalf of their spouses, others attempted to delay or protect the family property, as did Sarah Peirse. When Foy informed her of the reason for his visit, she "desired him to wait for a short time, tilling him that I expected my husband home soon." Disregarding Peirse's request, Foy began claiming furniture and household goods, in accordance with the writ's instructions. Partway through the episode, Edward Peirse returned home, as did another woman who lived in the house, widow Elizabeth Heart.[76]

Sarah and Edward Peirse and Elizabeth Heart all engaged in heated negotiations with Foy that attested to their familiarity with legal procedures. According to Sarah Peirse, upon his arrival, Foy declared that he "had a writ against my husband." When Foy then laid claim to a desk, looking glass, and mahogany table, Peirse protested that these items did not belong to her husband. Foy replied that "he did not care whether they were or not, for he would take them." Peirse's opposition and her recollection of Foy's retort reflected her understanding of the writ's significance. She knew that such an instrument authorized Foy to seize her husband's belongings, but not those of other residents.[77]

Once Edward Peirse arrived home, he, too, sparred with Foy. The husband reiterated that the belongings in question were not his. Knowing that defendants who possessed insufficient property to provide security were required to post bail, Edward Peirse instead offered to locate bondsmen. Foy rejected each name that Peirse proposed. The constable declared that the first possibility "could not be found at that time of night," and that the second "lived two far of [off]." Running out of excuses when Peirse suggested they visit a man who lived "at the corner of the Lane" and could provide bond "in a minuet," Foy replied that "he had got security & would not goe" to the neighbor's house.[78]

Finally, Elizabeth Heart, who came onto the scene at some point during the commotion, intervened. Demonstrating the same knowledge of writs as her fellow residents, she admonished Foy, declaring that "the goods which he had attach'ed was all her property," and, according to Sarah Peirse's testimony, warned him that he could "touch or remove them upon his peril."[79] The phrase "upon his peril" and related variants refered to the assumption of risk and responsibility and were of great significance. They appeared repeatedly in legal texts and forms from that period. Witness depositions recounted numerous men and women issuing identical cautions in similar confrontations with local officials.[80] Whether Heart and other bystanders used this exact wording, they knew enough to notify sheriffs and constables with sufficient clarity that any eventual witness testimony would contain the term. Heart's warning gave Foy pause. It was at this point that he asked Starr whether he accepted legal responsibility for the evening's events. Starr's affirmative response would become highly significant later on in the dispute.[81]

Other New Englanders deployed additional tactics in their interactions with local law enforcement. As laypeople calculated their responses to those purporting to serve writs, they evaluated whether such individuals were indeed acting in an official capacity, rather than as private citizens. While the law required sheriffs and constables to bring writs with them to defendants' residences, it notably did not mandate that officials read such documents aloud immediately upon their arrival.[82] Some men and women interrogated officials about the writs' contents and demanded to either see the documents or hear them read.[83] In addition, because the law specified that sheriffs and constables could not forcibly invade residents' homes to serve writs, defendants and their allies sometimes rushed to lock doors and hide belongings when officials arrived. Ruth Loring and Elizabeth Goddard, a boarder and a servant who sided with the Hewes family in their protracted dispute surrounding their Boston tannery (see chapter 1), showed such knowledge of the law when they shut the door on the sheriff, rather than accepting one writ, and hurried to lock shops and outbuildings to prevent him from seizing property in fulfillment of another.[84] Given the frequency with which sheriffs served writs in eighteenth-century New England, familiarity with legal procedures was vital for protecting the interests of oneself and one's allies or superiors.

For his part, Foy appeared intent on staging all possible elements of the episode to his advantage. The law allowed constables to serve writs in the evening, and Foy's decision to do so most likely was deliberate. The cover of February darkness may have enhanced Foy's ability to surprise and intimidate Sarah Peirse, and nighttime provided a convenient excuse for rejecting possible bondsmen. (Peirse noted that her husband returned home between 9 and 10 pm, so the entire episode unfolded late in the evening, especially by the standards of eighteenth-century Boston.) Foy also highlighted the scene's gender dynamics. In response to Elizabeth Heart's challenges, he reminded her of his superior physical strength, proclaiming that "he would carry [the goods] away if she was not stronger than he."[85] While it is possible that Foy was simply intent on fully exercising the powers of his minor local office, his strong commitment to seizing valuable goods suggests that he may have possessed a vested financial interest in assisting Benjamin Starr, Edward Peirse's creditor.

Foy left the Heart and Peirse residence with a considerable haul: a desk, tea table, and stand—all made out of mahogany, a luxury wood—as well as a looking glass and brass kettle.[86] He delivered all of these items to Benjamin Starr, who was to hold them as security until his case was resolved. At the Court of Common Pleas two months later, Elizabeth Heart sued Benjamin Starr for taking her property, a decision that followed from Starr's verbal promise to accept responsibility for Foy's actions. It was this lawsuit in which Sarah Peirse testified.[87]

Elizabeth Heart's lawsuit and the events of that February night underscore that the service of writs touched many individuals who were not officially parties in a given debt case, drawing them into both casual interactions and heated confrontations with representatives of the law. The record does not specify whether the Peirses or Elizabeth Heart owned the house that Foy visited, but, given that the two parties were apparently unrelated, it is almost certain that one rented from the other. If the valuable furniture seized by Foy belonged to Elizabeth Heart, it is probable that the dwelling was hers, and that she was among the roughly one-third of taxpaying Boston widows who counted on rent as an important source of their income.[88]

If Elizabeth Heart was indeed a landlord, she was part of a larger coterie of female entrepreneurs who became entangled with the law as a result of their proximity to others' property. In addition to engaging in her own many lawsuits, in 1754, Newport shopkeeper Sarah Rumreil dealt with local officials in a lawsuit between two male merchants. The defendant, William Stoakesberry, was a resident of the Mosquito Coast in the West Indies, but he had left some of his assets with Rumreil. Officials accordingly served Rumreil with the writ arising from this case, and she surrendered £81 of his property. This episode was uneventful, but evaluating local officials' demands involved the same sort of legal knowledge demonstrated by Sarah and Edward Peirce and Elizabeth Heart.[89]

Whether women were tenants or landlords, their property could become intermixed with that of their fellow residents. In the episode that gave rise to Elizabeth Heart's lawsuit, this was particularly evident when Joseph Foy's tour of the residence reached the kitchen. As Foy eyed the large brass kettle, Heart attempted to redirect him, insisting that the kettle was hers, but that a nearby table belonged to Edward Peirse.[90] With multiple residents' belongings located within arm's reach of each other, local officials' tasks included distinguishing ownership of a household's many contents. Given the high possibility of mixups, men and women had to protect their own property when officials came to serve writs on other residents in their households.

Heart's and the Pierces' legal challenges, arising from women's involvement in urban rental and service economies, resembled those faced by a Newport widow, Joanna Chapman, three decades earlier. Chapman assumed custody of George Lawton's property, as she housed and cared for him during a period of worsening illness, lasting from 1729 until his death in 1732. Theirs was a business arrangement—Chapman charged for her services and later sued Lawton's estate for payment—but one whose daily practicalities involved considerable intimacy.[91] While her tenant was sick, Chapman assumed de facto control of his locked red leather trunk, which contained money, financial records, and assorted fabrics. When Lawton was too unwell to settle with creditors who came to him, he gave the trunk's key to his female landlord and caretaker. On several occasions, Chapman opened the trunk, got out the necessary money, and paid Lawton's creditors.[92] Chapman's access to Lawton's belongings led to confusion after his death. The Newport Town Council summoned her to testify regarding the inventory of Lawton's estate, and Lawton's administrator sued her, alleging that she was unlawfully withholding her late tenant's trunk and its contents. In apparent acknowledgement of the fact that Chapman's conduct was within normal business practices, the administrator lost this suit.[93] Renting rooms may have enhanced the incomes of women, including Joanna Chapman and Elizabeth Heart, but it also drew them into confrontations with local officials.

It is equally possible that Sarah and Edward Peirse and Elizabeth Heart were co-conspirators. New Englanders sometimes temporarily "sold" their property to others, in order to shield it from creditors' claims, and the Peirse couple, with assistance from Heart, may have engaged in a variant of this practice.[94] Sarah

Peirse may have cleverly insisted that the house's furniture belonged to Heart as a way to deter Foy from seizing it, and, whether as a result of prior planning or attentive improvisation, Edward Peirse and Elizabeth Heart may have continued the ruse. If Foy and Starr suspected such a scheme, this would explain their insistence on carrying away the property in question.

Ultimately, the court ruled in favor of Heart, ordering that Starr pay her £6 in damages for seizing the property involved in the lawsuit.[95] Regardless of whether Elizabeth Heart was an innocent victim or a savvy accomplice, her saga highlights that even seemingly straightforward debt cases rippled beyond the named parties. In a process that was repeated hundreds of times per court term, officials fanned out in search of the defendants named in writs. When they arrived at their destinations, they often encountered other members of the relevant households, including women, and seizing a defendant's property could require sorting through the residents' intermingled belongings. Even for those women and men who were unlikely to personally receive court summonses, the biannual or quarterly serving of writs was a familiar and potentially treacherous aspect of life within the highly litigious societies of colonial Boston and Newport. Laypeople's ability to protect their persons and property hinged on their familiarity with legal procedure and their ability to advocate for themselves in confrontations with local officials. Women were among those forced to respond when the constable or sheriff arrived.

Conclusion

Within the highly litigious societies of colonial Boston and Newport, debt suits touched the lives of most residents. Plaintiffs and defendants were at the heart of the court proceedings. Between 1730 and the Revolution, those who initiated or respond to lawsuits faced a shifting legal landscape. The courts increasingly prioritized questions of law when adjudicating disputes, and they generally sided with parties who advanced technically compliant claims and substantiated them with sufficient evidence. Women and men both navigated these changes. Whereas men became plaintiffs and defendants in roughly equal proportions, the vast majority of female litigants were creditors, and therefore plaintiffs, in straightforward lawsuits. They overwhelmingly won their cases, typically without any challenges from their opponents. Status as both a creditor and a plaintiff enabled women to gain public visibility within the official setting of the courts, and it allowed them to lay claim to others' bodies and property. The small number of women who were sued for unpaid debts, however, were positioned on the opposite side of this same system, and thus had only limited abilities to counter their creditors' demands.

Fully taking stock of women as skilled legal actors also requires expanding our view beyond the courtroom. By mid-century, professional lawyers were ubiquitous in debt suits, and much of the workings of litigation outside of court occurred as lawyers and laypeople coordinated their activities through conversations and correspondence. Examining the mechanics of such attorney-client collaborations revises the standard narratives of professionalization and its implications for gender. Lawyers needed a large number of clients, among whom were both *femes sole* and *femes covert*, in order to maintain profitable practices. Employing an attorney had varying meanings for women. For an elite proprietor like Abigail Stoneman, attorneys' fees were small, relative to other transactions, and partnering with a lawyer meant moving within existing social circles. In contrast, less-affluent women, like Mary Searing and Phebe Hinckly, interacted with their social betters and faced burdensome fees as they sought the assistance of lawyers. For all of these women, as well as for men, an attorney-client partnership was a form of principal-agent relationship. Necessarily characterized by flexibility, it required the litigants' ongoing oversight. Female plaintiffs and defendants, far from simply losing their voice within the legal system as male attorneys rose to prominence, demonstrated skill in hiring lawyers and supervising their conduct.

Debt litigation's consequences also extended beyond the litigants and their attorneys, reaching those who became caught up in local officials' efforts to summon defendants to court. Since women were frequently at home when sheriffs and constables called, Sarah Peirse and Elizabeth Heart were among those who demonstrated skill in responding to such officials' pronouncements. Within crowded urban quarters in which renting was common, such efforts included preventing the sheriff from seizing property that ostensibly belonged to uninvolved residents. Even as male lawyers and legal technicalities became increasingly important to debt litigation during the mid-eighteenth century, women were integral participants in this changing system, using its attributes to their advantage and driving its changes.

CHAPTER 4

"I saw and heard"

The Knowledge and Power of Witnesses

In July 1731, Mary Asten watched and listened with interest as Peter Weast settled his account with a fellow male landowner to whom he was indebted. The conversation unfolded at Weast's residence in South Kingstown, Rhode Island, one town over from Asten's home in North Kingstown.[1] Asten spectated as the two men compared their records, then heard the pair agree that Weast would give his creditor a bond for the £3.10 he owed. Once the parties had drafted the instrument, Asten listened as the creditor read its text aloud. She observed Weast sign it and affix his seal, and then saw two other men add their signatures as witnesses. When the debt became the subject of a lawsuit two years later, Mary Asten appeared before a justice of the peace and testified to all of these details.[2]

Asten's narrative recounted numerous practices that, as previous chapters have shown, constituted relationships between creditors and debtors outside of court. These included traveling through one's community, haggling over the terms of agreements, and producing and scrutinizing financial records, often within mixed-use residential spaces. As we have seen, attending to these everyday activities reveals women's extensive, skilled contributions within credit networks, whether as creditors and debtors in their own right or as representatives of their households. Yet Asten's testimony spotlights an additional and often-overlooked group of female actors within the economy and the legal system:

witnesses. Asten, a *feme covert* of no apparent relation either to Weast or his creditor, observed and subsequently described in depth the negotiations between the two men. In so doing, she both acquired and displayed knowledge of credit, debt, and the law. In chronicling the mechanics of settling a debt, Asten shaped her narrative in acknowledgement of the court's priorities and facilitated the clerk's recording of the salient details in her written deposition.

Between the seventeenth and eighteenth centuries, changes within New England courtrooms shifted the content and significance of witnesses' testimonies. As part of their aim to repair fractured community bonds, the first generations of judges and magistrates encouraged witnesses to speak freely regarding all aspects of cases and parties' relationships. By the mid-eighteenth century, the court's increasing emphasis on adherence to English law, coupled with the justices' concern for swiftly dispensing with the high volume of debt cases, seemingly narrowed the relevant details about which witnesses could testify. Such changes also aligned with Europeans' and colonists' growing embrace of Enlightenment ideals of rationality during the same period. Within the intensely spiritual world of seventeenth-century New England, men and women commonly recounted and took seriously experiences rooted in magic and wonder, including in their courtroom testimonies. By the turn of the eighteenth century, however, New Englanders increasingly privileged empirical knowledge that emerged from sensory experience. Some have argued that these changes led women's authority as witnesses to wane between the seventeenth and eighteenth centuries.[3] Examining the activities of witnesses like Mary Asten, however, underscores the participatory nature of the eighteenth-century economy and legal system, as well as the strong sense of legal-mindedness possessed by ordinary men and women.

New England's witnesses to financial transactions also fit within a broader story of early modern observers and reporters. Throughout the Atlantic World, myriad forms of witnessing allowed individuals, particularly those who were geographically or socially marginal, to cultivate authority and public personalities. Evangelicals' embodied experiences of religious conversion enabled women as well as men to become church members, preachers, prophets, or visionaries.[4] As collectors of specimens and chroniclers of scientific phenomena, people from throughout North America, including women, blacks, and Natives, inserted themselves into elite cultures of science and natural history.[5] Patients contributed to a knowledge of disease and bodies by interpreting their symptoms to learned physicians.[6] Thus, far from excluding ordinary people from religious and scientific discourse, the Enlightenment's high valuation of firsthand observation afforded them a central role in knowledge production. Moreover, observing matters of credit and debt endowed New England men and women with information and influence within their communities. Just as examining these other forms of witnessing sheds light on early modern gender relations, so, too, does the study of financial witnessing elucidate the nature and extent of women's economic involvement.

Significant overlaps characterized women's and men's activities as witnesses from 1730 to the Revolution. Although New Englanders sometimes preferred to enlist male observers for settlements outside of court, the household was a hub of regularized financial activity that gave rise to multiple layers of witnessing for all inhabitants. Routinely surrounded by others who were transacting business, handling documents, or discussing financial matters, women and men gained knowledge of both specific credit relationships and standard procedures for borrowing and lending. Such informal observations, in turn, yielded formal witnessing, including solidifying transactions by signing documents and shaping case outcomes by testifying in court. Free white women performed both activities at lower rates than men, but their involvement in formal, documented forms of witnessing bespeaks their skilled contributions to the wider universe of credit transactions outside of court.

One's gender also shaped the significance of becoming a witness. Men faced few limitations on their ability to become creditors, debtors, and litigants. Many women, in contrast, lacked the ability to independently borrow and lend, due to their legal status as *femes covert*, even though they did use credit and debt extensively in their daily lives. In addition, schooling and apprenticeships afforded boys more extensive opportunities than girls to gain literacy, numeracy, and the associated financial and legal skills. Through witnessing, married and unmarried women from across the class spectrum were drawn into credit networks and litigation. In the process, they cultivated practical skills that were vital for navigating these arenas. Whereas men engaged in numerous forms of legal and political speech, testifying before officers of the law was among the few ways in which free women could publicly and officially appraise others' reputations.

Becoming a Witness

Within credit transactions and debt litigation, witnessing encompassed three categories of activity: observing or overhearing matters of financial and legal significance, signing legally binding documents, and testifying in lawsuits. Of these three practices, only two—signing and testifying—generated an archival record. And just one, giving depositions before officers of the law, yielded sources documenting the circumstances and nature of witnesses' involvement outside of court. Nonetheless, these forms of witnessing built upon one another. Creditors and debtors enlisted some of the many observers of financial transactions to serve as signatories on documents. Women and men could not necessarily foresee which debts would become the subject of litigation, and, in the rare instances when disputes yielded contested lawsuits, litigants strategically summoned by-standers or signatories to testify to their recollections. We can therefore read backward from depositions and, to a lesser extent, from signed financial instruments, in order reconstruct underlying patterns of third parties' roles within relationships of indebtedness. Because households were centers of financial activity, and because legal principles allowed a broad range of individuals to sign documents and testify, witnessing in all of its forms was accessible to a wide range of free white women, including dependents and lower-class women who were unlikely to become creditors or debtors themselves. Even though fewer women than men signed documents and testified in court, the presence of female witnesses within the legal record underscores that informal observations of everyday transactions drew a diverse group of women into the credit economy and legal system.

Women made up small but significant percentages of those documented witnesses who signed financial instruments and testified in court. Between 1730 and the Revolution, they composed 10 percent of those who signed bonds and promissory notes in both Newport and Suffolk counties.[7] During that same period, women made up 10 percent of the witnesses who testified in debt cases in the Newport Court of Common Pleas, and 16 percent of those in the Suffolk Court of Common Pleas.[8] In comparison with other kinds of cases and jurisdictions, these figures are certainly low. As a result of women's unique authority to interpret their anatomy, conflicts concerning the female body or occurring between women were much more likely to privilege female witnesses' testimonies. In courts in early modern Britain and France, for instance, women formed nearly half of the witnesses in cases concerning marriage, sex, and sexual slander.[9] On the other hand, the figures for financial witnessing are consistent with the broader patterns of women's formal legal involvement in matters of credit and debt. As we have seen, female litigants made up roughly 10 percent of the parties in debt cases in colonial Boston and Newport.[10] Much like this consistent visibility of women on dockets and in court sessions, the persisting minority of female witnesses reminded New Englanders that credit networks and the courts were heterosocial realms. Just as statistics about debt litigation tell only part of the story of women's contributions to borrowing and lending, the documentary record reflects only the tip of the iceberg regarding their roles as witnesses within everyday life.

Using depositions to access practices outside of court underscores the importance of households as sites that facilitated women's as well as men's involvement in credit transactions. Depositions typically began by noting the places where individuals observed the events in question, and residences were by far the most frequently cited places in both men's and women's statements. Among witnesses who specified where they had seen or heard the events at issue, roughly two-thirds mentioned houses, whether their own or those of others.[11] Samuel Hicks, for example, noted in 1761 that he "happened to be at Edward Wantons house" when he saw two men "talking about settling accounts." Patricia Cornell likewise recalled in 1736 that while at the "house of John Lawton," she heard a creditor and debtor "have some discourse about a bond." In 1756, Katherine West, a Newport widow, remembered that Thomas Chadwick "came to her house" and spoke with her about a debt he owed to another resident. Highlighting households' significance as sites of business activity, Sarah Greenman stated that she discussed a debtor's account for wholesale bread purchases "att the hous of Jeremiah Child the baker" in 1762.[12] Each of these scene-setting statements was typical in its level of detail. Witnesses tended not to specify the rooms in which financial negotiations occurred, however, and they typically neglected to explain why they were present or whether someone had summoned them. Regardless of the circumstances that led bystanders to observe financial activities, witnesses' generalized statements affirmed the importance of houses as sites of financial activity and normalized the presence of observers of both genders.

After houses, shops were the second–most common places in which women gleaned information about others' finances and transactions. Some of these women were entrepreneurs, making mental notes in the course of their own business dealings. In the early 1750s, Newport shopkeeper Alice Gould listened attentively as three young sisters in her shop insisted that their purchases should be charged to their mother's account. Gould later testified to these interactions in a lawsuit in which she was not an interested party. Other episodes emerged from the collaborative dimensions of shopping and the shops' function as gathering places. In 1755, Temperance Grant, the widow and retailer who launched the slander suit against a ship captain (see chapter 1), was at her shop when she listened in on a woman asking a man for payment of a debt. In 1761, Mary Brown and Susannah Hazard accompanied their friend Eunice Rhodes to the shop of a Newport furniture-maker and watched the two haggle over prices (see chapter 2). Women's routine presence in city shops not only attested to their own uses of credit, but also led them to become knowledgeable about other residents' affairs.[13]

Depositions and credit instruments indicate that witnessing engaged broad cross-sections of the female population. First, married as well as unmarried women routinely observed conversations and dealings concerning credit. Wives sometimes observed matters of financial consequence along with their husbands, which reflects the importance of family ties in facilitating economic activities. In the late 1730s, Timothy and Frances Whiting, a married couple, were both at their house in Newport when another man visited and described an agreement with his landlord. In 1765, two Rhode Islanders recruited both Elizabeth

Phillips and her husband, a mariner, to sign a contract as witnesses.[14] Legal documents typically required two witnesses, so enlisting a married couple like the Phillipses was a convenient way to secure both witnesses at once. Overall, in roughly one-quarter of the instances where women signed financial documents, they did so along with their husbands.[15] Yet wives also moved through their communities and observed economic activities apart from their spouses, as the opening example of Mary Asten indicates. Asten's husband, Edmund, appears not to have been present during Peter Weast's negotiations with the creditor, and he was never summoned to testify in the resulting case.[16]

Witnessing was also a form of economic activity that was accessible to youthful women. Numerous female deponents explained that they had observed the events in question while at the residences or shops of their fathers or widowed mothers. In 1728, Sarah and Dorcas Fowler and Elizabeth Kimball were all at their father's house in Ipswich, Massachusetts, when he settled his account with a local physician. Eunice and Elizabeth Brown overheard their mother, the proprietor of a Boston boardinghouse, negotiate with her landlord in 1744. Ann Bowers was working at her father's shop in Newport in 1752 when customers made purchases that would later become the subject of a lawsuit.[17] These and other young women's attention to their parents' finances arose in part from the period's living arrangements, with many daughters residing with their fathers or mothers until marriage. It equally came about from the importance of children within systems of family labor, which included activities surrounding credit, debt, and record-keeping.[18] Elizabeth Kimball stored her father's receipt for safekeeping after he finished settling with the doctor, and Ann Bowers sold cloth to her father's customers and spoke with them about payment.[19] Because young women living as dependents could not borrow or lend themselves, acting as witnesses to their parents' transactions was an important way in which they engaged with credit.

Female witnesses also included lower-class servants dwelling with their masters, and boarders living in the residences of their more affluent landlords. Excluding obvious familial ties, witnesses' connections with borrowers and lenders are seldom revealed in financial instruments and depositions. Nonetheless, because unrelated individuals routinely lived together within urban households, labor and rental arrangements facilitated at least some women's witnessing. Depositions occasionally identify boarders or servants. For example, Mary Potter, a married woman, explained in her testimony that she was a tenant in the residence of Joshua Coggeshall in the early 1730s when she observed his family's divisions of financial labor. In the controversy surrounding Abigail Hewes, the pregnant tanner's wife (see chapter 1), a boarder, Ruth Loring, and a servant, Elizabeth Goddard, were among those who watched Hewes's arguments with Nathaniel Cunningham and testified in the resulting dispute.[20] Given that less-affluent

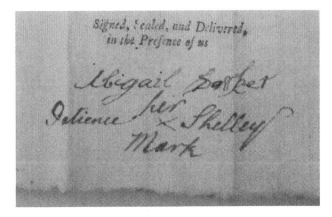

Figure 4.1. Witness signatures on bond of Fones Haszard to Margaret Holmes. *Holmes v. Easton*, Newport County Court of Common Pleas, May 1751, #227, Rhode Island Supreme Court Judicial Records Center. Photo by the author

women possessed circumscribed abilities to extend and receive credit in their own names, witnessing within households enlarged their involvement in credit networks, including in larger or more-formal transactions than those in which they might otherwise participate.

With elite and middling women receiving more extensive training in writing than did their lower-class counterparts, female witnesses' varying abilities in this regard further suggest that they came from a range of social classes. Between 10 and 20 percent of the women who were witnesses to bonds and promissory notes used marks as opposed to signatures (fig. 4.1).[21] Likewise, 25 percent of those who testified in court signed with marks.[22] While female witnesses were more likely to be able to sign their names than New England's overall female population, the percentage of such witnesses who used marks is nonetheless striking.[23] They included lower-class women and female laborers who mobilized forms of knowledge and skill not encompassed by narrow definitions of literacy.

At the same time as the study of witnessing underscores the participatory nature of the credit economy, it also reveals the gendered and class-based patterns of economic activity that shaped which transactions women could observe, certify, and describe. Although many witnesses, both male and female, recounted local credit transactions occurring in residences and shops, men also testified in debt suits concerning large and complicated transatlantic ventures. Such male witnesses tended to be from elite merchant families, and they observed their peers engaging in ritualized procedures for forming agreements and settling accounts. While some of these gatherings convened in merchants' homes, others, located in non-residential settings, compounded their masculine nature.

In 1746, a group of merchants gathered at a "publick house" in Boston's North End to watch a leading merchant, Thomas Goldthwait, contract with two shipbuilders, who agreed to build him a 400-ton vessel. As the shipbuilders later recounted, "for that purpose witnesses were called in," and the agreement was "laid on a large table," where it could be examined by all present. Three years later, Royall Pierce was present "in the counting house of Mr John Banister," a leading Newport merchant, when Banister and another merchant settled accounts arising from their jointly financed shipping venture. Banister, "after some conversation," agreed to sell his share of the investment, and Pierce watched as Banister's bookkeeper drafted a memorandum of the agreement. The record contains no indication that women were present for either of these episodes, and no female witnesses recounted similar proceedings. In such instances, both the content of the negotiations and the spaces in which they were conducted set them off from other heterosocial forms of urban commerce.[24]

Apart from mercantile settlements, men and women also made choices about whom to enlist as witnesses, and gender could be one factor in such decisions. Depositions often suggest that people became observers of financial negotiations seemingly because they happened to be present or were nearby, where they could be easily summoned. In other instances, individuals asked their friends or neighbors to serve as witnesses, either because they desired assistance from neutral third parties, or because they feared that disputes would eventually reach the court. When recruiting their witnesses in advance, men and women both chose men to accompany them to settlements. Whereas one-fifth of male witnesses who testified about financial settlements recalled that they had been enlisted to assume a formal role, no female witnesses offered similar explanations for their presence during financial activities.[25] Some of these men noted that creditors and debtors had requested their presence, whether to serve as witnesses or to evaluate competing accounts. David Daniels narrated that Jonathan Draper had asked him to "go to [Draper's] house and be witness" to his "reckoning" with another man in 1749. Jacob Richardson remembered that when Matthew Cozzens and Philip Burgen "were disputing about the settlement of their accounts & could not agree upon the balance" in 1769, they asked him to "look over their accounts & say what was due to Burgen."[26] By recruiting men such as Daniels and Richardson to assist them, creditors and debtors pressured their adversaries to conduct above-board negotiations and ensured that their allies could testify if matters advanced to court. Other male witnesses noted that they had drafted financial and legal documents at the request of creditors and debtors, or, in appeals of cases previously decided through arbitration, testified to their prior roles as referees or arbitrators.[27] Even though credit suffused the daily lives of all colonists, they saw systematic involvement by neutral parties to be the domain of men.

Microlevel dynamics of particular negotiations—including the use of spaces within households and parties' choices of witnesses from among available individuals—could, in rare instances, shape and curtail women's activities as witnesses. In March 1766, two men attempted to limit Susannah Brownell's involvement in a land sale. John Palmer and another man met at the Brownell residence in Little Compton, Rhode Island, to negotiate their agreement. Susannah Brownell was present in the house on that day. So, too, was her husband, whom court documents identified as a yeoman, as well as two other men, a schoolmaster and an elite landholder. As the three male witnesses later recounted, Palmer "asked for a room," because he had some "bisiness to due" and "desired" the other men present to accompany the pair into that room in order to "take notice" of their agreement. Susannah Brownell echoed this description, explaining that the men were in a room "by themselves." It was only when the parties were ready to sign the promissory note that Palmer asked Susannah Brownell to come into the room and serve as a witness. Palmer's actions appear to have been strategic. When the transaction later resulted in a lawsuit, it was revealed that the promissory note in question was intentionally vague in ways that benefited Palmer. It was to his advantage to have at least one witness who could not testify to the full terms of the oral agreement that preceded the note. As a result of her limited access to the room in which the negotiations occurred, Susannah Brownell recounted the episode in much less detail than the men.[28]

The law dictated men's and women's eligibility to engage in documented forms of witnessing. Whereas the archive reveals the range of places where financial activities occurred and the cast of characters who participated in them, it offers only a partial view of bystanders' involvement. In colonial British America, status as a free person was a prerequisite for attesting to the legality of transactions or shaping the course of lawsuits. Just as enslaved people could not be parties to legal agreements, so, too, did the law exclude them from signing such documents, including financial instruments, as witnesses. Enslaved men and women also could not testify in court cases, except in support of criminal accusations against other slaves. Meanwhile, free blacks and Natives were among those who could technically assume roles as formal witnesses, although the Boston and Newport records do not clearly identify people of color serving in these capacities.[29] As other historians have noted, this sharp legal distinction between free and enslaved people's ability to testify was a crucial underpinning in the violence and terror of chattel slavery, and it additionally circumscribed such people's involvement in the credit economy.[30]

The law's prohibition on witnessing by enslaved people was particularly consequential in northern port cities, including Boston and Newport, where their work and living arrangements placed them in close proximity to free whites' credit transactions. Most Boston and Newport slaveholders owned one or two enslaved laborers, and these bound men and women typically lived in the households of their captors. Artisans and retailers—individuals who very routinely used credit and debt in the course of their business activities—were among those who commonly possessed slaves. Regardless of how frequently enslaved women watched or even took part in the circumstances surrounding credit transactions, whites consistently excluded them from signing financial documents and testifying in court.[31]

Moll, an enslaved woman who, at different times, resided in several commercially active Newport households, was among those who repeatedly encountered these legal barriers to her power as a witness. In the 1730s and early 1740s, Moll and her son, Cato, lived with physician John Brett and his wife Mary in the couple's residence. In November 1744, two months after her husband died in the gunpowder explosion (see chapter 1), Newport widow Temperance Grant purchased Moll and Cato from John Brett. The pair lodged with Grant until 1755. At that point, Mary Brett, then widowed, sued for and regained possession of the enslaved mother and son. We know about Moll and the households she moved between only because of this property dispute between Temperance Grant and Mary Brett.[32]

Despite the limited archival record surrounding Moll's life, speculation about her daily activities highlights the ways in which the laws surrounding witnessing circumscribed enslaved people's economic involvement and legal personality. Moll, like many other women in her situation, may well have sold small quantities of goods or her own labor within Newport's informal economy. Regardless of whether she did this, she gained additional knowledge of economic value, record-keeping, and other residents' creditworthiness through her close proximity to the businesses of John Brett and Temperance Grant. Moll very likely observed physician John Brett receive and extend credit when he purchased medical supplies and treated patients. At Temperance Grant's shop, Moll would have similarly overheard this shopkeeper haggling with suppliers and customers over prices and the terms of loans. At both locations, Moll may have tracked the evolution of financial relationships as she watched Brett and Grant draft accounts, receipts, and other commercial records.[33]

Although Moll was unable to intervene in the slander suit that Grant brought against ship captain Simeon Potter (see chapter 1), she may well have harbored crucial information in that case. Both Potter's insult and the eventual lawsuit concerned Grant's sales of goods to Dutch sailors, and Moll possibly looked on from the corner or listened in an adjacent room as Grant sold goods to the men in March 1745. While none of the free white witnesses who ultimately testified could offer conclusive evidence on this point, Moll perhaps knew whether the sailors had willingly signed over their bills of sale, or whether Grant had tricked or persuaded the men to do so. Yet any knowledge Moll possessed would have been of limited concern to Grant and Potter, as both knew that she could never be summoned to testify. In the slander suit and beyond, Grant, a free white woman, cultivated a level of notoriety and legal authority that was inaccessible to Moll as an enslaved woman. Despite all of her routine encounters with credit, Moll never assumed a documented role as a signatory on contracts or a deponent in litigation. By barring those like Moll from serving as official witnesses, free whites doubly reinforced the racial and gender hierarchies of slavery. They denied to enslaved individuals the forms of social authority that other witnesses accrued through their formal legal activities, and they permanently excluded such people's knowledge from the archive.[34]

In contrast, the law placed few restrictions on the ability of free adults, including women, to sign documents and testify in lawsuits. British common law held that free people over the age of fourteen could give sworn testimony as witnesses.[35] Neither gender nor marital status barred women from testifying. According to legal treatises and practical handbooks for justices of the peace, the law only prohibited free individuals from testifying if they lacked mental "competency," had demonstrated a "want of integrity" (e.g., by committing a serious crime), or were "interested" in case outcomes.[36] Within this framework, wives could become witnesses in all suits except those in which their husbands were parties, as, in such instances, the law assumed that husbands and wives were "one and the same person in affection and interest."[37] Coverture thus structured witnessing by *femes covert* much less significantly than it shaped the terms and documentation of married women's activities as creditors, debtors, and litigants. Because signatories on financial documents could eventually be called as witnesses in court, the same parameters that governed one's eligibility to testify structured the selection of individuals to sign as witnesses to such documents. Adult women could be signatories, regardless of their marital status, as long as wives did not witness their husbands' documents.

Common law's emphasis on using concepts of probability to evaluate the truthfulness of witnesses' testimonies created a framework in which statements by free adults of both genders could possess the same evidentiary weight. As eighteenth-century New England lawyers and judges increasingly sought to align their legal system with British models, they looked to treatises authored by British jurists who, like their contemporaries throughout Europe, standardized the law based on what they saw as principles of reason. Contributing to a shift toward probabilistic modes of thought that was simultaneously occurring among scientists, historians, and intellectuals, authors such as Matthew Hale and Geoffrey Gilbert set out quasi-mathematical criteria by which jurors should, in their words, "weigh" witnesses' testimonies. Initially published in 1754, Gilbert's *Law of Evidence*, the first treatise focusing exclusively on evidence-based law, discussed witness testimony in a chapter entitled "Probability." He noted that the word of two witnesses was generally stronger than that of a sole individual, and that one witness's testimony could be given greater or lesser weight in light of supporting or competing testimonies from others. Hale and Gilbert recommended that jurors should consider the "reasons and Accounts [witnesses] give of their knowledge," as well as their overall "credibility."[38] Through this emphasis on the deliberative process, these two authors allowed that jurors could accord the same importance to women's and men's testimonies.

While treatises on common law permitted married and unmarried women to become witnesses, New Englanders also encountered handbooks for lawyers and tradesmen that overwhelmingly depicted witnesses as male. In one manual, fictional male witnesses "John Simms" and "William Thomas" observed the creation of a bond. Other guides used allegorical men's names, underscoring the witnesses' obligations to be observant and truthful. "Nicholas Notice" signed a promissory note; "John Evidence" and "William Telltrue" added their names to a bill of debt.[39] In no instance did commercial handbooks include a sample credit instrument with a female witness.[40] The inclusion of male witnesses was part of such texts' more general depiction of commerce and law as masculine realms, paralleling leading merchants' choices to enlist their peers as audiences and arbitrators. Belying the fact that a wide array of people routinely observed credit transactions, models in handbooks reinforced borrowers' and lenders' occasional strategy of bringing male witnesses with them when settling accounts.[41]

One of the few texts that used an example of a female witness credited her with vital knowledge of the affair in question, while simultaneously playing on associations between femininity and flightiness. *The Attorney's Compleat Pocket-Book*, which was published in London in 1756 and circulated in the colonies, featured an "affidavit for want of a material witness" by a defendant seeking postponement of his trial because he could not locate his former female servant. Absences of key witnesses were among the reasons why Massachusetts and Rhode Island residents sought new trials or postponements of existing ones, and forms like this one shaped their arguments and thinking about witnesses.[42] The author of the sample document explained that the potential witness was away "in the County of L.," but that "in what part of L. she is, [he] does not know, nor can discover, although he has done his utmost Endeavour to find out where she is." He insisted that this female servant was a "material witness," and he could not "safely proceed to Trial" without her.[43] This rare reference to a female witness negatively portrayed her as a runaway, thereby calling into question women's suitability for legal positions as witnesses. At the same time, by featuring a female example in its only form pertaining to witnessing, the author of *The Attorney's Compleat Pocket-Book* allowed that women, including lower-class servants, could offer testimonies that would be vital to a party's case.

The affidavit in *The Attorney's Compleat Pocket-Book* encapsulates the paradoxes surrounding Boston and Newport women's activity as witnesses. Commercial handbooks coded witnessing as masculine, and parties sometimes intentionally selected men to act as neutral observers. Yet everyday practices, especially those within households, routinely led women of all ages and classes, both free and not, to see and hear the financial dealings of those around them. With the law allowing any free person of age to be a credible witness, convenience and strategy led New Englanders to enlist white women in the formal roles of signing documents and testifying in lawsuits, thus permanently inscribing their knowledge and authority within the historical record.

Learning through Observation

Within the eighteenth-century credit economy, observation was a powerful teacher. As women watched and overheard matters of financial consequence outside of court, they gained both ephemeral and lasting forms of knowledge. Some of this information was specific to the transactions at hand. Female witnesses learned about credit relationships between parties and, by extension, gleaned information regarding the financial standing and personal character of those individuals. At the same time, witnessing schooled women in skills than transcended any one dispute, such as how to bargain, draft and handle documents, and navigate debt litigation in the county courts.

As bystanders to conversations about finance, women discovered who was indebted to whom, and which individuals were presently able or unable to pay their debts. As a result of overhearing a discussion about a bond in 1735, Priscilla Cornell learned that Portsmouth, Rhode Island, resident John Lawton was indebted to Mary Langworthy, and that Lawton had already paid Langworthy £183, a portion of that debt. Freelove Tweedy, in contrast, discovered in the early 1750s that fellow Newport resident Joseph Whipple was "broke." Within earshot of Tweedy, a creditor repeatedly complained that he had dunned Whipple many times, and Whipple had offered only vague promises of in-kind payments of rum or molasses. The creditor, Tweedy would later recall, lamented that he was "afraid he should lose part of his debt." By assembling such prosaic details, women like Patricia Cornell and Freelove Tweedy familiarized themselves with the contours of credit networks and the financial standing of their fellow residents. Because colonists believed that dealing honorably with one's trading partners was a sign of good moral character, female witnesses' insights enabled them to assess others' reputations. The interaction witnessed by Patricia Cornell would have reflected well on John Lawton's credibility, while Freelove Tweedy would have looked askance on Joseph Whipple's insolvency and evasiveness.[44]

Watching and listening to others' transactions also equipped New Englanders to be savvy participants in the credit economy and the legal system. Books were relatively scarce, expensive possessions in colonial British America, so few Boston and Newport residents owned commercial and legal handbooks. Even when men and women could access these texts, their pages offered incomplete guidance on how to engage in credit transactions and debt litigation. Some books, such as Defoe's *The complete English Tradesman*, emphasized general principles for honest dealing, while others focused narrowly on the properties of legal forms. Within the latter category, *The Secretary's Guide, or Young Man's Companion*, a New York and Philadelphia handbook adapted from older London guides, sought to make its content digestible for novices by alternating sample forms with short explanatory rhymes. The text prefaced its sample bond with the admonition that bonds should be used in business transactions with possibly untrustworthy debtors: "Wherefore if debtors may uncertain be/ In Paying, when 'tis due, if thou can'st see/ Before hand, what thy lot in this case may be/ Chuse and accept a bond, without delay." Yet neither this doggerel nor the sample instrument itself instructed readers in countless other aspects of a bond's use, such as negotiating its terms, either drafting a version featuring the proper visual elements or enlisting someone to do so, storing the document after its creation, and demanding payment. Similarly, if a colonist consulted a handbook in an attempt to understand the step-by-step process of undertaking debt litigation, or the nuances of when to sue a debtor and when to grant forbearance, he or she would have been sorely disappointed. Given that printed sources provided, at best, only partial instruction on navigating one's economic world, watching others talk about and use credit was a far more common and practical form of financial and legal learning.

Observation was a more important source of knowledge for women than for men. Although a small number of New England writers and entrepreneurs took the reformist position that women should receive a practical education in "all the arts of Oeconomy, Writing, and Book-keeping," the dominant views on education held that practical schooling was less important for women than for men. While both boys and girls were taught to read, girls' educations generally stopped short of skills such as accounting. Apprenticeships, another form of financial learning, were also much less common for young women than for young men. To a greater extent than men, women primarily relied on informal learning, including witnessing, in order to develop the skills and savvy that were required to navigate the economy and the legal system.[45]

Looking closely at individual instances of witnessing suggests the forms of legal and financial knowledge that women gained through their proximity to others' transactions. Ruth Besse, a young woman from Wareham, Massachusetts, learned about the use of promissory notes because she was present at her father's home when he sold a horse to another man, "some years" before 1760. In a deposition she signed with her mark, Besse described how she listened as the two men negotiated the terms of their agreement, ultimately agreeing that the purchaser would deliver a specified quantity of iron as in-kind payment. She then spectated as her father drafted a promissory note, read it aloud to the purchaser, and gave it to him to sign. Finally, she saw the purchaser return the promissory note to her father, who kept it.[46]

Simply as a result of observing this brief exchange, Besse gained several pieces of financial knowledge. As did numerous other female witnesses, she learned about the value of goods—in this case, the relative worth of iron and the family's horse—as the potential trading partners haggled with each other. She encountered the content and form of a promissory note as her father read the document aloud, as well as when the two men passed the paper between themselves. When the purchaser handed the note back to her father at the end of the interaction, Besse was reminded that creditors kept promissory notes until debtors satisfied their obligations. Other female bystanders gained even greater familiarity with promissory notes and bonds when the involved parties asked them to sign such documents as witnesses. The act of signing allowed women to handle and examine the instruments, which, in turn, facilitated their ability to identify and scrutinize similar documents in the future.

Female witnesses also learned about the mechanics of both consensual and conflicting interactions between those seeking to settle accounts. As mentioned earlier in this chapter, three sisters—Sarah and Dorcas Fowler and Elizabeth Kimball—experienced the ordinary course of settling debts as they watched their father deal with a local physician in 1728. The physician's arrival at their house demonstrated to them the established practice of creditors dunning their debtors. Listening as the two men conversed, the sisters gleaned scripts by which creditors could request payment and debtors could acquiesce to pay. If, as was typical during the settlement of book debt, their father had examined the doctor's accounts, they would have been reminded of the importance of verifying the accuracy of the opposing party's records. The sisters then watched as their father tendered £3 to the physician and saw the doctor gave a signed receipt to him. The conclusion of this episode impressed upon all three women the relationship between paying a debt and obtaining a receipt, knowledge that they later displayed when they stated that the receipt was for payment "in full of all accounts."[47]

Whereas the Fowlers and Kimball watched their father willingly pay his physician, another young woman, Livine Love, learned about legal strategy when her mother, Margaret Tree, countered a creditor's claims. In 1759, Love was at Tree's home when a male friend arrived, warning Tree that a creditor "had got a writ for her" and advising her to launch a countersuit for a larger sum than her creditor demanded. When Tree replied that she had no written account tracking her opponent's debts, the friend instructed her in "how to make up her account" and suggested that she write the account "upon the side of the house in chalk." Tree followed these instructions, and her friend return the next day to copy down the account, which they then used as the basis for her countersuit. In her testimony in the eventual lawsuit, Livine Love insisted that the account was fabricated, the result of a conspiracy between Margaret Tree and her male ally to win money in court. Regardless of whether Love's reading of the incident was accurate, the episode contained many lessons about how to use credit, debt, and the courts. Tree's predicament reminded Love of the importance of using written accounts to track mutual indebtedness, and the male friend's instructions to Tree doubled as a lesson in bookkeeping for Love. Although Livine Love condemned her mother's actions, Margaret Tree's swift response to the writ against her highlighted how countersuits were a tool in combatting lawsuits over book debt.[48]

The knowledge that female witnesses gained through observation was necessarily piecemeal. By watching a single interaction unfold, a woman learned about one financial relationship and encountered one example, whether positive or negative, of how to manage a step within the lifespan of credit transactions. Yet, because women so regularly observed others using credit and debt, individual acts of witnessing added up to composite portraits of local credit networks and sound financial and legal practices. Witnessing served as a particularly useful training ground for young adults like Ruth Besse, Sarah and Dorcas Fowler, Elizabeth Kimball, and Livine Love, but it equally offered a source of knowledge for women of all ages. As women navigated the credit economy and the courts as borrowers, lenders, and litigants, they drew on the skills and savvy they gained by watching and listening to those around them.

Acquiring Legal and Social Power

At the same time as witnessing enabled free women to cultivate knowledge that was useful in their future dealings, it shaped their relationships with others in their communities. At the most basic level, taking note of financial activities equipped them with information they might later reveal if disputes progressed to court. The more formal variants of witnessing—signing documents and testifying in court—bestowed both ephemeral and lasting forms of authority. Signing a bond or a promissory note was a brief and formulaic act, but it was one that cemented permanent bonds between creditors and debtors. Testifying in contested cases enabled women to intervene in specific disputes and, by extension, bring public recognition to their legal and financial knowledge and shape litigants' reputations.

For women observing flexible and unscripted negotiations outside of court, observation could shade into direct intervention. In 1747, Jacob Marshall went to the home of his male landlord, a fellow Exeter, Rhode Island, resident, to discuss a lawsuit pending between them concerning Marshall's lease. Two men and two women from a neighboring town happened to be at the landlord's house when Marshall, his tenant, called. They watched and listened as the landlord and tenant spoke and ultimately agreed to settle matters outside of court. Near the conclusion of this conversation, one of the observers, Hannah Watson, intervened. Sensing trouble and seeing a reason to seek assurance from Marshall, Watson asked whether he had indeed "stopt the action." Marshall replied, "yeas for ever mour," and pledged that he and his landlord would "live in good naburwud [neighborhood] and in love," free of lawsuits, from then on. When Marshall nonetheless continued to press his case, the men and women who had overheard his verbal promise testified in favor of the landlord.[49] Marshall's lawsuit led Hannah Watson's pivotal remark to be captured within the legal record, and her pointed query probably stands in for countless other instances when female observers similarly shaped the course of financial negotiations and subsequent litigation.

Women who signed as witnesses on bonds and notes assumed a formal, official role in legitimating credit transactions. Bonds and bills obligatory (a variant of promissory notes) required witnesses' signatures in order to be valid.[50] Because borrowing and lending were such routine acts within colonial society, signing familiar credit instruments was in some ways a perfunctory act. Yet witnessing bonds and promissory notes was legally consequential. It solidified enduring financial obligations, and those parties who signed bonds and promissory notes could later be summoned to testify about these documents in court.[51] Within episodes involving these instruments, women—as bystanders and parties to credit transactions—played on these paradoxical dimensions of witnessing in order to gain power within the immediate context of financial relationships.

In their choice of witnesses, men sometimes enlisted women, in an attempt to take advantage of their supposedly limited knowledge and submissiveness. In two revealing instances, men appear to have chosen women to serve as witnesses on documents that were of uncertain legality. The first of these episodes occurred in 1750, when Abigail Thayer was at the Middleborough, Massachusetts, residence of Silvanus Barrows when a traveling retailer arrived. Barrows purchased some leather on credit, giving the vendor a bill obligatory as a promise of future payment. According to Massachusetts law, financial instruments could only establish debts using the colony's currency, so this bill specified that Barrows would pay the retailer in Massachusetts dollars. Both parties agreed, however, that Barrows could pay using other currency. Barrows's choice to enlist Thayer to witness the bill obligatory was strategic. His negotiations with the retailer spanned several hours as the two moved between Barrows's house, mill, and shop. At least two male laborers were present at the Middleborough house that day, but Barrows asked Thayer, who had not observed the conversation in its multiple phases and places, to serve as a witness. According to Thayer's eventual testimony, Barrows simply asked her to "set [her] hand as a witness to a paper," without specifying the document in question.[52]

In 1766, John McQuellen and Hannah Brayton similarly enlisted Brayton's tenants, Elizabeth Phillips and her husband Michael, as witnesses on a deed finalized at Brayton's residence in Newport. The deed would supposedly transfer property from McQuellen to Brayton only if the two married, but, as McQuellen's later remarks would reveal, he never intended to marry Brayton. In Elizabeth Phillips's telling, McQuellen and Brayton "brought in two papers" and asked her and her husband to serve as witnesses but "was very unwilling that I should know the contents of them."[53] In the instances involving both Thayer and Phillips, the parties in question attempted to circumvent the normal procedure of allowing witnesses to familiarize themselves with a document's contents prior to signing, perhaps thinking that women would not possess the knowledge or assertiveness to protest. Such evasiveness was suspect, given that other witnesses recounted agreements in which the parties read documents aloud as part of the routine course of events.[54]

Contrary to the men's expectations, Abigail Thayer and Elizabeth Phillips resisted the pressure to sign quickly. Thayer protested that "I would not set my hand to any paper unless I first heard it read." Barrows accordingly read it to her, and, demonstrating her familiarity with standard credit instruments and their legal implications, she readily identified the document as a bill obligatory, payable to the leather retailer. Only then did she scrawl her mark, an *A*, at the bottom of the page.[55] Elizabeth Phillips likewise "asked what [the documents] were." When the parties initially refused to reply, she insisted, according her later deposition, that "I would not sign any Instrument without knowing what it was." At this point, McQuellen and Brayton explained that the document was a deed, and Phillips signed it. Her forwardness is even more noteworthy, given that the parties had recruited both her and her husband to serve as witnesses, and the two of them were present for this conversation. In his own, separate deposition, Phillips's husband Michael agreed that she was the primary holdout. When he asked the parties to read the deed aloud and they refused, it was Elizabeth who more firmly asserted that "she would not sign until she had read it or heard it read." Maintaining her position more firmly than her husband did, Elizabeth Phillips, much like Abigail Thayer, possessed a strong sense of a witness's legal responsibility.[56]

These two episodes spotlight both the extent and the limits of women's power as signatories of financial documents. In certain respects, witnessing was a procedural activity. In its extreme form, this perspective led some, including Silvanus Barrows, Hannah Brayton, and John McQuellen, to assume that witnesses—particularly female witnesses enlisted during the final stage of negotiations—would even sign illegal or fraudulent documents. Yet both episodes also suggest the colonists' recognition of a witness's legal power. Bystanders' words could call into question suspect transactions, and parties could not finalize agreements without witnesses. It was this predicament that motivated the relevant parties' attempts to cut signatories like Abigail Thayer and Elizabeth Phillips out of the negotiations surrounding documents. Because witnesses were expected to possess basic familiarity with the documents they signed, Abigail Thayer and Elizabeth Phillips could reasonably insist that the parties fully identify the documents in question. The ordinary course of financial transactions, however, only offered Thayer and Phillips a limited ability to protest further, and both women ultimately affixed their signatures as witnesses.

Through the seemingly simplistic act of signing financial documents, women also forged commercial and social alliances that were crucial to Boston's and Newport's development. While female signatories of all classes helped build connections, this function of witnessing is particularly visible on bonds that include clusters of creditors, debtors, and witnesses from prominent and interrelated families. As wealth and power became increasingly concentrated in the hands of port cities' commercial elites, the affluent women who signed financial instruments as witnesses contributed to the relationships manifested within them. For instance, when Newport lawyer Augustus Johnston borrowed money from Robert Hooper in the late 1750s, Elizabeth Honyman joined her husband James, another prominent Newport lawyer and the colony's eventual attorney general, as a witness on the bond. During the same decade, Temperance Grant witnessed a bond jointly with Andrew Heatley, her father's and her late husband's former business partner. The creditor named on the bond was kinsman Abraham Grant.[57] Elite women like Honyman and Grant helped build firms and partnerships as they married and had children, and they wielded social and political power as arbiters of reputations in their communities. Lending support to the connections manifested within financial documents was an additional form of their labor and influence.[58]

The female relatives of notaries and clerks also routinely signed bonds alongside their husbands and fathers. Mary Lyndon, the wife of Josias Lyndon, a longtime clerk of the Newport County courts and the Rhode Island General Assembly, signed many bonds as a witness, along with her husband. In 1751 alone, five debt cases, each with different plaintiffs and defendants, concerned bonds that Josias and Mary Lyndon had signed as witnesses.[59] Scrivener Joseph Fox, who ran his business out of his family's residence, alternately relied on two female dependents, Susannah and Abigail, to sign documents with him.[60] For Josias Lyndon, signing financial instruments was an extension of the notarial components of his appointed office, one that contributed to what historian Julie Hardwick has termed "the integrity of private transactions." Similarly, drafting and formalizing agreements was Joseph Fox's core business activity. By serving as a second witness on financial instruments and other legal documents, women such as Susannah and Abigail Fox and Mary Lyndon supported family enterprises and cultivated civic personalities in conjunction with male household heads.[61]

When disputes between creditors and debtors advanced to the county courts, women who had observed the parties' interactions outside of court or who had signed financial documents could be summoned to testify as witnesses. Becoming a witness was a formal, oftentimes public process, involving direct interactions with officers of the court.[62] In the weeks between the plaintiffs' filing of suits and the time when the court sat, sheriffs called witnesses to testify by coming to their homes and reading their summonses to them. Like the occasions when sheriffs served writs on defendants, calling witnesses to testify was visible to bystanders and signified that such individuals had firsthand knowledge of particular disputes.[63]

Near the turn of the eighteenth century, both Massachusetts and Rhode Island eased their requirements for all witnesses to personally appear in court, allowing them to testify in front of justices of the peace instead. Rhode Island witnesses could testify either before a justice of the peace or in court, while Massachusetts witnesses could submit written depositions if they lived more than thirty miles from the court or could not travel, due to "Age, Sickness, or other bodily Infirmity." According to the preamble of the Massachusetts law, its purpose was to ensure that "all Witnesses may indifferently testify to their certain Knowledge, and the whole Truth in the Cause they are to speak unto."[64] The law affirmed the evidentiary importance of witnesses' statements, even as it limited their opportunities to gain visibility in court.

Witnesses in the same case typically congregated at a justice of the peace's residence to testify on a single day, so even this practice contained public dimensions. When it was their turn to testify, witnesses gave their statements under oath, swearing to "speak the Truth, the whole Truth, and nothing but the Truth."[65] With the justice of the peace taking rough transcriptions of their words, they made their statements and, in some cases, answered questions posed by the plaintiff or defendant, or by their attorneys. They then signed at the bottom of their completed depositions.[66] This process was intended to guarantee the reliability of witnesses' testimonies and underscore the import of their words. For women, appearances before justices of the peace stood out as one of the few contexts in which they were invited to speak in an official capacity.

To an even greater extent than giving a deposition before a justice of the peace, testifying in open court amplified female economic and legal authority, as this involved holding forth publicly before the judges, court officers, involved parties, and observers assembled in the official setting of a courtroom. The court also compensated witnesses who testified in court for their time and for their travel, ultimately holding the losing party accountable for these expenses.

Women expected this compensation and specifically requested it when it was not received. For example, in 1762, two female witnesses wrote to attorney James Otis, asking that he "send me my money for [attending] court."[67]

The fact that witnesses were paid indicates that lawmakers and courts viewed their testimonies as essential. In the mid-eighteenth century, witnesses in Massachusetts received one shilling and six pence per diem, or two shillings if they lived more than three miles from court. In Rhode Island, witnesses garnered one shilling and six pence per diem, plus two pence for every mile traveled to court.[68] Except when witnesses travelled a great distance to court, their total income from testifying was small, less than a male laborer's average daily wages of three shillings.[69] Nonetheless, contemporary commentators made a connection between compensating witnesses and valuing the content of their testimonies, arguing that not paying witnesses to testify constituted a "great defect . . . in judicial administration," because it prevented the court from hearing all salient evidence and made it particularly difficult for "poor persons" to testify.[70] Paying women and men at the same rates indicated the courts' recognition that their testimonies were equally valuable. In a period in which women were less likely than men to work for pay, and tended to receive lower wages than men when they did, monetary compensation to female witnesses affirmed their legal importance.[71]

Regardless of whether female witnesses appeared before a justice of the peace or in court, their testimonies allowed them to pass judgment on others and potentially shape the outcomes of cases. Even seemingly mundane descriptions of credit transactions could indicate the integrity of plaintiffs or defendants. By detailing purchases charged to accounts or recounting the creation of bonds or promissory notes, female witnesses legitimated the creditors' claims and depicted the debtors as delinquent and, thus, dishonorable. Conversely, by describing the settlements reached, payments made, or receipts issued, female witnesses could lend support to the debtors' insistence that they had already paid their due, and that their opponents were avaricious and untrustworthy. Women also directly impugned others' character by testifying to dramatic and revealing outbursts. In 1762, Eunice Hill, of Massachusetts, recounted that one man urged another to "pretend" he had not received a loan and thus "cheat" a creditor. In a post-Revolutionary suit concerning book debt, Patience Macomber, a married woman from Tiverton, Rhode Island, described the male debtor's brash insistence that he would "cheat every man both rich and poor: if he could get any thing by it for he intended to live well if he went to hell at last." Whereas most depositions simply summarized conversations about credit, Hill's and Macomber's testimonies presented the men's nefarious statements as verbatim quotations and, in so doing, amplified the scandal associated with their words.[72]

Female witnesses engaged even more directly in social evaluation when lawsuits concerned gendered conflicts between women and men. Testifying in such cases offered them an official forum in which to defend other women's actions and question men's behavior, thereby critiquing imbalances of gendered power. In 1751, Elizabeth and Eunice Brown came to the defense of their mother, widow Lydia Brown, in her dispute with leading merchant William Bowdoin. Lydia Brown operated a boardinghouse out of the residence she owned, located on a choice plot of land in the center of Boston. In the spring of 1744, Bowdoin approached Brown and asked her to move out as soon as possible, orally promising to pay her the considerable sum of £500 in return. Brown accordingly left soon thereafter, but Bowdoin never paid her. Six years later, she sued him. Elizabeth and Eunice Brown testified individually before a justice of the peace, because they were too ill to go to court. Both supported their mother's claims. The sisters insisted that Bowdoin had pledged to compensate their mother for her swift departure and stated that she had relocated quickly for this reason. Exposing the links between gender, class, and reputation, Elizabeth Brown added that her mother had believed "she might depend on Mr. Bowdoin's word and honour," clarifying that the dispute involved Bowdoin's character, as well as his economic behavior.[73]

Extant records make it difficult to conclusively link the testimony of any witness, whether male or female, to a given case's outcome. Jury verdicts, which were often recorded on small strips of paper, simply noted that the assembled bodies found "for the plaintiff" or "for the defendant," without providing explanations for these decisions. Whereas, in some instances, women's narratives seemingly lent support to winning arguments, in others, their words fell on the losing side of cases. Male witnesses similarly testified in favor of and against parties that eventually won lawsuits. Even if we cannot definitively link women's statements to case outcomes, the words of female witnesses like Patience Macomber, Eunice Hill, and the Brown sisters were powerful. During this same period, New Englanders routinely initiated slander suits against those who allegedly mischaracterized their economic behavior. Testimonies by women, given under oath and thus protected from allegations of slander, possessed the legal system's imprimatur and enabled assessments of others' reputations.

At the same time as witnesses in debt suits intervened in disputes immediately at hand, their words served a broader function. Through their testimonies, witnesses publicly demonstrated their capacity to interpret and recollect activities involving credit and debt. The sources arising from witnesses' oral statements—the depositions added to case files—were collaborative productions of the deponents themselves and the officials who recorded what was said. Depositions reflected the witnesses' understandings and experiences and, equally, emerged from the officials' knowledge of the law and of what kinds of statements could plausibly be attributed to witnesses. Recorded testimonies, variously written in the first and third persons, incorporated the witnesses' recollections into smooth narratives, obscuring any hesitations or interjections from bystanders.[74] Overall, such depositions by women and men are far more similar than different. Because evidence law insisted that only details seen and heard firsthand constituted solid evidence, all witnesses established their credibility by vividly recounting the settings, sights, and words of financial negotiations. The official act of testifying magnified financial and legal skills, and depositions indicated New Englanders' recognition that all women, even those who were youthful or lower-class women, could possess a savvy similar to that of men.[75]

The principles of common law maintained that witnesses' testimonies were most reliable when they were grounded in concrete, plausible details, acquired through firsthand experience. Gilbert's *Law of Evidence* argued that evaluations of witnesses' statements should be based on "the Reasons and Accounts they give of their Knowledge." The most reliable witness was one who provided "plain and evident Marks and Signs of his Knowledge."[76] In contrast, testimonies by witnesses were "suspect" or marked by "incredibility" if they seemed "contrary to all manner of Experience and Observation"—that is, if the witnesses failed to explain the sources of their beliefs, or if they purported to recall events that occurred long ago without explaining why or providing sufficient detail.[77] Although early modern courts did not consistently adhere to his prescriptions, Gilbert also asserted that hearsay evidence was inadmissible. He insisted that a witness must testify "to what he knows," rather than to the "uncertain Reports of the Talk and Discourse of others."[78] Subsequent legal treatises echoed Gilbert's privileging of firsthand knowledge arising from specific details, and this emphasis on observation was consistent with other Enlightenment-era disciplines, particularly the natural sciences.[79]

In acknowledgement of this framework, depositions established their credibility by situating witnesses in relation to the events about which they testified. Their opening lines located witnesses, together with creditors and debtors, at places and times specified with as much precision as possible. Ann Aston's deposition combined these common elements when it noted that she was "at Elisha Cards in the year 1739 in October," when "John Freeborn came to said Card's house." Seth Adams recounted that "some time in the year 1745 I was at the house of Edward Clark Esq in Medway and Jonathan Draper and David Darling were both there." Samuel Carr stated that "some time last fall being in Channing['s] kitchen [he] heard some discours between John Burt and John Curtleo."[80] Using standard phrases such as "being at," "I was at," or "I saw," this scene-setting reflected early modern legal culture's high valuation of knowledge based on direct eyewitnessing.

The opening lines of witness depositions served a second purpose: depicting the involved parties as engaging in customary practices of financial negotiation or account settlement. Some witnesses reported seeing the parties come to one another's homes with the intention of discussing financial matters, such as when Ruth Freeman recalled that Oliver Cook "Came to my house . . . to enquire of one Alexander Clayton who lives with me concerning a note," or when Joseph and Benjamin Sheffield testified that "Rodes Havens brot his book to my fathers house in order for a settlement with him."[81] Other witnesses similarly reported observing the parties "in the shop talking and writing," "sitting at the table with books and papers before them talking about settling accounts," or "setting at a table whereon lay their books of account, this being as the deponent understood a settlement."[82] Describing scenes in ways that comported with standard conduct, witnesses conveyed that the parties involved were forging binding financial agreements, rather than merely engaging in conversation. Furthermore, by emphasizing their own ability to interpret scenes of financial and legal significance as they occurred ("this being as the deponent understood a settlement"), witnesses depicted themselves as astute observers of what was unfolding.

Depositions portrayed all witnesses as able to carefully observe and interpret financial transactions. Many of these descriptions focused on financial papers. Men and women reported on the contents of such documents and on telltale gestures that indicated the progress of settlements. Witnesses recounted that a party "shewed a paper therein containing an account of sundrys" or "shewed his account," and they assessed whether the parties had reached agreements. In a settlement between Jonathan Draper and David Pond, a male witness explained that after Draper "[gave]" Pond a promissory note as payment for a debt, Pond, in turn, "gave [Draper] a sined discharge" and "gave up" another promissory note documenting Draper's debt to him. Sarah and Dorcas Fowler likewise noted that James Hayward did "receive of my . . . father the sum of three pounds of bills of exchange and did at the same time give my father a receipt for the same." Concentrating on those elements that concerned the court, these women stressed their "certain knowledge" that "Dr Heyward signd with his own hand." Eunice Hill, in contrast, cited Oliver Pond and Mary Cook's handling of documents as proof that they had failed to put their agreement into effect. She explained that "after the note was written & signed & the discharge was wrote & signed each party kept their own obligations in their own hands."[83] As male and female witnesses described such transactions to the court, they demonstrated their ability to identify financial documents by name and interpret both the documents' content and the significance of how they were handled.

Moreover, depositions depicted both genders as equally able to comprehend and faithfully recount conversations between creditors and debtors. Similarities between men's and women's depositions are apparent, particularly when multiple witnesses overheard and described the same conversation. In a relevant case mentioned earlier in this chapter, Abigail Thayer described hearing Silvanus Barrows and Hezekiah Bilding hash out their agreement. Her statement included the same details as those by two men. In their depositions, William Thomas and David Sears informed the court of details not formally included in Barrows's promissory note to Bilding. They heard Barrows ask Bilding how to pay him, and Bilding's reply that he would "send him a letter" instructing him "where he should leave the money." Sears additionally reported that Bilding promised to "take other government[s'] money" from Barrows, even though the promissory note specified Massachusetts dollars. Abigail Thayer echoed these points in her deposition. She recounted that before she signed the note as a witness, Barrows said that it would be paid in a different colony's currency from that specified on its face. She also recalled that Barrows asked Bilding to "send him a letter whare he should send the money."[84]

In a 1767 dispute between prominent Newport tavernkeeper Abigail Stoneman and her landlord, William Stoddard, both male and female witnesses recalled similar details. All concurred that Stoddard told Stoneman to deduct the cost of house repairs from her rent and promised to pay expenses that exceeded the amount of her rent. The deposition of Stoneman's daughter, Mehitable Downs, explained that she "heard said Stoddard desire her said mother to repair the house," and that "if any balance should be due to her said mother at year's end he'd pay her." Thomas Brenton similarly "understood" that Stoneman could deduct the repairs from the rent and Stoddard would cover any outstanding costs. He heard Stoddard tell Stoneman to "let [the carpenters] do what is wanting to be done & I will see you satisfied." Downs also recalled that she heard Stoddard tell the carpenters that "if Mrs. Stoneman's pay was not good he'd pay them." Corresponding language was present in the deposition of a carpenter who worked on the home. Elisha Norton heard Stoddard promise to "satisfy him if Mrs. Stoneman's pay did not sute."[85] When women such as Thayer and Downs overheard the same conversations as men, they proved to be equally capable of distilling them for court officers. To the extent that witnesses' similar narratives resulted from efforts to align their stories, women as well as men joined in such coordination. Resulting depositions depicted all laypeople as attuned to key components of financial transactions, including modes and means for the payment of debts.

Female and male witnesses also demonstrated their attentiveness when they recalled comments about whether debts remained unpaid. New Englanders discussed financial matters outside of direct negotiations between creditors and debtors, and hearers of these conversations could testify about them in court. Benjamin Whipple, for example, stated that Daniel Northup "told me that he and Greene had seteled" and that "he did justly ow said Greene two dolors or more." Peleg Spooner reported that shopkeeper Sueton Grant said the late William Bennet had once owed him "a large sum" but had subsequently paid all but "about fifteen pounds" of his account.[86] Female witnesses' depositions contained similar details and numerical precision. Margaret Curtelo, for example, happened to have "heard John Bert say that he owed Mr Marks three pounds." Sarah Cook explained that she was at Nathaniel Haws's home when "Nathaniel Ingraham came in and among the rest of his discourse said that he never paid Oliver Pond one penny toward the note."[87] The depositions of all of these individuals depicted them as knowledgeable and credible witnesses. The details in their narratives conveyed that women, like men, possessed enough numerical and financial skill to recognize the import of creditors' and debtors' statements when hearing them and, later, to recollect them with precision.

While women's depositions typically attested to their independent skill in assessing financial and legal matters, clerks' and justices' record-keeping practices occasionally assigned secondary importance to wives' testimonies in cases in which their husbands also testified. Officials generally took each man's deposition individually and recorded it full. In contrast, legal records sometimes positioned wives as simply confirming their husbands' testimonies. In roughly half of the cases in which husband-wife pairs testified, married women signed statements affirming that their husbands' testimonies were true.[88] Situating men's testimonies as the primary version of events resonated strongly with the principle of coverture. At the same time, this practice still reflected the law's emphasis on direct, detailed observation. In their short affirmations of their husbands' testimonies, married women insisted that they were "also present & heard" the events in question, and they verified that their husbands' statements were true "in every article."[89] By sometimes recording separate depositions for each spouse, court officers also allowed that married women could independently assess financial activities.[90]

When women signed credit instruments or testified in lawsuits, they assumed forms of authority that built on their power as observers outside of court. When enlisted to sign bonds and promissory notes, they took their role seriously in ratifying legally binding obligations, thus forging economic networks. When summoned to appear in debt cases, women spoke publicly and under oath before legal officials, attorneys, creditors, debtors, and lay audiences. Describing and interpreting what they had seen and heard, female deponents evaluated others' characters and displayed similar forms of knowledge as their male counterparts. By engaging in witnessing in all of its forms, women helped to both establish and sever ties that carried social as well as financial and legal significance.

Conclusion

Although borrowers and lenders often assume center stage in our analysis of credit networks, many other men and women helped confer legitimacy on and enforce financial obligations. Expanding our angle of vision to encompass such witnesses further elucidates the extent to which gender shaped patterns of legal and economic activity in colonial British America. In Suffolk and Newport Counties, women composed a small but consequential minority of those who signed documents and testified in lawsuits, and residents' pre-planned selections of witness reflected the prescriptive literature of the period's definition of witnessing as a masculine activity. Yet it is equally significant that women's involvement in documented forms of witnessing emerged from widespread practices of observation outside of court. Throughout New England, and especially in the crowded households of port cities, both women and men were surrounded by credit transactions other than their own. Simply by turning a watchful eye on events or keeping one's ears pricked, a New Englander could learn the state of others' finances and scrutinize their characters. Spectating and eavesdropping also trained bystanders in how to use credit and debt, as well as navigate the courts, and such informal learning was especially important for women, given their limited access to formal schooling and apprenticeships.

For free women and men, their proximity to credit transactions yielded written records of their roles in signing documents and testifying in court. Because colonial women were excluded from political and civic offices and these positions' associated speech, formal witnessing uniquely enlarged their social influence and enabled them to demonstrate their financial and legal savvy. Women could become formal witnesses, even if they possessed only a limited ability to access credit in their own names. Female witnesses notably represented a wide range of social classes and had varying levels of reading and writing ability. Women—whether married, daughters still residing in their parents' households, boarders, or servants—were among those who signed documents and testified in court. Their clearly delineated legal roles authorized and encouraged them to behave similarly to men. Both when helping to finalize contracts and when intervening in lawsuits, women as well men evinced a keen awareness of the varieties of financial records and their significance, and of the relationship at law between oral negotiations and written agreements. All those who testified, moreover, recounted key events in ways that conformed to the courts' privileging of sensory experience and legal technicalities.

Witnessing fits within a broader matrix in which women's skilled financial activities, many of which occurred in households, enhanced their authority within their communities. Witnesses' frequent testimonies about what went on within residences affirm the household's importance as a locus of financial activity and public scrutiny, one that facilitated the extensive engagement of women with finance and the law. Just as borrowers and lenders demonstrated skill and savvy as they established and navigated their relationships, so, too, did witnesses reveal their facility in interpreting the financial activities of others. Witnessing, like many other actions involving credit, intersected with and even temporarily disrupted social hierarchies that were based on gender, age, and class. Much like creditors, who traveled through their cities and made forceful demands in the course of collecting debts, witnesses asserted themselves within credit transactions, whether by clarifying agreements or refusing to sign until the parties read the instruments aloud. In an era when the conduct of creditors and debtors reflected on their characters, it followed that men and women who testified in lawsuits could evaluate and shape others' reputations. Through witnessing, a wide range of women and men proved to be adept at navigating their legal and financial worlds.

CHAPTER 5

"Laboring under many difficulties and hardships"

The Problem of Debt and Vocabularies of Grievance

By the middle of the eighteenth century, widening credit networks, growing economic volatility, and an increasingly regimented legal system posed crucial questions of political economy for Bostonians and Newporters. Residents of both cities had used written credit to forge new ties and finance new commercial ventures. During recurring currency crises and the boom and bust cycles of war and peace, some women and men found themselves overextended and unable to pay their debts. This problem was particularly acute in Boston, which spiraled steadily into economic depression from 1740 onward. In both Massachusetts and Rhode Island, the legal system offered limited relief. The colonies lacked comprehensive and permanent bankruptcy laws through which overextended individuals could start anew, and the courts consistently favored procedural adherence and creditors' interests. As debtors faced property seizure or imprisonment, laypeople and lawmakers alike evaluated the circumstances under which individuals deserved special dispensations from standard procedures. Especially amid the port cities' growing social problem of female poverty, such questions contained another significant angle. The view that women were entitled to special protection conflicted with the legal system's privileging of creditors' claims.[1]

Petitioning was an important area in which New Englanders collectively grappled with this newly mechanistic character of debt litigation and its gendered dimensions. While most relationships of indebtedness ended uneventfully, appeals to colony legislatures offered late-stage resorts within protracted legal battles. During the middle third of the eighteenth century, precisely the same decades in which the courts increasingly emphasized legal technicalities, a growing number of litigants protested the outcomes of debt cases through petitions to the Massachusetts General Court and the Rhode Island General Assembly. Whereas Massachusetts legislators received only 16 petitions in this regard in the 1730s, they received 61 such petitions only one decade later. In Rhode Island, the number of petitions concerning debt roughly doubled in every decade between the 1730s, when legislators heard 21 such appeals, and the 1760s, when they entertained 169 requests. Most petitioners were debtors and, among female ones, many were also widows and administrators or executors.[2] All petitions were read aloud in the presence of and evaluated by the colonies' highest officials. In the process, the grievances in them called attention to the law's privileging of creditors' interests above those of all others, particularly widows. Christian frameworks insisted that women who had lost their husbands were uniquely deserving of charity, yet creditors' claims conflicted with the widows' ability to inherit and retain family wealth.[3]

Appeals of debt suits fit within broader early modern European legal cultures, which held that petitioning was a right. The genre of the petition was sufficiently flexible that it could accommodate a wide range of concerns. Through this legal action, individuals and groups throughout the Atlantic World demanded formal recognition of their varied grievances and made requests to which authorities were obligated to reply. Even those who fell outside the body politic or were of dependent legal status claimed this right. Thus petitions were especially important tools for marginalized groups, including women, blacks, and indigenous peoples. Petitions and their outcomes both shaped and reflected understandings of law and justice.[4]

In eighteenth-century Massachusetts and Rhode Island, petitioning evolved to offer a narrowly delimited safety valve within a legal system that aimed to facilitate debt collection. As petitioners drafted their requests, and as legislators ruled on them, they assessed whether the litigants had encountered circumstances beyond their control and, therefore, deserved relief. Through their appeals, some female petitioners voiced the unique obstacles that women could face in financial disputes. Yet petitions by both women and men, composed with an awareness of successful arguments, increasingly coalesced around standard narratives of injustice, most of which hinged on their claims to competence, as opposed to ineptitude. The consequences of such narratives cut in multiple directions. In one respect, petitioning reinforced a cultural recognition that free white women, as well as men, were capable users of credit and the law. Yet this process also legitimated the all-male legal profession and men's business pursuits, and it failed to fundamentally disrupt a legal system that privileged creditors, regardless of their gender.

The struggles of one Newport widow, Ann Maylem, serve as this chapter's centerpiece and offer a unique opportunity to situate petitions and their language within the workings of the eighteenth-century's economy and its legal system. Eighteenth-century women, including Maylem, had access to numerous registers of grievance, and protracted financial disputes demanded that they use all of them. From 1742 to 1748, Maylem clashed with her late husband's creditors. She published a broadside airing her complaints, rallied attorneys to her cause, sparred with her opponents through lawsuits, and repeatedly petitioned the Rhode Island General Assembly. Following Maylem through print, correspondence, the courts, and the legislature reveals that she varied her self-presentation both within and across these different forums. Any one of Maylem's statements only partially encapsulated her skills and experience. At times she identified herself as a distressed widow, while elsewhere she positioned herself as a competent and savvy economic actor. Ultimately, Maylem's distinctive circumstances fell outside the standard grounds for redress of grievances. Her repeated attempts to obtain justice, including through petitioning, were unable to compensate for her early error in the administration of her husband's estate.

Navigating Indebtedness: Ann Maylem's Legal Battles

In March 1742, the Newport Town Council appointed Ann Maylem to administer the estate of her late husband, John.[5] It was in this capacity that she entered a protracted conflict with another Newport resident, rum distiller George Gardner. Maylem's struggles reveal the challenges faced by indebted widows within a legal system that favored creditors, as well as illuminate the avenues of protest that were accessible to them in protecting their families' assets. Women, including Maylem, had access to multiple languages of grievance, and they varied their self-presentation as they pursued justice in different forums.

Both Ann (née Low) and John Maylem came from families of moderate means. The Low family owned property in Rhode Island, and Ann inherited one-sixth of her father's land, a parcel valued at £132, in 1720. John Maylem was the son of a Boston bricklayer, and his family possessed sufficient wealth and status to enable him to attend Harvard College.[6] Throughout the more than twenty years of their marriage, Ann and John Maylem moved between Boston, Newport, and New Hampshire, where they purchased property and pursued commercial investments.[7]

Like other middling and elite New England women, Ann Maylem possessed reading and writing skills that facilitated her involvement in financial transactions.

By 1742, she wrote with a consistent hand, which suggested that she did so regularly and comfortably. As one who signed her name frequently and recognized the seriousness of doing so, she had cultivated a distinctive way of signing documents. Maylem's telltale signature, exemplified on one of her several petitions to the Rhode Island General Assembly, included a majuscule *A*, with ornamental flourishes, at the start of her first name (fig. 5.1). (Ann Maylem was also the only writer who spelled her surname "Maylam," and this further enables us to identify her signature.) As we shall see, Maylem penned certain documents in their entirety. She also affixed her name to other sources, including petitions, that were drafted by individuals with formal training in law and penmanship.[8] For Maylem, collaborating with allies was both a strategic choice and a means of shaping her own self-presentation.

In the fall of 1739, John and Ann Maylem returned to Newport, where they sought to benefit from that city's growing prosperity amid the economic stimulus of imperial warfare. John Maylem participated in one of the port's major industries, which embodied its growing involvement in Atlantic commerce: distilling Caribbean molasses into rum. The production of rum was a costly, complicated enterprise. Many distillers of the period were established merchants, able to use the profits and connections from their other ventures to finance and coordinate this particular business. John Maylem was not a merchant, so his entry into this trade required him to assume significant debt and considerable risk. He purchased his distillery from George Gardner on credit, signing two bonds and a mortgage. The distillery, its associated supplies, and the surrounding land were expensive—they cost £1,360, more than twice the value of all John Maylem's other belongings—and Maylem hoped his venture would prove to be profitable.[9]

In 1742, less than three years after the couple's return to Newport, John passed away unexpectedly. Ann was in her mid-forties at the time and was the mother of four children, ranging in age from three to twelve. Following her appointment as administrator of John's estate, Ann confronted the consequences of her family's financial overreaching.[10] John died possessing a sizeable personal estate that was valued at £659, excluding the rum distillery. His estate, however, was insolvent, as his debts significantly exceeded his assets, and he had no debtors from whom Ann could obtain payment. In addition, it was uncertain

Figure 5.1. Signature on petition of Ann Maylem [as "Maylam"] (September 1744). Petitions to the Rhode Island General Assembly, vol. 6, 13, Rhode Island State Archives. Courtesy of the Rhode Island State Archives

whether the Maylem family's most valuable asset, the distillery, was owned outright by them, or whether the property remained mortgaged to another Newport resident.[11]

Torn between preserving her family's wealth and satisfying her late husband's
creditors, Ann Maylem faced a predicament that was governed by colony-specific
inheritance laws. Both Massachusetts and Maylem's home jurisdiction of Rhode
Island took as their starting point the British common law principle of dower,
which stipulated a widow's right to receive one-third of her late husband's estate. Dower distinguished between personal estates (belongings) and real estate
(land). Widows received outright ownership of their husbands' belongings but
only lifetime use of real estate, meaning that they could occupy such land or
enjoy any resulting profits, but they could not sell or bequeath it to others.
Dower automatically applied for those widows, including Maylem, whose husbands died intestate. Widows whose husbands wrote wills could, if they chose,
reject such wills and assert their dower rights. In theory, dower ensured a widow's
ability to support herself and her family.[12]

Colonial officials assessed whether dower thirds were calculated before or
after creditors received their due, and their determinations diminished the property rights of Maylem and other widows. Under English common law, widows'
dower rights superseded creditors' claims to land. Creditors' claims to moveable
property, however, took precedence over allowances for widows. English legal
principle held that widows would inherit one-third of only that personal property which remained after the payment of debts. Massachusetts and Rhode Island, like other North American colonies, adapted this legal framework to
benefit creditors. Whereas a 1648 Massachusetts law had protected widows' real
property from creditors' claims, by 1692, Massachusetts stipulated that widows
would receive one-third of what remained of their husbands' estates *after* all
creditors were paid. In 1718, Rhode Island likewise required widows to surrender all but their most basic necessities in order to satisfy creditors. Massachusetts and Rhode Island further eroded dower by establishing procedures by
which administrators, including widows, could obtain permission to sell land
in order to pay an estate's debts.[13] By mid-century, commercial investments resulted in many residents, John Maylem included, dying in a state of financial
overreach. New Englanders thus frequently confronted this acute tension between widows' and creditors' interests. None of a widow's property was sacro-
sanct. Beset by creditors' demands, a widow was forced to choose between
selling her most valuable assets (most likely her land), or those over which
she retained greater control (her personal belongings, which provided daily
comfort).

As of the early 1740s, New England colonies lacked laws establishing procedures through which insolvent individuals or estates could seek relief, and this

further intensified Ann Maylem's plight. Given that eighteenth-century British Americans viewed an inability to pay one's debts as reflecting moral failings, John Maylem was probably loath to publicly admit his precarious financial state during his lifetime. Even if he had been willing to do so, legal channels for debt forgiveness did not yet exist. Through mid-century, debtors could seek private compositions (meetings of their creditors) or petition colonial legislatures for individual acts of insolvency, but such channels simply allowed insolvent individuals to surrender their assets for division among creditors in proportion to the amounts they were owed. These proceedings ended any ongoing lawsuits but did not permanently extinguish individuals' debts so they could start anew.[14]

Amid the unstable economic climate of the Seven Years' War and its aftermath, lawmakers' views shifted. Beginning to recognize that insolvency could result from macroeconomic causes beyond one's control, Rhode Island and Massachusetts established bankruptcy laws for individuals in 1756 and 1757, respectively. (Massachusetts repealed its law, then in its second iteration, in 1768). In Rhode Island, a 1758 law additionally codified procedures through which commissioners could proportionately divide an insolvent estate's assets among its creditors. By taking part in insolvency proceedings and accepting their shares, creditors agreed not to press further claims against an estate. This law did not alter widows' dower rights, but it at least established a mechanism through which they could stop creditors from pursuing their late husbands' estates indefinitely.[15] Yet all of these protections for debtors came too late for the Maylem family. John Maylem could not set his finances right during his lifetime, nor could Ann Maylem stop creditors from pursuing her family's assets following John's death. If Ann could not find sufficient liquid assets to pay John's creditors in full, she would be required to sell the family's belongings, and perhaps even its land.

Forced to forge her own strategies for responding to creditors' demands, Ann Maylem recognized that her family's distillery was of great importance, since producing and selling rum offered her a source of income. The same day that her husband died, Maylem employed George Gardner to make all of the molasses stored at the distillery into rum. Given that nothing about the distilling process required her to act so quickly, this choice reflected a concerted financial and legal strategy, perhaps even shaped by an awareness of her shaky hold on the distillery. In the short term, she could use the profits from the sale of the rum to pay her husband's creditors. If she could retain the business in the longer term, it offered the prospect of ongoing revenue. As Maylem may well have feared, George Gardner and his associates short-circuited these plans when they claimed the distillery as theirs.[16] Arising from the combination of her husband's insolvency and the distillery's importance, Maylem's plight drove her subsequent tenacity in challenging her opponents.

The ways in which John Maylem financed his purchase of the distillery shaped Ann's challenges as his administrator. Men routinely formed partnerships when entering the complex business of rum distilling, but these alliances were unstable and prone to conflict.[17] When John initially bought the distillery in 1739, Ann's brother-in-law, merchant Jacob Dehane, co-signed one of the bonds. The following year, Maylem acquired a new partner, carpenter Jonathan Diman. The pair mortgaged the distillery to merchant George Goulding to obtain funds for its operation. In return, Goulding gave Maylem and Diman a bond of defeasance. This crucial document bound Goulding to uphold his side of the mortgage agreement, in which he promised to relinquish ownership of the distillery to Maylem and Diman after they had paid off the mortgage, or else owe them a £1,600 penalty. At the time of John Maylem's death, he and his partner remained indebted to Goulding, and the Maylem family held the bond of defeasance.[18]

Ann Maylem's responsibilities as an administrator inserted her into her late husband's network of male business associates. Diman called on Maylem at her house to settle his accounts with the estate. She summoned Jacob Dehane and a second Newport distiller, Nathaniel Coggeshall, to assist in this process. The men determined that Diman owed £90 to John Maylem's estate.[19] Shortly thereafter, Ann Maylem gave Diman the bond of defeasance that Goulding had signed in 1740. Gardner also called on Maylem to demand several hundred pounds that he claimed were due on bonds from the estate. The written record suggests that Ann Maylem was the only adult woman present in each of these meetings.[20]

Maylem's surrender of the bond of defeasance to Diman—an act that took only seconds to complete—had tremendous consequences for her hold on the distillery and, by extension, on her financial standing. Acquiring the bond of defeasance enabled Diman to reconfigure the distillery's ownership. He jettisoned his former partners, the Maylems, in favor of distiller Ezekiel Burroughs and George Gardner, the same man from whom John Maylem had purchased the distillery in 1739. A few weeks after Diman had obtained the bond, he delivered it to Goulding, who cancelled it. Diman, Burroughs, and Gardner then purchased the distillery anew from Goulding. At this point, according to the written record, John Maylem's estate and his heirs no longer owned the distillery.[21]

For six years following her husband's death, Ann Maylem attempted to regain the distillery from its new owners. Gardner and his associates insisted that they paid Maylem for the bond of defeasance and, thus, for the purchase of her share of the distillery, adding that she had given her "free consent" and was "intirely satisfied" when she relinquished it.[22] Maylem, in contrast, maintained that that she had not surrendered the bond knowingly and voluntarily. Maylem published her broadside regarding the dispute in late 1742, sued Diman and

Gardner four times from 1743 to 1745, and submitted four petitions between 1744 and 1748.[23]

Maylem's difficulty in regaining the distillery had cascading financial consequences, limiting her ability to prevent other creditors from dismantling her dower and her family's inheritance. On three occasions in 1742, Maylem sold portions of her late husband's estate—including household goods, clothing, and an enslaved boy—at auction. In each instance, she used the profits to make a round of payments to creditors in the following days. In total, she paid £521 to seventeen different creditors. When Maylem submitted her account of these activities to the Newport Town Council, the document reflected the frenetic nature of selling the family's numerous low-value possessions in order to satisfy creditors. Whereas the councilors accepted most accounts of administration without comment, they criticized the form of Maylem's records. Exhibiting a scrutiny that was consistent with the legal system's concern for creditors' claims, this legal body protested that the account's catch-all references to sales of "sundry goods" at auction left individual transactions "so blended together" that it was "difficult to be particular in examining them." In this same document, Maylem reported that, as was consistent with a widow's right to retain a small number of necessary items, she had kept only a "small" bed and bedding, together valued at £10, for herself.[24]

Submitting an account of administration normally signaled the completion of an administrator's duties, but creditors persisted in scavenging John Maylem's estate. One of them signaled that he would stop seeking payment if the estate was proportionately divided among its creditors, but Maylem and the estate's various creditors never forged such an agreement.[25] Instead, in May 1743 and 1744, four creditors, each of whom had previously received small payments from Maylem, separately sued her for their balances. In lower court trials and appeals, Maylem argued that she was not liable for the debts, because she no longer had any of John's estate in her possession. The courts rejected Maylem's defenses, and, as a result of these rulings, sheriffs attempted to seize her few remaining belongings.[26] Meanwhile, Maylem continued her efforts to regain the bond of defeasance and, by extension, the distillery and its potential income.[27] Maylem's protracted conflicts with other Newport residents and her loss of property attest to the consequences of a legal system that favored satisfying creditors over protecting a widow's inheritance.

Aware of her limited options, Maylem first attempted to use public opinion to pressure Gardner and his associates. In the final months of 1742, she or her allies visited the shop of another Newport widow, printer Ann Franklin, to enlist her services.[28] The resulting broadside, entitled *A short Narrative of the unjust Proceedings of Mr. George Gardner of Newport Distiller, against Ann Maylem Widow and Administratrix to the Estate of John Maylem late of Newport Distiller deceased*, enumerated her grievances against Gardner (fig. 5.2). At this point, Maylem had sold much of her husband's estate at auction, but some creditors still awaited payment and Gardner, Diman, and Burroughs claimed ownership of the distillery. Print allowed Maylem to shame her opponents and elicit sympathy from others. Copies of the broadside probably circulated among Newport's residents and appeared in conspicuous locations throughout the city. In the short term, the document's claims led the Newport Town Council to summon Gardner to testify. In the years that followed, the broadside served as a concise record of the quarrel, which Maylem then circulated in her bid to secure legal representation.[29]

In publishing a stand-alone narrative, Maylem pushed beyond customary uses of print by women. Female administrators routinely placed notices in newspapers, but Maylem's authorship of a longer text was exceptional. Only twenty-six freestanding works by women were published in British America between 1640 and 1755. Most were either posthumous works or reprints of French or British ones. Only eight texts were published by colonial women in their own lifetimes. The content of Maylem's broadside also set her apart. Prior to the imperial crisis, most female-authored texts concerned religious experiences, and evangelical lay leader Sarah Osborn penned the only other mid-century text by a Newport woman. Printed in 1755, and based on a manuscript letter composed in 1753, Osborn's *The Nature, Certainty, and Evidence of True Christianity* identified her only as "a gentlewoman in New England," adding that she had agreed to publication "provided her Name and Place of abode remain concealed."[30] Maylem's broadside, in contrast, named her in its title and used the first person throughout. Its text declared that she had drafted it for publication because she "thought proper to inform the World" of her suffering. In these regards, Maylem's text most closely resembled the broadsides, pamphlets, and newspaper essays that men sometimes published during protracted financial and legal disputes.[31]

Maylem's broadside marshaled extensive financial detail in order to suggest that she, and not George Gardner, was in the right. Its opening lines explained that Maylem had "been laboring under many difficulties and hardships ever since the Death of my Husband" and was treated "cruelly" by Gardner. The rest of its first paragraph traced the commercial relationship between Gardner and John Maylem. The middle third was a tabular account of Ann Maylem's payments surrounding the distillery. The final third recounted her interactions with Gardner and the repercussions from them. These three parts yield a convoluted picture for modern readers, and this is one reason why historians have largely overlooked Maylem's publication. The broadside probably even confused its eighteenth-century audience. The final third of the publication references numerous technical documents, and tracking Gardner's alleged abuses of Maylem

A fhort Narrative of the u juft Proceedings of
Mr. *George Gardner* of *Newport* Diftiller,
againft *Ann Maylem* Widow and Adminiftra-
trix to the Eftate of *John Maylem* late of
Newport Diftiller Deceafed.

AS I have been labouring under many difficulties and hardfhips ever fince
the Death of my Hufband *John Maylem*, I have thought proper to inform the World how cruelly I have been dealt with by Mr. *George
Gardner* of the Town of *Newport* Diftiller, which is as follows. In
the Year 1739, my Hufband bought of faid *Gardner*, a Lot of Land, Still-
Houfe, two Stills, their Heads, Worms, Cifterns, &c. for £1360 giving him
at the fame time his Bond for £370. Brother *Debane* and Mr *Maylem*, gave
him alfo a joint Bond for £200 and at the fame time Mr. *Maylem* Mortgaged
the Still-Houfe abovementioned to faid *Gardner*, for £900 taking a Bond of
Defeazence Obliging him the faid *Gardner* to Reconvey to Mr. *Maylem* faid
Still-Houfe again.

The following is an Account of fundry Payments made towards faid Still-Houfe.

Viz. 1742 To a Bond taken up dated; *Nov.* 23*d.* 1739	370	00	00
June 7 To Cafh paid in part of a Bond Sued laft			
Tuefday of May paft given to *George*			
Gardner by *Debane* and *Maylem*,	100	00	00
Nov. 19 To fo much paid by Mr. *Debane* in full of			
the above Bond and Execution.	118	08	00
	218	08	00
To Cafh paid on Bond *Maylem* to *Gardner*,	181	11	11
To half the Stock in the Still-Houfe at the			
time of Mr. *Maylems* Deceafe, being 53 ſ			
Gallons at 7 ſ. pr. Gallon,	185	17	00
Omiffions in the Acc. delivered in to *Geo. Gardner*,	9	15	00
To my Negroe working 8 Days in the Still-Houfe			
after Mr *Maylem* Died.	4	00	00
	969	11	11

The Day Mr. *Maylem* Died which was the 13*th* of March 1741,2 I fent to
Mr. *Gardner* to Still up the Stock which was then in the Still-Houfe; the Tuefday
following *Gardner* fends *Jonathan Dimon* to me defiring I would let him have the
Bond of Defeazence that he juft wanted to look at it and that he would fend it back
to me immediately, with a great deal of perfwafion I let him have it, and thus getting
the Strength out of my Hands he makes ufe of the Stock and all my other intereft
in the Still-Houfe and never Accounts with me for one farthing of the fame. At the
time when I was making up my Accounts for the Town Council Mr. *Gardner* came
and defired I would take the abovementiond Bond of £181 11 11 that it might
appear to them as fo much paid and that he had no other end or View in
fo doing but only to ferve me he knowing the trouble I was then in, and by
his perfwading me fo to do I was obliged to pay it over again as alfo the
above £100 and that thro' the means of *David Richards* who was then my
Attorney. *N. B.* the above £370 was paid and Difcharged in Mr. *Maylems*
life time after which Mr. *Gardner* had not the leaft demand on Mr. *Maylem*
except that £181 11 11 which he Crowded into my hand in the above
Fraudulent manner and after the Difcharge of the £370 Mr. *Maylem* and Mr.
Gardner made a Settlement and Mr. *Gardner* being at that time in Debt to
Mr. *George Goulding* the Mortgage was then made to faid *Goulding* from whom
Mr. *Maylem* got the Bond of Defeazence which is the fame that faid *Gardner*
fo unjuftly withholds from me.

Figure 5.2. Ann Maylem, *A short Narrative of the unjust Proceedings of Mr. George
Gardner of Newport Distiller, against Ann Maylem Widow and Administratrix to the
Estate of John Maylem late of Newport Distiller Deceased* (Newport, RI: Ann Franklin,
1742), quarto sheet, c. 31 cm × 23.2 cm. Collection of the Massachusetts Historical
Society

requires cross-referencing these instruments' sums with the account entries. In addition, this paragraph is not strictly chronological. Its lengthy final argument ("*N.B.* the above £370 . . .") backtracks to provide clarifying details about the bonds in question. Even—or perhaps especially—for those readers who did not fully engage with the broadside's substance, its style and form, including the central placement of an account, accorded with Ann Maylem's financial mastery. Her *Short Narrative* was the product of an intellectual framework that increasingly privileged empiricism and numerical specificity, and it suggested that the written record unambiguously supported her claims.[32]

Maylem's broadside further vilified Gardner in the way that it narrated two episodes concerning the handling of financial documents. In one—the incident that became the subject of Maylem's petitions—Diman and Gardner obtained the bond of defeasance. In the other, Gardner forced Maylem to pay the same debt twice. The broadside maintained that Diman and Gardner had deliberately misled her in both instances. It claimed that Gardner had "[sent]" Diman to obtain the instrument, and that Gardner had extracted the double payment by persuading Maylem that he had "no other end or View . . . but only to serve me." In keeping with its overall portrayal of Maylem as assertive and financially savvy, the text depicted her as skeptical during her interactions with the two men: Diman used a "great deal of perswasion," and Gardner obtained the duplicate payment only after "perswading" Maylem of his plan. Both confrontations contained embodied and tactile dimensions. Maylem characterized the men as "getting the Strength out of my Hands" when she gave them the bond of defeasance, and she accused Gardner of having "Crowded into my hand" the bond that she paid twice. Such descriptions, evoking violence by men toward a woman, accentuated Gardner's and Diman's wrongdoing. Yet the broadside equally characterized Ann Maylem as a formidable opponent by implying that the men only carried out their plans following a struggle.[33]

Ann Maylem next turned to the courts, where the technical requirements of common law pleading led to muted, compartmentalized versions of her claims. In November 1745, she sued Diman, demanding that he return the bond of defeasance and pay £2,000 in damages. Maylem's case was an action of detinue, a type of suit in which she sued Diman for unlawfully detaining her property—in this instance, the bond itself.[34] According to the complaint that Maylem's attorney filed, she "casually lost the said bond" on March 16, 1742, then "afterward on said day the same came to the hands of the [defendant] by finding," and he thereafter refused to return it.[35] Because the legal issue in the case was Diman's failure to return the bond, Maylem's declaration to the court gave no indication of her heated conversation with him. It lacked the themes of misplaced trust and intentional trickery present in the broadside.

Maylem's three lawsuits against Gardner were similarly narrow. Each was an action of account in which she insisted that he had never provided her with the profits from the molasses he had distilled. Yet in them, she never referenced the bond of defeasance or the competing claims to the distillery's ownership.[36] Maylem's lawsuits captured only a small slice of the disputes in which she was engaged, as each made separate allegations against specific individuals. Litigation offered Maylem the prospect of compensation for her losses, but it required her to blunt her critiques of Gardner's and Diman's conduct.

Unable to obtain relief in the county courts, Maylem pursued a final strategy by petitioning the Rhode Island legislature. This led her and her collaborators to narrate her difficulties at length. (Maylem's petitions, like most, were drafted in a formal hand by someone with legal expertise. She personally signed at least two petitions, however, and this attests to her direct involvement in her appeal.[37]) A standard petition began by greeting the receiving body and identifying the petitioner, and closed by presenting its specific request. Petitions' intervening lines, which could span multiple pages, were open ended, chronicling the signers' difficulties and enumerating the reasons why the authorities should grant their requests.

The middle sections of Maylem's petitions stressed her vulnerability. In so doing, they aligned with her broadside's opening lines, which vilified Gardner. But whereas the broadside quickly shifted to financial details, Maylem's petitions more uniformly depicted a "distressed" widow whose creditors threatened to "ruin" her. Within Maylem's petitions, George Gardner and his "accomplice," Jonathan Diman, were guilty of "fraud & craft" and "wicked" acts.[38] Details of Maylem's and the men's interactions concerning the bond of defeasance supported these characterizations. Maylem characterized herself in the broadside as savvy enough to challenge Diman's request for the bond, but she downplayed that assertiveness when appealing to the legislature. One petition explained that, while Maylem was "full of Trouble & Concern for the loss of her husband" in the days immediately following his death, she "inadvertently" allowed Diman to "carry away" the crucial bond.[39] In another version of the events, Diman asked for the bond and "promised to bring the same again very quickly." Maylem, "doubting nothing of his fidelity and being then in great trouble for the Death of her husband," surrendered the instrument.[40] While these accounts differed in their specificity, both emphasized Maylem's passivity. She claimed to be a widow in the throes of mourning who at no point resisted Diman's request for the bond.

Maylem's repeated appeals in the county courts and before the colony's legislature led her to hire numerous lawyers, including Massachusetts attorney James Otis. Seven of Maylem's letters to Otis survive, and these letters are the fourth and final arena in which she represented herself and her predicament.

Maylem wrote to Otis in 1745 to engage him in matters unrelated to the distillery. In 1746, she again sought his representation, this time against Gardner and Diman. She contacted him six times as her appeals awaited hearings before the Superior Court and then the General Assembly. Maylem enlisted two different individuals with formal penmanship skills to draft her 1745 memorandum to Otis and her first overture in 1746, and she signed her name at the bottom of each of these completed letters (fig. 5.3).[41] She then, in her own hand, drafted five additional missives to Otis, including four within a four-day span in September, in which she enjoined him to come to Newport in time for her hearings (fig. 5.4). These letters ranged from four lines to a full page long. Given the time-sensitive nature of her requests, Maylem probably found it impractical to obtain assistance in writing her letters, and perhaps she possessed a greater sense

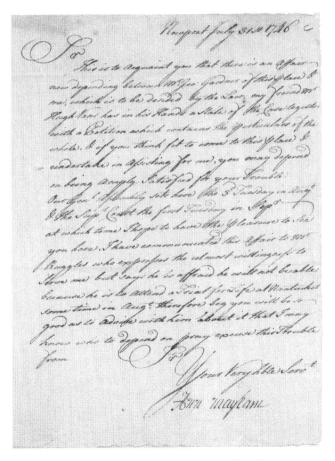

Figure 5.3. Ann Maylem to James Otis, July 31, 1746. Otis Family Papers, Massachusetts Historical Society. Collection of the Massachusetts Historical Society

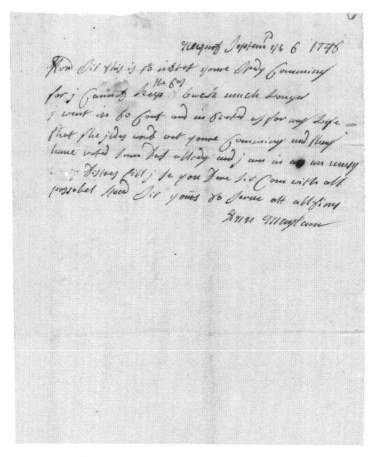

Figure 5.4. Ann Maylem to James Otis, September 6, 1746. Otis Family Papers, Massachusetts Historical Society. Collection of the Massachusetts Historical Society

of familiarity with Otis once he had agreed to take her case. (If Otis wrote to the widow, none of his letters survive.) These five letters, written in a consistent hand with occasional phonetic spellings, represent the only body of sources unquestionably drafted by Maylem herself.[42]

All of Maylem's letters from 1746 asked Otis to come to Newport, and she deployed multiple forms of self-presentation as she reiterated this request. Composed with an ally's assistance, her July letter referred to "an affair now depending between Mr. Geo. Gardner of this place & me." It promised that Otis would be "amply satisfied" if he thought "fit to come to this place & undertake in assisting me." As was typical of polite commercial correspondence, such concise, unemotional phrasing positioned Maylem as a knowledgeable client whose cases fit within the ordinary course of a lawyer's business.[43]

In contrast, the letters drafted by Maylem herself emphasized her imperiled state and contained greater urgency. In them she employed evaluative language regarding her dispute with Gardner, referencing "the case whare I sow unjustly lost 8 hundred pounds" and insisting that there was "full evidens clere and strong in my favore." She reformulated the first letter's pledges of compensation as a frantic plea, insisting in August that "I am under the greatest Disadvantages in Life and shall be absolutely ruind if you Don't Come and there for [therefore] for Gods Sack Com and I shall fully reward you." In September, she reiterated that she faced "unesy distress" and wrote "in grat hast" to urge Otis's "speedy comming," adding that "I cannot tack one moments rest till I se you."[44] Emphasizing her dependence on Otis, Maylem's own rhetorical choices reflected her desperation in seeking to secure her attorney's loyalty as her court date approached. In their emphasis on her linked financial and emotional peril, the letters penned by Maylem also aligned more closely with her petitions than with her broadside or lawsuits. Perhaps Maylem's own words inflected her petitions' content, or perhaps her familiarity with her petitions shaped her letters to Otis. Either way, parallels between the letters and the petitions suggest that the image of the distraught and financially vulnerable widow was well known to both Maylem and her collaborators.

Maylem's self-authored letters also positioned her as a public, active adversary in her lawsuits. In addition to reminding Otis that she was a paying client, she provided precise information about the location and timing of her hearings and detailed her efforts to postpone her trials until he arrived. She informed Otis that she "went into Court" and insisted "as for my life that the judge would wait your coming." Two days after her court appearance, she visited Gardner's attorney to ask him to delay the proceedings. Dissatisfied with his response, she then called on the court clerk. When the deputy governor's brother came to her house to inform her that her case would be heard the following day, she visited Gardner's lawyer again, persuading him to stay the trial for an additional twenty-four hours.[45] The necessity of updating Otis about her case's timing led Maylem to reveal her movements through Newport and her negotiations with court officers, even as this complicated her self-presentation as a distressed and dependent widow.

Overall, in the course of settling John Maylem's affairs, Ann Maylem encountered two interrelated sets of difficulties that yielded lasting consequences. First, as a widow administering the insolvent estate of her late husband within the context of a legal system that privileged creditors' interests, she struggled to respond to demands for payment. She sold the family's belongings in order to pay John's debts, and she faced lawsuits from creditors even after doing so. Second, early on in her term as an administrator, she lost possession of her family's most valuable asset, the distillery, and with it the potential for ongoing profit.

In those multiple genres of writing, Ann Maylem and her collaborators spilled much more ink on the specific conflict with Gardner than on her general financial difficulties. In her broadside, lawsuits, petitions, and letters to her attorney, Maylem concentrated on regaining the distillery and the value of its stock from Gardner, as well as obtaining the bond of defeasance as a means to this end. As the broadside suggested when referring to the bond as Maylem's source of "Strength," colonists' heightened emphasis on written records of debt meant that a momentary decision could have lasting consequences.[46] In order for other Boston and Newport women to administer estates and use credit and debt without incident, they needed to demonstrate mastery of the key documents and avoid the sort of error committed by Maylem.

Ann Maylem's focus on the distillery and the bond of defeasance made financial sense, but it also reflected the constraints of a legal system that prioritized adjudicating individual conflicts. Maylem, as we have seen, occasionally referenced her financial straits when she noted that she was a "distressed" widow facing "ruin."[47] She did so, however, to buttress her specific claims against Gardner, Diman, and other creditors, rather than call attention to the structural problem of widowhood within an economy and a legal system that privileged creditors' rights. The eighteenth-century legal landscape provided women with numerous outlets for seeking redress for grievances, but it also circumscribed their expression of those perceived injustices.

While the aggregate evidence about Ann Maylem suggests the challenges encountered by widows whose husbands left behind extensive debts, comparisons across different source types underscore how women, including Maylem, presented themselves differently in various forums. The most savvy and authoritative version of Maylem's persona emerged in her unconventional broadside, which portrayed her as resisting Gardner and Diman in person and mastering relevant financial details thereafter. Meanwhile, Maylem's lawsuits couched her grievances within legal language that eschewed narration, while her petitions depicted her as an imperiled widow who needed the legislators' assistance to stand up to Gardner's and Diman's plot. Lastly, the missives to James Otis included polite requests, anxious pleas, and evidence of direct engagement in her affairs.

Taken together, these sources position women's financial and legal capabilities in a new light. By following women, including Ann Maylem, across multiple venues, such bodies of records reveal them to be savvy, active players in their affairs. Varying one's presentation in different forums was a crucial legal skill, one that required alignment with individuals who possessed the relevant expertise. As was common during the eighteenth century, Maylem produced many of her narratives in collaboration with others, whether printers, lawyers, or skilled laypeople. For female debtors, including Ann Maylem, combatting a legal system that favored creditors demanded not only mastering multiple vocabularies and genres, but also forging alliances with those in their cities and beyond.

Providing Relief and Constructing Competency: Petitions for New Trials

In August 1748, six years after her husband died, Ann Maylem proffered her fourth petition to the Rhode Island General Assembly. Emphasizing once more that she was "poor injured and distressed," she asked the legislators to grant her a "fair trial" in the lower courts, so she could regain the bond of defeasance. This petition represented Maylem's last resort. All of her prior efforts had failed. Following Maylem's publication of the broadside, the Newport Town Council summoned Gardner to testify but declined to intercede on Maylem's behalf. She also lost every one of her court cases. The Rhode Island General Assembly declined to act on her prior petitions, dismissing some of them outright and letting others languish. That legislative body's response to her 1748 petition was no different. The lawmakers postponed consideration of this petition until their next session and summoned George Gardner to appear. They took no further action on Maylem's petition, however, and she never again sued Gardner or Diman in Newport's county courts.[48]

At first glance, the Rhode Island lawmakers' unwillingness to intercede on Maylem's behalf may seem surprising. Foregrounding her gender and marital status, Maylem's petitions cast her as a vulnerable widow wronged by conspiring men, one whose plight could only be relieved through the benevolent intervention of other men—namely, the colony's legislators. As was typical of the genre's conventions, Maylem's petitions embedded assertive claims within supplicatory, deferential rhetoric. Their content also seemingly aligned with eighteenth-century understandings of patriarchy. Yet situating Maylem's four appeals within the larger corpus of petitions concerning debt litigation helps explain the Rhode Island legislators' repeated unwillingness to grant her requests. It also sheds light on those documents' legal functions and cultural consequences.[49]

Ann Maylem's four petitions were part of a steady stream of requests concerning debt litigation received by the Massachusetts and Rhode Island legislatures. For the period from 1730 to 1776, 472 petitions by men and 30 petitions by women survive. These sources represented an important avenue of protest within a legal system that favored creditors. Petitioners tended to advance one of several standard arguments that satisfied the legal criteria for appeals, and these increasingly standardized narratives positioned both women and men as fundamentally competent in disputes surrounding credit. Yet this premise of laypeople's competence, forged through petitions, also contained gendered nuances. Key subsets of petitions elevated lawyers' legal expertise and legitimated men's commercial activities, while acknowledging that women, especially those acting as their husbands' agents or as estate administrators, could face heightened but temporary difficulties as debtors and defendants. The unwieldy tales in Maylem's petitions, in their intense focus on the dispute with Gardner and Diman, failed to comport with other petitioners' increasingly standardized arguments for new trials. Her exceptional, highly specific appeals contributed to her eventual defeat.

By petitioning the Rhode Island legislature, Maylem sought to benefit from a process that softened colonial legal systems' privileging of creditors over debtors. Like Maylem, the overwhelming majority—more than 80 percent—of those petitioning with regard to financial disputes were debtors.[50] (Because creditors won more then 90 percent of their cases, they seldom had reason to petition.) Whereas the county courts processed their high volumes of routine debt cases quickly and often issued judgments based on assessments of legal technicalities, petitions and the resulting proceedings were more flexible. Their middle sections could incorporate any arguments the authors believed were advantageous to their causes, and colonial assemblies evaluated petitions based on principles of equity, which enabled broader consideration of the cases' issues than did common law. Legislators typically did not issue their own judgments on the lawsuits detailed in petitions. Instead, they invalidated prior case outcomes and ordered new hearings in the county courts. While legislators' interventions were not necessarily permanent victories for petitioners, they at least protected debtors' assets until new hearings took place. Unlike Ann Maylem, roughly three-quarters of those who requested re-hearings of debt cases successfully obtained new trials.[51]

In comparison with other women's petitions concerning legal disputes, Maylem's was atypical in its overwhelming emphasis on her gender and marital status. In Massachusetts and Rhode Island between 1730 and the Revolution, only two other petitions for new trials explicitly contended that legislators should grant the requests because they would be aiding vulnerable widows. Susannah Hood's document urged officials not to "set her adrift again especially as she has lost her pilot" and claimed that a "poor widow and fatherless children would be very much wronged" if they denied her request for a new trial. Elizabeth Tiffany's appeal likewise explained that her husband was "killed in one moment and she left with a family and small children" and requested that legislators "take special care to do justice to the widow and the fatherless" by granting her a new trial in a debt case. Although the record does not contain the legislators' eventual decision, Hood's opponent strenuously opposed her petition. And, as they did for Maylem, officials refused to grant Tiffany's request.[52]

Fully elaborated discussions of widowhood were uncommon and unsuccessful strategies in women's petitions, because, at least in themselves, they did not satisfy the criteria for the issuance of new trials. Even though legislators possessed greater discretionary power than county court judges, legal principles nonetheless shaped the colonial assemblies' handling of petitions. Treatises from the period specified that litigants could obtain new hearings only when they suffered from "defects of justice" that fell into one of three categories: "surprise," "accident," or "mistake." "Surprise" referred to circumstances in which the litigants were not notified of proceedings against them; "accident" and "mistake" encompassed instances in which outside forces or errors by individuals other than the defendant had led to the resulting outcomes of such cases. Parties notably did not deserve new trials when losses arose from "laches"—that is, the litigants' negligence in the performance of legal duties.[53] Those who drafted petitions and rebuttals were sufficiently aware of this legal framework that they sometimes invoked it explicitly, such as when debtors insisted that they had committed "no laches," or when creditors retaliated that a petitioner sought to "take advantage of his own latches" or had lost as a result of his "laches and faults."[54] While descriptions of widows' plights may have elicited the legislators' sympathy, they were not, in themselves, grounds for a new trial.

The law's seemingly binary distinction between "defects of justice" and "laches" hinged on subjective expectations surrounding laypeople's financial and legal competencies. What constituted "defects of justice" that were beyond the litigants' control, and when did outcomes result from the litigants' own neglect? And to what extent were particular capabilities and difficulties uniquely masculine or specifically feminine? Massachusetts and Rhode Island residents collectively addressed these questions when litigants and their allies strategically drafted petitions, when opponents countered requests for new trials, and when assembly members granted or denied petitions' requests. Through their decisions to mobilize and accept certain arguments and reject others, they formed a consensus over time.

In recognition of the legal distinction between injustice and negligence, petitioners' narratives eventually converged around five categories of obstacles. The vast majority of petitions cited one or more of the four most common arguments: defendants' inability to attend court, attorneys' failure to represent their clients, the unavailability of crucial evidence, or erroneous judgments by the courts (table 5.1). Such grounds for new trials were so well established that, as early as 1739, a creditor accused his opponent of petitioning "in a commonplace way" by the latter's mechanistically rehearsing standard arguments that "he was not in court when the case was called and that he was surprised and the like," even though they did not apply.[55] A fifth impediment, litigants' unfamiliarity with relevant aspects of the law, appeared less frequently than the others and required more-nuanced positioning by petitioners, but it nonetheless was also stylized.

The vast majority of petitions for new trials reinforced understandings of men and women as equally capable of winning debt cases. Men and women

TABLE 5.1.
Reasons cited in petitions for re-hearings of debt cases, 1730–1776

	Petitions (*N*)	Prevented from arguing case (%)	Problems with attorney (%)	Evidentiary issues (%)	Court error (%)	Unfamiliarity with law (%)
Women	30	43	30	20	17	17
Men	472	45	30	29	15	7

Sources: For Rhode Island petitions, see Rhode Island Petitions, vols. 2–16 and 25.2, Rhode Island State Archives. For Massachusetts petitions, see Massachusetts Archives Collection, vols. 17–19B, 41–44, 105, 303, Massachusetts State Archives.

Notes: This table reflects all extant petitions for re-hearings of debt cases that were submitted exclusively by women or exclusively by men to the Rhode Island or Massachusetts legislatures from 1730 to 1776. Rhode Island petitions exist for throughout this entire period, while Massachusetts petitions are only extant for 1730 through 1757. To facilitate comparisons between men's and women's petitions, this table excludes a small number submitted jointly by women and men. Because some petitioners advanced multiple arguments in their petitions, percentages total more than 100.

cited the most common arguments for new trials—litigants' being unable to attend their trials, attorneys' failures, missing evidence, and erroneous court judgments—in roughly equal frequencies (table 5.1). In acknowledgment of the law's insistence that willful negligence was not grounds for a new trial, all four arguments hinged on the premise that, but for identifiable obstacles, the defendants would have successfully refuted the plaintiffs' claims. Standard petitions by both men and women began by enumerating the difficulties they had encountered, confidently asserted that they could win their cases if they were granted re-hearings, and then concluded by asking colonial assemblies to grant their requests.

Male and female petitioners referenced similar underlying premises in their most common argument for new trials: that unforeseen circumstances had prevented the litigants from attending court. In mid-century Rhode Island, illness kept Silas Tallman and Bethiah Hedge from responding to debt suits against them. Each enlisted an individual with legal expertise to draft a petition for a new trial, and the resulting process of translating their experiences into legal lexicons downplayed the significance of gender. In 1746, Tallman's boilerplate petition explained that for "sometime before" and "a long time after" the court session, he was "so very ill that he was unable to go to said Court, or even to leave his house without the great danger of loss of his life." Tallman stood to be "greatly injured" if forced to pay the debt at issue, and such an outcome would be "contrary to the meaning of [the] law." Hedge's 1738 petition similarly recounted that she defaulted in a debt case when she "by reason of her sickness was not able to go to Newport to put in an answer." It asked that the legislators grant her "a fair Trial upon the merits of the cause." The standard opening lines of Hedge's petition identified her as the wife of the late John Hedge, but the document otherwise did not reference her femininity or widowhood. Through their insistence that illness alone prevented them from winning their cases, Tallman's and Hedge's petitions cast them as being familiar with the necessary legal procedures as well as with the substance of their cases. Their demands, both of which were granted by the General Assembly, rested on the assumption that both men and women could competently defend themselves in debt cases.[56]

When petitioners and scribes delved into additional detail, they articulated nuanced understandings of financial and legal skills that aligned with the imperative to cast litigants as victims of circumstance. Like Silas Tallman and Bethiah Norton, Deborah Johnson, who petitioned for a re-hearing of a debt case in 1743, could not attend court due to illness. She was "very sick," and others in her family had died or were "at the point of death." Johnson's petition, mined in chapter 2 for its evidence of women's strategies during face-to-face settlements, labored to cast her as a capable manager of her affairs, one whose loss arose due to "the hand of Providence." The petition noted that Johnson "could neither read or write," but every other aspect—from its description of the account in question to its recounting of her use of witnesses—provided evidence of her attentiveness.[57] As the petitions' creators marshaled details showing that "defects of justice" had led to case outcomes, they decoupled practical skills from formal literacy and showed that any layperson could be a capable litigant.

The second most common argument made in petitions, that lawyers had failed to represent their clients, reinforced the necessity of attorneys' professional services within lawsuits. All manner of impediments seemingly prevented lawyers from getting to court. Women's petitions recounted instances in which an attorney "neglected" their cases, "mistook the week on which the court was to have sat," was "obliged to attend" other courts that were meeting simultaneously, was "sick," or could not reach the court in time "thro' the difficulty of the season" or because he "lived at so great a distance" away from the courthouse.[58] Men's petitions similarly explained the myriad reasons why their attorneys had not represented them: "the weather was so severe" that travel was impossible; a lawyer was "sick" and "could not possibly" go to court; he was detained by "business out of the government" or at another court session "held the same day"; or an "oversight and omission" amid his "great multiplicity of business" let a case slip through the cracks.[59] Petitions presented attorneys as unreliable figures, prone to missing court dates due to acts of nature and the structure of legal practices.

While such petitions, on their surface, discredited the legal profession, they ultimately normalized laymen's and -women's decisions to hire attorneys. In recognition of the legal distinction between "defects of justice" and laches, petitioners cited employing lawyers as evidence of their own attentiveness. Mary Carr explained in 1742 that she "made application to an attorney to file an answer which was by him neglected." In 1762, John Congdon likewise recalled that he had "engaged an attorney to file an answer" and that the lawyer "promised me he would take care and do it."[60] Petitions concerning attorneys' failures thus established that hiring lawyers was the first step in responding to lawsuits, and references to their busy practices reinforced this message. Creditors who opposed their debtors' petitions accepted the same logic and only disputed the petitions' factual claims. When Susanna Waldo sought a new trial in 1743, her opponent countered that Waldo had never hired the two lawyers whom her petition accused of neglecting her case.[61] In suggesting that litigants' losses directly resulted from their hired attorneys' absences, petitions and responses implied that lawyers provided skills and services that were vital to winning cases.

The large body of petitions concerning attorneys' lapses also created institutional protections for women and men who hired lawyers. As legislators responded favorably to the vast majority of such petitions, they created an additional incentive to engage attorneys. Their decisions reinforced the view that lawyers and their clients were separate entities, and that lapses by an attorney did not indicate negligence on the part of the client. This aspect of the petitioning process becomes even clearer when we recognize that litigants often employed lawyers to assist them in drafting their petitions. In some instances, the attorneys who penned petitions were the same ones who had lost the original lawsuits.[62] By positioning their lapses as excusable and helping their clients obtain new trials, lawyers advanced their professional ambitions. Aware of the success of such petitions, savvy eighteenth-century litigants came to recognize that attorneys brought valuable expertise to their cases and offered built-in possibilities for new trials.

When blaming lawyers for litigants' losses, petitions made sharper distinctions between laypeople and legal professionals than between women and men. The implications of such narratives thus cut in two directions. On the one hand, these narratives elevated the standing of the all-male legal profession. Strengthening associations between masculinity and lawyerly expertise, they marked courtrooms and formal pleadings as male arenas in ways that obscured the richness of New Englanders' involvement in the larger process of debt litigation, both inside and outside of court. On the other hand, the petitions' attention to the mechanics of litigation also meant that they necessarily acknowledged this broader universe of legal activity. Like other common arguments, those concerning attorneys' lapses stipulated that women as well as men could competently participate in debt litigation, in this case by hiring and directing lawyers.

Even as petitions acknowledged that both genders could capably pursue litigation, variant details within broadly similar arguments acknowledged and thus perpetuated several differences between men's and women's economic positions. First, petitions allowed greater geographic mobility to men than to women. When arguing that they deserved new trials because circumstances beyond their control impeded them from attending their hearings, both male and female petitioners cited illness, inclement weather, travel difficulties, and officials' and opponents' failures to notify them of proceedings. Yet some men's petitions offered an additional explanation for their absences, one not cited by women who missed court sessions—namely, that men's economic pursuits took them away from home, and thus they had not learned of debt suits against them until after the court sessions had ended. One leading Newport merchant petitioned for a new trial in 1747 because the initial proceedings occurred "whilst he was absent & out of the Government," preventing him from defending himself "as he could have done provided he had been present & had early notice of s[ai]d actions."[63] Another insisted in 1768 that he missed his court date when he was "not able to leave his business" because he had "a vessel of great consequence" concurrently arriving in another port.[64] Other men repeated variations on the argument that they faced "urgent business" or explained that the proceedings against them had unfolded while they were "absent on a fishing voyage," "in his majesty's service," or "obliged to take a voyage to sea."[65] Reflecting the movements of Boston's and Newport's sizeable populations of merchants, ship captains, and sailors, such petitions coded "business" and overseas travel as masculine activities.

Married women's petitions concerning lawsuits against their husbands affirmed the routine nature of men's absences. Echoing the language of men's petitions, wives explained that their husbands were "obliged to go to sea" or were "bound to sea" and thus had not been able to defend themselves against creditors' lawsuits.[66] Some of these female petitioners sought re-hearings in which they would respond in their husbands' names. Such requests implied that procedural irregularities, not the women's inability to act for their husbands, yielded the cases' initial outcomes.[67] Other married women asked the assemblies to grant re-hearings that would take place after their husbands had returned. In 1769, Lydia Manchester explained that a creditor sued her husband after he had left Rhode Island to captain a ship. Insisting that the creditor must have made "some very great Mistake," which she was "not able to demonstrate wherein," she noted that her husband was expected home by spring at the latest. At that point, "the whole Affair may be settled without Prejudice to either Party."[68] Women's social standings and the complexity of their husbands' affairs did not necessarily correlate with the approaches pursued in their petitions. For example, although Lydia Manchester sought to divest herself from a complicated suit concerning her husband's partial ownership of a vessel, other ship captains' wives insisted on their ability to represent their husbands in equally sophisticated cases concerning commercial credit.[69]

As they narrated men's absences from court, petitioners established routines and legal protections surrounding men's business travels. In their efforts to prove that the male defendants in question were not negligent, petitions by husbands and their wives established standard tactics that seafarers might undertake prior to their departures. These included attempting to settle with known creditors or hiring attorneys for pending lawsuits.[70] Such divergences reflected gender differences in the scales of movement that occurred during routine economic activities, and the petitioning process itself reinforced these patterns. If men's pre-travel precautions failed—if a creditor reneged on a verbal promise not to sue, if a new creditor emerged, or if an attorney missed a court date—the petitioning process offered an additional layer of protection. Each time that legislators granted re-hearings for mariners or merchants who spent time "at sea," they affirmed the economic importance of such activities and gave license to men's overseas travel, a crucial facet of economic life in port cities.

Petitions also established that female administrators faced heightened but ultimately surmountable difficulties in gaining control of written evidence. In their most common form, petitions concerning unavailable evidence explained that the court had overlooked crucial documents or witness testimony, or that new witnesses or papers had subsequently "appeared" or been "discovered."[71] A 1752 petition by Samuel Boone was representative of this category of appeal. Having lost a case concerning book debt, Boone noted that he was now "able by good witnesses to prove that he tendered the full sum due," and that he "found some new evidence" to support his claims. He offered no explanation, however, for why he previously lacked such witnesses and materials.[72] Whereas men claimed to have located additional evidence in cases where they were litigants in their own right or were administrators of estates, all of the women who did so were estate administrators. Such narratives by female petitioners were more descriptive than those by male petitioners, but they were nonetheless standardized. Female administrators explained that they had recently assumed control of their late husbands' affairs, and thus they had only just located documentation that was relevant to their cases.

Two widows and estate administrators, Martha Hart of Newport and Sarah Staniford of Boston, were among those who initially did not prevail in cases launched by creditors, because they lacked key financial documents. In 1749, Hart lost by default in a lawsuit brought by Providence cooper Caleb Potter, who alleged that Hart's late husband, a mariner, had never delivered a barrel of tallow. She consulted an attorney, but without the requisite evidence, the lawyer did not even try to refute Potter's claim. Only later, when Hart had located several receipts, did she challenge Potter's demands and petition for a re-hearing.[73] Boston widow and administrator Sarah Staniford faced similar difficulties when John Calef demanded a debt supposedly owed by her husband's estate. When Calef first called on the widow to settle the account, she could not find the records that disproved his claims. Calef then sued Staniford and won. Later, when she had more thoroughly examined her husband's accounts, she found that

Calef owed a debt to the estate, so she sought a new trial.[74] Without their husbands' receipts and accounts, Hart and Staniford could not definitively refute the creditors' claims themselves, nor could they properly direct their attorneys' activities or challenge the creditors' demands in court.

Female estate administrators, including Martha Hart and Sarah Staniford, emphasized their temporary unfamiliarity with their husbands' transactions. According to Hart's petition, Potter sued her "soon after [she] had taken administrat[io]n," when she remained "unacquainted with the affairs of the deceased." Staniford likewise "never knew" about the accounts in question prior to her husband's death. Calef called on her when the matter was "new, and she unacquainted with the affair." Both widows then suggested that they had surmounted their early difficulties. Hart claimed that she "found satisfactory proof that the demand of the said Potter is altogether wrong." Staniford had simply needed "a little time to look into the accounts among [my] husband's papers." Once she did so, she could convincingly prove that Calef was "not intitled" to his lawsuit, and actually was a net debtor to the estate. In keeping with the parameters for obtaining new trials, Hart and Staniford depicted their ignorance as a short-lived state, rather than as a product of innate female capabilities. Explaining what the specific records had enabled them to prove, Hart's and Staniford's petitions proclaimed their ability to interpret financial documents and realize the ensuing legal implications. The Rhode Island and Massachusetts legislators granted both petitioners' requests.[75]

Female administrators' narratives about discovering revelatory documents were both descriptive and prescriptive. Estate administration required rapidly mastering the deceased individual's affairs. Within an economy and a legal system that privileged written documentation, this required orienting oneself within often-voluminous bodies of financial records. This task became all the more daunting when the administrators' everyday practices did not involve the same spaces, records, or business associates as those of the deceased. One group that was especially prone to such challenges was composed of widow-administrators whose husbands had engaged in commercial transactions or overseas travel. Ann Maylem's struggles surrounding the distillery reflected such obstacles. Another Newport widow, Phebe Battey, experienced similar impediments. In 1753, William Battey, a ship captain, died off the coast of Surinam, aboard the *Charming Abigail*. Battey's shipboard death inserted his wife into far-flung networks and distant affairs. As the administrator of William's estate, Phebe struggled to gain control of his financial papers. While the ship was still at sea, the first mate of the *Charming Abigail* assumed custody of a day book and ledger previously maintained by the late captain. Following the sloop's return to Newport, Phebe Battey sued the first mate for refusing to return the crucial volumes, which she claimed contained her late husband's personal records, rather than those of the voyage.[76] Lawsuits like Phebe Battey's, which high-lighted widows' difficulties accessing their late husbands' records, lent plausi-bility female petitioners' arguments concerning newly located evidence.

Petitions, however, collectively overstated the extent to which mastery of the relevant records was a challenge specific to and common among women. As we have seen, countless other examples suggest wives' involvement in producing and safeguarding the records of family businesses, including for commercial transac-tions that we might assume were the exclusive domain of men. Petitions' insistence on the widow-administrators' sudden "finding" of relevant papers obscured these broader documentary practices. In addition, rifling through unfamiliar document boxes and paging through unknown account books were tasks completed by all administrators, not just widows. In some cases, women possessed greater familiar-ity with their late husbands' affairs than did men administering other men's es-tates. By attaching the difficulties of estate administration only to widows, peti-tions elided the complexities of everyday life, overstating the divergence between men's and women's initial capabilities as administrators. As legislators granted widow-administrators' requests for new trials, their decisions reinforced the cultural power of this narrative. Favorable outcomes encouraged other female petitioners to present their experiences within this same framework of initial ignorance and subsequent mastery.[77]

Among the five standard arguments found in petitions, one of them—litigants' unfamiliarity with the law—fit uneasily within equity and common law principles. While the Massachusetts and Rhode Island legislatures were just as likely to grant petitions based on this argument as those advancing other ones, petitioners who mobilized this particular narrative needed to carefully position themselves to deflect charges of negligence.[78] Men were very reluctant to claim that they deserved new trials because they were unfamiliar with the law. This position was not popular among women, either (table 5.1). Although the num-bers are too small to make a definitive judgment about whether women were more prone to use this argument than men, the different uses petitioners made of it forged tentative links between masculinity and competency. This subset of requests for new trials thus sat in tension with most other petitions and belied the heterosocial nature of everyday financial practices.

Women's petitions concerning their unfamiliarity with the law insisted that their gender led to a general lack of legal knowledge. In 1755 and 1765, Anne Clarke explained that she was sued for a debt owed by a bond, and that, "being a woman and ignorant of the laws in such case," she "suffered the said action to go by default." Such gendered statements of ignorance also appeared in women's petitions for retrials in other kinds of suits. Ann Carr explained in 1750 that she lost a case concerning a servant's employment because she was "a woman totally ignorant of the Law Business." In 1754, Hannah Curtis recounted that, "being a woman" and "being ignorant of the law," she did not appeal her conviction for theft. Such petitions, presenting female litigants as unfamiliar with the law in general, rather than with its specific provisions, reveal a tension between the vocabularies accessible to the documents' creators and the realities of women's daily lives in communities suffused by credit transactions and litigation.[79]

Men framed their ignorance of the law much more narrowly than women. Three-quarters of male petitioners citing this argument explained that they were unfamiliar with specific laws, often because they had recently arrived in Massachusetts or Rhode Island, or because the statutes were new. Men explained that they were "altogether ignorant of the law of this Colony that enjoins all persons who are sued to file their answer six days before the sitting of [the] Court," or that they were "not knowing of a late law . . . requiring the adverse party to be notified" before a litigant swore to the accuracy of his books. Others described not residing "so long in this Province as to have heard of the law" or "residing in another colony," therefore being "a stranger to the method and proceedings of the courts of [Massachusetts]." By casting their ignorance as temporary or limited in scope, these petitioners suggested that such circumstances did not reflect badly on their manly virtue and competence.[80]

Only a few men professed ignorance of the law in the broad terms sometimes found in women's petitions. All cited their poverty, their youth, or their status as men of color. One lost because he was "an ignorant mollatto also being poor." Others were "a sailor & wholly unacquainted with the law," and "an infant and ignorant in what manner to conduct himself." Such arguments were analogous to female petitioners' claims of ignorance by virtue of "being a woman." These male petitioners rested their lack of specific knowledge on their status. Their marginal social status meant that they did not possess standard forms of masculine competence.[81]

Respondents almost always protested that men's arguments concerning ignorance of the law were invalid. In 1747, Bostonian John Fairservice railed against his male opponent's claim that he deserved a new trial because he was "wholly ignorant" of a relevant law. Citing the legal standard for obtaining new trials, Fairservice countered that "maxims not disputed" held that "every man is presumed to know the laws especially where he is immediately concerned." If his opponent "was ignorant[,] he should have taken measures to be informed." While the legislature ultimately granted the male petitioner's request for a new trial, Fairservice's response suggested that true men had no excuse for ignorance, and that gaps in their knowledge marked them as incompetent and unmanly.[82]

During the 1740s, the decade in which Ann Maylem repeatedly appealed to the Rhode Island General Assembly, that legislative body also heard forty-four other petitions concerning debt cases. Those by Maylem, as we can now see, diverged from all of these other requests for new trials. Even though Maylem's difficulties concerned the bond of defeasance, they did not fit within the simplistic narratives of female administrators who acquired new, valuable evidence that undermined prior court outcomes. Whereas most petitions articulated concise reasons for the litigants' prior losses, all four of Maylem's petitions offered sprawling chronicles of her struggles surrounding the distillery. Rather than seeking a re-hearing for a specific case, Maylem's first petition vaguely pled for "some remedy," so Maylem might be "let into the law in order to recover what has been so unjustly detained." It referenced none of the five most common narratives advanced in other petitions about debt litigation.[83] Maylem's second petition contained a variation on the genre's standard discussion of attorneys. Whereas such narratives typically foregrounded that a lawyer had inadvertently lost track of an individual case, or that uncontrollable events had prevented him from attending court, Maylem's petition merely mentioned in passing that an attorney "withdrew" her first case against George Gardner, "but for what reason she cannot tell." Undermining its own effort to attribute an otherwise-competent litigant's difficulties to her attorney's actions, the petition then noted that Maylem had sued Gardner anew using a different attorney, and that the court had dismissed that case, too.[84]

Maylem's third and fourth petitions incorporated a variation on the common argument that the court had made an incorrect judgment. They complained that Maylem had lost her cases against Jonathan Diman because the court had allowed Gardner to testify, even though he was "notoriously interested" in the suits. Appreciating Maylem's claims, however, required in-depth engagement with the dispute surrounding the distillery, a matter that was much less straightforward than typical justifications for new trials.[85] Because Maylem publicly battled Gardner and Diman for many years, Rhode Island officials' outside knowledge of her affairs may well have contributed to their refusal to grant her requests. Nonetheless, her petitions' failure to conform to standard, straightforward narratives undoubtedly hampered her cause.

In the long run, Ann Maylem's inability to obtain redress against Gardner and Diman limited her family's living standard and diminished her children's inheritance.[86] She entered into a variety of living arrangements in attempts to make ends meet. At one point, she took in a tenant for several months. Another time, she rented a room from a male relative. She also obtained formal appointments as the guardian of her children and, later, her grandson. These posts allowed her to claim compensation for the care of her offspring.[87] In the 1760s, Maylem entered a second protracted legal battle, this time with two of her nephews, in attempts to claim her late sister's estate. Her limited financial means probably intensified her determination to claim the property at issue.[88]

Ann Maylem's saga illustrates that petitions offered an incomplete remedy within colonial New England's legal system, one that increasingly favored creditors. In the course of her dispute with Gardner and Diman, Maylem displayed her legal savvy in countless ways, including through the publication of her broadside, her dogged pursuit of her opponents within the legal system, and her hiring of and extensive correspondence with lawyers. Given her demonstrated knowledge and her partnerships with lawyers, ignorance and naivete cannot explain her petitions' departures from standard narratives. Instead, John Maylem's tangled finances and the complexities of his widow's subsequent conflicts were a poor match for the most common arguments in petitions. Although petitioning provided relief for some debtors, it could not accommodate more complex circumstances, such as those of Ann Maylem.

At the same time as legislators' handing of petitions mattered for individual women and men, such decisions also carried broader cultural consequences. Throughout the petitioning process, laypeople, attorneys, and legislators collectively evaluated when debtors deserved re-hearings, and, by extension, what skills laymen and -women could reasonably be expected to possess. Men's and women's requests for re-hearings, drafted with an awareness of the legal framework concerning new trials, overwhelmingly attributed losses to specific events, rather than to generalized impediments. Such imperatives to highlight litigants' attentiveness and delineate narrow explanations for defeats meant that colonial petitions acknowledged laypeople's general competence in financial matters and debt litigation. At the same time, however, these documents reinforced certain gendered divisions of labor. They elevated the importance of male attorneys' services, sanctioned men's travels for business matters, and recognized the unique difficulties faced by female administrators.

Conclusion

By the mid-eighteenth century, New Englanders had adapted their court system in response to the proliferation and quickening pace of credit transactions. The courts, no longer evaluating cases based solely on their individual particularities, rapidly dispensed with uncontested cases and those in which one party had deviated from legal technicalities. In this way, the courts enabled large numbers of creditors to register and enforce debts they were owed in the absence of other institutional means of doing so. But this efficiency had negative consequences for debtors. One inopportune event—an unexpected spring snowstorm, a bout of the flu, a receipt separated from its case file—could lead the court to swiftly rule in a creditor's favor. In addition, the legal system made minimal allowances for insolvency. This was particularly problematic for widows such as Ann Maylem, whose future comfort and livelihood hinged on the same assets eyed by their late husbands' creditors.

Within this context, petitions to the Massachusetts General Court and the Rhode Island General Assembly offered partial remedies. Litigants, whether male or female, who had initially lost their debt suits could obtain re-hearings in the lower courts. Legislators used equity law to assess petitions for new trials, and this encouraged those submitting them to cite specific reasons for their defeats. The petitions' genre conventions and legal frameworks flattened their content, leading most most of those concerned to offer variations on stock explanations for their defeats. For those litigants who could narrate their experiences in accordance with the standard grounds for a new trial, petitions had precisely their desired intent: slowing or halting debt collection within a system that favored creditors. Yet, unlike other kinds of petitions, these requests for new trials did not facilitate collective action. The individualistic and stylized nature of petitions concerning debt litigation deflected attention away from structural problems of indebtedness, including for widows.

Because colonial legislatures heard requests for new trials at each legislative session, and because petitioners included women as well as men, this form of legal activity crystallized cultural understandings of laypeople's capabilities. Successful petitions insisted that, aside from specific and enumerated obstacles, free men and women alike were savvy users of credit who possessed the requisite knowledge to win their lawsuits. In contrast, in the rare circumstances in which women, such as Ann Maylem, advanced sprawling gendered arguments of being imperiled widows persecuted by men, legislators declined to grant re-hearings. Shaped by the framework of equity law, petitioners' strategies and legislators' decisions molded cultural understandings of masculinity and femininity. Far from reifying essentialist notions of gender, petitions reinforced the expectation that free adults could—and should—competently engage with credit. Yet this emphasis on men's and women's parallel responsibilities also had significant limits, as, over time, petitions legitimated men's long-distance business pursuits and the all-male legal profession's centrality to litigation.

As women and men petitioned for new trials, they generated a rich archive that, for historians, illuminates everyday practices surrounding financial settlements and litigation. By pinpointing reasons for litigants' defeats, petitions disaggregate settlements and debt litigation into their separate components, highlighting tasks that other laypeople completed successfully. Ann Maylem's complaint that her attorney withdrew a lawsuit against Gardner, for example, suggests that female litigants needed to maintain good communication with their lawyers. Petitions concerning the illnesses of Deborah Johnson and Bethiah Hedge highlight the importance of women's own attendance at court sessions. Martha Hart's and Sarah Staniford's narratives concerning recently discovered documents underscore that mastering relevant records was vital when disputing creditors' claims. Commonalities between women's and men's petitions, moreover, remind us that these fundamental skills were the same ones that the economy and the legal system demanded of its male participants. Through mastery of written records, familiarity with legal procedure, and collaborations with attorneys, either women or men could gain the upper hand in disputes surrounding credit.

Finally, while much can be gleaned by analyzing petitions alone, for eighteenth-century litigants, such requests for new trials always functioned within a larger legal strategy. A petitioner's goal could be as straightforward as delaying payment of a single debt. It could also be as complex as that of Ann Maylem, who moved between the worlds of print, manuscript, the courts, and legislative sessions in attempts protect her family's assets, especially the distillery, from creditors' claims. As free white women, including Maylem, navigated these arenas, they necessarily presented themselves in different ways, whether in attempts to elicit fellow residents' sympathy, solidify alliances, or obtain victory at law. While women's efforts to collaborate with others and fashion compelling narratives are particularly visible in petitions, strategic choices undergirded their divergent self-presentations across all of the forums in which they transacted business and litigated disputes. Female petitioners displayed their savvy within a system that made limited allowances based on either gender or indebtedness, and their protests bespeak the skill of countless other women who never had to avail themselves of the genre.

CHAPTER 6

"According to your judgments"

Redefining Financial Work
in the Late Eighteenth Century

In 1765, Boston and Newport residents organized in opposition to the Stamp Act as the imperial crisis escalated. By the time the Continental Congress issued the Declaration of Independence eleven years later, city dwellers had confronted countless alterations to everyday economic life.[1] The British army's occupations of Boston and Newport led many residents to flee; shortages of goods and a volatile monetary system disrupted routine exchanges for those who remained in the cities; and the county courts, long a key institution of debt collection, temporarily closed their doors. Following the Revolution, residents of Boston and Newport began reconstituting their credit networks and resuming the associated financial and legal practices. As vital contributors to colonial port economies and as the majority of both cities' free adult populations before and after the war, women were among those forced to respond to the upheaval of the Revolution.

We are accustomed to thinking about the Revolutionary era as occasioning both short-term consequences and lasting shifts for women. During the war itself, Patriot, Loyalist, African American, and Native women all confronted distinctive opportunities and challenges as they sought to protect their families, households, and property during an era characterized by violence and shifting political paradigms.[2] Throughout the late eighteenth and early nineteenth centuries, elite and middling Americans gradually reshaped gendered cultural understandings of politics, work, and the household. Emerging notions of republican motherhood and partisanship located women's political influence within their families, rather than through direct participation in formal institutions, while definitions of productive labor narrowed to encompass only market-oriented and cash-earning activities undertaken by men.[3]

While we know a great deal about the changing status of women during and after the Revolution, we understand much less about how women's involvement in credit transactions and debt litigation—central realms of economic and legal life—transformed during this same period. This chapter uses two approaches to investigate the extent to which gendered financial and legal practices evolved during the Revolutionary era. First, continuing to examine women's everyday financial labors reveals both persistence and change during and following the war. Second, interrogating elites' handling of complex financial matters sheds light on shifting understandings of gendered divisions of financial and legal labor.

Just as the Revolution disrupted countless other aspects of women's lives and required them and their families to act strategically in response to new exigencies, so, too, did the war temporarily strain practices surrounding credit and debt, which relied heavily on women's labor. The British occupation of Boston and Newport, financial instability, the closure of the courts, and the separation of family members all complicated creditor-debtor relationships. Both in Boston and Newport, as well as in the surrounding towns to which many former city dwellers scattered, women redoubled their reliance on skills cultivated during the colonial period, including exercising financial savvy outside of court and coordinating with the members of one's household or family. Such wartime disruptions were short lived. Following the return of peace to New England, Boston and Newport residents resumed their prior patterns of financial and legal activity. Free women, both in their own right and as members of households, once again negotiated with creditors and debtors, navigated the courts, hired and supervised attorneys, and served as witnesses for legally binding credit transactions.

From the 1760s to the 1790s, elites in Boston and Newport and beyond also drove a reevaluation of gendered divisions of labor in ways that would have lasting cultural consequences. It is often suggested that the notions of class and gentility that crystalized during the second half of the eighteenth century led elite women to withdraw themselves from the technicalities and controversies of legal activity, yet we lack a fine-grained analysis of this transition.[4] Close readings of three families' correspondence suggest that, as of the 1780s, elite women's relationships to finance and the law remained situational and were shot with contradictions. As prominent families collaborated with lawyers and other agents regarding long-distance affairs, they at times cast such women, especially widows, as being entitled to remove themselves from financial and legal concerns. In so doing, they asserted the beginnings of a gendered class identity stipulating that professional men would oversee and protect the interests of female elites. Standing in contrast to lower-class and middling women's continued involvement in urban borrowing and lending, genteel women's supposed retreat from finance signaled their class as well as their gender privileges. At the same time, their practices in many ways resembled those of their colonial predecessors. Portrayals of elite femininity were largely strategic, allowing men and women alike to secure attorneys' and other professional agents' assistance in gender- and class-appropriate ways. Yet high-status women themselves continued to engage in the skilled and opinionated monitoring of their affairs in ways that defied their supposed reliance on male agents.

Wartime Disruptions and Postwar Continuities

Boston, Newport, and the surrounding New England communities experienced economic as well as political upheaval during the Revolutionary era. Following the Seven Years' War, Boston and Newport residents organized in opposition to imperial policies, and the metropolitan government targeted both cities in efforts to subdue this mounting colonial protest. The British quartered troops in Boston from 1768 onward, and they formally occupied the city and closed its port between 1774 and 1776. Newport, meanwhile, experienced a British naval blockade in the summer and fall of 1775, and the British army occupied that city and garrisoned troops there from 1776 to 1779.[5] These shocks disrupted economic life in Boston and Newport and led many urbanites, both Patriot and Loyalist, to depart their communities. In the cities and their surrounding towns, women were among those who shouldered the brunt of the war's economic challenges. Many *femes sole* lacked the resources to leave their cities, and, in a continuation of colonial women's support of men's maritime labor and military service, wives often assumed responsibility for their households when their husbands left for distant posts. The economic and social disruptions of war proved to be temporary, however. Following the Revolution, woman as well as men again facilitated the workings of credit networks and debt litigation.

The American Revolution dispersed family members, and this was particularly the case in port cities, including Boston and Newport. Throughout North America, Patriot wives remained behind as their husbands took up posts in state militias, the Continental Army, and the fledging American government. Some married women also continued to reside on their families' property as a way to protect it while their Loyalist husbands fled.[6] In Boston and Newport, the blockades and military occupations prompted those who could leave to do so. Thousands of city residents escaped to surrounding towns, where they either joined family or friends or took up rented quarters. Loyalists relocated to other places in the British Empire. Both Boston's and Newport's populations plummeted. Boston fell from a peak of more than 16,000 residents in 1771 to only 2,719 in 1776. More than half of Newport's 11,000 residents left the city.[7]

Gender, social class, and connections all shaped who remained in the cities and who fled. Unmarried women of limited means were among those who had the least ability to leave occupied cities. By 1782, Newport's female majority became even more pronounced than during the colonial period. Adult white women composed 30 percent of Newport's population, whereas just 17.6 percent consisted of adult white men.[8] Those who remained in Boston and Newport confronted disordered urban governments, shortages of food and firewood, limited access to imported goods, and the complicated politics of daily interactions between soldiers and civilians.[9] Sarah Osborn, an informal leader of Newport's evangelical community who was in her sixties at the time of the Revolution, was among the women who struggled economically when she remained in her city. Forced to close the school that she ran for many years, Osborn and her family lacked money for food and firewood. They took refuge in a friend's home in Newport, joining fifteen others who were similarly displaced by the war. In 1778, Osborn's husband died, and her adult children moved to a neighboring town, leaving her alone in Newport. When she died in 1792, the value of her very small estate barely exceeded her debts.[10]

Boston's and Newport's unmarried female entrepreneurs also faced economic challenges as the imperial crisis and the Revolution disrupted their supply and credit chains. As the British blockades limited the flow of imported goods into cities, these shopkeepers' retail stocks dried up. And, to the extent that they did acquire merchandise to sell, boycotts of British items meant that potential customers often declined to buy them. Jane Mecom, Benjamin Franklin's sister, experienced such difficulties firsthand in Boston when she attempted to open a millinery shop in 1767. By the time she had stocked her shop and advertised her business, Bostonians had begun boycotting British goods to protest the Townsend Acts, leading her to lament that "it Proves a Litle unlucky for me that our People have taken it in their Heads to be so Excesive Frugal."[11] The city's newspapers attacked other shopkeepers who continued to sell imported wares, including sisters Anne and Elizabeth Cuming, whom the *Boston Gazette* labeled as "Enemies to their country," and Jane Eustis, who stopped her business in response to such criticism. Elizabeth Murray, long a mentor to other female shopkeepers, struggled to facilitate her younger relatives' continued involvement in retail. Her niece, Anne Murray, ultimately closed her Boston shop during the British occupation in 1774.[12]

Women who ran boardinghouses likewise suffered as their cities' populations decreased. Although some created new opportunities by renting rooms to British soldiers, many others found that their clienteles dwindled. Jane Mecom, a landlady as well as an aspiring milliner, lost an important source of tenants when Massachusetts's royal governor dissolved that colony's assembly in 1768.[13] Mary Almy, another boardinghouse-keeper, described the bleak scene in Newport during the late stages of the British occupation in 1778: "No business going forward; all the shops still kept shut; nothing is to be seen in the streets, but carts and horses and some old worn out-drivers."[14] During the colonial period, female entrepreneurs had found ready customers and clientele among the port cities' cosmopolitan and mobile populations. As Almy's lament suggests, the imperial crisis and the Revolution disrupted the facets of urban economies that had previously facilitated women's business activities.

Middling and elite families responded to the war by redoubling their reliance on the family as an economic unit, and this led wives to continue or even expand their involvement in financial matters. The activities of one elite Boston couple, Susannah and William Palfrey, illustrate these larger trends. Both Susannah and William descended from affluent families, and William was a merchant and business partner of the famed John Hancock. During the Revolution, William left Massachusetts to serve as paymaster general of the Continental Army, while Susannah and their children temporarily relocated to Marlborough, a town in central Massachusetts.[15] Families' social class and economic pursuits shaped the scale and complexity of the transactions in which married women participated, so Susannah assumed an especially wide range of responsibilities in William's absence. She independently forged new credit relationships as she purchased provisions for her family, and, in coordination with William, she conducted in-person negotiations with the family's creditors and debtors. William's mercantile business meant that on many occasions, Susannah collected and delivered large sums of money. She also facilitated William's involvement in complex and costly partnerships for privateering ventures.[16] Just as the spouses of merchants, captains, and mariners managed their households while their husbands were at sea during the colonial period, married women like Susannah Palfrey played a crucial role in stabilizing households and financial relationships during wartime.

As had occurred during the colonial period, such involvements in credit transactions led wives to produce and manage technical financial records. Susannah Palfrey generated receipts and other documents in the course of her financial dealings, and she used formal bookkeeping to track her family's incoming and outgoing monies, as well as to send William reports on their family's finances.[17] She additionally served as the custodian of William's commercial records while he was away, safeguarding some documents per his instructions and forwarding others upon his request. In 1776, William called on Susannah to "send my pocket book to me," but asked her to first remove and store the financial instruments that were kept inside it, including a lottery ticket. On another occasion, William asked Susannah to forward him a loan office certificate, an instrument that was sold by the Continental Congress to fund the war effort and was redeemable at interest. In addition to trusting Susannah to locate this crucial record, he directed her to have the couple's children copy the certificate prior to sending it to him, as well as to supervise them to be sure that they transcribed it correctly. All of these activities were extensions of married women's routine uses of financial documents prior to the Revolution, and such previous experiences enabled them to locate and appropriately handle the records their husbands described in letters.[18]

Regardless of whether women remained in cities or relocated, they confronted disruptions to financial and legal structures. The imperial crisis and the war destabilized the county courts, which had long served as the primary institution through which creditors held their debtors accountable. Between the Stamp Act's passage by the British Parliament in March 1765 and its repeal the following February, controversy surrounding this legislation created uncertainty about whether Massachusetts's and Rhode Island's courts would meet. Legal documents were among those papers subjected to the act's tax, and some argued that the courts should remain closed as a means of abstaining from business involving stamped paper.[19] Both Boston's and Newport's courts shut down for extended periods during and following the British occupation. The Suffolk County Courts closed from September 1774 to 1780, and the Newport County Courts heard no new business between 1777 and 1780.[20]

While the courts were not in session, creditors, including women, were forced to rely more heavily on extralegal methods of debt collection—namely, pressuring their debtors through in-person conversations and letters. The movements of individuals and households during the war complicated such efforts, and some families coordinated in order to confront those who owed them funds during the narrow windows of time in which they returned home from distant posts with money in hand. In 1776, Lieutenant Dudley Colman informed his wife Mary, who remained at the family home in Newbury, that a man indebted to them "is discharged from the Service & gone or going home," so "if you should see him get the money."[21] Even when debtors could be located, some declined to pay, either due to their own financial struggles or because they knew their creditors lacked enforcement mechanisms. In 1774, Abigail Adams explained to her spouse John that she was financially "distressed," because "no person thinks of paying any thing." The following year, Sally Paine likewise reported to her husband, Robert Treat Paine, that "Debts[,] I have not been able to collect any worth mentioning."[22] As Adams's complaint suggests, women on the home front experienced such difficulties in collecting debts particularly acutely, as they relied in part on such payments to keep their households afloat.

The financial instabilities of war further tested women's economic strategies. Colonial New Englanders were accustomed to multiple circulating currencies that fluctuated in value, and this monetary landscape became increasingly complex and volatile during the Revolution. At first the Continental Congress and the states, including Massachusetts and Rhode Island, printed large quantities of paper money to finance the war effort. This currency quickly became devalued, and subsequent legislative efforts to curtail inflation were ineffective.[23] The federal and state governments also began issuing bonds in attempts to generate additional revenue. Women, most notably Abigail Adams, were among those who speculated in these instruments, in attempts to turn a profit.[24]

This disordered financial system inserted new considerations into negotiations between debtors and creditors. As women had done prior to independence, they tracked fluctuating currency and bond values and evaluated barter as an alternative to cash-based exchanges. Despite laws establishing state currencies as legal tenders, some creditors declined to accept devalued paper money. Widow Rebecca Baldwin of Weston, Massachusetts, confronted this situation in 1779. As the administrator of her late husband's estate, Baldwin visited a male creditor to pay him a debt owed by bond. As Baldwin later recalled, she "beg'd" the creditor to "receive his pay in such as I had." but, refusing to accept devalued paper money, he insisted he "would have none but silver or gold." Female creditors, on the other hand, evaluated debtors' offers of payment. To the extent that they collected such debts, they received sums that were considerably diminished in value.[25]

Uncontrolled inflation and fluctuating prices also compounded women's difficulties as consumers and as participants in businesses, roles that likewise included borrowing and lending. The costs of food and labor rose dramatically, leading Sally Paine to complain in 1776 that one would "need to have a wagon Load of money" to purchase provisions for the winter. As managers of households, Paine and others carefully tracked shifting currency values and prices, attempting to exchange currencies when rates were favorable and purchase provisions when prices were low. As shopkeepers and participants in family businesses, women also applied similar strategies in choosing when to purchase and sell retail goods. Mary Colman, for example, continued to run her family's shop during her husband's army service. She sold certain goods promptly, while stockpiling others for which prices were likely to rise.[26] While participation in commerce and credit transactions always required a careful monitoring of market conditions, the need to do so became even more pressing amid the economic volatility of the Revolution.

As combat shifted to southern theaters and the United States and Britain negotiated their settlement, New Englanders reconstructed their communities, economies, and legal systems. While we are often accustomed to thinking of the

Revolution as a starting or ending point, American independence did not occasion dramatic shifts in the everyday practices surrounding credit. Instead, Newport's and Boston's populations began to rebuild, slowly at first and then more rapidly in Boston. As late as 1800, the city of Newport had fewer than 7,000 residents, a significant decrease from its pre-war high of over 9,000. In 1780, Boston had 10,000 residents, only two-thirds of its pre-war population. That city's inhabitants then numbered a new high of 18,000 in 1790 and continued to multiply during subsequent decades.[27] When the Suffolk and Newport courts reopened in 1780, each body initially received a trickle of new lawsuits. As the decade progressed, caseloads gradually rebounded to pre-war court levels, and neither received a massive influx of cases concerning debts from the 1770s. This suggests that New Englanders had settled some of their wartime debts outside of court, and that creditors viewed others as unenforceable, given that so much time had passed and so many people had moved away during the Revolution.[28]

Throughout the 1780s and into the 1790s, Boston and Newport women resumed their involvement in the gendered political economies of their cities and regions, continuing to use credit regularly as entrepreneurs, borrowers, and lenders. As they had prior to the Revolution, female shopkeepers sold goods to customers on credit and entered their purchases into accounts. For instance, from 1785 to 1786, Newport widow Susannah Mumford sold various goods—including fabric, thread, gloves, and lavender—to Jonathan Banister and charged his purchases to an account. One decade later, Newport resident Jabez Champlin visited widow Elizabeth Miller's shop every few months to buy tea, sugar, rum, and wine. Miller entered these numerous small purchases into an account that totaled £6.7.[29] Landladies, such as Bostonian Mary Lobb, likewise persisted in providing housing to tenants and tracking the resulting financial relationships. She rented a room to another Boston woman, Bulah Edes, on credit for several months in 1789. Lobb accepted a combination of cash and labor from Edes as rent. On days when the pair settled their accounts, Lobb provided signed receipts to Edes as proof of payment.[30] Still others used bonds and promissory notes to provide loans to others in their community, or, as the example of Bulah Edes suggests, accessed credit in order to purchase necessary goods and services.[31] As was the case during the colonial period, entering into such credit relationships required women to skillfully negotiate the terms of loans and proposed settlements, as well as to handle and interpret the records associated with their transactions.

Wives' labor also remained vital in establishing and maintaining credit relationships, with Boston and Newport residents accepting the involvement of *femes covert* in financial transactions even as they produced records that, on first glance, obscured such activities. In 1783, for instance, Newport laborer Gideon Hoxie sued a Newport shipwright for failing to pay him for his work in constructing a vessel. Yet, as witness testimonies made clear, Hoxie's agreement was not with the male defendant named in the lawsuit, but rather with a woman identified in the records only as Mrs. Chapin, the wife of Seth Chapin. (He was another ship-builder overseeing the project.) Mrs. Chapin went to the residences of Hoxie and another male laborer, Daniel Watts, in attempts to hire them. Hoxie and Watts were not at their homes when Mrs. Chapin called, so they visited the Chapin residence later. There, the shipbuilder's wife and the two men haggled over appropriate compensation, ultimately agreeing that Hoxie and Watts would each receive eight shillings per day. Moreover, Mrs. Chapin was not the only woman who took part in this arrangement. When she went to the Watts residence, she spoke with the wife of Daniel Watts, who relayed the proposed labor agreement to her husband. Even shipbuilding, an industry requiring extensive capital and labor, remained tied to household-based systems of labor and credit, and wives were among those who facilitated crucial financial agreements.[32]

Women also continued to navigate the courts in order to collect debts and rebut creditors' claims. By the early 1790s, when both the Newport and Suffolk courts had resumed their normal business, women were parties in approximately the same percentage of suits as during the late colonial period. As we have seen, between 1730 and the Revolution, female litigants took part in roughly 12 percent of the debt suits in Newport County and 9 percent of those in Suffolk County. During sampled terms from the early 1790s, 19 percent of the debt cases in Newport County and 11 percent of those in Suffolk County named female litigants.[33] Similar to the colonial period, such litigants included married women appearing alongside their husbands, widows serving as administrators and executors, and *femes sole* acting as litigants in their own right. We know about the business activities of female entrepreneurs, including shopkeepers Susannah Mumford and Elizabeth Miller and landlady Mary Lobb, because they later took part in lawsuits concerning their transactions.

For both the late eighteenth century and the colonial period, attending to the component practices of litigation reveals additional evidence of legal activity by women, especially wives. In the 1780s and 1790s, they actively followed their cases through the courts and supervised the legal professionals whom they hired for assistance. The efforts of Mary Whipple, for instance, closely resemble those of sailors' and ship captains' wives who took care of their families' legal affairs during the colonial period. In 1785, Whipple's husband, a captain, left Rhode Island on a voyage to the West Indies. When a creditor initiated a lawsuit against him during his absence, Mary Whipple responded to the suit. Knowing that, as she later explained, there was "nothing due" from her husband to the litigating creditor, Whipple "consulted some friends" to plot her next steps. Based on their advice, she hired a lawyer to file an answer in the case. When the lawyer did not do so on time, and Whipple lost the case by default, she petitioned for a new trial. In that request, which the Rhode Island General Assembly granted, Whipple asked to "have a day in court" so she could "abundantly make it appear" that her husband owed nothing to the supposed creditor. At every stage of the affair, Whipple, like her colonial predecessors, skillfully drew on networks of legal knowledge, including both other laypeople and professional attorneys, in order to protect her family's assets.[34]

As the county courts resumed their operation, the renewed relationship between everyday practices and debt litigation again led women to assume legally consequential roles as witnesses. For example, in the dispute concerning the Newport shipbuilders' hiring of laborers Gideon Hoxie and Daniel Watts, Elizabeth Dunham was the only witness present at the Chapin residence to overhear the crucial conversation concerning the laborers' wages. When the matter advanced to the court, Dunham, who signed her deposition with her mark, recounted the negotiations with precision. She recalled that Hoxie and Watts requested wages of eight shillings per day. She then added that Mrs. Chapin responded by saying she "did not think" the rate would cause "any difficulty," while the other shipbuilder found the wages to be too high and declared that he would have "nothing to do with" paying the laborers.[35] Dunham's testimony was part of a larger pattern of continued female involvement in financial transactions as witnesses. During the 1780s and 1790s, women continued to compose between 4 and 11 percent of the signatories on financial documents and the witnesses in debt cases in Newport and Suffolk Counties.[36] Similar to the colonial period, such small but significant percentages bespoke broader patterns of financial activity. The heterosocial nature of everyday transactions and negotiations, especially those occurring within households, continued to facilitate women's power as witnesses.

Overall, the Revolution temporarily altered financial and legal practices in Boston and Newport, leading all New Englanders to redeploy skills and strategies cultivated during the colonial period in response to new challenges. Following the war, urban residents gradually returned to their prior patterns of financial and legal activity, including the regular use of personal credit and frequent recourse to the courts to enforce obligations. As they did so, women once again helped drive the dynamic world of intrapersonal negotiations outside of court as borrowers and lenders, skillfully initiated and responded to lawsuits as plaintiffs and defendants, and ratified transactions and intervened in disputes as witnesses. While the Revolution brought about dramatic political change, the family and household structures and demographic realities that undergirded urban women's financial and legal activities persisted during the early decades of the newly formed United States.

Making Financial Work Masculine

During the same decades in which all Boston and Newport residents responded to the temporary upheavals of the imperial crisis and war, elites in these cities and beyond reappraised gendered divisions of financial and legal labor. Acting in ways that both served short-term strategic imperatives and had lasting cultural consequences, wealthy families at times cast professional men as uniquely equipped to engage in large, complex financial matters and associated legal disputes. Within this framework, elite women's withdrawal from such technical, controversial affairs arose from their limited knowledge and signaled their class and gender privilege. Spanning both sides of the Revolution, such viewpoints were seemingly precursors to nineteenth-century notions of feminine domesticity that viewed women's rightful place as in the home rather than in the commercial marketplace.[37] As of the late eighteenth century, however, the supposed distancing of elite women from finance and the law sat uneasily with their continued assertions of well-developed financial knowledge and opinions.

Attending to the tensions inherent in these women's relationship to finance requires shifting our focus from court records to the sustained correspondence of specific families. Because elites and their agents relied heavily on letters to coordinate their activities, these sources offer an ideal window into gendered divisions of responsibility. Furthermore, as an arena for self-fashioning and a forum through which writers attached social and cultural meanings to women's and men's tasks, correspondence itself served as an instrument of change.[38] In order to look closely at how correspondents shaped gendered understandings of financial labor, this section moves chronologically through the affairs of three women, each of whom was the author, subject, and recipient of numerous letters over an extended time period. From 1750 to the mid-1780s, Elizabeth Fletcher and her husband William worked both jointly and separately to protect their assets from creditors. Widow Hannah Laycock endeavored to settle her deceased husband's affairs during the late 1760s and early 1770s. Another widow, Martha Stevens, managed land and its associated credit relationships from 1776 to 1785. While a significant component of each story unfolded in Boston or Newport, the financial concerns of the Fletcher, Stevens, and Laycock families also encompassed other places, including Britain, the Caribbean, and additional North American ports and inland towns. Extending beyond any single locale, the intertwined processes of class differentiation and changing gender norms that are exemplified in these case studies occurred throughout British North America and the Atlantic World.

Elizabeth Fletcher, Hannah Laycock, and Martha Stevens all engaged in complex commercial matters that differed from the everyday financial practices of other eighteenth-century white women, including most of those discussed thus far in this book. Whereas we have largely seen women adeptly engaging in local and regional transactions that were crucial building blocks of the broader Atlantic economy, the distant business connections of the Fletcher, Laycock, and Stevens families reflect two intertwined trends in the late eighteenth century: increasingly dense webs of Atlantic commerce, and improved communication networks that enabled distant associates to more extensively coordinate their activities through correspondence.[39] In addition, as these three women faced legal quagmires concerning very large sums and considerable amounts of property, their affairs engaged key issues of political economy that remained unsettled during the 1750s through the 1780s, including institutional remedies for insolvency and the relationship between land ownership, credit, and taxation.[40] Such long-distance, tangled concerns led Elizabeth Fletcher, Hannah Laycock, and Martha Stevens to partner with lawyers and agents more extensively than did women engaged in straightforward local debt suits.

As laypeople and lawyers began to reshape understandings of elite masculinity and femininity, they grappled with related questions concerning the nature of the attorney-client bond and its gendered dimensions. Beginning in the 1760s, the development of New England's legal profession accelerated as more men became lawyers and joined bar associations. As attorneys built up the overall size of their practices, they simultaneously sought to insinuate themselves into the social and business circles of those mercantile elites whose dealings yielded the most protracted cases.[41] Meanwhile, laypeople like Elizabeth and William Fletcher, Hannah Laycock, and Martha Stevens sought to secure attorneys' attentive services while acting in ways that were consistent with their gender identities. Lawyers and elites jointly grappled with the extent to which attorney-client relationships were professional, transactional ones, or, like most eighteenth-century commercial connections, remained rooted in bonds of personal trust and friendship. Elites' and their agents' use of the "familiar letter," a genre that encouraged a combination of pragmatic details and affective language, intensified such ambiguities. Familiar letters connected distant "friends," and in eighteenth-century parlance this term could refer to either egalitarian or hierarchical relationships.[42] With this vocabulary of friendship, letter writers alternately downplayed or emphasized the use of attorneys in ways that were deeply gendered. An elite woman's reliance on a lawyer seemingly comported with gendered social hierarchies, whereas men sought to avoid such dependence and its associated connotations of effeminacy.

In 1755, William Fletcher fled his hometown of Boston, attempting to escape financial disgrace. This set off a multidirectional correspondence between himself, his wife Elizabeth, and two attorneys that continued until 1789. William Fletcher, a prominent member of Boston's commercial elite, was a merchant engaged in the shipping trade to the Caribbean and a member of the Massachusetts legislature. By the early 1750s, as Boston's economic depression worsened, he ran his business into debt. Fletcher hoped to recoup his losses, but the city's economic troubles consistently thwarted his efforts. Conflict and currency short-ages disrupted commercial networks during the Seven Years' War, and high rates of failure persisted afterward, due to the postwar economic downturn and the disruption of port economies during the imperial crisis and Revolution. The absence of permanent bankruptcy laws also prevented Fletcher from extinguish-ing all of his debts and starting anew.[43]

The immediate reason for William Fletcher's departure—and the affair that consumed the bulk of his agents' efforts—was a dispute with another elite Bos-tonian, William Tudor. Fletcher had mortgaged his house to Tudor, in order to persuade the latter to serve as surety in a protracted and highly publicized def-amation suit. The year he left Boston, Fletcher lost the case and was unable to pay his opponent. As Fletcher's bondsman, Tudor surrendered the substantial sum of £2,000 to the victor of the suit. In the years that followed, Tudor con-tinually sought to either collect this debt from Fletcher or seize the mortgaged property.[44] Life abroad thus offered Fletcher the prospect of recouping his losses while escaping controversy and sheltering his assets from creditors. Fletcher trav-eled to London, and then to the Dutch colony of St. Eustatius. Despite his perpetual optimism that "very brisk & flourishing" commerce would soon en-able him to right his finances and return to New England, he resided in the Ca-ribbean until his death, more than thirty years after his departure from Boston.[45]

William's wife, Elizabeth, remained in Boston with the couple's children until 1764. Along with two legal professionals, she assumed responsibility for the Fletcher family's affairs and assets in Boston. Early in 1755, William granted broad powers of attorney to Elizabeth. He authorized her to act for him "in all business whatsoever wherein I am concerned both in and out of court." By ex-empting her from common law restrictions on wives' control over property during marriage, he empowered her to sell his land and belongings in order to pay his debts.[46] William also relied on two men with legal expertise: Edmund Trowbridge, a leading attorney; and John Cushing, a judge in the Plymouth County Superior Court.[47] As William Fletcher, Elizabeth Fletcher, and the two lawyers collaborated, the elite men's insistence on Elizabeth Fletcher's passivity obscured her significant acumen as a financial manager.

William Fletcher turned to Edmund Trowbridge, John Cushing, and Eliz-abeth Fletcher for distinct tasks. He relied on Trowbridge to protect his prop-erty against lawsuits by creditors, including Tudor, and provide advice about legal technicalities.[48] Meanwhile, Elizabeth Fletcher managed her household's finances. She purchased food, clothing, and provisions for herself and their children, making countless decisions that prevented her family from plunging further into debt. Elizabeth personally negotiated with the creditors William had evaded when he left Boston, many of whom came to the family home to demand payment. She dunned William's debtors; maintained custody of his account books and records; received the cash, goods, and bills of exchange that he sent home; and reported on all of these activities in letters to her husband.[49] All of these labors, characterized by ongoing uses of credit and money, were paramount to her household's financial survival and resembled the financial work of other urban women whose husbands went abroad throughout the colonial period.

The activities of Trowbridge, Cushing, and Elizabeth Fletcher often overlapped, as a result of the legalistic dimensions of credit and debt and the challenges of transatlantic correspondence. All three negotiated with Tudor in attempts to reach both a long-term settlement and short-term agreements to allow the Fletcher family to remain in their mortgaged residence.[50] In addition, because letters took roughly six weeks to travel between St. Eustatius and Boston and sometimes miscarried, William Fletcher sought to exchange the most current information through all available channels. He sometimes responded to reports from Elizabeth in his letters to Trowbridge, or he wrote detailed instructions to Elizabeth and directed Trowbridge to speak with her for full information.[51]

William Fletcher's financial predicament yielded conflicting representations of Elizabeth in his correspondence with Cushing and Trowbridge. Of necessity, William and his male agents discussed Elizabeth's active role in financial negotiations. In such moments of pragmatic coordination, he portrayed his wife as a capable manager. In a letter in which he instructed Trowbridge to pay his Boston-area creditors, he matter-of-factly noted that Elizabeth would undertake one settlement.[52] William likewise directed Trowbridge to consult an "account in my desk, which my wife can show you," and, describing his handling of the profits from a ship's cargo, explained, "I instantly directed my wife to save £2000 . . . to give to Tudor."[53] Through such passing references to Elizabeth, William Fletcher acknowledged her responsibility for his family's records and assets.

At moments when William Fletcher was reflecting on his circumstances, as opposed to coordinating specific matters, these same letters depicted Elizabeth as the distressed victim of Tudor's cruelty. In keeping with the tendency of eighteenth-century male merchants to castigate their opponents as unmanly conspirators, William Fletcher condemned Tudor as "the devil" and as someone who was "at the bottom of some scheme" against him.[54] Within this worldview, one hallmark of unmanly behavior was mistreating women. He emphasized that Tudor's threats to seize the Fletchers' home were "greatly to the disturbance of my wife's comfort" and led her to write "many anxious letters." Such statements by William Fletcher in part reflected the reality that Elizabeth and the couple's children would be cast out of their residence if Tudor seized it. His remarks also shifted attention away from his own indebtedness to Tudor. Tasking Trowbridge and Cushing with helping Elizabeth in the conflict with Tudor and with "[keeping] her easy & [keeping] her spirits up," William positioned himself and his two male allies as Elizabeth's chivalrous protectors.[55] In so doing, he emphasized Elizabeth's passivity, a characterization that was at odds with his pragmatic statements elsewhere in his letters.

William's depictions of his wife as a long-suffering victim belied her sophisticated response to her family's predicament. In the early 1760s, Elizabeth Fletcher, along with two of the couple's sons, joined William in the Caribbean. They lived first in St. Eustatius for several years, and then relocated to St. Martin in the late 1760s, where they remained until at least 1789.[56] Elizabeth's move reconfigured correspondence networks and alliances between herself, her husband, and Trowbridge. While William Fletcher sent Trowbridge letters that he increasingly filled with wistful reminiscences, Elizabeth Fletcher separately corresponded with the Boston attorney. She drafted her own letters, insisting that "I can't writ nor spell [but] I don't car to let anni boddei writ for me." She also directed Trowbridge to mail her letters in care of a neighbor, so William could not intercept them.[57]

Elizabeth Fletcher used this direct communication with Trowbridge to support herself and her sons apart from her husband. As she explained to Trowbridge, she disapproved of William's failure to provide for their sons, and his constant pursuit of "new schemes" inevitably led to "ruin."[58] She accordingly carried out a plan to deceive William about his landholdings. At some point prior to Elizabeth's move to the Caribbean, Trowbridge had assisted the Fletchers in purchasing two farms in Cambridge, Massachusetts, property that would be free of Tudor's claims. Once in St. Eustatius, Elizabeth lied, asserting that the land was purchased in Trowbridge's name, as this prevented her husband from selling it. Feigning ignorance of the land's value, Elizabeth refused to show William accounts pertaining to its purchase. Meanwhile, she directed Trowbridge to maintain the ruse and rent out the land, so its profits could support the couple's other children, who remained in New England.[59] Paradoxically, Elizabeth Fletcher's closer proximity to her husband and greater distance from Trowbridge allowed her new opportunities for autonomy, at least within the historical record.

In order to secure Trowbridge's assistance, Elizabeth mobilized the same vocabularies of friendship and supplication that her husband had previously deployed. William had repeatedly asserted his trust in Trowbridge by interspersing his directives with statements such as "I doubt not the continuance of your friendship."[60] Elizabeth likewise referred to Trowbridge as her friend and entreated him to assist her. On one occasion, Elizabeth wrote to Trowbridge, "Dear sir I must beg you still to be my frind." In another letter, she expressed her "trust" that Trowbridge would "continnu [as] that frind I allwas take you for" and "deu every thing in your power for my intrest." Such statements often preceded specific instructions, such as Elizabeth's requests that Trowbridge use some of her land's profits to pay for the care of her children in Boston, or that he lie to her family about who owned the property.[61] Trowbridge played along with Elizabeth's plan. He wrote social letters to William, while taking "no other person's word" except hers concerning her financial wishes.[62] Building on the personal connection she had established while in Massachusetts, Elizabeth effectively mobilized the conventions of men's correspondence as she maintained her alliance with Trowbridge across the Atlantic.

In their letters to Trowbridge, William and Elizabeth Fletcher separately expressed their hopes to return to Boston—William to visit old friends, and Elizabeth to escape a marriage and a place that she increasingly resented.[63] The record contains no evidence that either William or Elizabeth ever carried out these plans. Nonetheless, their example begins to suggest the way in which correspondence offered not only a means of coordination, but also a forum for interpreting and recasting women's financial contributions. As William Fletcher attempted to rehabilitate his manliness and secure Trowbridge's assistance in the face of mounting debts, he characterized his wife as the ultimate victim of unforgiving creditors. Elizabeth herself chose not to adopt this discourse. Instead, the conventions of mid-century correspondence were sufficiently flexible for her to position Trowbridge as her loyal friend and ally, just as William did in his own letters.

By the 1760s and the Revolutionary era, elite women selectively used gendered discourses of vulnerability to their own strategic advantage. As the cases of Hannah Laycock and Martha Stevens exemplify, those who did so were often widows. They specifically linked their financial precariousness and emotional distress to their altered marital state, as opposed to more-general notions of feminine fragility. In so doing, they entered a longstanding cultural conversation on widows. Throughout the early modern period, Europeans and colonists fixated on such women as a group who fit uneasily within patriarchal frameworks. Referenced in plays, sermons, and pamphlets, one archetypical widow was the pitiable, often impoverished woman who had lost her husband. Discussions of imperiled widows often cited the scriptural injunction that "the widow and the fatherless" were especially deserving of charity and, in so doing, relocated widows within structures of patriarchal protection.[64] As we have seen, Boston and Newport widows occasionally made use of such notions throughout the colonial period, including when writing to lawyers to seek their assistance or when petitioning legislatures for re-hearings of their cases. Unlike Ann Maylem and other mid-century widows who stressed their vulnerability, Hannah Laycock and Martha Stevens were elite creditors, not insolvent or imperiled debtors. The extensive correspondences maintained by Laycock and Stevens illuminate the function and consequences of such discourses of widowhood within late eighteenth-century legal affairs.

In 1768, Hannah Laycock, who was then in her mid-sixties, suffered the loss of her husband and became the administrator of his estate. While the Laycock family resided in Halifax, England, roughly 170 miles northwest of London, the financial ties of Hannah's husband, merchant Godfrey Laycock, extended across the Atlantic Ocean to British North America, and especially to Newport. During the same decades in which Elizabeth Fletcher struggled to protect her insolvent household from creditors, Hannah Laycock encountered the flip side of this problem as an administrator. She scrambled to collect from her late husband's North American trading partners, some of whom were insolvent, before other creditors seized their remaining assets. In 1768, she granted a power of attorney to William Pollard, a Philadelphia merchant and former Halifax resident, and to Pollard's Philadelphia partners, merchants Thomas and Samuel Wharton.[65] These men, in turn, hired fledgling Newport lawyer Henry Marchant to collect the estate's debts in that city. While Marchant went on to become a very prominent attorney, he was admitted to the Rhode Island bar only one year before taking on Hannah Laycock's cases and thus, at that point, was eager to build up his practice.[66] Laycock at times stressed her dependence on these male agents with whom she collaborated, and this strategy had greater consequences than she anticipated.

Like Elizabeth Fletcher and free white women in colonial Boston and Newport, Hannah Laycock was a savvy participant in her family's finances, including through her active oversight of the three Philadelphians, Pollard and the Whartons. Laycock's initial overtures to these men were emblematic of her direct involvement. She enlisted a Halifax attorney to draft a power of attorney appointing Pollard and the Whartons as her agents, but she insisted on penning her own introduction, which would arrive by the same vessel. In this letter, Laycock directed the Philadelphia merchants to update her directly, urging them to write to her in Halifax "as often as it sutes."[67] In her subsequent correspondence, she instructed Pollard and the Whartons about individual matters, often based on her review of her husband's records in Halifax. When a landlord continued to demand payment for housing provided to Godfrey Laycock during his visits to North America, Hannah Laycock reported that she "found no memorandums" about the outstanding debt. She instructed the Whartons and Pollard to ask the landlord whether he received payment "for 28 weeks in [17]60, at my husband's return to America in [17]62," and copied into her letter lines from her husband's account indicating that the landlord remained indebted to the estate.[68] While distance precluded Laycock from settling directly with her husband's creditors and debtors, she nonetheless maintained detailed oversight of all accounts.

In the same letters in which she issued specific directives to Pollard and the Whartons, Hannah Laycock sometimes strategically emphasized her feminine dependence on her male agents. Although she was quite affluent, Laycock lamented that her husband's delinquent creditors "sought to deprive a poor widow" and repeatedly labeled estate administration as a "perplexing" task in which she was "altogether incapable" of directing her agents in North America.[69] Within this framework, the Whartons' and Pollard's assistance to Hannah Laycock comported with Christian teachings. She characterized their service as an "act of generosity and compassion to a distressed widow," deserving of "a reward adequate to such noble actions of Christian benevolence."[70] Even though estate administration was burdensome to Laycock in her advanced age, such statements functioned strategically to simultaneously secure her male agents' sympathy and loyalty.[71]

The structure and content of the Philadelphia merchants' collaboration with lawyer Henry Marchant further diminished Hannah Laycock's active involvement in settling her late husband's affairs. Whereas men often enlisted mutual acquaintances to make connections with distant attorneys with whom they then communicated with directly, Hannah Laycock and Marchant notably never wrote to one another. Instead, she exchanged letters with the Philadelphia merchants, the Whartons and Pollard, who, in turn, hired and corresponded with the Newport lawyer. Such correspondence among Marchant and the Philadelphia men focused on strategies to collect from Godfrey Laycock's debtors, with many letters never mentioning Hannah Laycock by name. In 1769, for instance, William Pollard sent the Whartons a multipage missive about negotiations with Godfrey Laycock's debtors in which he referred to her only in his concluding lament, "so you see what a poor situation the widow is in." That same year, Marchant sent the Philadelphia merchants an equally long letter referencing Hannah Laycock only in its closing pledge, "I am in earnest to secure the widow's just demand."[72] Were one to read such letters without prior familiarity with the Laycock family's affairs, it would be difficult to recognize Hannah Laycock's role as client and engaged supervisor.

The correspondence between the male agents, containing a slippage between "the widow" as a practical descriptor and a potent signifier, mobilized the same figure of the distressed widow found in Laycock's own letters. Attorney Henry Marchant, in particular, often portrayed himself as emotionally as well as professionally invested in Hannah Laycock's case. On one occasion he reflected, "My spirits are damp'd to think of entering into the state of the poor widow's cause when I see full reason to fear that by one scheme and another, that she will never reap the fruits of her labor."[73] Here and elsewhere, Marchant fused discourses of widowhood with vocabularies of sympathy and conspiracy that were common in men's letters about financial difficulties.[74] Similar to how William

Fletcher cast himself and Edmund Trowbridge as jointly protecting Elizabeth Fletcher, Marchant's characterizations of Hannah Laycock doubly reinforced his own masculinity. He positioned himself as aiding a woman who otherwise lacked patriarchal protection, and, even though he could only partly fulfill his professional obligation to assist her in collecting debts, he remained a man of feeling who was distressed by her plight.

These writings by Laycock's male agents fit within broader patterns of men corresponding about widows' legal affairs. In letters from the 1760s onward, other laymen and lawyers likewise appealed to one another's sense of manly obligation. Flattering one another by stating that "I know you are fond of helping the widow and the fatherless," men sought aid for an unnamed "poor widow" who desperately needed help collecting what others would consider a "trifling" sum, or for "a widow whom Providence has thrown considerably into my care." Such appeals, rooted in gendered concepts of paternalism, reinforced oppositions between masculine competence and the passivity and vulnerability of widows.[75]

The tensions between seeing Hannah Laycock as a savvy principal and a vulnerable widow are most evident in the estate's dispute with Thurston and Company, insolvent Newport merchants with whom her late husband had extensive dealings. Hannah Laycock initially told the Pollards and Wharton that she was "incapable" of directing them in that conflict and that, in keeping with their power of attorney, they should "transact the whole affair according to your judgments."[76] When the Philadelphia merchants subsequently negotiated with the Thurstons without her input, this arrangement ostensibly followed her wishes. Yet Laycock later expressed frustration when attorney Henry Marchant reached a final settlement without consulting her. She lamented that the agreement excused the Thurstons from paying for the "expences attending this affair" and costs associated with "the ship & cargo" that were central to the dispute.[77] Once Laycock had stressed her incapacity as a widow, regardless of the extent to which she had done so genuinely or strategically, it was difficult for her to disclaim such language and regain a greater say in her affairs.

Roughly one decade after understandings of widowhood structured Hannah Laycock's involvement in estate administration, Boston widow Martha Stevens used similar scripts to both distance herself from financial concerns and control her male agents. She was part of a larger group of women who became significant landholders during the Revolutionary and early national periods.[78] Descended from a wealthy mercantile family, Stevens became sole owner of more than two thousand acres of land in Ashford, in northeastern Connecticut, following her third husband's death in 1776. Until her own demise in 1785, Stevens resided in Boston and rented out her Ashford land, which was subdivided into many smaller plots, to tenants. As an absentee landlord, she collaborated with two male agents based in Connecticut.[79] She relied on a leading lawyer, Charles Church Chandler, primarily for technical legal matters, such as representing her in lawsuits arising from her land ownership.[80] She also employed layman Ebenezer Byles to conduct much of the daily work of managing her acreages, especially in reporting on events in Ashford and collecting rent from her many tenants.[81] At the same time as she remained a demanding and attentive client, Stevens strategically invoked her gendered persona as a widow, in order to shape her relationships with both men.

The economic instability of the Revolutionary era posed ongoing challenges to Martha Stevens and her agents regarding the Ashford properties. When Connecticut, like other state governments, raised land taxes in attempts to pay for the war, Stevens's income became increasingly inadequate to pay such assessments. As a landowner, she was bound up in chains of credit and debt. She owed taxes to her state government, and she functioned as creditor to her tenants, whom she allowed to pay rent retroactively, rather than at the start of each month. As the printing of paper money by multiple state governments sparked massive inflation, the value of debts long unpaid by Stevens' tenants decreased in relation to her more recently imposed tax liabilities. Then, when the amount of currency in circulation decreased in the early 1780s, tenants struggled even further to pay their rent on time, and they refused to pay the taxes directly, even when they were included in the terms of their leases. Byles concisely described this "great Deal of Difficulty" in 1781 in one of his many letters to Stevens, noting that "the officers come to me and demand pay" for taxes, and "when I shall git it from the Tenants I can't tell."[82]

Martha Stevens's financial troubles were intertwined with political and social challenges. During the late eighteenth century, revolutionary rhetoric inserted new dimensions into republican political frameworks in which the independent yeoman farmer embodied the ideals of citizenship and proper manhood.[83] Yet, as a result of growing inequality and speculators driving up land prices, many men could not afford land. Ashford residents came to resent Martha Stevens for being an elite absentee landlord. Byles reported to Stevens that "many people are evely [evilly] affected toward you," and he devoted many letters to the problem of "continuall trespass" on her land by squatters and pillagers.[84] He noted that tenants would not pay their rent "until the law makes them," which placed her in a bind at a time when many court sessions were cancelled.[85] Stevens's gender may have intensified the hostility and resistance she faced from Ashford residents, as her wealth and profit-seeking seemingly barred less affluent men from property ownership and, by extension, full masculinity. The economic turmoil of war and its aftermath offered Stevens limited possibilities for escaping this predicament. Prospective buyers were scarce, and rapid inflation made it difficult for Stevens and her agents to evaluate purchasers' bids.[86]

Within these challenging circumstances, Martha Stevens cultivated a multifaceted persona. On the one hand, just as Elizabeth Fletcher and Hannah Laycock continued the practices of colonial women by engaging with the details of their finances, the Boston widow carefully oversaw Byles's and Chandler's activities through both in-person conversations and frequent letters.[87] She offered detailed inputs on virtually all aspects of her affairs, including tax assessments, rents, land surveys, suits against delinquent tenants and trespassers, and prices at which she was willing to sell her acreage. Such directives routinely reflected significant levels of financial knowledge, including understandings of exchange rates and property values.[88] Byles acknowledged Stevens's skilled oversight by responding to her in depth.[89]

At the same time, much like Hannah Laycock, Martha Stevens strategically referenced her widowhood when decrying her financial difficulties. When protesting against the high taxes assessed on her land, she asked whether the assessors believed "the judge of all the Earth approves this oppression of the widow." On another occasion she lamented, "Perhaps no act was ever carried into Execution with greater severity and oppression as this has been, especially to the widow and the fatherless."[90] By aligning herself with the figure of the imperiled widow, Stevens softened her political critiques and downplayed her status as a wealthy landholder. Moreover, by portraying herself as a pitiable figure deserving of charitable protection, such statements helped reinforce her male agents' assistance.

Additional gendered tensions pervaded Martha Stevens's relationships with the men acting for her. Stevens's sole ownership of the Ashford lands occurred during a period of transition in the nature of male agents' work. Many eighteenth-century financial collaborations, including those of Elizabeth Fletcher and Hannah Laycock, contained strong personal dimensions, with correspondents appealing to the language of friendship. Yet, as the law continued to gain strength as a profession during and after the Revolution, attorneys' relationships with their clients also became more predictably transactional.[91] Stevens and her agents accordingly disagreed on whether Byles and Chandler were hired professionals or friends performing favors.

Ambiguity about the nature of Byles's services yielded conflict surrounding his compensation. In keeping with the genre of the familiar letter, Stevens and Byles corresponded as friends, exchanging pleasantries and news of mutual acquaintances in the same missives in which they discussed the Ashford lands. Yet Stevens also repeatedly offered to pay Byles if he furnished her with an itemized account.[92] Although Byles embraced numerical precision in all of the other aspects of his post, he declined to attach fees to his labor. He only sent Stevens lists of the many services he performed. These included spending numerous days with Chandler leasing out farms and negotiating with tenants; traveling to neighboring towns to attend court and have writs served; and measuring, carting, and selling grain grown on Stevens's land. He characterized this time-consuming work as favors provided by "a friend and a well-wisher to you" and insisted that "if you please to give me anything for my trouble it shall be thankfully received."[93] Such statements frustrated Stevens, who repeatedly protested that Byles's accounts "contained many articles carried out blank which is not in my power to fill up" and that she merely wished to provide him "ample satisfaction" for his "trouble."[94] In this aspect of the pair's relationship, it was Byles who rooted his work within friendship, rather than market exchanges.

Stevens manipulated these same understandings of friendship in order to prevent Byles from resigning his post, despite his repeated attempts to do so from 1778 onward. Byles recommended that Stevens either become more involved in her affairs or grant full responsibility for her lands to Chandler, whom he cast as "more capable than myself," or to another trusted agent.[95] Stevens refused to accept Byles's resignation, insisting that "I will not allow this" and instructing him never to "mention" or even "think of" leaving. She viewed Chandler as an inadequate replacement, protesting that the lawyer was "very dilatory" with his updates and "scarce thinks it worth while to answer my letters."[96] Just as Stevens strategically referenced her widowhood when voicing political opposition to tax policy, she also did so in order to diffuse tension with Byles. Immediately after one of the many instances in which she barred him from stepping down, Stevens expressed the hope that Byles, still unpaid as a result of the accounting dispute, would be rewarded in the afterlife for "pleading the cause of the widow."[97] Resembling Hannah Laycock's thanks to the Philadelphia merchants, Martha Stevens's statement similarly situated men's labor within gendered hierarchies and religious understandings of charity. Ultimately, Byles acted as Stevens's agent in Ashford until her death in 1785, and he assisted her estate's administrators in managing the land for the better part of a decade thereafter.[98]

As a female landowner collaborating with distant agents, Martha Stevens proved to be demanding and even manipulative. Stevens was immersed in her affairs, issuing specific directives and posing pointed queries to her agents from afar. She insisted that they provide her with frequent updates. While Byles met this expectation with his numerous lengthy letters, Chandler apparently did not. Byles's letters and accounts frequently referenced work performed by Chandler, and the latter appears have filed legal documents and represented Stevens in court as needed.[99] Yet, by taking on Stevens's affairs within his larger legal practice, Chandler did not grant her the extensive attention that she expected, a level of regard that was based in friendship, as opposed to the professionalized attorney-client relationship.

Stevens monitored her affairs on her own terms. She refused to travel to Connecticut personally to attend to issues regarding her land, in part because doing so would have directly inserted her into the political controversies surrounding tenancy and taxation. She also refused to let Ebenezer Byles resign, an action that would have forced her to become more involved in the management of her land, at least in the short term. Had Stevens replaced Byles with a different agent, it is unlikely that she would have enjoyed the same kind of control and power, which were grounded in longstanding affective ties. When Stevens died in 1785, her estate remained plagued by high taxes and insufficient rental income. Yet, partially due to her success in collaborating with Chandler and Byles, her property holdings remained considerable, and she bequeathed significant legacies to numerous heirs.[100]

Collectively, the experiences of Elizabeth Fletcher, Hannah Laycock, and Martha Stevens allude to the renegotiations of elite women's relationships to commerce and finance that were underway between the imperial crisis and the early national period. Each of their correspondence networks suggests that exchanges of letters, under certain circumstances, encouraged men and women to intentionally cultivate gendered personas as they worked to secure distant allies' loyalties. Understandings of femininity were at times central to the ways in which elite women or those around them depicted women's relationships to financial matters. Elite men referenced female fragility and the norms of patriarchal protection when discussing the Fletcher family's plight. Hannah Laycock and her male collaborators emphasized her standing as a widow deserving of protection. Martha Stevens invoked her widowhood to critique tax policy and retain Ebenezer Byles's assistance.

Women continued to demonstrate financial skill and legal savvy despite their and others' occasional claims that they relied entirely on exertions by professional men. Although William Fletcher averred that his wife depended on men to protect her from creditors, Elizabeth Fletcher assumed significant responsibilities as her household's representative in Boston, and she later conspired with Edmund Trowbridge to protect her family's property. Hannah Laycock asserted well-developed opinions on her late husband's affairs, at the same time as she and her North American agents cast her as unable to participate in such matters. Martha Stevens remained a discerning and demanding supervisor of Ebenezer Byles and Charles Chandler, even though she claimed that she was reliant upon their assistance. It is also noteworthy that the two women who explicitly professed their reliance on men—Hannah Laycock and Martha Stevens—stressed their vulnerability as widows, thus invoking their age and marital status, as well as their gender. As late as the 1780s, associations between femininity and withdrawal from financial matters remained partial and uneven.

Conclusion

On the surface, the history of women's financial work during the late eighteenth century seemingly contains two distinct threads. First, the political and economic turmoil of the imperial crisis and warfare splintered families and disrupted both personal credit networks and the important role that the county courts played in such obligations, forcing free women to redeploy their existing legal and economic skills in response to new challenges. Once the British army withdrew from Boston and Newport and peace returned to New England, city residents resumed their pre-war financial and legal practices, with women once again serving as skilled participants and vital conduits in urban commercial networks and the court system. Second, during the decades on either side of the war, elites with strong connections to Boston and Newport positioned technical, high-stakes financial matters as the purview of lawyers and other skilled men. Women, these elites suggested, were both ill-equipped to handle the intricacies of such affairs and entitled to remove themselves from the associated stressors. Both men and women articulated this gendered division of labor within their long-distance correspondence, often doing so in order to secure the assistance or loyalty of others. The different chronologies of these two narratives further heighten the apparent distance between them. While the imperial crisis and war disrupted urban financial practices in the short term, evolutions within elites' correspondence occurred over the longer duration of the Revolutionary era.

These two components of women's financial practices—the temporary disruptions of the Revolution and emerging understandings of class and gender—have more in common than these preliminary contrasts suggest. Whether in preserving businesses and households during wartime, rebuilding urban commercial networks following the return of peace, or managing technical affairs over great distances, ordinary people and elites alike mobilized financial and legal skills and shaped their activities in response to economic exigencies. While new political languages and their deployment by various groups are important components of the Revolutionary era, economic and legal practices and their gendered dimensions proved to be remarkably resilient during this same timeframe, creating continuities between the colonial and early national periods.

In addition, everyday urban activities and elite notions of masculinity and femininity were interrelated. The ongoing involvement of lower-class and middling women in credit networks and the courts served as an implied point of contrast at those moments when elites attempted to distance women from financial matters. William and Elizabeth Fletcher, Hannah Laycock, and Martha Stevens, all preoccupied with their own affairs, never explicitly commented on other households' gendered divisions of labor. Nonetheless, elite women's extended partnerships with professionals served as a marker of their privilege, differentiating them from their middling and lower-class counterparts who trudged through city streets, personally haggled with creditors and debtors, or attended crowded court sessions. Wealthy families' appeals to notions of elite womanhood, in other words, proved to be strategic and culturally powerful only because of the continued visibility of middling and lower-class women's everyday financial and legal activities.[101]

By positioning these concerns as the domains of professional men, affluent families implicitly located women within their households, where they supervised financial relationships through letter writing. While much more work remains to be done about women's changing relationship with finance during the early national period, the ordeals of Elizabeth Fletcher, Hannah Laycock, and Martha Stevens suggest that elites and their allies shaped this era's broader reappraisal of gendered divisions of labor. As early industrialization and wage labor took hold during the nineteenth century, Americans increasingly cast only men's work as productive, while ignoring the economic value of women's unpaid work. These changes took numerous forms, ranging from political leaders' economic plans for the newly created United States to struggling male artisans' clamors for increased wages. By the War of 1812, in contrast to the Revolutionary era, patriotic rhetoric did not acknowledge the political significance of women's household production or consumer choices. This redefinition of work culminated in new ideologies of privacy and domesticity during the early nineteenth century, which located women within the home, a place cast as a refuge from the masculine arenas of public life and the commercial marketplace. Glossing over the fact that skilled female labor remained crucial to households' economic viability, the identities of elite and middle-class families hinged on their supposed abilities to enact this idealized vision.[102] Through occasional and strategic insistences that the rightful place for women was outside of the contentious, masculine realms of financial markets and the courts during the 1760s to 1780s, elites articulated one component of the gendered ideologies that took hold during the early nineteenth century.

The gendered negotiations occurring within wealthy families' correspondence also raise important questions about the relationship between cultural understandings and the new institutions of the early national period. During the late eighteenth and early nineteenth centuries, Americans established numerous financial and legal systems that gradually supplanted interpersonal negotiations and litigation in the county courts. These included banks to facilitate lending, insurance companies and credit bureaus to mitigate risk, and a new federal court system in which parties argued cases concerning interstate commerce.[103] Men dominated every occupational level of these bodies, from directors and judges to white-collar clerical workers. Men also increasingly used legal strictures, such as trusts and prenuptial agreements, to limit women's control over wealth within these new institutions.[104] To be sure, female assets and labor continued to undergird capitalism during the nineteenth century, as women maintained households, invested in banks, and supplied the connections and wealth that undergirded New England's dynastic merchant families.[105] Yet the gendered political economy of the Early Republic increasingly differed from that of the colonial period, when the residents of New England's port cities accepted that the direct and skilled involvement of women and men alike undergirded networks of personal credit.

Conclusion

In the century following the American Revolution, elected officials, activists, and the press reappraised the legal powers of women and their involvement in finance. One of the most critical transformations began in the late 1830s, when state legislatures began enacting Married Women's Property Acts, laws that enhanced the ability of wives to own and control property. These statutes' goals and scopes in part reflected paternalistic impulses. As officials passed this body of legislation in the wake of the Panic of 1837, they aimed to protect married women's assets, especially property inherited from their fathers, from seizure by their husbands' creditors. The laws, however, left intact other aspects of the legal and cultural framework of coverture, including restrictions on married women's ability to independently engage in litigation, and documentary practices that obscured wives' everyday financial labor within their households. Yet the various acts of the 1830s through 1870s nonetheless eroded one cornerstone of marriage law—a wife's inability to own property—and women's rights activists were among those who lobbied for this legislation.[1]

Some of these activists also began to challenge men's economic and political power, which arose from their control of financial institutions. The first female-owned brokerage firm opened its doors on New York City's Wall Street in 1870. Run by Victoria Woodhull (who would become the first woman to run for the US presidency) and her sister, Tennessee Claflin, the firm was part of the pair's feminist agenda. Woodhull described the enterprise as a "female invasion of the masculine precincts of finance." Newspapers condemned and satirized this venture. The sisters' entry into finance, the press insisted, was akin to sexual immorality and threatened the gendered social order. A cartoon in New York's *Evening Telegraph* characterized Woodhull and Claflin's business as the "Wall Street Hippodrome" and depicted them brazenly driving a carriage drawn by a team of bulls and bears, topped with male human heads. While Woodhull, Claflin, and Company was a short-lived enterprise, the controversy over it crystallized female activists' and critics' shared recognition of finance as a masculine realm. Women pushed against the gendered cultural understandings that the male-dominated press strenuously defended.[2]

These two nineteenth-century milestones—the Married Women's Property Acts and the turmoil surrounding Woodhull and Claflin's firm—at first glance fit within a narrative of the gradual expansion of female legal and economic power within the history of the United States. Indeed, legislators and judges have continued to dismantle coverture through laws and court decisions. Similarly, women have slowly entered the financial sectors since the founding of Woodhull, Claflin, and Company; today, they compose 41 percent of those who work in finance. Yet critics might well note that it was not until 1974, with the passage of the Equal Credit Opportunity Act, that Congress barred lenders from considering women's marital status when issuing loans, and the gender gap in the financial sector remains vast at the executive levels.[3] Depending on one's perspective, this is a story either of steady progress or the stubborn persistence of patriarchy.[4]

Rather than conforming to trajectories of linear progress or patriarchal continuity, the eighteenth century forces us to acknowledge an uneven and contingent narrative. Recognizing the full extent of women's financial labor reframes our understandings of legal and economic developments and of gendered social hierarchies. Between roughly 1730 and the Revolution, British North America—especially its port cities, including Boston and Newport—underwent intertwined economic and legal transitions in which women's work, skills, and assets played crucial roles. As Boston and Newport became nodes that linked New England's hinterlands with the Atlantic World, the pace of market-oriented exchange quickened. Free whites increasingly used written credit to structure their economic relationships. Gender conditioned all individuals' engagement with borrowing and lending, and cultural understandings of credit mobilized oppositions between masculinity and femininity. Yet it is telling that, even amid legal and cultural strictures, women's extensive use of personal credit facilitated vital exchanges of goods and services. In a period characterized by economic risk and turmoil, New Englanders necessarily accepted that female labor protected family wealth and stabilized financial networks in the face of men's deaths and departures from home. Women's uses of credit also stoked the two major legal changes of the pre-Revolutionary period: the formalization of law, and the development of the legal profession. Free women and men turned to the courts in increasing numbers to hold one another accountable for their promises to pay, and this dramatic influx of cases fed lawyers' businesses and reinforced the courts' emphasis on formal procedures and legal technicalities. The development of nineteenth-century institutions of industrial and financial capitalism, including the markets that Victoria Woodhull and Tennessee Claflin sought to infiltrate, hinged on the direct involvement of both women and men in the transitions of the previous century.

Woodhull and Claflin's challenge to gendered spatial dimensions of nineteenth-century finance would have been impossible and unintelligible in eighteenth-century Boston and Newport, where the intermixing of domestic life and business activities within the household meant that all of its members could be drawn into the labor surrounding credit transactions. Women routinely handled the finances for family businesses, received payments from debtors, evaluated creditors' claims, witnessed transactions, and tangled with local law enforcement. Credit transactions led them to enter a wide range of other urban places. Women who dunned debtors or sought out creditors traversed city streets and visited shops and others' houses. Female litigants and witnesses visited lawyers' and clerks' offices and attended county courts and legislative sessions. While credit and debt were most accessible to free white women of at least moderate means, lower-class women, including servants and the enslaved, at times used credit and debt in the course of their labor relations, and they served as informal observers to credit disputes. Households and extra-household settings alike functioned as heterosocial, public arenas of financial and legal activity for all city residents.

Much like the way Woodhull and Claflin took on the specifically nineteenth-century institution of Wall Street, so, too, did antebellum reformers seek to modify coverture from its distinctive nineteenth-century form. Although common law's opposition between *feme sole* and *feme covert* originated in medieval England, jurists and laypeople modified coverture in ways that were specific to particular times and places. In colonial British North America, coverture indeed curtailed married women's abilities to own and transmit property and shaped record-keeping practices, such that sources often positioned male household heads as autonomous borrowers, lenders, and litigants. Yet married women were crucial players in a system in which kinship ties structured the financial networks of all colonists, regardless of gender, and in which households functioned as vital economic units and labor systems. Especially as seafaring and imperial warfare depleted Boston and Newport of adult men, the residents of these cities necessarily accepted and relied on wives' labors in matters of credit and debt. At the level of everyday practice, married women's activities in port cities closely resembled those of *femes sole*. Wives negotiated with creditors and debtors, maintained financial records, hired and supervised lawyers, signed documents, and testified as witnesses. Prior to the dissemination of William Blackstone's influential legal treatise, *Commentaries on the Laws of England*, and the creation of law schools with standardized curricula in the Early Republic, laypeople and their lawyers invoked coverture inconsistently and strategically within individual lawsuits.[5] The development of colonial and Atlantic economies and financial networks hinged on the skilled contributions of all participants. When we emphasize only the strictures of coverture, we risk replicating the logic of the archive, rather than interrogating early modern systems of labor relations.

Power dynamics within credit networks and the courts were highly situational, shaped by the immediate context of financial and legal relationships, as well as by gender, race, and social class. Close attention to everyday practices reveals extensive similarities between the activities of women and men surrounding credit and debt. As did free white men, free white women conducted and observed transactions using all forms of credit and debt, including the formal instruments—such as bonds, promissory notes, and bills of exchange—that were the hallmarks of the developing commercial economy. Standing as a creditor, debtor, client, or witness authorized laypeople to behave in ways that were specific to those roles, which, in turn, shaped relations between women and men. As creditors and debt collectors, New Englanders exercised significant power over others, making forceful demands on their debtors in person and in writing, and achieving high rates of success in litigation. Such outcomes enabled them to lay claim to debtors' bodies and belongings. As clients, women and men supervised male attorneys and demanded their loyalty. Female witnesses, like their male counterparts, helped solidify financial relationships, evaluated others' reputations, and shaped case outcomes.

Within this system, where specific powers and expected behaviors inhered in one's economic and legal roles, women's vulnerability as debtors stands out. All debtors, whether male or female, possessed limited means with which to challenge properly documented debts. Thus they typically lost or did not contest suits brought against them in county courts. Yet, in light of coverture and women's tendency to outlive men, the increasing privileging of creditors' claims by colonial courts had different consequences for women than for men. Unable to control or renounce their spouses' financial decisions, wives became accountable for their husbands' debts when creditors seized household goods and property, and widows and estate administrators struggled to protect their inheritance from their late husbands' creditors.

At times, women called attention to their vulnerability within financial relationships and legal disputes, and situating such instances within the full spectrum of everyday practices helps us understand them. Some female petitioners and letter-writers highlighted their financial and legal peril or their limited knowledge in order to seek men's assistance. Even within these genres, however, gendered language was one available register among many, and women often cited their specific difficulties as indebted widows, rather than broad deficiencies arising from their femininity. While such language reflected legal realities, it equally functioned strategically. Vulnerability and expertise were not opposing ends of a spectrum. Instead, women's situational defenselessness or power was intertwined with their exercise of skill and strategy. Navigating credit relationships and the courts required numerous practical abilities, and, while high-level numeracy or extensive reading and writing abilities could be advantageous, they were not prerequisites for interpreting others' activities or favorably resolving one's affairs. Choosing to invoke one's vulnerability in accordance with standard tropes was, in itself, a form of competence, one of many that women deployed within their financial dealings.

Women's participation in the credit economy had tremendous significance for eighteenth-century gender relations and social order. To observe this fact is not to return to earlier arguments that the colonial period represented a "golden age" for women.[6] Colonial society was fundamentally patriarchal. Boys enjoyed greater access to formal schooling and apprenticeships than did girls. Adult white men participated fully in political and civic life, and they exercised social and legal authority over the dependent members of their households. Adult white women were largely excluded from formal politics, and they possessed limited authority over men, particularly those who were not laborers in their own households. Through their involvement in the credit economy and the courts, however, women gleaned and deployed vital practical knowledge, acquired visibility and governmental recognition, and exercised authority over others when they acted as creditors, clients, and witnesses. Reconstructing such everyday practices underscores that fluidity was a defining element in eighteenth-century social relations and highlights the importance of ordinary financial and legal dealings as a source of power for women.

As late as the 1780s, finance and the law remained heterosocial realms. While harbingers of change were visible, it was not yet clear that finance would wholly consist of "masculine precincts," as Woodhull and Claflin so decisively claimed ninety years later. During the American Revolution, women redoubled their reliance on existing forms of financial savvy and strategies for informal dispute resolution. After British troops ended their occupation of Boston and Newport, urban credit networks and the courts resumed their normal functioning again, with all members of households, including women, as crucial contributors. Especially from mid-century onward, however, laypeople were beginning to relate to finance and the law in new ways. Petitions for new trials elevated business activity and the practice of law as realms of masculine expertise, and elite women at times suggested that delegating their technical, contentious financial affairs to professional men was a marker of class and gender privilege. Yet these same women simultaneously demonstrated their own financial and legal knowledge as they asserted well-developed opinions about how their affairs should be conducted by such men. In so doing, they continued practices that resembled those of their mothers and grandmothers.

When we sift carefully through the eighteenth century's historical record, especially through the prosaic documentation of everyday life, we encounter abundant evidence of women's contributions to financial and legal systems. By intentionally aggregating such evidence, we can see that their skilled labor undergirded urban political economies and Atlantic capitalism. Within the context of any one study that is not expressly about women, it is often easy to dismiss these shards of evidence—and thus female labor—as marginal. But in so doing, we preserve portraits of the economy and the legal system as masculine, thus shaping our understanding of subsequent periods and the present day. Resisting narratives that emphasize either unbroken continuity or a gradual improvement in the status of women, the study of eighteenth-century economic and legal practices pushes us to attend to changing policies and cultural understandings across historical epochs. Equally importantly, it reminds us of the crucial role that microlevel negotiations played both in individual women's lives and in gendered power relations writ large.

Sources and Sampling for the Quantitative Analysis of Debt Cases

During a typical term, litigants brought hundreds of cases to the Suffolk and Newport County Courts of Common Pleas. A quantitative analysis of these cases and their litigants therefore requires sampling. This appendix outlines the sampling procedures used for the quantitative analysis of debt litigation in chapters 3 and 6.

In order to quantify the percentage of cases concerning debt, men's and women's participation rates, the outcomes of lawsuits by men, and the kinds of debts at issue in men's cases, I constructed a database containing all cases from one term of the Newport and Suffolk County Courts per decade. (The Newport County Courts met twice per year, while the Suffolk County Courts met four times per year until the 1790s, then twice per year thereafter.) For Newport County, I used the May term in the first year of each decade, beginning with 1731 and ending with 1791, with the exception of 1731, when I employed the November term, because the records for May are incomplete. For Suffolk County, I included the July terms of 1730, 1740, 1750, 1760, 1770, 1780, and 1790. Because available records for 1756 through 1776 do not consistently report case outcomes, I excluded 1760 and 1770 from my analysis of the outcomes of men's debt cases.

I used the record books to identify debt cases brought to the Newport County Court of Common Pleas. For Suffolk County, I drew on the record books for 1730, 1740, 1750, 1780, and 1790 to build my database. Record books for the Suffolk County Court of Common Pleas are not extant for 1756 through 1776, but the court has constructed an index online—*Suffolk County Court of Common Pleas, Index to Cases 1756–1776*, American Ancestors, New England Historic Genealogical Society, available at americanancestors.org—based on its extant case files. I used this index for my analysis of 1760 and 1770. I excluded these years from my analysis of the outcomes of men's debt cases, however, as the index does not consistently include case outcomes. For both Newport and Suffolk Counties, I cross-referenced record books and indexes with docket books and individual case files when necessary.

TABLE A.I.
Cases in the Newport County Court of Common Pleas

Year	All cases (*N*)	Debt cases (%)	Other (%)	Unknown (%)
1731	153	77	9	14
1741	223	76	22	2
1751	430	78	21	1
1761	262	69	31	0
1771	362	78	21	1
1781	167	64	34	2
1791	217	68	38	4
All years	1,814	74	24	3

Sources: Case Files, Record Books, and Docket Books, Newport County Court of Common Pleas, Rhode Island Supreme Court Judicial Records Center.
Note: Due to rounding, percentages may not total 100.

Two components of record book entries allowed me to identify debt cases. First, Newport clerks recorded the kinds of financial obligations that gave rise to the cases, and some Suffolk County clerks also did so. For those years when the clerks included such detail in their records, I counted as debt cases all of those suits involving accounts, promissory notes, bonds, bills of exchange, or rent. Second, I used legal actions (technical categories of complaint) to identify debt cases in Suffolk County in 1750, 1780, and 1790, as Suffolk County clerks did not record the financial obligations giving rise to lawsuits in these years.

When relying on the kinds of legal actions to estimate the percentage of cases concerning debt, I counted all "actions of debt" and "actions on the case" as debt cases. Plaintiffs used "actions of debt" only in suits concerning unpaid debts arising from bonds and rent. They employed "actions of trespass on the case" (alternately referred to in the records as "actions on the case") when collecting on accounts and promissory notes. "Trespass on the case" and "action on the case" were broad categories of legal redress that could also involve disputes unrelated to debt, but, based on research in more-detailed records, we know that more than 90 percent of the actions on the cases concerned debts. Other kinds of legal actions (e.g., actions of account, covenant, or promise) indirectly concerned debt, but I did not count them as debt cases.*

Tables A.1 and A.2 list the total number of cases per term sampled for the Newport and Suffolk Courts of Common Pleas, respectively, as well as the percentage of these that were debt cases, based on the assumptions spelled out above. By coincidence, my sample included the same grand total for the number of cases heard in Suffolk and Newport Counties.

---

*On the use of actions of trespass on the case to sue for debts, see Simon Middleton, "Private Credit in Eighteenth-Century New York City: The Mayor's Court Papers, 1681–1776," *Journal of Early American History* 2 (2012): 154–55.

TABLE A.2.
Cases in the Suffolk County Court of Common Pleas

Year	All cases (*N*)	Debt (%)	Other (%)	Unknown (%)
1730	401	80	14	6
1740	579	76	14	10
1750	223	80	20	0
1760	131	81	18	1
1770	138	86	12	2
1780	37	62	30	8
1790	305	56	26	18
All years	1,814	75	8	17

Sources: Record Books and Case Files, Suffolk County Court of Common Pleas, Massachusetts State Archives; *Suffolk County Court of Common Pleas, Index to Cases 1756–1776*, online database, American Ancestors, New England Historic Genealogical Society, americanancestors.org.

I created a supplemental database that included additional debt cases involving female litigants, in order to engage in a more detailed quantitative analysis of their demographic attributes, such as marital status, whether they were administrators or executors, and the outcomes of their cases as plaintiffs and defendants. For Suffolk County, I examined all debt cases with female litigants in the following terms: July 1730, 1740, and 1750; January, July, and October 1760 and 1770; and July 1780 and 1790. (As in my general analysis of debt litigation, I excluded 1760 and 1770 from my investigation of the outcomes of women's cases.) For Newport County, I used all debt cases with female litigants in the first year of each decade, beginning with 1731 and ending with 1791.

Abbreviations

AAS	American Antiquarian Society, Worcester, MA
CHS	Connecticut Historical Society, Hartford, CT
Houghton	Houghton Library, Harvard University, Cambridge, MA
HSP	Historical Society of Pennsylvania, Philadelphia, PA
Kent CCP	Kent County Court of Common Pleas
MA Archives	Massachusetts Archives Collection
MHS	Massachusetts Historical Society, Boston, MA
MSA	Massachusetts State Archives, Boston, MA
Newport CCP	Newport County Court of Common Pleas
Newport SCJ	Newport County Superior Court of Judicature
Newport TC	Newport Town Council Records
NHS	Newport Historical Society, Newport, RI
Providence SJC	Providence Superior Court of Judicature
RIHS	Rhode Island Historical Society, Providence, RI
RIJRC	Rhode Island Supreme Court Judicial Records Center, Pawtucket, RI
RI Petitions	Petitions to the Rhode Island General Assembly
RISA	Rhode Island State Archives, Providence, RI
Suffolk CCP	Suffolk County Court of Common Pleas
Suffolk SCJ	Suffolk County Superior Court of Judicature
WMQ	*William and Mary Quarterly*, 3rd series

Introduction

1. George Fisher, *The American Instructor: or, Young Man's Best Companion*, 9th ed. (Philadelphia: B. Franklin & D. Hall, 1748), LCP, Am 1748 Fis Api 748.

2. Fisher, *American Instructor*, iv, 375, 376.

3. The Library Company of Philadelphia holds 14 books containing Morris's inscription. Key works portraying eighteenth-century commerce as a male realm include Thomas Doerflinger, *A Vigorous Spirit of Enterprise: Merchants and Economic Development in Revolutionary Philadelphia* (Chapel Hill: University of North Carolina Press, 1986); David Hancock, *Citizens of the World: London Merchants and the Integration of the British Atlantic Community, 1735–1785* (Cambridge: Cambridge University Press, 1995); David Hancock, *Oceans of Wine: Madeira and the Emergence of Atlantic Trade and Taste* (New

Haven, CT: Yale University Press, 2009). Studies emphasizing women's diminishing economic authority during the eighteenth century include Cornelia Hughes Dayton, *Women Before the Bar: Gender, Law, and Society in Connecticut, 1639–1789* (Chapel Hill: University of North Carolina Press, 1995); Deborah Rosen, *Courts and Commerce: Gender, Law and the Market Economy in Colonial New York* (Columbus: Ohio State University Press, 1997); Elaine Forman Crane, *Ebb Tide in New England: Women, Seaports, and Social Change, 1630–1800* (Boston: Northeastern University Press, 1998).

4. On Deborah Morris, see Elizabeth Jones-Minsinger, "Out of the Shadows: Uncovering Women's Productive and Consuming Labor in the Mid-Atlantic, 1750–1815" (PhD diss., University of Delaware, 2017), esp. 27, 45–48, 212–16, 191–92, 201–2, 212, 222–32. On unmarried women's economic activities in Pennsylvania, see also Karin Wulf, *Not All Wives: Women of Colonial Philadelphia* (Ithaca, NY: Cornell University Press, 2000).

5. Fisher, *American Instructor*, iv.

6. Fisher, *American Instructor*, 153.

7. Fisher, *American Instructor*, 376.

8. Fisher, *American Instructor*, v. Also see Eve Tavor Bannet, *Empire of Letters: Letter Manuals and Transatlantic Correspondence, 1688–1820* (Cambridge: Cambridge University Press, 2005), 191–92.

9. For overviews of the early American economy, see Stephen Innes, ed., *Work and Labor in Early America* (Chapel Hill: University of North Carolina Press, 1988); John J. McCusker and Russell R. Menard, *The Economy of British America, 1607–1789* (Chapel Hill: University of North Carolina Press, 1985); Cathy Matson, ed., *The Economy of Early America: Historical Perspectives and New Directions* (University Park: Pennsylvania State University Press, 2006). On transformations in markets and trading networks, see Emma Hart, *Trading Spaces: The Colonial Marketplace and the Foundations of American Capitalism* (Chicago: University of Chicago Press, 2019); Sheryllynne Haggerty, *The British-Atlantic Trading Community, 1760–1810: Men, Women, and the Distribution of Goods* (Leiden, Neth.: Brill, 2006). On New England, see especially Daniel Vickers, *Farmers & Fishermen: Two Centuries of Work in Essex County, Massachusetts, 1630–1850* (Chapel Hill: University of North Carolina Press, 1994); Margaret Ellen Newell, *From Dependency to Independence: Economic Revolution in Colonial New England* (Ithaca, NY: Cornell University Press, 1998); Virginia Dejohn Anderson, "Thomas Minor's World: Agrarian Life in Seventeenth-Century New England," *Agricultural History* 82, no. 4 (Fall 2008): 496–518. On changing consumer practices, see Richard Bushman, *The Refinement of America: Persons, Houses, Cities* (New York: Knopf, 1992); T. H. Breen, *The Marketplace of Revolution: How Consumer Politics Shaped American Independence* (New York: Oxford University Press, 2004); Amanda Vickery and John Styles, eds., *Gender, Taste, and Material Culture in Britain and North America, 1700–1830* (New Haven, CT: Yale University Press, 2006); Jan de Vries, *The Industrious Revolution: Consumer Behavior and the Household Economy, 1650 to the Present* (Cambridge: Cambridge University Press, 2008); Ann Smart Martin, *Buying into the World of Goods: Early Consumers in Backcountry Virginia* (Baltimore: Johns Hopkins University Press, 2009).

10. On ports, see Elaine Forman Crane, *A Dependent People: Newport, Rhode Island in the Revolutionary Era* (New York: Fordham University Press, 1985); Gary B. Nash, *The Urban Crucible: Social Change, Political Consciousness, and the Origins of the American Revolution* (Cambridge, MA: Harvard University Press, 1979); Ellen Hartigan-O'Connor,

The Ties that Buy: Women and Commerce in Revolutionary America (Philadelphia: University of Pennsylvania Press, 2009); Serena Zabin, *Dangerous Economies: Status and Commerce in Imperial New York* (Philadelphia: University of Pennsylvania Press, 2009); Emma Hart, *Building Charleston: Town and Society in the Eighteenth-Century British Atlantic World* (Charlottesville: University of Virginia Press, 2010); Mark Peterson, *The City-State of Boston: The Rise and Fall of an Atlantic Power, 1630–1865* (Princeton, NJ: Princeton University Press, 2019).

11. Bruce Mann, *Neighbors and Strangers: Law and Community in Early Connecticut* (Chapel Hill: University of North Carolina Press, 1987); Mary M. Schweitzer, *Custom and Contract: Household, Government, and the Economy in Colonial Pennsylvania* (New York: Columbia University Press, 1987); Craig Muldrew, *The Economy of Obligation: The Culture of Credit and Social Relations in Early Modern England* (New York: St. Martin's, 1998); Mary Poovey, *Genres of the Credit Economy: Mediating Value in Eighteenth- and Nineteenth-Century Britain* (Chicago: University of Chicago Press, 2008); Simon Middleton, "Private Credit in Eighteenth-Century New York City: The Mayor's Court Papers, 1681–1776," *Journal of Early American History* 2, no. 2 (2012): 150–77; Simon Middleton, *From Privileges to Rights: Work and Politics in Colonial New York City* (Philadelphia: University of Pennsylvania Press, 2006); Hartigan-O'Connor, *Ties that Buy*, 69–100; Zabin, *Dangerous Economies*, 10–31. On the variety of monetary and nonmonetary economic relationships existing in early America, see Laurel Thatcher Ulrich, *A Midwife's Tale: The Life of Martha Ballard, Based on her Diary, 1785–1812* (New York: Random House, 1990); Daniel Vickers, "Errors Excepted: The Culture of Credit in Rural New England, 1750–1800," *Economic History Review* 63, no. 4 (Nov. 2010): 1032–57. On paper money, see B. L. Anderson, "Money and the Structure of Credit in the Eighteenth Century," *Business History* 12, no. 2 (July 1970): 85–101; Hartigan-O'Connor, *Ties that Buy*, 101–28; Katherine Smoak, "The Weight of Necessity: Counterfeit Coins in the British Atlantic World, circa 1760–1800," *WMQ* 74, no. 3 (July 2017): 471–76.

12. Mann, *Neighbors and Strangers*; Dayton, *Women Before the Bar*, 69–104; Claire Priest, "Currency Policies and the Nature of Litigation in Colonial New England" (PhD diss., Yale University, 2003); Rosen, *Courts and Commerce*; Schweitzer, *Custom and Contract*; Middleton, *From Privileges to Rights*; Middleton, "Private Credit." For a similar rise in debt litigation in England one century earlier, see Muldrew, *Economy of Obligation*. On the legal profession, see especially Gerald W. Gawalt, *The Promise of Power: The Emergence of the Legal Profession in Massachusetts, 1760–1840* (Westport, CT: Greenwood Press, 1979); John M. Murrin, "The Legal Transformation: The Bench and the Bar of Eighteenth-Century Massachusetts," in *Colonial America: Essays in Politics and Social Development*, 3rd ed., ed. Stanley N. Katz and John M. Murrin (New York: Alfred A. Knopf, 1983), 540–71; A. G. Roeber, *Faithful Magistrates and Republican Lawyers: The Creation of Virginia Legal Culture, 1680–1810* (Chapel Hill: University of North Carolina Press, 1981); Mary Sarah Bilder, *The Transatlantic Constitution: Colonial Legal Culture and the Empire* (Cambridge, MA: Harvard University Press, 2004); Martha G. McNamara, *From Tavern to Courthouse: Architecture and Ritual in American Law, 1658–1860* (Baltimore: Johns Hopkins University Press, 2004).

13. Toby L. Ditz, "Shipwrecked; or, Masculinity Imperiled: Mercantile Representations of Failure and the Gendered Self in Eighteenth-Century Philadelphia," *Journal of American History* 81, no. 1 (June 1994): 51–80; Muldrew, *Economy of Obligation*; Tawny

Paul, *The Poverty of Disaster: Debt and Insecurity in Eighteenth-Century England* (Cambridge: Cambridge University Press, 2019).

14. For helpful discussions of political economy, see "Forum: Rethinking Mercantilism," *WMQ* 69, no. 1 (Jan. 2012): 3–70; Newell, *Dependency to Independence*, 8; Peterson, *City-State of Boston*, 87. On the centrality of gender to the political economy, see Ellen Hartigan-O'Connor, "The Personal Is Political Economy," *Journal of the Early Republic* 36, no. 2 (Summer 2016): 335–41.

15. Even as the present study analyzes the ways in which individuals, identified in the records as men or women, shaped gender relations through their economic practices, eighteenth-century New Englanders possessed a wider range of self-understandings. On gender as a form of "external recognition," see Jen Manion, *Female Husbands: A Trans History* (Cambridge: Cambridge University Press, 2020), esp. 11–12.

16. Recent studies of merchants have similarly reconstructed routine practices and exemplify the analytical payoffs of this approach. See Cathy Matson, "Putting the *Lydia* to Sea: The Material Economy of Shipping in Colonial Philadelphia," *WMQ* 74, no. 2 (Apr. 2017): 303–32; Emma Hart and Cathy Matson, "Situating Merchants in Late Eighteenth-Century British Atlantic Port Cities," *Early American Studies* 15, no. 4 (Fall 2015): 660–82.

17. Other historians are doing crucial work to situate lower-class, Native, and black women, both free and enslaved, within formal and informal economies and legal regimes. On lower-class and black women in the Atlantic economy, see especially Robert Olwell, *Masters, Slaves & Subjects: The Culture of Power in the South Carolina Low Country* (Ithaca, NY: Cornell University Press, 1998), 141–80; Zabin, *Dangerous Economies*, 57–80; Hartigan-O'Connor, *Ties that Buy*, 53–55, 165–67; Nancy Christie, "Merchant and Plebeian Commercial Knowledge in Montreal and Quebec, 1760–1820," *Early American Studies* 13, no. 4 (Fall 2015): 856–80; Marisa J. Fuentes, *Dispossessed Lives: Enslaved Women, Violence, and the Archive* (Philadelphia: University of Pennsylvania Press, 2016), 44, 64–69; Justene Hill, "Felonious Transactions: Legal Culture and Business Practices of Slave Economies in South Carolina, 1787–1860," *Enterprise and Society* 18, no. 4 (Dec. 2017): 772–83; Erin Trahey, "Among Her Kinswomen: Legacies of Free Women of Color in Jamaica," *WMQ* 76, no. 2 (Apr. 2019): 257–88; Shauna J. Sweeney, "Market Marronage: Fugitive Women and the Internal Marketing System in Jamaica, 1781–1834," *WMQ* 76, no. 2 (Apr. 2019): 197–222; Jessica Marie Johnson, *Wicked Flesh: Black Women, Intimacy, and Freedom in the Atlantic World* (Philadelphia: University of Pennsylvania Press, 2020). On the nineteenth century, see Brian P. Luskey and Wendy A. Woloson, eds., *Capitalism by Gaslight: Illuminating the Economy of Nineteenth Century America* (Philadelphia: University of Pennsylvania Press, 2015). On the relationship between slavery and white women's economic activities, see Stephanie Jones-Rogers, *They Were Her Property: White Women as Slaveholders in the American South* (New Haven, CT: Yale University Press, 2019); Christine Walker, *Jamaica Ladies: Female Slaveholders and the Creation of Britain's Atlantic Empire* (Chapel Hill: University of North Carolina Press, 2020).

18. Nash, *Urban Crucible*, 112, 313; Lynne Withey, *Urban Growth in Colonial Rhode Island: Newport and Providence in the Eighteenth Century* (Albany: State University of New York Press, 1984), 115.

19. Crane, *Dependent People*; Stephen Innes, *Creating the Commonwealth: The Economic Culture of Puritan New England* (New York: W. W. Norton, 1995); Newell, *From Dependency to Independence*; Barry Levy, *Town Born: The Political Economy of New*

England from its Founding to the Revolution (Philadelphia: University of Pennsylvania Press, 2009); Peterson, *City-State of Boston.*

20. For examples of the study of free and enslaved women's productive and reproductive labor, see Laurel Thatcher Ulrich, *Good Wives: Image and Reality in the Lives of Women in Northern New England, 1650–1750* (New York: Alfred A. Knopf, 1982); Jeanne Boydston, *Home and Work: Housework, Wages, and the Ideology of Labor in the Early Republic* (Oxford, UK: Oxford University Press, 1990); Ulrich, *Midwife's Tale*; Gloria L. Main, "Gender, Work, and Wages in Colonial New England," *WMQ* 51, no. 1 (Jan. 1994): 39–66; Jennifer L. Morgan, *Laboring Women: Reproduction and Gender in New World Slavery* (Philadelphia: University of Pennsylvania Press, 2004). Recent studies advancing more-capacious frameworks for analyzing women's work include Maria Ågren, ed., *Making a Living, Making a Difference: Gender and Work in Early Modern European Society* (Oxford, UK: Oxford University Press, 2016); Maria Ågren, *The State as Master: Gender, State Formation and Commercialization in Urban Sweden, 1650–1780* (Manchester, UK: Manchester University Press, 2017).

21. Key studies of male merchants include Doerflinger, *Vigorous Spirit of Enterprise*; Hancock, *Citizens of the World*; Cathy Matson, *Merchants & Empire: Trading in Colonial New York* (Baltimore: Johns Hopkins University Press, 1998); Hancock, *Oceans of Wine.* For broader approaches to the study of colonial economies, see Cathy Matson, ed., "Ligaments: Everyday Connections of Colonial Economies," special issue, *Early American Studies* 13, no. 4 (Fall 2015).

22. On women as active participants in both urban economies and transatlantic networks, see especially Hartigan-O'Connor, *Ties that Buy*; Zabin, *Dangerous Economies*; Susanah Shaw Romney, *New Netherland Connections: Intimate Networks and Atlantic Ties in Seventeenth-Century America* (Chapel Hill: University of North Carolina Press, 2014). On family and kinship networks, see Naomi R. Lamoreaux, *Insider Lending: Banks, Personal Connections, and Economic Development in Industrial New England* (Cambridge: Cambridge University Press, 1994); Richard Grassby, *Kinship and Capitalism: Marriage, Family and Business in the English-Speaking World, 1580–1720* (Cambridge: Cambridge University Press, 2001); Julie Hardwick, Sarah M. S. Pearsall, and Karin Wulf, "Introduction: Centering Families in Atlantic Histories," *WMQ* 70, no. 2 (Apr. 2013): 205–22. On female investors, see Robert E. Wright, "Women and Finance in the Early National U.S.," *Essays in History* 42 (2000); Margaret Hunt, "Women and the Fiscal-Imperial State in the Late Seventeenth and Early Eighteenth Centuries," in *A New Imperial History: Culture, Identity, and Modernity in Britain and the Empire, 1660–1840*, ed. Kathleen Wilson (Cambridge: Cambridge University Press, 2004), 29–47; Woody Holton, "Abigail Adams, Bond Speculator," *WMQ* 64, no. 4 (Oct. 2007): 821–38; Anne Laurence, Josephine Maltby, and Janette Rutherford, eds., *Women and their Money, 1700–1950* (London: Routledge, 2009); Amy M. Froide, *Silent Partners: Women as Public Investors during Britain's Financial Revolution, 1690–1750* (Oxford, UK: Oxford University Press, 2016); Misha Ewen, "Women Investors and the Virginia Company in the Early Seventeenth Century," *Historical Journal* (2019): 1–22. On female entrepreneurs, see especially Patricia Cleary, *Elizabeth Murray: A Woman's Pursuit of Independence in Eighteenth-Century America* (Amherst: University of Massachusetts Press, 2000); Douglas Catterall and Jodi Campbell, eds., *Women in Port: Gendering Communities, Economies, and Social Networks in Atlantic Port Cities, 1500–1800* (Leiden, Neth.: Brill, 2012). On household economies

and family businesses, see especially Margaret R. Hunt, *The Middling Sort: Commerce, Gender and the Family in England, 1680–1780* (Berkeley: University of California Press, 1996); Julie Hardwick, *Family Business: Litigation and the Political Economies of Daily Life in Early Modern France* (Oxford, UK: Oxford University Press, 2009); Alexandra Shepard, *Accounting for Oneself: Worth, Status, and the Social Order in Early Modern England* (Oxford, UK: Oxford University Press, 2015); Jones-Minsinger, "Out of the Shadows."

23. For recent essays highlighting these issues, see Seth Rockman, "What Makes the History of Capitalism Newsworthy?," *Journal of the Early Republic* 34, no. 3 (Fall 2014): 439–64; Alexandra Shepard, "Crediting Women in the Early Modern English Economy," *History Workshop Journal* 79, no. 1 (2015): 1–24; Hartigan-O'Connor, "Personal Is Political Economy"; Amy Dru Stanley, "Histories of Capitalism and Sex Difference," *Journal of the Early Republic* 36, no. 2 (Summer 2016): 343–50.

24. Paula R. Backscheider, "Defoe's Lady Credit," *Huntington Library Quarterly* 44, no. 2 (Spring 1981): 89–100; Carl Wennerlind, *Casualties of Credit: The English Financial Revolution, 1620–1720* (Cambridge, MA: Harvard University Press, 2011), 186–88, 191–93; Hartigan-O'Connor, *Ties that Buy*, 70.

25. Mary Beth Norton, "Gender and Defamation in Seventeenth-Century Maryland," *WMQ* 44, no 1. (Jan. 1987): 3–39; Laura Gowing, *Domestic Dangers: Women, Words, and Sex in Early Modern London* (Oxford, UK: Clarendon Press, 1996); Catherine Ingrassia, *Authorship, Commerce, and Gender in Early Eighteenth-Century England: A Culture of Paper Credit* (Cambridge: Cambridge University Press, 1998); Liz Bellamy, *Commerce, Morality, and the Eighteenth-Century Novel* (Cambridge; Cambridge University Press, 1998); Ditz, "Shipwrecked"; Alexandra Shepard, "Manhood, Credit, and Patriarchy in Early Modern England, c. 1560–1640," *Past and Present* 167, no. 1 (May 2000): 75–106; Toby L. Ditz, "Secret Selves, Credible Personas: The Problematics of Trust and Public Display in the Writing of Eighteenth-Century Philadelphia Merchants," in *Possible Pasts: Becoming Colonial in Early America*, ed. Robert Blair St. George (Ithaca, NY: Cornell University Press, 2000): 219–42; Donna Merwick, "A Genre of Their Own: Kiliaen van Rensselaer as a Guide to the Reading and Writing Practices of Early Modern Businessmen," *WMQ* 64, no. 4 (Oct. 2008): 669–712; Clare Crowston, *Credit, Fashion, Sex: Economies of Regard in Old Regime France* (Durham, NC: Duke University Press, 2013); Paul, *Poverty of Disaster*.

26. On the categories of public and private, see especially Mary Beth Norton, *Founding Mothers & Fathers: Gendered Power and the Forming of an American Society* (New York: Alfred A. Knopf, 1996); Mary Beth Norton, *Separated by their Sex: Women in Public and Private in the Colonial Atlantic World* (Ithaca, NY: Cornell University Press, 2011). On the gendering of household and non-household spaces, see also Ulrich, *Good Wives*; Ulrich, *Midwife's Tale*.

27. Laura Gowing, *Domestic Dangers: Women, Words, and Sex in Early Modern London* (Oxford, UK: Clarendon Press, 1996); Julie Hardwick, *The Practice of Patriarchy: Gender and the Politics of Household Authority in Early Modern France* (Philadelphia: University of Pennsylvania Press, 1998); Laura Gowing, *Common Bodies: Women, Touch, and Power in Seventeenth-Century England* (New Haven, CT: Yale University Press, 2003); Hartigan-O'Connor, *Ties that Buy*; Hardwick, *Family Business*; Amanda Vickery, *Behind Closed Doors: At Home in Georgian England* (New Haven, CT: Yale University Press, 2010); Emma Hart, *Building Charleston: Town and Society in the Eighteenth-Century British Atlantic World* (Charlottesville: University of Virginia Press, 2010), 98–129; Sonya

Lipsett-Rivera, *Gender and the Negotiation of Daily Life in Mexico, 1750–1856* (Lincoln: University of Nebraska Press, 2012); Caylin Carbonell, "Fraught Labor, Fragile Authority: Households in Motion in Early New England" (PhD diss., William & Mary, 2020).

28. Works emphasizing the distinctive social position of *femes sole* in early North America include Suzanne Lebsock, *The Free Women of Petersburg: Status and Culture in a Southern Town* (New York: W. W. Norton, 1984); Lisa Wilson, *Life after Death: Widows in Pennsylvania, 1750–1850* (Philadelphia: Temple University Press, 1992); Wulf, *Not All Wives*; Linda L. Sturtz, *Within Her Power: Propertied Women in Colonial America* (New York: Routledge, 2002); Vivian Bruce Conger, *The Widow's Might: Widowhood and Gender in Early British America* (New York: New York University Press, 2009). For early modern England, see especially Judith M. Bennett and Amy M. Froide, eds., *Single Women in the European Past, 1250–1850* (Philadelphia: University of Pennsylvania Press, 1999); Amy M. Froide, *Never Married: Singlewomen in Early Modern Europe* (Oxford, UK: Oxford University Press, 2005).

29. Ulrich, *Good Wives*, 9, 36.

30. On property law, see especially Marylynn Salmon, *Women and the Law of Property in Early America* (Chapel Hill: University of North Carolina Press, 1986). On coverture and its limitations, see Margot Finn, "Women, Consumption, and Coverture in England, 1760–1860," *Historical Journal* 39, no. 3 (Sept. 1996): 703–22; Craig Muldrew, "'A Mutual Assent of Her Mind'? Women, Debt, Litigation, and Contract in Early Modern England," *History Workshop Journal* 55 (2003): 47–71; Nicola Phillips, *Women in Business, 1700–1850* (Woodbridge, UK: Boydell, 2006), 23–47; Holly Brewer, "The Transformation of Domestic Law," in *The Cambridge History of Law in America*, vol. 1, *Early America*, ed. Michael Grossberg and Christopher Tomlins (Cambridge: Cambridge University Press, 2008), 288–323; Alexandra Shepard, "Minding Their Own Business: Married Women and Credit in Early Eighteenth-Century London," *Transactions of the Royal Historical Society* 25 (2015): 53–74.

31. Ross W. Beales and E. Jennifer Monaghan, "Literacy and Schoolbooks," in *A History of the Book in America*, vol. 1, *The Colonial Book in the Atlantic World*, ed. Hugh Amory and David D. Hall (New York: Cambridge University Press, 2000), 380. See also Kenneth A. Lockridge, *Literacy in Colonial New England: An Enquiry into the Social Context of Literacy in the Early Modern West* (New York: W. W. Norton, 1974); Gloria Main, "An Inquiry into When and Why Women Learned to Write in Colonial New England," *Journal of Social History* 24, no. 3 (Spring 1991): 579–89.

32. On New England's distinctive religious culture, see David D. Hall, *Worlds of Wonder, Days of Judgment: Popular Religious Belief in Early New England* (Cambridge, MA: Harvard University Press, 1990). On reading and writing in colonial America, see especially Lockridge, *Literacy in Colonial New England*; Main, "An Inquiry"; Beales and Monaghan, "Literacy and Schoolbooks," 380–87; E. Jennifer Monaghan, *Learning to Read and Write in Colonial America* (Amherst: University of Massachusetts Press, 2005); Konstantin Dierks, *In My Power: Letter Writing and Communications in Early America* (Philadelphia: University of Pennsylvania Press, 2009), 141–88.

33. On literacy and numeracy, see Monaghan, *Learning to Read*; Patricia Cline Cohen, *A Calculating People: The Spread of Numeracy in Early America* (Chicago: University of Chicago Press, 1982). On legal literacy as a skill set, see Tim Stretton, "Women, Legal Records, and the Problem of the Lawyer's Hand," *Journal of British Studies* 58, no. 4

(Oct. 2019): 684–700; Mary Bilder, "The Lost Lawyers: Early American Legal Literates and the Transatlantic Legal Culture," *Yale Journal of Law and the Humanities* 11, no. 1 (1999): 47–117. On laypeople's involvement in science and medicine, see, for instance, Christopher M. Parsons, *A Not-So-New World: Empire and Environment in French Colonial North America* (Philadelphia: University of Pennsylvania Press, 2018); Cameron Strange, *Frontiers of Science: Imperialism and Natural Knowledge in the Gulf South Borderlands, 1500–1850* (Chapel Hill: University of North Carolina Press, 2018); Sarah Knott, "The Patient's Case," *WMQ* 67, no. 4 (Oct. 2010), 634–76; Susan Scott Parrish, *American Curiosity: Cultures of Natural History in the Colonial British Atlantic World* (Chapel Hill: University of North Carolina Press, 2006).

34. See, for instance, Carole Shammas, "Anglo-American Household Government in Comparative Perspective," *WMQ* 52, no. 1 (Jan. 1995): 104–44; Kathleen M. Brown, *Good Wives, Nasty Wenches, and Anxious Patriarchs: Gender, Race, and Power in Colonial Virginia* (Chapel Hill: University of North Carolina Press, 1996), 4–5.

35. The most influential study arguing that the development of formal institutions led to a decline in status for colonial North American women is Dayton, *Women Before the Bar*. The present study challenges Dayton's arguments that women's involvement in the credit economy and debt litigation declined, beginning in the 1720s, and that the formalization of both law and credit relationships necessarily led to such declines. It concurs, however, with Dayton's arguments that elite women increasingly distanced themselves from financial practices during the late eighteenth century, and that economic and legal changes contributed to the redefinition of civic life as a masculine arena by the Early Republic. See also Rosen, *Courts and Commerce*; Crane, *Ebb Tide*.

36. Studies emphasizing cultural and political shifts include Martha Howell, *Women, Production, and Patriarchy in Late Medieval Cities* (Chicago: University of Chicago Press, 1986); Martha Howell, *The Marriage Exchange: Property, Social Place, and Gender in the Cities of the Low Countries* (Chicago: University of Chicago Press, 1998). On the broad consequences of the Age of Revolutions, see Rachel Weil, *Political Passions: Gender, the Family, and Political Argument in England, 1680–1714* (Manchester, UK: Manchester University Press, 1999); Sarah C. Chambers, *From Subjects to Citizens: Honor, Gender, and Politics in Arequipa, Peru, 1780–1854* (University Park: Pennsylvania State University Press, 1999); Linda Kerber, *No Constitutional Right to Be Ladies: Women and the Obligations of Citizenship* (New York: Hill & Wang, 2001); Arlene J. Díaz, *Female Citizens, Patriarchs, and the Law in Venezuela, 1786–1904* (Lincoln: University of Nebraska Press, 2004); Mary P. Ryan, *Mysteries of Sex: Tracing Women and Men through American History* (Chapel Hill: University of North Carolina Press, 2006), 147–201; Christopher Tomlins, *Freedom Bound: Law, Labor, and Civic Identity in Colonial English America, 1580–1865* (Cambridge: Cambridge University Press, 2010).

37. On trade, see Bernard Bailyn, *New England Merchants in the Seventeenth Century* (Cambridge, MA: Harvard University Press, 1955); Crane, *Dependent People*; Nash, *Urban Crucible*; Newell, *From Dependency to Independence*; Levy, *Town Born*; James W. Roberts, "'Yankey Dodle Will Do Verry Well Here': New England Traders in the Caribbean, 1713 to circa 1812" (PhD diss., Johns Hopkins University, 2011); Peterson, *City-State of Boston*. On Newport's involvement in the slave trade, see Jay Coughtry, *The Notorious Triangle: Rhode Island and the African Slave Trade, 1700–1807* (Philadelphia: Temple University Press, 1981); Rachel Chernos Lin, "The Rhode Island Slave Traders: Butchers, Bakers, and Candlestick

Makers," *Slavery and Abolition* 23, no. 3 (Dec. 2002): 21–38; Gregory E. O'Malley, "Beyond the Middle Passage: Slave Migration from the Caribbean to North America, 1619–1807," *WMQ* 66, no. 1 (Jan. 2009): 159–65; Christy Clark-Pujara, *Dark Work: The Business of Slavery in Rhode Island* (New York: New York University Press, 2016).

38. On Boston's and Newport's economies generally, see Crane, *Dependent People*; Nash, *Urban Crucible*; Newell, *Dependency to Independence*; Levy, *Town Born*; Peterson, *City-State of Boston*. On women's contributions to New England port economies, see also Cleary, *Elizabeth Murray*; Ellen Hartigan-O'Connor, "'She Said She Did Not Know Money': Urban Women and Atlantic Markets in the Revolutionary Era," *Early American Studies* 4, no. 2 (Fall 2006): 322–52; Hartigan-O'Connor, *Ties that Buy*, 39–68; Conger, *The Widow's Might*. For comparisons with other port cities, see Wulf, *Not All Wives*; Sheryllynne Haggerty, "'Miss Fan can tun her han!': Female Traders in Eighteenth-Century British American Atlantic Port Cities," *Atlantic Studies* 6, no. 1 (Apr. 2009): 29–42; Zabin, *Dangerous Economies*; Sophie White, "'A Baser Commerce': Retailing, Class, and Gender in French Colonial New Orleans," *WMQ* 63, no. 3 (July 2006), 517–70; Catterall and Campbell, eds., *Women in Port*.

39. On Boston's and Newport's demographics, see Crane, *Ebb Tide*, 11–12, 14–16. On seafaring communities, see Crane, *Dependent People*, 69–75; Ruth Wallis Herndon, "The Domestic Cost of Seafaring: Town Leaders and Seamen's Families in Eighteenth-Century Rhode Island," in *Iron Men, Wooden Women: Gender and Seafaring in the Atlantic World, 1700–1920*, ed. Margaret S. Creighton and Lisa Norling (Baltimore: Johns Hopkins University Press, 1996), 55–69; Lisa Norling, *Captain Ahab Had a Wife: New England Women and the Whalefishery, 1720–1870* (Chapel Hill: University of North Carolina Press, 2000); Daniel Vickers, with Vince Walsh, *Young Men and the Sea: Yankee Seafarers in the Age of Sail* (New Haven, CT: Yale University Press, 2005). On widows and single women in other port cities, see Froide, *Never Married*; Wulf, *Not All Wives*.

40. Nash, *Urban Crucible*, 166; Hunt, "Women and the Fiscal-Imperial State"; Hartigan-O'Connor, *Ties that Buy*.

41. Crane, *Dependent People*; Nash, *Urban Crucible*; Catherine A. Brekus, *Sarah Osborn's World: The Rise of Evangelical Christianity in Early America* (New Haven, CT: Yale University Press, 2013), 198.

42. Newell, *Dependency to Independence*, 107–236, esp. 128–29, 186–87, 197–98, 232; Christine Desan, *Making Money: Coin, Currency, and the Coming of Capitalism* (Oxford, UK: Oxford University Press, 2015); Peterson, *City-State of Boston*, esp. 85–88.

43. Nash, *Urban Crucible*, 61–63, 112–15, 174, 316–19.

44. Nash, *Urban Crucible*, 115, 317–18; Claire Priest, "Currency Policies and the Nature of Litigation in Colonial New England" (PhD diss., Yale University, 2003); Claire Priest, "Currency Policies and the Nature of Litigation in Colonial New England," *Journal of Economic History* 64, no. 2 (June 2004): 563–69.

45. Gawalt, *Promise of Power*, 313–58; Murrin, "Legal Transformation"; Charles McKirdy, "Massachusetts Lawyers on the Eve of the American Revolution: The State of the Profession," in *Law in Colonial Massachusetts, 1630–1800*, ed. Daniel R. Coquillette (Boston: Colonial Society of Massachusetts, 1984); McNamara, *From Tavern to Courthouse*; Bilder, *Transatlantic Constitution*. On court days, see also Roeber, *Faithful Magistrates*.

46. On printing and the book trade, see especially Amory and Hall, eds., *A History of the Book in America*, vol. 1.

47. Crane, *Dependent People*, 49–52; Withey, *Urban Growth*, 115; Benjamin Carp, *Rebels Rising: Cities and the American Revolution* (Oxford, UK: Oxford University Press, 2007), 25, 27–28; Hartigan-O'Connor, *Ties that Buy*, 15–23.

48. Withey, *Urban Growth*, 130; Nash, *Urban Crucible*, 194; Sharon V. Salinger and Charles Wetherell, "Wealth and Renting in Prerevolutionary Philadelphia," *Journal of American History* 71, no. 4 (Mar. 1985): 829; Edward A. Chappell, "Housing a Nation: The Transformation of Living Standards in Early America," in *Of Consuming Interests: The Style of Life in the Eighteenth Century*, ed. Cary Carson, Ronald Hoffman, and Peter J. Albert (Charlottesville: University Press of Virginia, 1994), 186–90; Hartigan-O'Connor, *Ties that Buy*, 13–38.

49. On women's economic activities in rural New England, see especially Ulrich, *Good Wives*; Ulrich, *Midwife's Tale*; Marla R. Miller, *Entangled Lives: Labor, Livelihood, and Landscape in Rural Massachusetts* (Baltimore: Johns Hopkins University Press, 2019).

50. In comparison with Dutch, French, and Spanish legal regimes, distinguishing features of British law included coverture and the absence of a notarial system by which private transactions received state imprimatur. On the distinctiveness of English law, see Amy Louise Erickson, "Coverture and Capitalism," *History Workshop Journal* 59 (Spring 2005): 1–16. For comparisons with other European empires, see Hardwick, *Practice of Patriarchy*; Jane E. Mangan, *Trading Roles: Gender, Ethnicity, and the Urban Economy in Colonial Potosi* (Durham, NC: Duke University Press, 2005); Hardwick, *Family Business*; Catterall and Campbell, eds, *Women in Port*; Romney, *New Netherland Connections*. For comparisons with the British Caribbean, see Christine Walker, "Pursuing Her Profits: Women in Jamaica, Atlantic Slavery and a Globalising Market, 1700–60," *Gender & History* 26, no. 3 (Nov. 2014): 478–501; Erin Trahey, "Free Women and the Making of Colonial Jamaican Economy and Society" (PhD diss., University of Cambridge, 2018). For comparisons between England and British North America, see Lindsay R. Moore, *Women Before the Court: Law and Patriarchy in the Anglo-American World, 1600–1800* (Manchester, UK: Manchester University Press, 2019).

51. See especially Dayton, *Women Before the Bar*; Rosen, *Courts and Commerce*. Other studies that rely extensively on court records include Hartigan-O'Connor, *Ties that Buy*; Zabin, *Dangerous Economies*.

52. On "legal ephemera," see Tom Johnson, "Legal Ephemera in the Ecclesiastical Courts of Medieval England," *Open Library of Humanities* 5, no. 1 (Feb. 2019), https://olh.openlibhums.org/articles/10.16995/olh.334/.

53. Fuentes, *Dispossessed Lives*, 2.

54. While slavery was central to social hierarchies throughout colonial British America, New England cities' involvement in the slave trade did not lead them to have larger enslaved populations than other cities or surrounding towns. Boston's and Newport's populations included roughly the same percentage of slaves as other northern North American ports, and they had a lower percentage of slaves than did surrounding Massachusetts and Rhode Island towns that used slave labor for farming and dairying. See Crane, *Dependent People*, 57, 75–83; Withey, *Urban Growth*, 71–2; William D. Pierson, *Black Yankees: The Development of an Afro-American Subculture in Eighteenth-Century New England* (Amherst: University of Massachusetts Press, 1988), 13–22; Nash, *Urban Crucible*, 107, 320; Hartigan-O'Connor, *Ties that Buy*, 19–20, 202–3n13; Jared Hardesty, "'The Negro at the Gate': Enslaved Labor in Colonial Boston," *New England Quarterly* 87, no. 1

(Mar. 2014): 72–98; Jared Hardesty, *Unfreedom: Slavery and Dependence in Eighteenth-Century Boston* (New York: New York University Press, 2016).

55. Nash, "Urban Wealth and Poverty," 112–13, 125, 128, 161–97, 246–64, 313–15; Benjamin Carp, *Defiance of the Patriots: The Boston Tea Party and the Making of America* (New Haven, CT: Yale University Press, 2010), 32–33; Brekus, *Sarah Osborn's World*, 191–247.

56. According to Newport's 1774 census, 18% of the city's population was black, mulatto, or Native, with free blacks composing 1.7% of the population. Roughly 8% of Boston's residents were enslaved and, in total, 10% of that city's population consisted of people of color. See Crane, *Dependent People*, 82; Ellen Hartigan-O'Connor, *The Measure of the Market: Women's Economic Lives in Charleston, SC and Newport, RI, 1750–1820* (PhD diss., University of Michigan, 2003), 32–33.

57. John Wood Sweet, *Bodies Politic: Negotiating Race in the American North, 1730–1830* (Baltimore: Johns Hopkins University Press, 2003); Beverley Lemire, *The Business of Everyday Life: Gender and Social Politics in England, c. 1600–1900* (Manchester, UK: Manchester University Press, 2005), 56–109; Seth Rockman, *Scraping By: Wage Labor, Slavery, and Survival in Early Baltimore* (Baltimore: Johns Hopkins University Press, 2008), 158–93; Zabin, *Dangerous Economies*, 57–80.

58. Account of Administration, Estate of Ann Kees, Jan. 7, 1745, Newport TC, vol. 9, 100, NHS. See also the payment to "Mrs Hull's negro woman" in Account of Administration, Estate of Patience Williams, Mar. 27, 1757, Newport TC, vol. 12, 161, NHS; the account of "Dinah" with shopkeeper Martha Salisbury, in Martha Salisbury Account Book, 1753–1773, Salisbury Family Papers, octavo vol. 4, AAS. Dinah's account was the only one for which Martha Salisbury did not record a last name, a detail which strongly suggests that she was either a free or enslaved black woman. On financial records kept by Cesar Lyndon, an enslaved man in Newport, see Tara Bynum, "Cesar Lyndon's Lists, Letters, and a Pig Roast: *A Sundry Account Book*," *Early American Literature* 53, no. 3 (Fall 2018): 839–49.

59. *Freeman v. Easton*, Newport CCP, May 1746, #156, RIJRC. The promissory note included only the standard phrasing whereby Easton promised to pay Freeman in exchange "for value received."

60. Daniel Vickers, "The First Whalemen of Nantucket," *WMQ* 40, no. 4 (Oct. 1983): 560–83; Jean M. O'Brien, *Dispossession by Degrees: Indian Land and Identity in Natick, Massachusetts, 1650–1790* (Cambridge: Cambridge University Press, 1997), 132–43; David J. Silverman, "The Impact of Indentured Servitude on the Society and Culture of Southern New England Indians, 1680–1810," *New England Quarterly* 74, no. 4 (Dec. 2001): 622–66; Sweet, *Bodies Politic*, 36–43; Margaret Newell, *Brethren by Nature: Indians, Colonists, and the Origins of American Slavery* (Ithaca, NY: Cornell University Press, 2015); Linford D. Fisher, "'Why Shall Wee Have Peace to Bee Made Slaves': Indian Surrenders during and after King Philip's War," *Ethnohistory* 64, no. 1 (Jan. 2017): 91–114. On the blurred line between slavery and indentured servitude, see Sweet, *Bodies Politic*, 83–87, 225–67. On systems of indentured and enslaved labor, see also Tomlins, *Freedom Bound*.

Chapter 1 · Women and the Urban Credit Economy

1. Deposition of Samuel Welsh ("wrong"), Deposition of David Moore ("before severall people," "in the street"), Deposition of John Lawrence, and Deposition of Job Bennet, *Grant v. Potter*, Newport CCP, May 1746, #87, RIJRC. On slanderous speech against women, see Mary Beth Norton, "Gender and Defamation in Seventeenth-Century Maryland," *WMQ*

44, no 1. (Jan. 1987): 3–39; Kathleen M. Brown, *Good Wives, Nasty Wenches, and Anxious Patriarchs: Gender, Race, and Power in Colonial Virginia* (Chapel Hill: University of North Carolina Press, 1996), 306–18; Laura Gowing, *Domestic Dangers: Women, Words, and Sex in Early Modern London* (Oxford, UK: Clarendon Press, 1996); Bernard Capp, *When Gossips Meet: Women, Family, and Neighborhood in Early Modern England* (Oxford, UK: Oxford University Press, 2003).

2. On taverns and coffeehouses as public spaces, see David W. Conroy, *In Public Houses: Drink and the Revolution of Authority in Colonial Massachusetts* (Chapel Hill: University of North Carolina Press, 1995); David Shields, *Civil Tongues and Polite Letters in British America* (Chapel Hill: University of North Carolina Press, 1997), 55–98; Sharon V. Salinger, *Taverns and Drinking in Early America* (Baltimore: Johns Hopkins University Press, 2002); Bryan Cowan, *The Social Life of Coffee: The Emergence of the British Coffeehouse* (New Haven, CT: Yale University Press, 2005); Benjamin Carp, *Rebels Rising: Cities and the American Revolution* (Oxford, UK: Oxford University Press, 2007), 62–98.

3. *Grant v. Potter*, Newport CCP, May 1746, #87, RIJRC.

4. On widows, see Lisa Wilson, *Life after Death: Widows in Pennsylvania, 1750–1850* (Philadelphia: Temple University Press, 1992); Linda L. Sturtz, *Within Her Power: Propertied Women in Colonial America* (New York: Routledge, 2002); Vivian Bruce Conger, *The Widow's Might: Widowhood and Gender in Early British America* (New York: New York University Press, 2009). On never-married women, see Karin Wulf, *Not All Wives: Women of Colonial Philadelphia* (Ithaca, NY: Cornell University Press, 2000); Amy M. Froide, *Never Married: Singlewomen in Early Modern Europe* (Oxford, UK: Oxford University Press, 2005).

5. On Boston and Newport, see especially Elaine Forman Crane, *A Dependent People: Newport, Rhode Island in the Revolutionary Era* (New York: Fordham University Press, 1985); Gary B. Nash, *The Urban Crucible: Social Change, Political Consciousness, and the Origins of the American Revolution* (Cambridge, MA: Harvard University Press, 1979); Elaine Forman Crane, *Ebb Tide in New England: Women, Seaports, and Social Change, 1600–1800* (Boston: Northeastern University Press, 1998); Mark Peterson, *The City-State of Boston: The Rise and Fall of an Atlantic Power, 1630–1865* (Princeton, NJ: Princeton University Press, 2019). On maritime communities, see also Daniel Vickers, with Vince Walsh, *Young Men and the Sea: Yankee Seafarers in the Age of Sail* (New Haven, CT: Yale University Press, 2005); Lisa Norling, *Captain Ahab Had a Wife: New England Women and the Whalefishery, 1720–1870* (Chapel Hill: University of North Carolina Press, 2000).

6. Crane, *Ebb Tide*, 9–20.

7. On women's networks, see Laurel Thatcher Ulrich, *Good Wives: Image and Reality in the Lives of Women in Northern New England, 1650–1750* (New York: Alfred A. Knopf, 1982); Laurel Thatcher Ulrich, *A Midwife's Tale: The Life of Martha Ballard, Based on Her Diary, 1785–1812* (New York: Random House, 1990); Beverly Lemire, *The Business of Everyday Life: Gender, Practice and Social Politics in England, c. 1600–1900* (Manchester, UK: Manchester University Press, 2005), 16–55.

8. For an overview of gender relations in colonial British America, see Mary Beth Norton, *Founding Mothers & Fathers: Gendered Power and the Forming of American Society* (New York: Vintage Books, 1996).

9. Petition of Joseph Prince, MA Archives, vol. 43, 461–63, MSA; *MacDaniel v. Fry*, Newport CCP, May 1741, #132, RIJRC.

10. Marylynn Salmon, *Women and the Law of Property in Early America* (Chapel Hill: University of North Carolina Press, 1986); Lindsay R. Moore, *Women Before the Court: Law and Patriarchy in the Anglo-American World, 1600–1800* (Manchester, UK: Manchester University Press, 2019), 21–38. On gender and archival silences, see Marisa J. Fuentes, *Dispossessed Lives: Enslaved Women, Violence, and the Archive* (Philadelphia: University of Pennsylvania Press, 2016).

11. William Blackstone, *Commentaries on the Laws of England*, vol. 1 (Oxford, UK: Clarendon Press, 1765), 430.

12. Craig Muldrew, "'A Mutual Assent of Her Mind'? Women, Debt, Litigation, and Contract in Early Modern England," *History Workshop Journal* 55 (2003): 47–71; Nicola Phillips, *Women in Business, 1700–1850* (Woodbridge, UK: Boydell, 2006), 23–47; Holly Brewer, "The Transformation of Domestic Law," in *The Cambridge History of Law in America*, vol. 1, *Early America*, ed. Michael Grossberg and Christopher Tomlins (Cambridge: Cambridge University Press, 2008), 288–323.

13. [John Barnard], *A Present for an Apprentice: Or, a Sure Guide to gain both Esteem and Estate*, 4th ed. (Philadelphia: B. Franklin & D. Hall, 1749), ("whole happiness") 86, ("fair wife") 91. See also Margaret R. Hunt, *The Middling Sort: Commerce, Gender, and the Family in England, 1680–1780* (Berkeley: University of California Press, 1996).

14. Deposition of Joseph Nichols, *Grant v. Bennet*, Newport CCP, May 1741, #134, RIJRC.

15. David Hancock, *Citizens of the World: London Merchants and the Integration of the British Atlantic Community, 1735–1785* (Cambridge: Cambridge University Press, 1995); Margaret R. Hunt, *The Middling Sort: Commerce, Gender, and the Family in England, 1680–1780* (Berkeley: University of California Press, 1996); Julie Hardwick, *The Practice of Patriarchy: Gender and the Politics of Household Authority in Early Modern France* (Philadelphia: University of Pennsylvania Press, 1998); Peter Mathias, "Risk, Credit, and Kinship in Early Modern Enterprise," in *The Early Modern Atlantic Economy*, ed. John J. McCusker and Kenneth Morgan (Cambridge: Cambridge University Press, 2000), 15–35; Richard Grassby, *Kinship and Capitalism: Marriage, Family, and Business in the English-Speaking World, 1580–1720* (Cambridge: Cambridge University Press, 2001); Julie Hardwick, *Family Business: Litigation and the Political Economies of Daily Life in Early Modern France* (Oxford, UK: Oxford University Press, 2009); Ellen Hartigan-O'Connor, *The Ties that Buy: Women and Commerce in Revolutionary America* (Philadelphia: University of Pennsylvania Press, 2009), 69–100; Lindsay Mitchell Keiter, "Uniting Interests: The Economic Function of Marriage in America, 1750–1860" (PhD diss., College of William and Mary, 2016). On the importance of families in the Atlantic World, see also Sarah M. S. Pearsall, *Atlantic Families: Lives and Letters in the Later Eighteenth Century* (Oxford, UK: Oxford University Press, 2008); Julie Hardwick, Sarah M. S. Pearsall, and Karin Wulf, "Introduction: Centering Families in Atlantic Histories," *WMQ* 70, no. 2 (Apr. 2013): 205–24; Jane E. Mangan, *Creating the Bonds of Family in Conquest-Era Peru and Spain* (Oxford, UK: Oxford University Press, 2015).

16. "Reply to a Piece of Advice," *Pennsylvania Gazette*, Mar. 4, 1734/1735.

17. Cotton Mather, *Ornaments for the Daughters of Zion* (Cambridge, MA: S. G. & B. G., 1692), 82–83; *Reflections on Courtship and Marriage [. . .]* (Philadelphia: B. Franklin, 1746), 46; [Barnard], *A Present for an Apprentice*, 89–90; [Mary Wray, or Richard Steele and George Berkeley?], *The Ladies Library*, 6th ed. (London: J. & R. Tonson & S. Draper,

1751), vol. 1: 95–97; [George Savile], *The Lady's New-year's Gift; or, Advice to a Daughter* (London: T. Caxton, 1758), 31–33; [William Kenrick], *The Whole Duty of Woman [. . .]* (London, repr. Boston: Fowle & Draper, 1761), 33, 43.

18. Benjamin Franklin, *Autobiography of Benjamin Franklin*, in *The Life of Benjamin Franklin*, vol. 1, ed. John Bigelow (Philadelphia: J. B. Lippincott, 1875), 205. See also Joseph M. Adelman, *Revolutionary Networks: The Business and Politics of Printing the News* (Baltimore: Johns Hopkins University Press, 2019), 22–26.

19. Hartigan-O'Connor, *Ties that Buy*, 69–100, 129–60.

20. Answer of Abigail Fry, *MacDaniel v. Fry*, Newport CCP, May 1741, #132, RIJRC. See also Nash, *Urban Crucible*, esp. 16, 19, 63–64, 115; Crane, *Dependent People*, 63–68; Billy G. Smith, *The "Lower Sort": Philadelphia's Laboring People, 1750–1800* (Ithaca, NY: Cornell University Press, 1990), 4, 113–14; Daniel Vickers, *Farmers & Fishermen: Two Centuries of Work in Essex County, Massachusetts, 1630–1850* (Chapel Hill: University of North Carolina Press, 1994), 184–88; Margaret Hunt, "Women and the Fiscal-Imperial State in the Late Seventeenth and Early Eighteenth Centuries," in *A New Imperial History: Culture, Identity, and Modernity in Britain and the Empire, 1660–1840*, ed. Kathleen Wilson (Cambridge: Cambridge University Press, 2004), 29–47; Vickers, *Young Men and the Sea*, esp. 107, 117.

21. Salmon, *Women and the Law of Property*, 58–80; Crane, *Ebb Tide*, 190–96; Clare Lyons, *Sex among the Rabble: An Intimate History of Gender and Power in the Age of Revolution* (Chapel Hill: University of North Carolina Press, 2006), 14–58.

22. On the law of necessaries, see Margot Finn, "Women, Consumption, and Coverture in England, 1760–1860," *Historical Journal* 39, no. 3 (Sept. 1996): 709–14; Muldrew, "Mutual Assent," 60–64; Hartigan-O'Connor, *Ties that Buy*, 137. On pawning, see Jane E. Mangan, *Trading Roles: Gender, Ethnicity, and the Urban Economy in Colonial Potosí* (Durham, NC: Duke University Press, 2005), 119–26; Hartigan-O'Connor, *Ties that Buy*, 93–94, 114, 137–38, 167; Serena Zabin, *Dangerous Economies: Status and Commerce in Imperial New York* (Philadelphia: University of Pennsylvania Press, 2009), 73–75. On the MacDaniels' goods, see *MacDaniel v. Fry*, Newport CCP, May 1741, #132, RIJRC.

23. Petition of Joseph Prince, MA Archives, vol. 43, 461–63, MSA; Answer of John Wheelwright, MA Archives, vol. 43, 466–67, MSA.

24. "An Act, for Granting Administrations to the Wives of Persons Three Years absent, and unheard of" (1711) and "An Act for the Explanation of, and further Enlargement of an Act Passed by the General Assembly . . . for the Granting of Administrations to the Wives of Persons Three Years absent, and not heard of" (1717), *Acts and Laws of His Majesties Colony of Rhode-Island, and Providence-Plantations in America* (Boston: John Allen, 1719), 67–68, 81–83. Petitions by sailors' wives include Petition of Frances Child (1748), RI Petitions, vol. 7, 17, RISA; Petition of Sarah Mason (1753), RI Petitions, vol. 8, 99, RISA; Petition of Mary Center (1757), RI Petitions, vol. 9, 195, RISA; Petition of Martha Salisbury (1768), RI Petitions, vol. 13, 28, RISA. See also Ruth Wallis Herndon, "The Domestic Cost of Seafaring: Town Leaders and Seamen's Families in Eighteenth-Century Rhode Island," in *Iron Men, Wooden Women: Gender and Seafaring in the Atlantic World, 1700–1920*, ed. Margaret S. Creighton and Lisa Norling (Baltimore: Johns Hopkins University Press, 1996), 55–69; Norling, *Captain Ahab Had a Wife*, 15–50.

25. Nash, *Urban Crucible*, 169–72, 242–43; Crane, *Ebb Tide*, 12, 14; Peterson, *City-State of Boston*, 247–93.

26. Nash, *Urban Crucible*, 172, 245; Crane, *Ebb Tide*, 13–17; Hunt, "Women and the Fiscal-Imperial State."

27. Nash, *Urban Crucible*, 184–97.

28. Petition of Joseph Prince, MA Archives, vol. 43, 461–63, MSA.

29. *MacDaniel v. Fry*, Newport CCP, May 1741, #132, RIJRC.

30. Declaration of Bryan MacDaniel, *MacDaniel v. Fry*, Newport CCP, May 1741, #132, RIJRC; Answer of Abigail Fry and Account of Bathiah MacDaniel with Abigail Fry, *MacDaniel v. Fry*, Newport CCP, May 1741, #132, RIJRC.

31. Answer of Abigail Fry, *MacDaniel v. Fry*, Newport CCP, May 1741, #132, RIJRC.

32. *Prince v. Wheelwright* (1748), Suffolk Files, 64,887, MSA.

33. Petition of Joseph Prince, MA Archives, vol. 43, 461–63, MSA.

34. Answer of John Wheelwright, MA Archives, vol. 43, 466–67, MSA.

35. Answer of Job Lawton, *Chapman v. Lawton*, Newport SCJ, Sept. 1733, RIJRC.

36. Crane, *Ebb Tide*, 168–69.

37. Judgment, *MacDaniel v. Fry*, Newport CCP, May 1741, #132, RIJRC.

38. Action on Petition of Joseph Prince, MA Archives, vol. 43, 468, MSA.

39. Finn, "Women, Consumption, and Coverture," 707.

40. On the Grant residence, see Hoke P. Kimball and Bruce Henson, *Governor's Houses and State Houses in Colonial America, 1607–1783: An Historical, Architectural, and Archeological Survey* (Jefferson, NC: Macfarland, 2017), 203.

41. For the initial explosion, see "Newport, Sept. 21" ("sorrowful accident"), *Boston Gazette*, Sept. 25, 1744, [2]; "Newport, Rhode-Island, September 21," *American Weekly Mercury*, Oct. 4, 1744, [2]; "Newport, Rhode-Island, September 14," *Pennsylvania Journal, or Weekly Advertiser*, Oct. 4, 1744, [2]. For Grant's death, see "Newport, Sept. 28," *Boston Evening Post*, Oct. 1, 1744, [1–2]. For the final return of Grant's vessel, the *Prince Frederick*, to Newport prior to the merchant's death, see "New-Port, Sept. 14th 1744," *Boston Weekly Post-Boy*, Sept. 17, 1744, [2]. On privateering, see Nash, *Urban Crucible*, 165–69.

42. *Temperance and Patrick Grant v. Job Caswell*, Nov. 1751, Record Book, Newport CCP, vol. E, 778, RIJRC; Account of Administration, Estate of Mr. Sueton Grant to Temperance Grant, May 18, 1764, Newport TC, vol. 14, 33, NHS.

43. Toby L. Ditz, *Property and Kinship: Inheritance in Early Connecticut, 1750–1820* (Princeton, NJ: Princeton University Press, 1986), 146–47; David E. Narrett, *Inheritance and Family Life in Colonial New York City* (Ithaca, NY: Cornell University Press, 1992), 106; Wilson, *Life after Death*, 112–13.

44. "An Act for the Probate of Wills, and Granting of Administrations" (1662), *Acts and Laws of His Majesties Colony of Rhode-Island, and Providence-Plantations in America* (Boston: John Allen, 1719), 13–14; "An Act for the Settlement and Distribution of Estates of Intestates" (1692), *Acts and Laws of Her Majesties Province of the Massachusetts Bay in New England* (Boston: B. Green, 1714), 2–4.

45. In 1740–41, 50% of administrators ($N = 64$) were women; in 1750–51, 38% ($N = 53$); in 1760–61, 39% ($N = 78$); and in 1770–71, 45% ($N = 104$). See Newport TC, vols. 8–16, NHS.

46. For those estates where a female administrator's or executor's relationship to the decedent is known ($N = 89$), 84% of female administrators and executors were widows administering their husbands' estates. The remaining female administrators and executors were entrepreneurs assuming their office by virtue of their status as the estates' largest creditors, or were executors for friends or family members, many of whom were

fellow single women. See Newport TC, vols. 8–16, NHS. On co-administrators, see Sara T. Damiano, "'To Well and Truly Administer': Female Administrators and Estate Settlement in Newport, Rhode Island, 1730–1776," *New England Quarterly* 86, no. 1 (Mar. 2013): 93.

47. Elaine Forman Crane, *The Poison Plot: A Tale of Adultery and Murder in Colonial Newport* (Ithaca, NY: Cornell University Press, 2018), 123–24, 141–42; Temperance Grant to Sueton Grant, Oct. 21, 1735, Grant Champlin Mason Family Papers, box 127, unmarked folder, NHS, reproduced in Crane, *Poison Plot*, 141.

48. Daniel Defoe, *The complete English Tradesman, in familiar letters; directing him in the several parts and progressions of the trade*, vol. 1 (London: Charles Rivington, 1725), 291.

49. Account of Administration, Estate of Mr. Sueton Grant to Temperance Grant, May 18, 1764, Newport TC, vol. 14, 33, NHS. Patrick Grant died in 1756. See Inventory, Estate of Patrick Grant, Feb. 2, 1756, Newport TC, vol. 12, 13–14, NHS.

50. This percentage is based on a sample of all men's court appearances ($N = 10,151$) in Newport County in the first two years of each decade between 1731 and 1779.

51. In Newport County, 38% of female litigants in sampled debt cases ($N = 213$) were administrators; 71% were non-administrators. In Suffolk County, 32% of female litigants in sampled debt cases ($N = 154$) were administrators; 68% were non-administrators. Because some women appeared in court both as administrators and as non-administrators, percentages for Newport County total more than 100%. On sampling, see the appendix.

52. One Warwick, Rhode Island, widow and administrator, Barbara Greene, complained that she was "obliged to deliver her bed &c to the sheriff" to satisfy the demands of one of her late husband's creditors, because his estate otherwise consisted of so little. Another, Dinah Cahoon, expressed concern that creditors would seize her husband's estate and sell it "for much less than the true value," thus limiting the assets remaining for her family. See Petition of Barbara Greene (1782), RI Petitions, vol. 19, 71, RISA; Crane, *Ebb Tide*, 162.

53. *Grant v. Potter*, Newport CCP, May 1746, #87, RIJRC. On New England's female shopkeepers, see especially Patricia Cleary, *Elizabeth Murray: A Woman's Pursuit of Independence in Eighteenth-Century America* (Amherst: University of Massachusetts Press, 2000); Conger, *The Widow's Might*; Hartigan-O'Connor, *Ties that Buy*, 39–68.

54. Nash, *Urban Crucible*, 166; Vickers, *Young Men and the Sea*, 131–62; Susanah Shaw Romney, *New Netherland Connections: Intimate Networks and Atlantic Ties in Seventeenth-Century America* (Chapel Hill: University of North Carolina Press, 2014), 30–40.

55. Hunt, "Women and the Fiscal-Imperial State"; Ellen Hartigan-O'Connor, "'She Said She Did Not Know Money': Urban Women and Atlantic Markets in the Revolutionary Era," *Early American Studies* 4, no. 2 (Fall 2006): 327–30; Romney, *New Netherland Connections*, 26–65.

56. Deposition of Hezekiah Usher, Deposition of John Bazin, and Deposition of John Clark, *Grant v. Potter*, Newport CCP, May 1746, #87, RIJRC.

57. My analysis excludes debts listed on accounts of administration that were incurred by administrators and executors, including funeral expenses and administrative fees associated with settling estates.

58. Deceased individuals appearing in probate records are, as a group, older and wealthier than the general population.

59. $N = 1,026$ debts. These figures are based on every third legible account of administration for Newport men's estates between 1735 and 1776, as contained within volumes 8–18 of the Newport Town Council Records, NHS. This sample consists of fifty-two accounts containing a total of 1,026 debts not contracted during estate administration.

60. $N = 143$ debts. These figures are based on every legible account of administration for Newport women's estates between 1735 and 1776, as contained within volumes 8–18 of the Newport Town Council Records, NHS. This sample consists of twenty-one accounts containing a total of 143 debts not contracted during estate administration.

61. For examples of studies depicting economic networks as masculine, see Thomas Doerflinger, *A Vigorous Spirit of Enterprise: Merchants and Economic Development in Revolutionary Philadelphia* (Chapel Hill: University of North Carolina Press, 1986); David Hancock, *Citizens of the World: London Merchants and the Integration of the British Atlantic Community, 1735–1785* (Cambridge: Cambridge University Press, 1995); Cathy Matson, "Putting the *Lydia* to Sea: The Material Economy of Shipping in Colonial Philadelphia," *WMQ* 74, no. 2 (Apr. 2017): 303–32. On women's networks, see Ulrich, *Good Wives*, 51–67; Ulrich, *Midwife's Tale*, 29–30, 72–101. Many exchanges between women were not captured in probate records, either because they occurred through face-to-face barter or an unwritten "memory economy," or because probate records attributed married women's transactions to their husbands.

62. Petition of Simeon Potter (1749), RI Petitions, vol. 7, 61, RISA.

63. Declaration of Temperance Grant, *Grant v. Potter*, Newport CCP, May 1746, #87, RIJRC; Deposition of Samuel Welsh, *Grant v. Potter*, Newport CCP, May 1746, #87, RIJRC.

64. Deposition of Hezekiah Usher, Deposition of John Bazin, and Deposition of John Clark, *Grant v. Potter*, Newport CCP, May 1746, #87, RIJRC.

65. Deposition of Samuel Welsh, *Grant v. Potter*, Newport CCP, May 1746, #87, RIJRC.

66. Defoe, *The complete English Tradesman*, vol. 1, 274–92 (quotations, 275); Daniel Defoe, *The complete English Tradesman*, vol. 2, part 1 (London: Charles Rivington, 1727), 256–98. See also *Debtor and Creditor: Or a Discourse on the following Words: Have Patience with me, and I will pay thee all* (Boston: B. Mecom, 1762); Cotton Mather, *Fair Dealing Between Creditor and Debtor* (Boston: B. Green, 1716), 25–26. On meanings of credit, see Craig Muldrew, *The Economy of Obligation: The Culture of Credit and Social Relations in Early Modern England* (New York: St. Martin's, 1998).

67. Declaration of Temperance Grant, *Grant v. Potter*, Newport CCP, May 1746, #87, RIJRC; Norton, "Gender and Defamation." For a rare example of gendered threats on the body of a female trader, see Zabin, *Dangerous Economies*, 52–56.

68. Declaration of Temperance Grant, *Grant v. Potter*, Newport CCP, May 1746, #87, RIJRC; Norton, "Gender and Defamation." On the relationship between personal credit and the absence of financial institutions, see especially Bruce Mann, *Neighbors and Strangers: Law and Community in Early Connecticut* (Chapel Hill: University of North Carolina Press, 1987); Hardwick, *Practice of Patriarchy*; Muldrew, *Economy of Obligation*; Hardwick, *Family Business*.

69. Declaration of Temperance Grant, *Grant v. Potter*, Newport CCP, May 1746, #87, RIJRC.

70. Declaration of Temperance Grant, *Grant v. Potter*, Newport CCP, May 1746, #87, RIJRC; Defoe, *The complete English Tradesman*, vol. 1, 152.

71. Conger, *The Widow's Might*; Declaration of Temperance Grant, *Grant v. Potter*, Newport CCP, May 1746, #87, RIJRC. Forty-seven years after Sueton Grant's death, Temperance Grant's obituary noted that the gunpowder explosion was "still recollected by many of this town with painful emotion." See "Died, on Thursday morning last," *Newport Herald*, May 21, 1791, [3].

72. Declaration of Temperance Grant, *Grant v. Potter*, Newport CCP, May 1746, #87, RIJRC.

73. Norton, "Gender and Defamation"; Toby L. Ditz, "Shipwrecked; or, Masculinity Imperiled: Mercantile Representations of Failure and the Gendered Self in Eighteenth-Century Philadelphia," *Journal of American History* 81, no. 1 (June 1994): 51–80.

74. Declaration of Temperance Grant, *Grant v. Potter*, Newport CCP, May 1746, #87, RIJRC; *Potter v. Grant*, Record Book, Newport CCP, vol. B, 800, RIJRC; *Potter v. Grant*, Record Book, Newport SJC, vol. C, 446, RIJRC.

75. For Temperance Grant's slaveholding, see *Brett v. Grant*, Newport SCJ, Mar. 1756, RIJRC. Temperance Grant continued to sell to sailors for several decades, and she administered the estates of three poor mariners in 1764, because she was the estates' largest creditor. See Accounts of Administration, Estates of John Calder, Thomas Jolly, and John Johnson, 1764, Newport TC, vol. 14, 37, NHS. For Grant's testimony about a conversation that took place in her shop, see Deposition of Temperance Grant, *Grant and Vernon v. Lawton*, Newport SCJ, 1755, RIJRC. For her debt suits, see *Grant v. Caswell*, Newport CCP, Nov. 1751, #186, RIJRC; *Grant v. Davids*, Newport CCP, Nov. 1751, #183, RIJRC; *Grant v. Caswell*, Newport CCP, Nov. 1751, #249, RIJRC; *Grant v. Caswell*, Newport CCP, Nov. 1751, #264, RIJRC; *Grant v. Wilson*, Newport CCP, Nov. 1751, #32, RIJRC. For Temperance Grant's death, see "Died, on Thursday morning last," *Newport Herald*, May 21, 1791, [3].

76. Alfred F. Young, "George Robert Twelves Hewes (1742–1840): A Boston Shoemaker and the Memory of the Revolution," *WMQ* 34, no. 4 (Oct. 1981): 572–73. George Robert Twelves Hewes was the son of George and Abigail Hewes.

77. For the initial partnership, see Bond, Nathaniel Cunningham to George and Robert Hewes (Jan. 16, 1634), Suffolk Files, 38,576, MSA; Articles of Agreement between Nathaniel Cunningham and George and Robert Hewes (Jan. 16, 1734), Suffolk Files, 38,587, MSA. For additional loans, see Bond, George and Robert Hewes to Nathaniel Cunningham (Dec. 10, 1734), Suffolk Files, 49,424, MSA; Bond, George and Robert Hewes to Nathaniel Cunningham (June 12, 1735), Suffolk Files, 50,187, MSA; Court Record, *Cunningham v. Hewes* (Oct. 2, 1739), Suffolk Files, 50,281, MSA. On tanners, see Smith, *The "Lower Sort,"* 5. On credit relationships linking merchants to artisans, see Nash, *Urban Crucible*, 316–18.

78. For the first lawsuit emerging from the dispute, see Summons of George and Robert Hewes (Jan. 26, 1740), Suffolk Files, 54,128, MSA.

79. For the parties' numerous petitions to the legislature, see MA Archives, vol. 41, 425, 562; vol. 42, 147, 153, 158, 448, 805; and vol. 43, 373, MSA. The Suffolk Files, MSA, also contain extensive file papers for the legal cases. For narratives of the dispute between the Hewes and Cunningham that emphasize class conflict and do not discuss women's involvement, see Alfred F. Young, *The Shoemaker and the Tea Party: Memory and the American Revolution* (Boston: Beacon, 1999), 17–18; Young, "George Robert Twelves Hewes," 572–75.

80. Nash, *Urban Crucible*, 102–28; Answer of Robert Hewes, MA Archives, vol. 43, 377–78, MSA.

81. Nash, *Urban Crucible*, 127; Ditz, "Shipwrecked."

82. "These are to inform all Merchants," *Boston Weekly News-Letter*, Sept. 1, 1737, [2].

83. "Inventory of sundry goods attached for Nathaniel Cunningham," MA Archives, vol. 41, 429, MSA; "All sorts of the best Tann'd and Curried Leather," *Boston Weekly News-Letter*, Mar. 25, 1736, [2]; "Choice good hard and soft Soap," *Boston Evening Post*, Apr. 11, 1737, [2]; "These are to inform all Merchants," *Boston Weekly News-Letter*, Sept. 1, 1737, [2]; "This is to inform all Gentlemen," *New England Weekly Journal*, Mar. 10, 1741, [2].

84. Depositions of John Blake (Aug. 1740) and John Stringer (Sept. 3, 1740), Suffolk Files, 52,392, MSA; Depositions of Elizabeth Goddard and Esther Blair (Jan. 1739), Deposition of John Russell and John Stringer (Feb. 22, 1739), Suffolk Files, 51,228, MSA. The Hewes brothers later sued Cunningham and his associates for illegally seizing the tannery's property. See Writ, *Hewes v. Cunningham, Royal, and Nichols* (June 15, 1739), Suffolk Files, 49,467, MSA; Writ, *Hewes v. Cunningham and Barker* (Apr. 3, 1740) Suffolk Files, 52,392, MSA.

85. Deposition of James Hawkins (May 23, 1739), Suffolk Files, 49,424, MSA; Deposition of David Munroe (Apr. 20, 1739), Suffolk Files, 51,228, MSA.

86. Depositions of Abigail Sever, Elizabeth Goddard, and Esther Blair (Jan. 1739), Suffolk Files, 51,228, MSA; Depositions of Ruth Loring (Aug. 22, 1740, and Sept. 3, 1740), Suffolk Files, 52,392, MSA.

87. Depositions of Elizabeth Goddard (Jan. 1739) and Bartholomew Allen and John Squire (Jan. 1739), Suffolk Files, 50,767, MSA. The record does not specify whether George Hewes was still imprisoned in September. The Hewes later sued Cunningham and his associates for illegally seizing the tannery's property in the April and September incidents. See Writ, *Hewes v. Cunningham, Royal, and Nichols* (June 15, 1739), Suffolk Files, 49,467, MSA; Writ, *Hewes v. Cunningham and Barker* (Apr. 30, 1740), Suffolk Files, 52,392, MSA.

88. Quotations from Deposition of David Munroe (Apr. 20, 1739), Suffolk Files, 51,228, MSA. Also see Deposition of James Hawkins (May 23, 1739), Suffolk Files, 49,424, MSA.

89. Deposition of Ruth Loring (Aug. 22, 1740), Suffolk Files, 52,392, MSA.

90. Deposition of Abigail Sever ("Barbarous," "she and her children," "subsist") (Jan. 1739), Suffolk Files, 51,228, MSA; Deposition of Ruth Loring ("no body") (Aug. 22, 1740), Suffolk Files, 52,392, MSA; Deposition of Elizabeth Goddard ("noise") (Jan. 1739), Suffolk Files, 51,228, MSA.

91. Depositions of Elizabeth Goddard ("should go"), and Abigail Sever (Jan. 1739), Suffolk Files, 51,228, MSA; Deposition of Ruth Loring (Aug. 22, 1740), Suffolk Files, 52,392, MSA.

92. Depositions of Abigail Sever, Elizabeth Goddard, and Esther Blair (Jan. 1739), Suffolk Files, 51,228, MSA; Deposition of Ruth Loring (Aug. 22, 1740), Suffolk Files, 52,392, MSA; Laura Gowing, *Common Bodies: Women, Touch, and Power in Seventeenth-Century England* (New Haven, CT: Yale University Press, 2003); 149–76 (quotation, 151). See also Ulrich, *Midwife's Tale*, 61–62; Adrian Wilson, *The Making of Man-Midwifery: Childbirth in England, 1660–1770* (London: University College London Press, 1995), 1, 25; David Cressy, *Birth, Marriage, and Death: Ritual, Religion, and the Life-Cycle in Tudor and Stuart England* (New York: Oxford University Press, 1997), 16, 84.

93. Deposition of Abigail Sever (Jan. 1739), Suffolk Files, 51,228, MSA.

94. Deposition of Ruth Loring (Aug. 22, 1740), Suffolk Files, 52,392, MSA.

95. Elizabeth Goddard reported that "Mr Nathaniel Cunningham came into George Hewes house" on June 18, but she did not explain the circumstances that led him

to do so. Goddard and Esther Blair reported that on June 22, "Cunningham came to the house" and then "went up chamber to Mrs Hewes" after Goddard told him that "she was so bad she was not able to come down out of her chamber." See Depositions of Elizabeth Goddard and Esther Blair (all quotations from Blair deposition) (Jan. 1739), Suffolk Files, 51,228, MSA.

96. Summons of Nathaniel Cunningham (Apr. 2, 1740), Suffolk Files, 52,392, MSA.

97. Barbara Duden, *The Woman Beneath the Skin: A Doctor's Patients in Eighteenth-Century Germany*, trans. Thomas Dunlap (Cambridge, MA: Harvard University Press, 1991), 107–9, 140–49, 157–70; Cressy, *Birth, Marriage and Death*, 45, 87; Gowing, *Common Bodies*, 22, 122–38.

98. For one suit concerning a debt, see Writ (Feb. 28, 1739), *Hewes v. Cunningham*, MA Archives, vol. 41, 430, MSA. For the suit concerning the slaves, see Writ (Sept. 15, 1739), *Hewes v. Cunningham* (Sept. 15, 1739), Suffolk Files, 50,127, MSA.

99. Ulrich, *Midwife's Tale*, 102–33; Cornelia Hughes Dayton, "Taking the Trade: Abortion and Gender Relations in an Eighteenth-Century New England Village," *WMQ* 48, no. 1 (Jan. 1991): 19–49; Kathleen Brown, "'Changed . . . into the Fashion of Man': The Politics of Sexual Difference in a Seventeenth-Century Anglo-American Settlement," *Journal of the History of Sexuality* 6, no. 2 (Oct. 1995): 171–93; Gowing, *Domestic Dangers*; Norton, *Founding Mothers and Fathers*, 183–97; Gowing, *Common Bodies*; Sharon Block, *Rape and Sexual Power in Early America* (Chapel Hill: University of North Carolina Press, 2006), 88–125.

100. *An Abridgement of Burn's Justice of the Peace and Parish Officer* (Boston: Joseph Greenleaf, 1773), 125.

101. Depositions of Abigail Sever, Elizabeth Goddard ("very much Surprized"), and Esther Blair (Jan. 1739), Suffolk Files, 51,228, MSA; Depositions of John Loring ("weak woman," "well and better") (Aug. 1740), Ruth Loring ("well composed," "frightned away") (Aug, 22, 1740, and Sept. 3, 1740), and Jane Shaw ("Cunningham's frighting," "Weak & Low," "as miserable a Condition") (Aug. 1740), Suffolk Files, 52,392, MSA. Sever, Goddard, Blair, and Shaw emphasized Cunningham's harsh treatment of Abigail Hewes and stressed the poor health of the mother and child. John and Ruth Loring (not married, but probably kin) contended that Cunningham had not frightened Hewes, that she was generally in good health, and that any difficulties resembled those of her previous childbirths. For a notation that Abigail Hewes was present when a witness provided testimony, see Deposition of Ruth Loring (Aug. 22, 1740), Suffolk Files, 52,392, MSA.

102. As was typical for the period, the court's records do not explain the reasoning behind this verdict. See Reasons of Appeal, *Cunningham v. Hewes* (Feb. 1739), Suffolk Files, 51,228, MSA; Summons of Nathaniel Cunningham (Apr. 2, 1740), Suffolk Files, 52,392, MSA; Superior Court Record (Aug. 1740), Suffolk Files, 54,128, MSA; Writ of Execution, *Cunningham v. Hewes* (Feb. 18, 1741), Suffolk Files, 56,164, MSA.

103. Petition of Nathaniel Cunningham Jr. (Feb. 7, 1750), MA Archives, vol. 43, 373–376, MSA.

Chapter 2 · Credit Relations Outside of Court

1. On changing consumer practices, see especially Richard Bushman, *The Refinement of America: Persons, Houses, Cities* (New York: Knopf, 1992); T. H. Breen, *The Marketplace of Revolution: How Consumer Politics Shaped American Independence* (New York: Oxford

University Press, 2004); Jan de Vries, *The Industrious Revolution: Consumer Behavior and the Household Economy, 1650 to the Present* (Cambridge: Cambridge University Press, 2008); Ann Smart Martin, *Buying into the World of Goods: Early Consumers in Backcountry Virginia* (Baltimore: Johns Hopkins University Press, 2009).

2. Petition of John Slack (1755), MA Archives, vol. 19A, 278, MSA; Declaration, *Rumreil v. Spooner*, Newport CCP, Nov. 1746, #108, RIJRC; Account of Administration, Estate of Ann Kees (1745), Newport TC, vol. 9, 100, NHS.

3. Bruce Mann, "The Transformation of Law and Economy in Early America," in *The Cambridge History of Law in America*, vol. 1, *Early America*, ed. Michael Grossberg and Christopher Tomlins (Cambridge: Cambridge University Press, 2008), 389; Serena Zabin, *Dangerous Economies: Status and Commerce in Imperial New York* (Philadelphia: University of Pennsylvania Press, 2009), 12–14.

4. Bruce Mann, *Neighbors and Strangers: Law and Community in Early Connecticut* (Chapel Hill: University of North Carolina Press, 1987), 11–45; Cornelia Hughes Dayton, *Women Before the Bar: Gender, Law, and Society in Connecticut, 1639–1789* (Chapel Hill: University of North Carolina Press, 1995), 78–79.

5. Regarding women's preference for and greater access to liquid assets as opposed to land, see Amy Erickson, *Women and Property in Early Modern England* (London: Routledge, 1993), 61–78; Beverly Lemire, *The Business of Everyday Life: Gender, Practice and Social Politics in England, c. 1600–1900* (Manchester, UK: Manchester University Press, 2005), 16–55; Woody Holton, "Abigail Adams, Bond Speculator," *WMQ* 64, no. 4 (Oct. 2007): 821–38. For credit instruments viewed as being masculine, see Cornelia Hughes Dayton, *Women Before the Bar: Gender, Law and Society in Connecticut, 1639–1789* (Chapel Hill: University of North Carolina Press, 1995), 77–79; Deborah A. Rosen, *Courts and Commerce: Gender, Law, and the Market Economy in Colonial New York* (Columbus: Ohio State University Press, 1997), 95–110.

6. This percentage is based on all Newport County Court of Common Pleas debt cases with female plaintiffs or defendants concerning promissory notes ($N = 121$) and bonds ($N = 65$) in 1731, 1741, 1751, 1761, 1771, 1781, and 1791. See Record Books and Case Files, Newport CCP, RIJRC.

7. This percentage is based on all Suffolk County Court of Common Pleas debt cases with female plaintiffs or defendants concerning promissory notes ($N = 34$) and bonds ($N = 38$) in the following terms: July 1730, 1740, and 1750; January, July, and October 1760 and 1770; and July 1780 and 1790. See Record Books and Case Files, Suffolk CCP, MSA.

8. Women were plaintiffs in 53% of their cases concerning accounts in Newport County, and in 50% of their cases concerning accounts in Suffolk County. These percentages are based on a sample of all Newport County Court of Common Pleas debt cases with female plaintiffs or defendants concerning book debt ($N = 129$) in 1731, 1741, 1751, 1761, 1771, 1781, and 1791, and of all Suffolk County Court of Common Pleas debt cases by women concerning book debt ($N = 48$) in the following terms: July 1730, 1740, and 1750; January, July, and October 1760 and 1770; and July 1780 and 1790. See Record Books and Case Files, Newport CCP, RIJRC; Record Books and Case Files, Suffolk CCP, MSA.

9. "Newport, Rhode Island, April 18," *Boston Weekly Post-Boy*, Apr. 21, 1740, [3]; Inventory, Estate of Ann Kay (1740), Newport TC, vol. 8, 91, NHS; Account of Administration, Estate of Ann Kay (1746), Newport TC, vol. 8, 154, NHS.

10. Inventory, Estate of Ann Chaloner (1770), Newport TC, vol. 16, 109, NHS.

11. Account of Administration, Estate of Ann Kay (1746), Newport TC, vol. 10, 118, NHS; Inventory, Estate of Ann Kay (1740), Newport TC, vol. 8, 91, NHS.

12. Account of Administration, Estate of Patience Redwood (1747), vol. 9, 290, NHS.

13. Inventory, Estate of Barbara Trott (1740), Newport TC, vol. 8, 85, NHS.

14. Account of Administration, Estate of Barbara Trott (1748), Newport TC, vol. 10, 179, NHS.

15. Account of Administration, Estate of Sylvia Woodman (1746), Newport TC, vol. 10, 133, NHS.

16. Inventory, Estate of Elizabeth Duploise (1747), Newport TC, vol. 9, 295, NHS.

17. "A choice parcel," *New England Weekly Journal*, Apr. 24, 1732, [2]; Vivian Bruce Conger, *The Widow's Might: Widowhood and Gender in Early British America* (New York: New York University Press, 2009), 150–51; Rebecca Amory Receipt Book, Amory Family Papers, MHS.

18. Lane, Son, and Fraser to Martha Salisbury, Feb. 20, 1767, Sept. 21, 1767, June 20, 1768, Oct. 7, 1768, Feb. 9, 1769, Aug. 31, 1769, and Apr. 1, 1773, Salisbury Family Papers, AAS; Martha Salisbury Account Book, 1753–1773, Salisbury Family Papers, octavo vol. 4, AAS.

19. Ellen Hartigan-O'Connor, *The Ties that Buy: Women and Commerce in Revolutionary America* (Philadelphia: University of Pennsylvania Press, 2009), 129–60; Christina J. Hodge, "Widow Pratt's World of Goods: Implications of Consumer Choice in Colonial Newport, RI," *Early American Studies* 8, no. 2 (Spring 2010): 217–34; Kate Haulman, *The Politics of Fashion in Eighteenth-Century America* (Chapel Hill: University of North Carolina Press, 2011).

20. Margaretta Lovell, *Art in a Season of Revolution: Painters, Artisans, and Patrons in Early America* (Philadelphia: University of Pennsylvania Press, 2005), ch. 7.

21. Deposition of Mary Brown, *Goddard v. Hazard*, Newport SCJ, Nov. 1763, RIJRC.

22. Depositions of Susannah Hazard and Daniel Spencer, *Goddard v. Hazard*, Newport SCJ, Nov. 1763, RIJRC. See also Jennifer L. Anderson, *Mahogany: The Costs of Luxury in Early America* (Cambridge, MA: Harvard University Press, 2012).

23. Deposition of John Goddard ("ask M[rs.] Bristow") and Power of Attorney of John Bristow to Katherine Bristow (Jan. 1, 1742), *Bristow v. Phillips*, Newport SCJ, Aug. 1754, RIJRC. For the use of the *Willing Maid* in coastal trading, see Answer of Peter Phillips and Deposition of Abner Coffin, *Bristow v. Phillips*, Newport SCJ, Aug. 1754, RIJRC.

24. Deposition of Benjamin Mason ("of M[rs.] Bristow") and Deposition of Peleg Thurston ("of his wife"), Newport SCJ, Aug. 1754, RIJRC.

25. Deposition of Ann Aston ("objected") and Deposition of Charles Garrard ("considerable conference"), *Card v. Freeborn*, Newport CCP, May 1741, [unnumbered case], RIJRC. The case's documents never mention Elisha Card's wife by name.

26. *Goddard v. Hazard*, Newport SCJ, Nov. 1763, RIJRC; *Bristow v. Phillips*, Newport SCJ, Aug. 1754, RIJRC; *Card v. Freeborn*, Newport CCP, May 1741, [unnumbered case], RIJRC.

27. On the importance of written evidence, see Mann, *Neighbors and Strangers*. For representative examples of men's descriptions of drafting documents, see Deposition of Hezekiah Bilding (1754) regarding Petition of Silvanus Barrows (1753), MA Archives, vol. 43, 783, MSA; Depositions of Noah Smith, Ezra Day, and Samuel Day (1764) regarding Petition of Gideon Cornell et al. (1764), RI Petitions, vol. 11, 188, RISA.

28. William Bradford, comp., *The Secretary's Guide, or Young Man's Companion* (Philadelphia: Andrew Bradford, 1737), 126. See also John Mair, *Book-keeping Methodiz'd: or, a Methodical Treatise of Merchant-Accompts, According to the Italian Form* (Dublin: Isaac Jackson, 1750), 2; George Fisher, *The American Instructor, or Young Man's Best Companion*, 9th ed. (Philadelphia: B. Franklin & D. Hall, 1748), 153.

29. Toby L. Ditz, "Secret Selves, Credible Personas: The Problematics of Trust and Public Display in the Writing of Eighteenth-Century Philadelphia Merchants," in *Possible Pasts: Becoming Colonial in Early America*, ed. Robert Blair St. George (Ithaca, NY: Cornell University Press, 2000), 223.

30. Naomi R. Lamoreaux, "Rethinking the Transition to Capitalism in the Early American Northeast," *Journal of American History* 90, no. 2 (Sept. 2003): 440–45; Daniel Vickers, "Errors Excepted: The Culture of Credit in Rural New England, 1750–1800," *Economic History Review* 63, no. 4 (Nov. 2010): 1032–57.

31. John Vernon, *The Compleat Compting-house* (Dublin: George Grierson, 1741), 22.

32. The first printed promissory note I have located is from 1791. See *Pynchon v. Gridley*, Suffolk CCP, Apr. 1791, #66, MSA.

33. Promissory Note, *Stoneman v. Wickham*, Newport CCP, Nov. 1770, #97, RIJRC.

34. Promissory Note, *Underwood v. Campbell*, Newport CCP, May 1754, #597, RIJRC; Promissory Note, *Anthony v. Kean*, Newport CCP, May 1761, #201, RIJRC. "Old tenor" referred to currency issued in Rhode Island prior to 1740, the year in which the colony issued a new set of notes ("new tenor"). Rhode Islanders continued to use both old and new tenor throughout the mid-eighteenth century.

35. Deposition of Abigail Thayer (1753) regarding Petition of Silvanus Barrows (1753), MA Archives, vol. 43, 481–82, MSA; Deposition of Ruth Besse, *Burge v. Leonard* (Apr. 1760), Suffolk Files, 80,630, MSA; Deposition of George Lawton, *Lawton v. Durfey*, Newport CCP, May 1761, #64, RIJRC.

36. For promissory notes given by women and containing two different hands, see Promissory Note, *Johnson v. Simon*, Newport CCP, May 1771, #130, RIJRC; Promissory Note, *Rhodes v. Viscount*, Suffolk CCP, Jan. 1760, #157, MSA. For a promissory note that a female debtor signed with her mark, see *Brown v. Clark* (Aug. 1740), Suffolk Files, 53,988. For a promissory note on which a female creditor recorded payments on the back and signed it with her mark, see *Underwood v. Campbell*, Newport CCP, May 1754, #597, RIJRC.

37. For a notary's advertisement, see Richard Jennys, "Notice is hereby given," *Boston Gazette*, Aug. 15, 1763, [2]. For advertisements for printed bonds, see "BLANKS," *Providence Gazette*, June 16, 1770, 102; "To be sold by Knight Dexter," *Boston Post-Boy*, Sept. 24, 1759, [4]; "Bibles, large and small," *Boston Evening Post*, Dec. 19, 1748, [4]; "All gentlemen," *Weekly Rehearsal*, July 9, 1733, [2]. On printers selling blank forms, see Joseph M. Adelman, *Revolutionary Networks: The Business and Politics of Printing the News* (Baltimore: Johns Hopkins University Press, 2019), 32–33.

38. "To the Publishers of the Boston Evening Post," *Boston Evening Post*, May 18, 1767, [1].

39. Bond, John Mumford to Sarah Lancaster, *Bourse v. Mumford*, Newport CCP, May 1741, #97, RIJRC.

40. Account, *Rumreil v. Carr*, Newport CCP, May 1751, #207, RIJRC. Rumreil initially kept her own accounts but later trained her three sons to help with her bookkeeping. See Hartigan-O'Connor, *Ties that Buy*, 61.

41. Account, John Lyddiard to Lydia Barnard, *Barnard v. Lydiard*, Suffolk CCP, Apr. 1751, #131, MSA. For additional examples, see *Colter v. Watts*, Suffolk CCP, Apr. 1766, #99, MSA; *Allen v. Barrel*, Suffolk CCP, Oct. 1770, #275, MSA; Deposition of Livine Love (1762) regarding Petition of Margaret Tree (Sept. 1760), RI Petitions, vol. 11.2, 19, RISA.

42. Vernon, *Compleat Compting-house*; Mair, *Book-keeping Methodiz'd*; William Webster, *Essay on Book-keeping* (London, 1759); Mary Poovey, *A History of the Modern Fact: Problems of Knowledge in the Sciences of Wealth and Society* (Chicago: University of Chicago Press, 1998), 29–91.

43. Martha Salisbury Account Book, 1753–73, Salisbury Family Papers, octavo vol. 4, AAS.

44. Elizabeth [Murray] Smith to Dolly Murray, Feb. 17, 1762, Elizabeth [Murray] Smith to Mrs. Rowe, Apr. 24, 1770, and Elizabeth [Murray] Smith to Mrs. Deblois, Apr. 13, 1770, as quoted in Patricia Cleary, *Elizabeth Murray: A Woman's Pursuit of Independence in Eighteenth-Century America* (Amherst: University of Massachusetts Press, 2000), 96, 127, 128. For Murray's involvement in her nieces' education, see Cleary, *Elizabeth Murray*, 93–97, 125–33, 142–48.

45. For advertisements concerning bookkeepers for hire, see "A young Man," *Newport Mercury*, May 23, 1763, [3]; "If any Gentleman or Merchant," *Boston Gazette*, June 12, 1744, [3]; "This is to Notify," *New England Weekly Journal*, Apr. 4, 1733, [2].

46. Petition of Nicholas Williams and Answer of Daniel Ballard ("kept," "no other") (1741), MA Archives, vol. 41, 773–77, MSA. For similar examples, see Depositions of Sarah Greenman and Southcote Langworthy regarding Petition of Jeremiah Child (1764), RI Petitions, vol. 11.2, 78, RISA; Petition of Richard Smith (1754), MA Archives, vol. 105, 482–83, MSA; Account, *Davis v. Tomson*, Newport CCP, May 1736, #5, RIJRC; Account, *Hamilton v. Lassells*, Newport CCP, May 1766, #379, RIJRC.

47. Probate inventories listing credit instruments among the other household items provide suggestive evidence of where women kept their records. In other inventories, credit instruments are listed at the conclusion of the document, along with the estate's other most-liquid and valuable assets, including clothes and enslaved people. For example, see Inventory, Estate of Willoughby Hayden (1747), Newport TC, vol. 10, 88, NHS; Inventory, Estate of Elizabeth Coggeshall (1748), Newport TC, vol. 10, 167, NHS; Inventory, Estate of Mary Godspeed (1756), Newport TC, vol. 12, 57, NHS. For credit instruments, clothing, and an enslaved woman listed at the conclusion of an inventory, see Inventory, Estate of Elizabeth Almy (1770), Newport TC, vol. 16, 152, NHS.

48. Inventory, Estate of Patience Taylor (1765), Newport TC, vol. 14, 75, NHS. See also Ellen Hartigan-O'Connor, "'She Said She did not Know Money': Urban Women and Atlantic Markets in the Revolutionary Era," *Early American Studies* 4, no. 2 (Fall 2006), 322–23; Esther Jameson, "Lost, On Saturday," *Essex Journal*, May 24, 1776, [3].

49. Inventory, Estate of Barbara Trott (1740), Newport TC, vol. 8, 85, NHS; Inventory, Estate of Mary Brayton (1755), Newport TC, vol. 11, 249, NHS; Inventory, Estate of Joanna Dennis (1766), Newport TC, vol. 15, 27, NHS.

50. For financial records listed among dishware, see Inventory, Estate of Mary Coggeshall (1747), Newport TC, vol. 9, 216, NHS. For financial records kept in chambers used for sleeping, see Inventory, Estate of Joanna Dennis (1766), Newport TC, vol. 15, 27, NHS; Inventory, Estate of Ann Chaloner (1770), Newport TC, vol. 16, 109, NHS.

51. Margaret Hazly, "Lost the latter End of January last," *Boston News-Letter*, Mar. 17, 1763, [3]. For similar advertisements by men, see "Lost on Saturday last," *Boston Gazette*, Nov. 6, 1744, [3]; "Lost in Boston on the 27th of August last," *Boston Gazette*, Oct. 8, 1745, [4]; "Lost on Saturday the 27th of February last," *Boston News-Letter*, Mar. 3, 1748, [2]. On similar advertisements in Pennsylvania, see Dierks, *In My Power*, 94–95.

52. Margaret Hazly, "Lost, the Latter End of January last," *Boston News-Letter*, Mar. 17, 1763, [3]. For the location of Hart's shipyard, off of Lynn Street and near the ferry, see Mercy Copeland, "To be Sold," *Boston Gazette*, Aug. 11, 1766, [supplement 2]. For similar advertisements by men, see "Lost on Saturday last," *Boston Gazette*, Nov. 6, 1744, [3]; "Lost in Boston on the 27th of August last," *Boston Gazette*, Oct. 8, 1745, [4]; "Lost on Saturday the 27th of February last," *Boston News-Letter*, Mar. 3, 1748, [2].

53. Based on keyword searches of digitized Massachusetts and Rhode Island newspapers, I have identified and examined 169 advertisements concerning lost papers, pocketbooks, and notebooks that were published between 1730 and 1776. Six advertisements name women as the owners of the missing items. In addition to the advertisement by Margaret Hazly, see "Lost on the 26th of August," *Boston Evening Post*, Sept. 22, 1746, [3]; "Lost on the 4th of January," *Boston Gazette*, Jan. 17, 1763, [3]; "Lost last Monday," *Boston News-Letter*, Sept. 12, 1771, [2]; Esther Jameson, "Lost, on Saturday the 18th," *Essex Journal*, May 24, 1776, [3]; Mary Chapman, "Lost on the second," *Boston Evening Post*, Nov. 18, 1745, [3].

54. Daniel Defoe, *The complete English Tradesman, in familiar letters; directing him in the several parts and progressions of the trade*, vol. 1 (London: Charles Rivington, 1725), 279.

55. For examples of male debtors voluntarily settling with their creditors, see Depositions of Seth Spooner and Samuel Gray regarding Petition of Robert Bennet (1749), RI Petitions, vol. 7, 80, RISA; Petition of Caleb Corey (1752), RI Petitions, vol. 9.2, 32 RISA; Deposition of Samuel Hicks, *Wilcox v. Wanton*, Newport CCP, May 1761, #244, RIJRC; Deposition of Thomas Howland, *Wing v. Sisson*, Newport CCP, Nov 1756, #98, RIJRC. For examples of male creditors dunning their debtors, see Deposition of William Bowen, *Billings v. Hall*, Suffolk SCJ (Feb. 1751), Suffolk Files 67,741, MSA; Deposition of Benjamin Fowler, *Hayward v. Fowler*, Suffolk SCJ (Aug. 1730), Suffolk Files, 29,855, MSA; Depositions of Elizabeth Kimball and Sarah and Dorcas Fowler, *Hayward v. Fowler*, Suffolk SCJ (Aug. 1730), Suffolk Files, 29,918, MSA; Deposition of Major Fairchild, *Burt v. Potter*, Newport CCP, May 1731, #21, RIJRC.

56. William Blackstone, *Commentaries on the Laws of England*, vol. 2 (Oxford, UK: Clarendon Press, 1766), 477–78. See also Daniel Defoe, *The complete English Tradesman*, vol. 1, 197–225; Julian Hoppit, *Risk and Failure in English Business, 1700–1800* (Cambridge: Cambridge University Press, 1987), 30; Ditz, "Secret Selves," 224.

57. Account, *Smith v. Bayard*, Suffolk CCP, Oct. 1760, #188, MSA. In the months between the events discussed here and the date of the lawsuit, Elizabeth Murray Campbell remarried. Her new husband, James Smith, was thus a party in the resulting lawsuit.

58. For Campbell's travels on October 19, 1759, see Writ, *Smith v. Bayard*, Suffolk CCP, Oct. 1760, #188, MSA. For Elizabeth and James Campbell's divisions of responsibility within their business, see Cleary, *Elizabeth Murray*, 70–71. For Campbell's place of residence, see Elizabeth Campbell, "Imported in the last Ships," *Boston Gazette, and Country Journal*, Apr. 30, 1759, [2]. For the residence of Mehitable Bayard's father, Balthazar Bayard, on "Broomfield's Lane," see "To be sold by Public Auction," *Boston*

Gazette, June 13, 1763, [2]. For the location of Broomfield's Lane in Marlborough Ward, see Samuel Blodget, *Boston Evening Post*, July 21, 1760, [1].

59. Writ, *Smith v. Bayard*, Suffolk CCP, Oct. 1760, #188, MSA. For Mehitable Bayard's marriage to Frederick Porter, see *The New England Historical and Genealogical Register*, vol. 11 (Boston: Samuel G. Drake, 1857), 43. For Frederick Porter's residence in Roxbury at the time of his death in 1761, see "Boston," *Boston Evening Post*, Jan. 5, 1761, [4].

60. For Fuller's moniker "Irish Pegg," see Depositions of Charles Smith, Samuel Snell, and John and Patience Osbourn, *Fuller v. Howes*, Newport SCJ, [1731?], RIJRC. For Fuller's agreement with Howes, see Bond, *Fuller v. Howes*, Newport SCJ, [1731?], RIJRC. For Fuller's trip to Newport by boat, see Deposition of James Miller, *Fuller v. Howes*, Newport SCJ, [1731?], RIJRC. Extant records do not indicate when the Newport Superior Court heard *Fuller v. Howes*. The case originated in the Providence Court of Common Pleas in December 1730, making it likely that the Newport Superior Court considered the case on appeal in 1731.

61. Depositions of James Miller, Charles Smith, Samuel Snell, and John and Patience Osbourn, *Fuller v. Howes*, Newport SCJ, [1731?], RIJRC.

62. For women traveling to nearby towns to collect debts, also see *Sheffield v. Weast*, Newport SCJ, Apr. 1733, RIJRC; *Corp v. Rhoades*, Newport SCJ, 1739, RIJRC; *Wilkee v. Mancester*, Newport CCP, May 1761, continued cases file, RIJRC.

63. Daniel Defoe, *The complete English Tradesman*, vol. 1, 350.

64. For men visiting female administrators' houses to settle accounts, see Statement of Michael Dalton (Sept. 1, 1753), MA Archives, vol. 43, 737, MSA; Deposition of James Honyman, *Wilson v. Balfour*, Newport SCJ, Sept. 1734, RIJRC.

65. Jane Carter, "All Persons who have any Demands," *Boston Gazette*, June 11, 1745, [4]; Jane Hunting, "All Persons having any Demands," *Boston Evening Post*, Sept. 22, 1755, [3]; See also Martha, Rufus, and Benjamin Greene, "All Persons that are indebted," *Boston Gazette*, Aug. 15, 1763, [2]; Catherine Mellens, "All Persons having any Demands," *Boston Evening Post*, Oct. 27, 1755, [2]; Mary Sweetser, "All Persons Indebted," *Boston Gazette*, Sept. 24, 1745, [5].

66. Jane Brown et al., "Notice is hereby given," *Newport Mercury*, Jan. 23, 1764, [4]; Rebecca Briggs, "Notice is hereby given," *Newport Mercury*, July 13, 1772, [3]. A small number of women placed similar advertisements in their capacity as entrepreneurs, urging creditors and debtors to settle before they closed their businesses or relocated. For instance, see Jane Eustis, "Jane Eustis Will embark for England," *Boston Evening Post*, Nov. 20, 1769, [4]; Sarah Goddard, "The Subscriber proposing," *Providence Gazette*, Oct. 8, 1768, [4]; Abigail Stoneman, "To Be Sold," *Newport Mercury*, Sept. 12, 1774, [4].

67. For additional discussion, see Sara T. Damiano, "'To Well and Truly Administer': Female Administrators and Estate Settlement in Newport, Rhode Island, 1730–1776," *New England Quarterly* 86, no. 1 (Mar. 2013): 110–12. On gender and advertising, see Carl Robert Keyes, "Early American Advertising: Marketing and Consumer Culture in Eighteenth-Century Philadelphia" (PhD diss., Johns Hopkins University, 2008), 181–240.

68. Deposition of Ruth Randall (1749), Suffolk Files, 66,332, MSA; Depositions of David Clap and Benjamin Torrey (1749), Suffolk Files, 66,132, MSA; Depositions of Robert Barker, Joshua Lincoln, and Jonathan Meritt (1748), Suffolk Files, 64,172, MSA. For Tucker's charges against his opponent, see Writ, *Tucker v. Stuston* (May 30, 1748), Suffolk Files, 64,172, MSA. The case moved through a series of appeals, with the courts

alternately ruling in favor of Tucker or Stutson. After the Superior Court ruled in Tucker's favor, his opponent petitioned the legislature for a new trial. The case's file papers do not include the outcome of this re-hearing. See Petition of Joseph Stutson (1749), MA Archives, vol. 42, 808, MSA; Writ, *Stutson v. Tucker* (Oct. 5, 1749), Suffolk Files, 66,332, MSA.

69. Court records identified Mary Sheffield's late husband, Joseph, using the titles "Esquire" and "yeoman," indicating that he was probably a landowner. Peter Weast was merely described as a "yeoman." See Writ and Bond, *Sheffield v. Weast*, Newport SCJ, Sept. 1733, RIJRC.

70. Depositions of Joseph Wait ("whether," "answered yes"), Elizabeth Wait, Mary Case, and John Vaughan ("like his hand"), *Sheffield v. Weast*, Newport SCJ, Sept. 1733, RIJRC.

71. Sheffield lost her case in both the Court of Common Pleas and the Superior Court. Nonetheless, the unusually detailed record generated by the controversy attests to a female creditor's knowledge of the law and recourse to forceful interrogation tactics outside of court. See Court of Common Pleas Record and Superior Court Verdict, *Sheffield v. Weast*, Newport SCJ, Sept. 1733, RIJRC.

72. Grace Gardner, "All Persons indebted to Mrs. Grace Gardner," *Boston Post-Boy*, Apr. 3, 1758, [3]. On scarcities during the Seven Years' War, see Catherine A. Brekus, *Sarah Osborn's World: The Rise of Evangelical Christianity in Early America* (New Haven, CT: Yale University Press, 2013), 198.

73. Account, James Lewis to Thomas Rogers, *Lewis v. Rogers*, Newport CCP, Nov. 1766, #262, RIJRC. For additional examples, see *Withered v. Price*, Suffolk CCP, Jan. 1760, #180, MSA; *Perry v. Osborn*, Newport SCJ, 1731, RIJRC.

74. For a male creditor refusing payment from a female debtor, see Deposition of William Carpenter, *Corpe v. Rhoades*, Newport SCJ, 1739, RIJRC.

75. For the meeting between Brown and Clark, see Depositions of Mary Clark, John Metcalf, Isaac Adams, and Joseph Adams, *Brown v. Clark*, Suffolk SCJ (Aug. 1741), Suffolk Files, 53,988, MSA. For Clark's limited belongings, see Writ, *Brown v. Clark*, Suffolk SCJ (Aug. 1741), Suffolk Files, 53,988, MSA. On the scrutiny of accounts during settlement, see Ditz, "Secret Selves." Witnesses to settlements of accounts typically described seeing books spread on the table for both parties to examine. See Deposition of George Gardner, *Rhodes v. Sheffield*, Newport CCP, May 1761, #231, RIJRC; Deposition of Samuel Hicks, *Willcox v. Wanton*, Newport CCP, May 1761, #244, RIJRC.

76. Depositions of Mary Clark, John Metcalf, Isaac Adams, and Joseph Adams, *Brown v. Clark*, Suffolk SCJ (Aug. 1741), Suffolk Files, 53,988, MSA.

77. A jury ruled in Clark's favor in the Court of Common Pleas. Brown then appealed to the Superior Court, and the record does not contain the outcome of Brown's appeal. Court of Common Pleas Record (June 1741), *Brown v. Clark*, Suffolk SCJ (Aug. 1741), Suffolk Files, 53,988, MSA.

78. Jeremiah Condy to Robert Treat Paine, Jan. 10, 1764, Robert Treat Paine Papers, MHS. For a husband and wife's joint decision to delay paying a debt, see Deposition of John Andrews regarding Petition of Thomas Angell (1773), RI Petitions, vol. 15, 45, RISA.

79. R. Rooks to James Otis, May 27, 1732, Otis Family Papers, MHS; Robert Treat Paine to James Freeman, Jan. 24, 1757, in Stephen T. Riley and Edward W. Hanson, eds., *The Papers of Robert Treat Paine*, vol. 2 (Boston: Massachusetts Historical Society, 1992),

6–7. For additional payments made by wives and daughters, see Answer of John Fairservice (1747), MA Archives, vol. 42, 472–74, MSA; Petition of Joseph Prince (1751), MA Archives, vol. 43, 461–63, MSA; Petition of John Martin (1757), RI Petitions, vol. 10, 11, RISA.

80. William Redwood to William Ellery, May 21, 1774, Channing Papers, NHS.

81. Depositions of James Miller ("old dog," "ring"), Charles Smith, John and Patience Osbourn, and Mary Smith, *Fuller v. Howes*, Newport SCJ, [1731?], RIJRC.

82. Court of Common Pleas Record, *Fuller v. Howes*, Newport SCJ, [1731?], RIJRC. Thomas Howes appealed to the Superior Court, but surviving documents do not indicate the outcome of his case.

83. Depositions of Edward Richmond and Joanna Chapman, *Richard v. Lawton*, Newport CCP, Nov. 1731, #19, RIJRC.

84. Bethiah Norton to James Otis, Feb. 18, 1758, Otis Family Papers, MHS.

85. Noah Sprague to James Otis, Nov. 12, 1768, Otis Family Papers, MHS. Sprague described the resistance of his "sister Hammond" to paying Elnathan Hammond of Newport, presumably a relation. The letter does not contain Sprague's sister's full name or her place of residence.

86. Receipt, Elizabeth Barnes to Rebecca Amory, Sept. 17, 1732, Rebecca Amory Receipt Book, Amory Family Papers, MHS. At the time of her death, Elizabeth Barnes owned "a large double house" on Beacon Street in Boston. See John Arbuthnott, "To Be Sold," *Boston Evening Post*, Feb. 6, 1744. [2].

87. Receipt, Hannah Willard to Rebecca Amory, Dec. 9, 1732, Rebecca Amory Receipt Book, Amory Family Papers, MHS; Receipt, Mary Faneuil to Rebecca Amory, Apr. 28, 1737, Rebecca Amory Receipt Book, Amory Family Papers, MHS; Receipt, Mary Hill to Rebecca Amory, July 13, 1738, Rebecca Amory Receipt Book, Amory Family Papers, MHS.

88. Account of Ann Maylem with Ann Drake and Receipt, Ann Drake to Ann Maylem, Feb. 4, 1742, *Read v. Maylem*, Newport CCP, May 1743, #280, RIJRC. For an additional example, see Mary Malden to Rebecca Amory, July 24, 1734, Rebecca Amory Receipt Book, Amory Family Papers, MHS.

89. Receipt, Elesabth [Elizabeth] Noel, July 3, 1734, Rebecca Amory Receipt Book, Amory Family Papers, MHS.

90. For men's receipts on behalf of other men, see, for example, Receipt, Thomas Steel Jr., to Rebecca Amory, Jan. 10, 1733, Rebecca Amory Receipt Book, Amory Family Papers, MHS; Receipt, Richard Carey to Rebecca Amory, July 20, 1734, Rebecca Amory Receipt Book, Amory Family Papers, MHS.

91. Receipt on Promissory Note, *Carr v. Fairchild*, Newport CCP, May 1731, #141, RIJRC; Receipt, Magdalene Wroe to Rebecca Amory, Aug. 15, 1733, Rebecca Amory Receipt Book, Amory Family Papers, MHS.

92. Receipt, Deborah Eustice to Rebecca Amory, Dec. 26, 1735, Rebecca Amory Receipt Book, Amory Family Papers, MHS; Receipt, Sarah Newton to Ann Maylem, Oct. 30, 1742, *Read v. Maylem*, Newport CCP, May 1743, #280, RIJRC.

93. Petition of Deborah Johnson ("person," "credit") (1743), RI Petitions, vol. 5, 47, RISA. For related documents, see *John Walton v. Deborah Johnson*, Oct. Session 1743, RI Equity Court File Papers, vol. 6, RISA.

94. Rebecca Amory Receipt Book, Amory Family Papers, MHS. On Amory's receipt book, see also Conger, *The Widow's Might*, 150–51. While Amory was actively using her receipt book, its pages were bound in a simple manner. After it was full, she or another family

member had it bound in a more ornate fashion that was commensurate with the importance of its contents. The book's irregularly sized pages were trimmed to a uniform size, and a green leather cover and ornate gold clasp were added for decoration and protection.

95. Elizabeth Aborn to Thomas Wharton and William Pollard, Oct. 5, 1768, Wharton Family Papers, HSP. For Joseph Aborn's shopkeeping, see "Just Imported from England," *Newport Mercury*, Mar. 12, 1764, [1].

96. On understandings of "public" and "private," see Mary Beth Norton, *Separated by their Sex: Women in Public and Private in the Colonial Atlantic World* (Ithaca, NY: Cornell University Press, 2011).

Chapter 3 · Debt Litigation, Lawyers, and Legal Practices

1. On caseloads in the Suffolk and Newport County Courts, see the appendix. On these transitions elsewhere in New England, see Bruce H. Mann, *Neighbors and Strangers: Law and Community in Early Connecticut* (Chapel Hill: University of North Carolina Press, 1987); Cornelia Hughes Dayton, *Women Before the Bar: Gender, Law, and Society in Connecticut, 1639–1789* (Chapel Hill: University of North Carolina Press, 1995); Claire Priest, "Currency Policies and the Nature of Litigation in Colonial New England" (PhD diss., Yale University, 2003). On the professionalization of law, see especially Gerald W. Gawalt, *The Promise of Power: The Emergence of the Legal Profession in Massachusetts, 1760–1840* (Westport, CT: Greenwood Press, 1979); John M. Murrin, "The Legal Transformation: The Bench and the Bar of Eighteenth-Century Massachusetts," in *Colonial America: Essays in Politics and Social Development*, 3rd ed., ed. Stanley N. Katz and John M. Murrin (New York: Alfred A. Knopf, 1983), 540–71; Martha G. McNamara, *From Tavern to Courthouse: Architecture and Ritual in American Law, 1658–1860* (Baltimore: Johns Hopkins University Press, 2004).

2. Penelope Stelle, "All Persons indebted," *Newport Mercury*, June 10, 1765, [3]. Stelle's advertisement also ran on June 17, July 1, July 8, and July 15, 1765. For an earlier advertisement by Stelle, see Penelope Stelle, "All Persons who have any Demands," *Newport Mercury*, June 20, 1763, [3]; This advertisement also ran on June 27, July 4, and July 18, 1763. Stelle's first advertisement identified her husband, Isaac Stelle, as a "ship captain," while the second described him as a "merchant." Isaac and Penelope Stelle also engaged in other enterprises, including running a bakehouse. See Elaine Forman Crane, *Ebb Tide in New England: Women, Seaports, and Social Change, 1630–1800* (Boston: Northeastern University Press, 1998), 125.

3. Mary Tillinghast, "All persons indebted" ("trouble"), *Newport Mercury*, Jan. 23, 1764, [4]; Bathiah Oliver, "All Persons that have any Demands" ("expect") *Boston Gazette*, Jan. 28, 1760, [3]; Mehitable Buttolph, "All Persons who are Indebted" ("without any exceptions"), *Boston Gazette*, Sept. 15–22, 1740, [4].

4. *Stelle v. Cole*, Newport CCP, Nov. 1765, #92, RIJRC; *Stelle v. Lillibridge*, Newport CCP, Nov. 1765, #123, RIJRC; *Stelle v. Gavett*, Newport CCP, Nov. 1765, #194, RIJRC; *Stelle v. Robinson*, Newport CCP, Nov. 1765, #248, RIJRC; *Stelle v. Stelle*, Newport CCP, Nov. 1765, #268, RIJRC; *Stelle v. Emmons*, Newport CCP, Nov. 1766, #275, RIJRC; *Stelle v. Mawdsley*, Newport CCP, Nov. 1766, #275, RIJRC.

5. See especially Dayton, *Women Before the Bar*. See also Crane, *Ebb Tide*; Deborah Rosen, *Courts and Commerce: Gender, Law, and the Market Economy in Colonial New York* (Columbus: Ohio State University Press, 1997).

6. Legal histories of debt include Mann, *Neighbors and Strangers*; Mary M. Schweitzer, *Custom and Contract: Household, Government, and the Economy in Colonial Pennsylvania* (New York: Columbia University Press, 1987); Rosen, *Courts and Commerce*; Priest, "Currency Policies."

7. Suffolk County: $N = 1472$. Newport County: $N = 1430$. On sampling, see the appendix.

8. Suffolk County: $N = 1160$; Newport County: $N = 1084$. On sampling, see the appendix.

9. Suffolk County: $N = 153$; Newport County: $N = 252$. On sampling, see the appendix.

10. See Ellen Hartigan-O'Connor, *The Ties that Buy: Women and Commerce in Revolutionary America* (Philadelphia: University of Pennsylvania Press, 2009), 72–73; Sara T. Damiano, "Gendering the Work of Debt Collection: Women, Law, and the Credit Economy in New England, 1730–1790" (PhD diss., Johns Hopkins University, 2015), 64–66; Lindsay R. Moore, *Women Before the Court: Law and Patriarchy in the Anglo-American World, 1600–1800* (Manchester, UK: Manchester University Press, 2019), 133–58.

11. Suffolk County: $N = 153$; Newport County: $N = 252$. On sampling, see the appendix.

12. Dayton, *Women Before the Bar*, 94, 100.

13. Henry Marchant to Priscilla Card, Dec. 7, 1773, Henry Marchant Letter Book, 1772–1792, Henry Marchant Papers, RIHS. Out of approximately 1,210 taxpayers listed on the Newport tax assessment for 1772, Henry Marchant was the thirty-seventh highest taxpayer. See Elaine Crane, *A Dependent People: Newport, Rhode Island in the Revolutionary Era* (New York: Fordham University Press, 1985), 25–29.

14. In Suffolk County, male plaintiffs won 83% ($N = 892$) of their debt cases, with 98% of these favorable judgments occurring by default. Female plaintiffs won 77% ($N = 44$) of their debt cases, with 64% by default. In Newport County, male plaintiffs also won 83% of their debt cases ($N = 1,009$), with 97% by default. Female plaintiffs won 78% of their debt suits ($N = 163$), with 88% by default. On sampling, see the appendix.

15. On uncontested debt suits, see Mann, *Neighbors and Strangers*; Turk McCleskey and James C. Squire, "Knowing When to Fold: Litigation on a Writ of Debt in Mid-Eighteenth Century Virginia," *WMQ* 76, no. 3 (July 2019): 509–44.

16. *Burrington v. Macomber*, Newport CCP, Nov. 1771, #172, RIJRC. Macomber did not challenge two other suits that Burrington had also filed against him. See *Burrington v. Macomber*, Newport CCP, May 1771, #168, RIJRC; *Burrington v. Macomber*, Newport CCP, Nov. 1771, #249, RIJRC; Record Book, Newport CCP, vol. H, 726, RIJRC. For Burrington's other suits, see Docket Books, Newport CCP, May 1770–May 1774, RIJRC. For the inventory of Robert Burrington's estate, see *Durfee v. Burrington*, Newport CCP, May 1773, #399, RIJRC.

17. William Pynchon, *The Diary of William Pynchon of Salem*, ed. Fitch Edward Oliver (Boston: Houghton Mifflin, 1890), 216, quoted in McNamara, *From Tavern to Courthouse*, 40.

18. McNamara, *From Tavern to Courthouse*, 45–46, 49; Petition of Catherine Cunningham (1740), MA Archives, vol. 41, 737, MSA.

19. On the meeting places of the Boston and Newport courts, see Norman Morrison Isham, "The Colony House at Newport, Rhode Island," *Bulletin of the Society for the Preservation of New England Antiquities* 8, no. 2 (December 1917): 7–14; Antoinette F.

Downing and Vincent J. Scully, Jr., *The Architectural Heritage of Newport Rhode Island 1640–1915* (New York: Clarkson N. Potter, 1967), 60–65; McNamara, *From Tavern to Courthouse*, 14–20, 29–31, 46–53. Hartigan-O'Connor, *The Ties That Buy*, 15. On imprisonment for debt, see Mann, *Republic of Debtors*, 16, 24–31.

20. Writ and Promissory Note, *Swinnerton v. Harris*, Newport CCP, May 1751, #170, RIJRC.

21. Robert A. Feer, "Imprisonment for Debt in Massachusetts before 1800," *Mississippi Valley Historical Review* 48, no. 2 (Sept. 1961): 252–69; Laurel Thatcher Ulrich, *A Midwife's Tale: The Life of Martha Ballard, Based on her Diary, 1785–1812* (New York: Alfred A. Knopf, 1990), 262–85; Mann, *Republic of Debtors*, 79–81; James Roberts, "'Such Scandalous Fellows': Aaron Lopez and the Trevett Affair of 1773–74," *Rhode Island Jewish Historical Notes* 15, no. 3 (2009): 406–16.

22. Deposition of Joseph Seaby, *Brayton v. George*, Newport CCP, May 1761, #31, RIJRC. Court records described Benjamin Brayton as a mariner, but the family owned property that Hannah Brayton later advertised for sale or rent. See Hannah Brayton, "To Be Sold," *Newport Mercury*, Aug. 15, 1763, [4]. For a male debtor who was imprisoned as a result of a female creditor's lawsuit, see *Champlin v. Christy et al.*, Newport CCP, May 1776, #14, RIJRC.

23. In Suffolk County, male defendants ($N = 912$) lost 83% of their debt suits, with 98% of these unfavorable judgments occurring by default. Female defendants ($N = 25$) lost 76% of their debt suits, with 80% of these by default. In Newport County, male defendants lost 83% of their debt suits ($N = 1{,}048$), with 96% of these by default. Female defendants lost 75% of their debt cases ($N = 92$), with 84% of these by default. On sampling, see the appendix.

24. Writ, *Brown v. Clark*, Suffolk SCJ (Aug. 1741), Suffolk Files, 53988, MSA.

25. For the seizure of Simon's furniture and home, see Henry Marchant to John Knapp, Mar. 24, 1771, and June 18, 1771, Henry Marchant Letter Book, 1769–1772, 232, 302, Henry Marchant Papers, RIHS. For the lawsuits against Abigail Simon, see *Johnson v. Simon*, May 1771, Record Book, Newport CCP, vol. H, 702, RIJRC; *Barker v. Simon*, May 1771, Record Book, Newport CCP, vol. H, 717, RIJRC; *Osborne v. Simon*, May 1771, Record Book, Newport CCP, vol. H, 721, RIJRC; *Vernon v. Simon*, Nov. 1771, Record Book, Newport CCP, vol. I, 53, RIJRC. Abigail Simon's husband, Peter Simon, died in 1768. His considerable estate was valued at £288.19 lawful money, or nearly £7,513 old tenor. See Inventory, Estate of Peter Simon (June 8, 1768), Newport TC, vol. 15, 199, NHS.

26. Feer, "Imprisonment for Debt," 257–60.

27. Petition of Sarah Hunt (1757), MA Archives, vol. 44, 350, MSA. For the death of Sarah Hunt's husband, Richard Hunt, see Sarah Hunt, "All Persons Indebted," *New England Weekly Journal*, Apr. 1, 1740, [2]. For Sarah Hunt's commercial activities, see John Salmon and Sarah Hunt, "To be sold," *Boston Evening Post*, Mar. 26, 1753, [2]; John Salmon and Sarah Hunt, "To be sold," *Boston Evening Post*, Aug. 20, 1753, [4]. For Hunt's description of the partnership, see Petition of Sarah Hunt (1757), MA Archives, vol. 44, 350, MSA. For an advertisement by the commissioners who received the claims of the insolvent firm's creditors, see Richard Bill, John Winslow, and Thomas Gray, "All Persons indebted," *Boston Evening Post*, Dec. 23, 1754, [2]. For Sarah Hunt's death at age seventy-five, see "Died. Mrs. Sarah Hunt," *Boston Evening Post*, Jan. 27, 1772, [3]. For examples of women who were imprisoned for debt, see Petition of Anne Clark (1755), RI

Petitions, vol. 9, 76, 173, RISA; Petition of Catherine Cunningham (1740), MA Archives, vol. 41, 737, MSA; Hartigan-O'Connor, *Ties that Buy*, 89. For examples of women who feared imprisonment for debts, see Petition of Abigail Remington (1760), RI Petitions, vol. 10, 139, RISA; Petition of Hannah Norton (1750), RI Petitions, vol. 7, 79, RISA.

28. On standard narratives of failure, see Toby L. Ditz, "Shipwrecked; or, Masculinity Imperiled: Mercantile Representations of Failure and the Gendered Self in Eighteenth-Century Philadelphia," *Journal of American History* 81, no. 1 (June 1994): 51–80, esp. 58–61. On insolvency, see Mann, *Republic of Debtors.*

29. Petition of Sarah Hunt (1757), MA Archives, vol. 44, 350, MSA; Feer, "Imprisonment for Debt," 260.

30. For example, see Jean H. Quataert, "The Shaping of Women's Work in Manufacturing: Guilds, Households, and the State in Central Europe, 1648–1870," *American Historical Review* 90, no. 5 (Dec. 1985): 1122–48; Martha Howell, *Women, Production, and Patriarchy in Late Medieval Cities* (Chicago: University of Chicago Press, 1986); Ulrich, *Midwife's Tale*, 36–71, 235–61; Judith Bennett, *History Matters: Patriarchy and the Challenge of Feminism* (Philadelphia: University of Pennsylvania Press, 2006), 72–79.

31. Murrin, "Legal Transformation," 541–47; Mann, *Neighbors and Strangers*, 81–85, 93–100; Dayton, *Women Before the Bar*, 47–48; Mary Sarah Bilder, "The Lost Lawyers: Early American Legal Literates and Transatlantic Legal Culture," *Yale Journal of Law and the Humanities* 11, no. 1 (Winter 1999): 57–67; McNamara, *From Tavern to Courthouse*, 28–29.

32. Charles McKirdy, "Massachusetts Lawyers on the Eve of the American Revolution: The State of the Profession," in *Law in Colonial Massachusetts, 1630–1800*, ed. Daniel R. Coquillette (Boston: Colonial Society of Massachusetts, 1984), 316; Richard Brown, *Knowledge Is Power: The Diffusion of Information in Early America, 1700–1865* (New York: Oxford University Press, 1989), 85–86, 88; Mary Sarah Bilder, *The Transatlantic Constitution: Colonial Legal Culture and the Empire* (Cambridge, MA: Harvard University Press, 2004), 117–20; McNamara, *From Tavern to Courthouse*, 28–29.

33. Estimates regarding the number of attorneys practicing in pre-Revolutionary Suffolk and Newport Counties vary. Charles McKirdy counts sixteen lawyers in Suffolk County in 1775. See McKirdy, "Massachusetts Lawyers," 337. Thirteen lawyers were present at the first meeting of the Suffolk County Bar Association in January 1770. Between 1770 and 1775, eleven additional attorneys attended association meetings or were formally admitted to practice in the Court of Common Pleas or the Superior Court. See George Dexter, ed., "Record Book of the Suffolk Bar," *Proceedings of the Massachusetts Historical Society*, 1st ser., 19 (Dec. 1881): 147–52. For lawyers in Newport County, see Docket Books, Newport CCP, RIJRC, which clearly identify the attorneys involved in each case.

34. Some historians state that the Suffolk Bar Association was founded in 1770, as this was the first year the group kept regular minutes, but others find earlier evidence of its activities in attorneys' personal papers. See Gawalt, *Promise of Power*, 10, 13, 17, 19; McKirdy, "Massachusetts Lawyers," 323; Bilder, *Transatlantic Constitution*, 118–20; McNamara, *From Tavern to Courthouse*, 36–37.

35. The legal documents included in eighteenth-century Suffolk County and Newport County case files consistently bear lawyers' signatures and indicate the litigants' use of attorneys. On eighteenth-century attorneys, see Mann, *Neighbors and Strangers*, 93–100; Dayton, *Women Before the Bar*, 47–53; Robert Blair St. George, "Massacred

Language: Courtroom Performances in Eighteenth-Century Boston," in *Possible Pasts: Becoming Colonial in Early America*, ed. Robert Blair St. George (Ithaca, NY: Cornell University Press, 2000), 327–56; Bilder, *Transatlantic Constitution*, 26–28.

36. John Adams (Mar. 14, 1759) ("frequent visits"), *The Adams Papers, Diary and Autobiography of John Adams*, vol. 1, *1755–1770*, ed. L. H. Butterfield (Cambridge, MA: Harvard University Press, 1961), 78; L. Kinvin Wroth and Hiller B. Zobel, introduction to *Legal Papers of John Adams*, vol. 1, ed. L. Kinvin Wroth and Hiller B. Zobel (Cambridge, MA: Belknap Press of Harvard University Press, 1965), lxix–lxxiv. On lawyers' business practices, see Charles McKirdy, "Before the Storm: The Working Lawyer in Pre-Revolutionary Massachusetts," *Suffolk University Law Review* 11 (1976): 46–60; Brown, *Knowledge Is Power*, 93; Sally Hadden, "DeSaussure and Ford: A Charleston Law Firm of the 1790s," in *Transformations in American Legal History: Essays in Honor of Professor Morton J. Horwitz*, ed. Daniel W. Hamilton and Alfred L. Brophy (Cambridge, MA: Harvard University Press, 2009), 85–108.

37. "New-Port, September 5" ("polite and genteel"), *New York Gazette*, Sept. 19, 1774, [2]; Abigail Stoneman, "The Merchants Coffee House" ("gentlemen"), *Newport Mercury*, July 1, 1767, [1]. For additional advertisements by Stoneman, see Abigail Stoneman, "The Royal Exchange Tavern," *Boston Evening Post*, Dec. 10, 1770, [3]; Abigail Stoneman, "Abigail Stoneman," *Newport Mercury*, May 3, 1773, [4]; Abigail Stoneman, "Abigail Stoneman," *Newport Mercury*, Nov. 15, 1773, [1]; Abigail Stoneman, "Abigail Stoneman," *Newport Mercury*, May 30, 1774, [4]. For Stoneman's portrait, see *Stoneman v. Blodget*, Newport CCP, May 1772, #302, RIJRC. For lawyers' visits to Stoneman's tavern, see *Stoneman v. Johnston*, Newport CCP, Nov. 1769, #140, RIJRC; *Stoneman v. Helme*, Newport CCP, May 1770, #183, RIJRC. On sites of elite sociability, see especially David S. Shields, *Civil Tongues and Polite Letters in British America* (Chapel Hill: University of North Carolina Press, 1997).

38. Account of Abigail Stoneman, William Ellery Journal, 121, NHS. For the price of punch, see *Stoneman v. Helme*, Newport CCP, May 1770, #183, RIJRC. For the price of boarding, see *Stoneman v. Blodget*, Newport CCP, May 1772, #302, RIJRC.

39. Account of Mary Searing, William Ellery Journal, 122, NHS. For Searing's business activities, see Hartigan-O'Connor, *Ties that Buy*, 89.

40. Henry Marchant to Sarah Perkins, Apr. 1, 1771, Henry Marchant Letter Book, 1769–1772, 242, Henry Marchant Papers, RIHS.

41. Elizabeth Thomas to James Otis, Dec. 1, 1746, Otis Family Papers, MHS.

42. Petition of Ann Maylem (Sept. 1744), RI Petitions, vol. 6, 13, RISA.

43. On lawyers' businesses as household and family enterprises, see Hadden, "DeSaussure and Ford," 95–96.

44. Henry Marchant to Francina Muir, June 16, 1774, Henry Marchant Letter Book, 1772–1792, 130, Henry Marchant Papers, RIHS.

45. Henry Marchant to Francina Muir, June 16, 1774, Henry Marchant Letter Book, 1772–1792, 130, Henry Marchant Papers, RIHS. For representative examples of Marchant's initial correspondence with male clients, see Harford and Powell to Henry Marchant, Mar. 10, 1770, and Daniel Roberdeau to Henry Marchant, Apr. 20, 1782, Henry Marchant Papers, RIHS; Henry Marchant to John Wendall, Jan. 3, 1771, and Henry Marchant to Harford and Powell, Oct. 4, 1770, Henry Marchant Letterbook, 1769–1772, 151, 178, Henry Marchant Papers, RIHS.

46. Account, *Johnston v. Holmes*, Newport CCP, Nov. 1755, #262, RIJRC. Johnston acknowledged that the £10 fee was subjective, appending the phrase "I deserve" in parentheses. For additional examples of accounts documenting services that attorneys rendered to female clients, see Account, *Richards v. Forrester*, Newport CCP, May 1746, #248, RIJRC; Account, *Ward v. Pinnegar*, Newport CCP, Nov. 1749, #1, RIJRC; Account, *Richards v. Briggs*, Newport CCP, May 1754, #480, RIJRC; Account, *Marchant v. Greene*, Newport CCP, May 1757, #69, RIJRC.

47. Account, *Johnston v. Holmes*, Newport CCP, Nov. 1755, #262, RIJRC.

48. Petition of Margaret Elliott (1755), MA Archives, vol. 44, 147, MSA.

49. Petition of Margaret Elliott (1755), MA Archives, vol. 44, 147, MSA.

50. Petition of Margaret Elliott (1755), MA Archives, vol. 44, 147, MSA.

51. Martha Parker to James Otis, July 1, 1757, Otis Family Papers, MHS. For additional evidence of married women's use of attorneys, see Isaac Little to James Otis, Apr. 30, 1757, Otis Family Papers, MHS; Ichabod and Anne Johnson to James Otis, Oct. 30, 1766, Otis Family Papers, MHS.

52. John Woodbridge to James Otis, May 21, 1754, Otis Family Papers, MHS.

53. Oxenbridge Thatcher to Robert Treat Paine, Aug. 23, 1763, Robert Treat Paine Papers, MHS.

54. Statement of Richard Bollan (1741), *Cummings v. Jones*, MA Archives, vol. 41, 593, MSA. Instances regarding debt cases in which mariners' wives petitioned during their husbands' absences provide additional evidence of such women's partnerships with attorneys. See Petition of Mary Hause (1730), RI Petitions, vol. 2, 28, RISA; Petition of Lydia Manchester (1769), RI Petitions, vol. 13.2, 166, RISA; Petition of Elizabeth Heffernan for Jeremiah Heffernan (1776), RI Petitions, vol. 12, 42, RISA; Petition of Sarah Tarr for Richard Tarr (1741), MA Archives, vol. 41, 730, MSA; Petition of Jane Stevens (1743), MA Archives, vol. 42, 247, MSA.

55. On agents in early modern commerce, see especially Thomas M. Doerflinger, *A Vigorous Spirit of Enterprise: Merchants and Economic Development in Revolutionary Philadelphia* (Chapel Hill: University of North Carolina Press, 1986); David Hancock, "The Trouble with Networks: Managing the Scots' Early-Modern Madeira Trade," *Business History Review* 79, no. 3 (Autumn 2005): 467–91; David Hancock, "The Triumphs of Mercury: Connection and Control in the Emerging Atlantic Economy," in *Soundings in Atlantic History: Latent Structures and Intellectual Currents, 1500–1830*, ed. Bernard Bailyn and Patricia L. Denault (Cambridge, MA: Harvard University Press, 2009), 112–40; Sheryllynne Haggerty, *"Merely for Money"? Business Culture in the British Atlantic, 1750–1815* (Liverpool, UK: Liverpool University Press, 2012). On husbands and wives, see Sara T. Damiano, "Agents at Home: Wives, Lawyers, and Financial Competence in Eighteenth-Century New England Port Cities," *Early American Studies* 13, no. 4 (Fall 2015): 808–35; Sara T. Damiano, "Writing Women's History through the Revolution: Family Finances, Letter Writing, and Conceptions of Marriage," *WMQ* 74, no. 4 (Oct. 2017): 697–728. For sample letters between principals and agents in letter-writing manuals, see William Bradford, comp., *The Secretary's Guide, or Young Man's Companion* (Philadelphia: Andrew Bradford, 1737), 65, 71–72, 75; John Hill, *The Young Secretary's Guide, or, a Speedy Help to Learning* (Boston: Thomas Fleet, 1750), 42, 43. On letter writing, see especially Toby L. Ditz, "Formative Ventures: Mercantile Letters and the Articulation of Experience," in *Epistolary Selves: Letters and Letter-Writers, 1600–1945*, ed. Rebecca Earle (Aldershot, UK:

Ashgate, 1999), 59–78; Eve Tavor Bannet, *Empire of Letters: Letter Manuals and Transatlantic Correspondence, 1680–1820* (Cambridge: Cambridge University Press, 2006); Sarah M. S. Pearsall, *Atlantic Families: Lives and Letters in the Later Eighteenth Century* (New York: Oxford University Press, 2008); Konstantin Dierks, *In My Power: Letter Writing and Communications in Early America* (Philadelphia: University of Pennsylvania Press, 2009).

56. Martha Parker to James Otis, Aug. 18, 1757, and Aug. 5, 1761, Otis Family Papers, MHS. For additional examples of clients instructing their lawyers to sue, see Sarah Rumreil to James Otis, Mar. 21, 1746, Benjamin Hammond to James Otis, Apr. 15, 1756, and Perez Tillson to James Otis, Jan. 26, 1760, Otis Family Papers, MHS; Aaron Lopez to Robert Treat Paine, Aug. 29, 1763, Robert Treat Paine Papers, MHS.

57. Martha Parker to James Otis, Aug. 5, 1761, Otis Family Papers, MHS. For additional examples of clients instructing their attorneys to respond to lawsuits, see Samuel Thacher to James Otis, Apr. 27, 1742, and Elizabeth Thomas to James Otis, Dec. 1, 1746, Otis Family Papers, MHS; James Swan to John Lowell, Sept. 21, 1776, John Lowell Papers, Houghton; Daniel Rodman to William Channing, Oct. 29, 1783, Channing Papers, NHS.

58. Martha Parker to James Otis, Aug. 18, 1757 ("as soon as you can"), and Dec. 3, 1757 ("as soon as may be"), Otis Family Papers, MHS. For additional examples of clients urging their attorneys to act quickly, see Samuel Knowls to James Otis, Sept. 24, 1734, John Traill to James Otis, Feb. 24, 1748, Benjamin Hammond to James Otis, Apr. 15, 1756, and Jane Savell to James Otis, Nov. 3, 1757, Otis Family Papers, MHS; Mary Ward to Robert Treat Paine, Aug. 5, 1762, James Putnam to Robert Treat Paine, Jan. 8, 1763, John Foster to Robert Treat Paine, Jan. 10, 1764, Thomas Brown to Robert Treat Paine, Feb. 10, 1764, and John Freebody to Robert Treat Paine, Mar. 6, 1770, Robert Treat Paine Papers, MHS.

59. Sarah Bradford to James Otis, Feb. 8, 1747 ("if you think it be best"), William Tabor to James Otis, May 12, 1753 ("as you think fit"), and Ichabod and Anne Johnson to James Otis, Oct. 30, 1766 ("most proper"), Otis Family Papers, MHS. See also Caleb Philips to James Otis, July 3, 1742, and Ann Maylem to James Otis, Oct. 23, 1745, Otis Family Papers, MHS; Joseph Greenleaf to Robert Treat Paine, Sept. 30, 1762, and Thomas Smith to Robert Treat Paine, Mar. 4, 1766, Robert Treat Paine Papers, MHS.

60. Martha Parker to James Otis, Dec. 3, 1757, Otis Family Papers, MHS.

61. William Samuel Johnson to Rebecca Gibbons, Apr. 2, 1766, Letterbook XII, William Samuel Johnson Papers, CHS; Henry Marchant to Anne Devisme, Feb. 20, 1769, Henry Marchant Letter Book, 1769–1772, 7, Henry Marchant Papers, RIHS. For an analogous letter from an attorney to a male client, see Henry Marchant to Walter Franklin, Oct. 14, 1769, Henry Marchant Letter Book, 1769–1772, 46, Henry Marchant Papers, RIHS.

62. William Samuel Johnson to Rebecca Gibbons, Apr. 2, 1766, Letterbook XII, William Samuel Johnson Papers, CHS; Henry Marchant to Sarah Perkins, Apr. 1, 1771, Henry Marchant Letter Book, 1769–1772, 242, Henry Marchant Papers, RIHS; Henry Marchant to Francina Muir, June 16, 1774, Henry Marchant Letter Book, 1772–1792, 130, Henry Marchant Papers, Henry Marchant Papers, RIHS.

63. For instance, see James Otis to Walter Chase, July 23, 1750, Otis Family Papers, MHS; Henry Marchant to Samuel Broome and Company, Feb. 3, 1770, Henry Marchant Letter Book, 1769–1772, 71, Henry Marchant Papers, RIHS; Henry Marchant to John

Murray, Apr. 19, 1770, Henry Marchant Letter Book, 1769–1772, 90, Henry Marchant Papers, RIHS.

64. Sarah Rumreil to James Otis, Mar. 21, 1746, Otis Family Papers, MHS.

65. Hartigan-O'Connor, *Ties that Buy*, 61, 91; Marian Mathison Desrosiers, *John Banister of Newport: The Life and Accounts of a Colonial Merchant* (Jefferson, NC: McFarland, 2017), 82–83. If Rumreil obtained assistance in drafting her letter, her choice would have fit within her broader strategy of delegating some of the clerical tasks associated with her business (see chapter 2).

66. Elizabeth Thomas to James Otis, Dec. 1, 1746 ("intreat," "pray"), Otis Family Papers, MHS; Elesabeth Hammond to James Otis, Feb. 6, 1749 ("beg"), Otis Family Papers, MHS.

67. Phebe Hinckly to James Otis, Apr. 29, 1762, Otis Family Papers, MHS. The phonetic spelling of Hinckly's letter suggests that she wrote it herself, as does the fact that the letter and signature appear to be in the same hand.

68. Isaac Doane to James Otis, Jan. 1, 1739, Otis Family Papers, MHS.

69. Hannah Norton to James Otis, Mar. 1756, Elesabeth Hammond to James Otis, Feb. 6, 1749, and Anne Johnson to James Otis, Oct. 30, 1766, Otis Family Papers, MHS. "Harpies" were a common metaphor in merchants' letters about credit and debt. See Ditz, "Shipwrecked," 51, 54, 60–61.

70. For a controversy surrounding the service of writs in a credit dispute between men, see Elaine Forman Crane, *Witches, Wife Beaters, and Whores: Common Law and Common Folk in Early America* (Ithaca, NY: Cornell University Press, 2011), ch. 5. On the continued importance of local encounters with the law during the nineteenth century, see Laura F. Edwards, *The People and Their Peace: Legal Culture and the Transformation of Inequality in the Post-Revolutionary South* (Chapel Hill: University of North Carolina Press, 2009).

71. Deposition of Sarah Peirse, *Heart v. Starr*, Suffolk CCP, Apr. 1766, #286, MSA.

72. For example, see Writ (Sept. 15, 1739) and Statement of William Nichols (June 20, 1739), *Hewes v. Cunningham*, Suffolk Files, 51,228, MSA.

73. Deposition of Sarah Peirse, *Heart v. Starr*, Suffolk CCP, Apr. 1766, #286, MSA. For constables' obligations, see *Conductor Generalis: or, the Office, Duty, and Authority of Justices of the Peace*, 2nd ed. (Philadelphia: B. Franklin & D. Hall, 1750), 333–61. For lawsuits filed against sheriffs and constables, see Petition of Jane Stevens (1743), MA Archives, vol. 42, 247, MSA; Petition of Josiah Quincy (1752), MA Archives, vol. 43, 575, MSA; *Ward v. Brenton*, Newport CCP, Nov. 1765, #177, RIJRC.

74. Mann, *Republic of Debtors*, 21, 23. For an example of a layperson's awareness of court deadlines, see Petition of Stephen Norwood (1748), MA Archives, vol. 42, 747, MSA. Norwood complained that he missed the hearing for his case at the Superior Court because he "took for granted" that the session would occur "at the usual and stated time," but the court 's meeting time had moved. Providing insight into how ordinary people learned of court dates, Norwood added that he had "looked into his almanack" to check when the court met.

75. Petition of Joseph Harris (1770), RI Petitions, vol. 14, 43, RISA.

76. Deposition of Sarah Peirse, *Heart v. Starr*, Suffolk CCP, Apr. 1766, #286, MSA. For additional examples of wives served with writs, see *Brown v. Manchester*, Providence SCJ, Sept. 1769, RIJRC; *Jeffers v. Issacks*, Newport SCJ, Sept. 1769, RIJRC.

77. Deposition of Sarah Peirse, *Heart v. Starr*, Suffolk CCP, Apr. 1766, #286, MSA.

78. Deposition of Sarah Peirse, *Heart v. Starr*, Suffolk CCP, Apr. 1766, #286, MSA. For an additional example of negotiations between a defendant and local officials, see *Russell v. Hallett*, Suffolk CCP, Apr. 1756, #290, MSA.

79. Deposition of Sarah Peirse, *Heart v. Starr*, Suffolk CCP, Apr. 1766, #286, MSA.

80. For examples in legal texts, see *Conductor Generalis*, 25, 143, 227, 369, 439. For warnings issued during confrontations, see Deposition of David Monroe (Apr. 20, 1739), Deposition of Cornelius Campbell, James Brown, and Jane Blake (Sept. 30, 1739), Deposition of Daniel Bridges, Ephraim Baker, and Cornelius Campbell (Feb. 18, 1739), and Deposition of George Hewes (Feb. 1739), *Hewes v. Cunningham*, Suffolk Files, 51,228, MSA; Deposition of James Hawkins (May 13, 1739), *Hewes v. Cunningham*, Suffolk Files, 49,424, MSA; Deposition of Amos Hovey (July 1739), *Hewes v. Cunningham*, Suffolk Files, 49,536, MSA; Deposition of John Gardner (Mar. 1742), *Hewes v. Cunningham*, Suffolk Files, 56,824, MSA; Crane, *Witches, Wifebeaters, and Whores*, 150, 168.

81. Deposition of Sarah Peirse, *Heart v. Starr*, Suffolk CCP, Apr. 1766, #286, MSA.

82. *Conductor Generalis*, 338.

83. Deposition of Daniel Bridges, Ephraim Baker, and Cornelius Campbell (Feb, 18, 1739), and Deposition of George Hewes (Feb. 1739), *Hewes v. Cunningham*, Suffolk Files, 51,228, MSA.

84. *Conductor Generalis*, 338; Julian Hoppit, *Risk and Failure in English Business, 1700–1800* (Cambridge: Cambridge University Press, 1987), 30; Deposition of Bartholemew Allen and John Squire (Jan. 1739), *Hewes v. Cunningham*, Suffolk Files, 50767, MSA; Deposition of Ruth Loring (Sept. 3, 1740); *Hewes v. Cunningham*, Suffolk Files, 52,392, MSA. See also Deposition of Samuel Thornton on Petition of Immaneul Northup (1765), RI Petitions, vol. 12, 18, RISA.

85. *Conductor Generalis*, 338–39; Deposition of Sarah Peirse, *Heart v. Starr*, Suffolk CCP, April 1766, #286, MSA. Massachusetts laws forbade non-white servants and slaves from leaving their homes after 9 pm without their household heads' permission and allowed night watchmen to question any suspicious persons out after 10 pm. See "An Act to Prevent Disorders in the Night," (Boston: Secretary of the Commonwealth, 1703), https://archives.lib.state.ma.us/handle/2452/118975/; "An Act for Explanation, and in Addition to the Act for Keeping of Watches in Towns [. . .]" (Boston: Secretary of the Commonwealth, 1712), https://archives.lib.state.ma.us/handle/2452/119066/.

86. On mahogany, see Jennifer L. Anderson, *Mahogany: The Costs of Luxury in Early America* (Cambridge, MA: Harvard University Press, 2012).

87. Deposition of Sarah Peirse and Writ, *Heart v. Starr*, Suffolk CCP, Apr. 1766, #286, MSA.

88. Joan R. Gunderson, *To Be Useful to the World: Women in Revolutionary America, 1740–1790*, rev. ed. (Chapel Hill: University of North Carolina Press, 2006), 82. On renting, see also Gary B. Nash, "Urban Wealth and Poverty in Pre-Revolutionary America," *Journal of Interdisciplinary History* 6, no. 4 (Spring 1976): 550; Sharon V. Salinger and Charles Wetherell, "Wealth and Renting in Prerevolutionary Philadelphia," *Journal of American History* 71, no. 4 (Mar. 1985): 829; Ellen Hartigan-O'Connor, "'She Said She did not know Money': Urban Women and Atlantic Markets in the Revolutionary Era," *Early American Studies* 4, no. 2 (Fall 2006): 327–30; Cornelia H. Dayton and Sharon V. Salinger, *Robert Love's Warning: Searching for Strangers in Colonial Boston* (Philadelphia: University of Pennsylvania Press, 2014), 95–115.

89. Writ, *Saunders v. Stokesberry*, Newport SCJ, 1754, RIJRC.

90. Deposition of Sarah Peirse, *Heart v. Starr*, Suffolk CCP, Apr. 1766, #286, MSA.

91. For Chapman's lawsuit seeking payment for her services, see *Chapman v. Lawton*, Newport SCJ, 1733, RIJRC.

92. Depositions of Adam Hunt, Joseph Ward, and Samuel Collings, *Lawton v. Chapman*, Newport SCJ, 1733, RIJRC.

93. *Lawton v. Chapman*, Newport Superior Court, 1733, RIJRC. For Chapman's appearance before the Newport Town Council, see Minutes, Newport TC (Dec. 5, 1732), NHS; *Lawton v. Chapman*, Newport SCJ, 1733, RIJRC.

94. For example, see *Russell v. Hallett*, Suffolk CCP, Apr. 1756, #290, MSA.

95. Referees' Report, *Heart v. Starr*, Suffolk CCP, Apr. 1766, #286, MSA.

Chapter 4 · *The Knowledge and Power of Witnesses*

1. Deposition of Mary Asten, *Sheffield v. Weast*, Newport SCJ, 1733, RIJRC. To a greater extent than in previous chapters, this chapter expands its focus to encompass the towns surrounding Boston and Newport, in addition to these cities themselves. In so doing, it suggests that practices of witnessing occurred both in port cities and their environs. This approach reflects the nature of surviving sources about witnesses' involvement in credit transactions. Witnesses who resided a considerable distance from their county seats often testified before justices of the peace in advance of court sessions, and officials included the resulting written depositions in case files. In contrast, when witnesses provided oral testimonies in court, as Boston and Newport locals tended to do, officials did not produce a written record of their statements. On similar practices elsewhere, see Cornelia Hughes Dayton, *Women Before the Bar: Gender, Law, and Society in Connecticut, 1639–1789* (Chapel Hill: University of North Carolina Press, 1995), 5–6.

2. Deposition of Mary Asten, *Sheffield v. Weast*, Newport SCJ, 1733, RIJRC. It was Mary Sheffield, the widow of Weast's creditor, who later attempted to collect the debt and who ultimately sued Weast. For a discussion of Mary Sheffield's activities as an administrator, see chapter 2.

3. Bruce Mann, *Neighbors and Strangers: Law and Community in Early Connecticut* (Chapel Hill: University of North Carolina Press, 1987); David D. Hall, *Worlds of Wonder, Days of Judgment: Popular Religious Belief in Early New England* (Cambridge, MA: Harvard University Press, 1990); Dayton, *Women Before the Bar*, 8–11, 29–31, 59–60, 70, 80–81. Witnesses' testimonies in witchcraft trials exemplify the intertwining of law, religion, and magic during the seventeenth century. See Carol F. Karlsen, *The Devil in the Shape of a Woman: Witchcraft in Colonial New England* (New York: W. W. Norton, 1998); Mary Beth Norton, *In the Devil's Snare: The Salem Witchcraft Crisis of 1692* (New York: Alfred A. Knopf, 2002); Richard Godbeer, *Escaping Salem: The Other Witch Hunt of 1692* (New York: Oxford University Press, 2005).

4. Phyllis Mack, *Visionary Women: Ecstatic Prophecy in Seventeenth-Century England* (Berkeley: University of California Press, 1992); Susan Juster, *Disorderly Women: Sexual Politics and Evangelicalism in Revolutionary New England* (Ithaca, NY: Cornell University Press, 1994); Catherine A. Brekus, *Strangers and Pilgrims: Female Preaching in America, 1740–1845* (Chapel Hill: University of North Carolina Press, 1998); Susan Juster, *Doomsayers: Anglo-American Prophecy in the Age of Revolution* (Philadelphia: University of Pennsylvania Press, 2003); Sarah Rivett, *The Science of the Soul in Colonial New England*

(Chapel Hill: University of North Carolina Press, 2011); Catherine A. Brekus, *Sarah Osborn's World: The Rise of Evangelical Christianity in Early America* (New Haven, CT: Yale University Press, 2013).

5. Steven Shapin, *A Social History of Truth: Civility and Science in Seventeenth-Century England* (Chicago: University of Chicago Press, 1994); Joyce E. Chaplin, *Benjamin Franklin and the Pursuit of Genius* (New York: Basic Books, 2006); Susan Scott Parrish, *American Curiosity: Cultures of Natural History in the Colonial British Atlantic World* (Chapel Hill: University of North Carolina Press, 2006); Andrew J. Lewis, *A Democracy of Facts: Natural History in the Early Republic* (Philadelphia: University of Pennsylvania Press, 2011); Steven Shapin and Simon Shaffer, *Leviathan and the Air Pump: Hobbes, Boyle, and the Experimental Life* (Princeton, NJ: Princeton University Press, 2011).

6. Sarah Knott, "The Patient's Case: Sentimental Empiricism and Knowledge in the Early American Republic," *WMQ* 67, no. 4 (Oct. 2010), 634–76.

7. Newport figures are based on a sample consisting of all witness signatures ($N = 1,454$) present on financial documents submitted to the Newport County Court of Common Pleas as evidence in November 1731 and in the May terms of 1736, 1741, 1746, 1751, 1756, 1761, 1766, 1771, and 1776. I used the November term of 1731, because the May records are incomplete. Suffolk figures are based on a sample consisting of all witness signatures ($N = 408$) present on financial documents submitted to the Suffolk County Court of Common Pleas as evidence in the April terms of 1736, 1741, 1746, 1751, 1756, 1761, 1766, 1771, and 1776. Because the records of April 1741 are incomplete, I additionally included July 1741 in my sample.

8. These figures are based on all witnesses who testified in debt cases in the Newport County Court of Common Pleas ($N = 207$) and Suffolk County Court of Common Pleas ($N = 45$) during sampled court terms. Because officials recorded the depositions of witnesses who testified before justices of the peace but not those who testified in court, extant depositions provide an incomplete portrait of who served as witnesses. I used depositions, summonses, and accounts of court fees to identify male and female witnesses. For the terms consulted, see note 7.

9. Laura Gowing, *Domestic Dangers: Women, Words, and Sex in Early Modern London* (Oxford UK: Clarendon Press, 1996), 11–12, 49–50; Julie Hardwick, *Family Business: Litigation and the Political Economies of Daily Life in Early Modern France* (Oxford, UK: Oxford University Press, 2009), 98.

10. See chapter 3.

11. Of the witness depositions that referenced specific locations ($N = 207$), 69% described events occurring in houses. An additional 143 witnesses did not mention precise sites in their depositions. My sample of witness depositions includes those from all years covered in my systematic sampling (see note 7), as well as other witness testimonies that I came across during my research in the records of the Newport and Suffolk county courts and the Massachusetts and Rhode Island legislatures from 1730 to 1776.

12. Deposition of Samuel Hicks, *Wilcox v. Wanton*, Newport CCP, May 1761, #244, RIJRC; Deposition of Patricia Cornell, *Lawton v. Langworthy*, Newport CCP, May 1736, #103, RIJRC; Deposition of Katherine West, *Crossing v. Chadwick*, Newport SCJ, 1756, RIJRC; Deposition of Sarah Greenman, Deposition of Southcote Langworthy, and Petition of Sylvanus Greenman (1764), RI Petitions, vol. 11.2, 78, RISA.

13. Deposition of Alice Gould, *Bowers v. Bagnall*, Newport SCJ, 1755, RIJRC; Deposition of Temperance Grant, *Lawton v. Grant and Vernon*, Newport SCJ, 1755, RIJRC;

Depositions of Mary Brown and Susannah Hazard, *Goddard v. Hazard*, Newport SCJ, 1763, RIJRC. Mary Brown and Susannah Hazard engaged in practices of collaborative consumption that were common in eighteenth-century port cities. See Ellen Hartigan-O'Connor, "Collaborative Consumption and the Politics of Choice in Early American Port Cities," in *Gender, Taste, and Material Culture in Britain and North America, 1700–1830*, ed. Amanda Vickery and John Styles (New Haven, CT: Yale University Press, 2006), 125–50.

14. Deposition of Timothy and Frances Whiting, *Banister and Pelham v. Parry*, Newport CCP, May 1741, #60, RIJRC; Deposition of Elizabeth Phillips, *Brayton v. Mackullin*, Newport SCJ, 1766, RIJRC.

15. In Newport, 24% of female witnesses (*N* = 130) present on financial documents submitted to the Court of Common Pleas signed alongside men with the same last name and thus appear to be wives signing with their husbands. In Suffolk County, 26% of female witnesses (*N* = 39) present on financial documents submitted to the Court of Common Pleas signed alongside men with the same last name and thus appear to be wives signing with their husbands. On sampled terms, see note 7.

16. *Sheffield v. Weast*, Newport SCJ, 1733, RIJRC.

17. Depositions of Elizabeth Kimball and Sarah and Dorcas Fowler, *Hayward v. Fowler*, Suffolk SCJ (Aug. 1730), Suffolk Files, 29,918, MSA; Depositions of Elizabeth and Eunice Brown, *Brown v. Bowdoin*, Suffolk SCJ (Feb. 1750/1751 and Mar. 1750/1751,) Suffolk Files, 67,695, 67,704, 67,755, MSA; Deposition of Ann Bowers, *Bowers v. Bagnall*, Newport SCJ, 1755, RIJRC. For daughters as witnesses, see also Deposition of Mehitable Downs, *Stoddard v. Stoneman*, Newport CCP, Nov. 1767, #185, RIJRC; Deposition of Ruth Besse, *Burge v. Leonard*, Suffolk SCJ (Apr. 1760), Suffolk Files, 80,630, MSA; Depositions of Elizabeth Bosworth and Hannah Fales, *Paine v. Bailey*, Newport SCJ, 1766, RIJRC; Deposition of Mary Tillinghast, *Tillinghast v. Shelton*, Newport SCJ, 1734, RIJRC.

18. Patricia Cleary, *Elizabeth Murray: A Woman's Pursuit of Independence in Eighteenth-Century America* (Amherst: University of Massachusetts Press, 2000); Daniel Vickers, *Farmers & Fishermen: Two Centuries of Work in Essex County, Massachusetts, 1630–1850* (Chapel Hill: University of North Carolina Press, 1994); Margaret R. Hunt, *The Middling Sort: Commerce, Gender, and the Family in England, 1680–1780* (Berkeley: University of California Press, 1996); Laurel Thatcher Ulrich, "Martha Ballard and Her Girls: Women's Work in Eighteenth-Century Maine," in *Work and Labor in Early America*, ed. Stephen Innes (Chapel Hill: University of North Carolina Press, 1988), 70–105.

19. Depositions of Elizabeth Kimball and Sarah and Dorcas Fowler, *Hayward v. Fowler*, Suffolk SCJ (Aug. 1730), Suffolk Files, 29,918, MSA; Deposition of Ann Bowers, *Bowers v. Bagnall*, Newport SCJ, 1755, RIJRC.

20. Deposition of Mary Potter, *Wing v. Coggeshall*, Newport SCJ, 1736, RIJRC; Deposition of Ruth Loring (Aug. 21, 1740), Suffolk Files, 52,393, MSA; Deposition of Elizabeth Goddard (Jan. 1739), Suffolk Files, 51,228, MSA. On elite Pennsylvania women who enlisted their servants as witnesses, see Elizabeth Jones-Minsinger, "Out of the Shadows: Uncovering Women's Productive and Consuming Labor in the Mid-Atlantic, 1750–1815" (PhD diss., University of Delaware, 2017), 34–35.

21. On sampled financial documents submitted to the Newport County Court of Common Pleas, 10% of female witnesses (*N* = 130) signed with a mark. On sampled financial documents submitted to the Suffolk County Court of Common Pleas, 20% of female witnesses (*N* = 39) signed with a mark. On sampling, see note 7.

22. This figure is based on all surviving depositions by female witnesses ($N = 67$) that I have located in the course of my research. This set of witness depositions includes those who testified in debt cases in the Court of Common Pleas or the Superior Court of Suffolk and Newport County, or in hearings concerning debt cases before the Massachusetts and Rhode Island legislatures. It includes not only depositions from my systematic sampling of court terms, but also others that I came across in my research.

23. In the early eighteenth century, roughly 45% of white women in New England could sign their names. See Ross W. Beales and E. Jennifer Monaghan, "Literacy and Schoolbooks," in *A History of the Book in America*, vol. 1, *The Colonial Book in the Atlantic World*, ed. Hugh Amory and David D. Hall (New York: Cambridge University Press, 2000), 380. See also Gloria Main, "An Inquiry into When and Why Women Learned to Write in Colonial New England," *Journal of Social History* 24, no. 3 (Spring 1991): 579–89.

24. Answer of Samuel Vaughan and Moses Tyler (1749), MA Archives, vol. 43, 36–39, MSA; Deposition of Royall Pierce (1751), *Banister v. Cook*, Newport CCP, May 1751, #141, RIJRC. On spaces where merchants conducted commercial activities, see Thomas Doerflinger, *A Vigorous Spirit of Enterprise: Merchants and Economic Development in Revolutionary Philadelphia* (Chapel Hill: University of North Carolina Press, 1986); David Hancock, *Citizens of the World: London and the Integration of the British Atlantic Community, 1735–1785* (Cambridge: Cambridge University Press, 1995); Toby L. Ditz, "Secret Selves, Credible Personas: The Problematics of Trust and Public Display in the Writing of Eighteenth-Century Philadelphia Merchants," in *Possible Pasts: Becoming Colonial in Early America*, ed. Robert Blair St. George (Ithaca, NY: Cornell University Press, 2000), 219–43; Cathy Matson, "Putting the *Lydia* to Sea: The Material Economy of Shipping in Colonial Philadelphia," *WMQ* 74, no. 2 (Apr. 2017): 301–32.

25. My sample of male witnesses' depositions ($N = 242$) includes depositions from all years included in my systematic sampling (see note 7), as well as other witness testimonies that I came across during my research in the records of the Newport and Suffolk county courts and the Massachusetts and Rhode Island legislatures from 1730 to 1776.

26. Deposition of David Daniels (1750), MA Archives, vol. 43, 261–62, MSA; Deposition of Jacob Richardson (1770), RI Petitions, vol. 14, 8, RISA.

27. For the drafting of documents, see, for instance, Deposition of George Lawton (1761), *Lawton v. Durfey*, Newport CCP, May 1761, #64, RIJRC. For referees' activities, see Depositions of Joseph Crandall and Jedediah Austen (1765), RI Petitions, vol. 11.2, 134, RISA. On arbitration, see Harold J. Berman, *Law and Revolution: The Formation of the Western Legal Tradition* (Cambridge, MA: Harvard University Press, 1983), 347; Bruce L. Benson, "Justice without Government: The Merchant Courts of Medieval Europe and Their Modern Counterparts," in *The Voluntary City: Choice, Community, and Civil Society*, ed. David T. Beito, Peter Gordon, and Alexander Tabarrok (Ann Arbor: University of Michigan Press, 2002); Sally E. Hadden, "The Business of Justice: Merchants in the Charleston Chamber of Commerce and Arbitration in the 1780s and 1790s," in *The Southern Middle Class in the Long Nineteenth Century*, ed. Jonathan Wells and Jennifer R. Green (Baton Rouge: Louisiana State University Press, 2011), 17–18, 30.

28. Depositions of Susannah Brownell, John Brownell, Aaron Willbur, and Thomas Bowland, *Palmer v. Brownell*, Newport CCP, May 1766, #346, RIJRC. For male signatories selected from a group of bystanders that also included women, see Depositions of Mary Asten and Alice Weast, *Sheffield v. Weast*, Newport SCJ, 1733, RIJRC.

29. Lindsay R. Moore, *Women Before the Court: Law and Patriarchy in the Anglo-American World, 1600–1800* (Manchester, UK: Manchester University Press, 2019), 63–64. I have not located debt cases in which men or women described as Native, free black, or mulatto gave depositions or signed financial instruments. Given that court records often described witnesses only by name and place of residence, it is certainly possible that Natives and free blacks occasionally assumed these legal roles. At the same time, the absence of clear references to such individuals suggests that, in spite of free blacks' and Natives' integration into urban economies, white colonists reinforced racial hierarchies by overwhelmingly enlisting other whites to assume formal legal responsibilities as witnesses.

30. On the role of enslaved people's testimonies in uncovering supposed slave rebellions, see Jill Lepore, *New York Burning: Liberty, Slavery, and Conspiracy in Eighteenth-Century Manhattan* (New York: Random House, 2005); Richard Bond, "Shaping a Conspiracy: Black Testimony in the 1741 New York Plot," *Early American Studies* 5, no. 1 (Spring 2007): 63–94; Jason Sharples, "Discovering Slave Conspiracies: New Fear of Rebellion and Old Paradigms of Plotting in Seventeenth-Century Barbados," *American Historical Review* 120, no. 3 (June 2015): 811–43. On slavery and the law in the South, see also Robert Olwell, *Masters, Slaves, and Subjects: The Culture of Power in the South Carolina Low Country, 1740–1790* (Ithaca, NY: Cornell University Press, 1998); Ariela J. Gross, *Double Character: Slavery and Mastery in the Antebellum Southern Courtroom* (Princeton, NJ: Princeton University Press, 2000); Sally E. Hadden, *Slave Patrols: Law and Violence in Virginia and the Carolinas* (Cambridge, MA: Harvard University Press, 2001); Laura F. Edwards, *The People and Their Peace: Law and the Transformation of Inequality in the Post-Revolutionary South* (Chapel Hill: University of North Carolina Press, 2009).

31. On enslaved people in Boston and Newport households, see especially Elaine Forman Crane, *A Dependent People: Newport, Rhode Island in the Revolutionary Era* (New York: Fordham University Press, 1985), 76–83; Ellen Hartigan-O'Connor, *The Ties that Buy: Women and Commerce in Revolutionary America* (Philadelphia: University of Pennsylvania Press, 2009), 19–23; Gloria McCahon Whiting, "Power, Patriarchy, and Provision: African Families Negotiate Gender and Slavery in New England," *Journal of American History* 103, no. 3 (Dec. 2016): 586–87. On Boston slaveholders' occupations, see Jared Ross Hardesty, *Unfreedom: Slavery and Dependence in Eighteenth-Century Boston* (New York: New York University Press, 2016), 50.

32. *Brett v. Grant*, Newport SCJ, Mar. 1756, RIJRC. For similar disputes revealing the presence of enslaved men laboring in the shops and residences of Newport widows, see *Mitchell v. Robinson*, Newport SCJ, Aug. 1748, RIJRC; *Carr v. Rumreil*, Newport SCJ, Mar. 1763, RIJRC. Mary Brett later created a school for black children, an action that suggests she may have sued for ownership of Moll and Cato because she aimed to improve their condition. See "Notice is hereby given," *Newport Mercury*, Aug. 3, 1772, [3]; "Whereas a school was established," *Newport Mercury*, May 3, 1773, [1]. On female slaveholders, see Stephanie Jones-Rogers, *They Were Her Property: White Women as Slaveholders in the American South* (New Haven, CT: Yale University Press, 2019); Christine Walker, *Jamaica Ladies: Female Slaveholders and the Creation of Britain's Atlantic Empire* (Chapel Hill: University of North Carolina Press, 2020).

33. On enslaved women as participants in urban economies, see Olwell, *Masters, Slaves & Subjects*, 141–80; Hartigan-O'Connor, *Ties that Buy*; Serena Zabin, *Dangerous Economies: Status and Commerce in Imperial New York* (Philadelphia: University of

Pennsylvania Press, 2009); Marisa J. Fuentes, *Dispossessed Lives: Enslaved Women, Violence, and the Archive* (Philadelphia: University of Pennsylvania Press, 2016); Justene Hill, "Felonious Transactions: Legal Culture and Business Practices of Slave Economies in South Carolina, 1787–1860," *Enterprise and Society* 18, no. 4 (Dec. 2017): 772–83; Shauna J. Sweeney, "Market Marronage: Fugitive Women and the Internal Marketing System in Jamaica, 1781–1834," *WMQ* 76, no. 2 (Apr. 2019): 197–222.

34. *Grant v. Potter*, Newport CCP, May 1746, #87, RIJRC. See also Fuentes, *Dispossessed Lives*; Sophie White, *Voices of the Enslaved: Love, Labor, and Longing in French Louisiana* (Chapel Hill: University of North Carolina Press, 2019).

35. Holly Brewer, *By Birth or Consent: Children, Law, and the Anglo-American Revolution in Authority* (Chapel Hill: University of North Carolina Press, 2005), 150–80.

36. *An Abridgement of Burn's Justice of the Peace and Parish Officer* (Boston: Joseph Greenleaf, 1773), 124–25; Matthew Hale, *Historia Placitorum Cornonæ: The History of the Pleas of the Crown*, vol. 2 (London: E. & R. Nutt, & R. Gosling, 1736), 276–80; Geoffrey Gilbert, *The Law of Evidence* (London: Henry Lintot, 1756), 121–47.

37. By barring wives from testifying against their husbands, common law affirmed men's patriarchal authority and severely limited wives' ability to charge husbands who committed physical or sexual violence against them. Wives could only testify against their husbands in cases involving their spouses' grievous mistreatment of them, such as when men had coerced women into marrying them, or when husbands were accomplices to other men who had raped their wives. See *Abridgement of Burn's Justice*, 125. See also William Nelson, *The Office and Authority of a Justice of Peace* (London: E. & R. Nutt, & R. Gosling, 1729), 268; George Webb, *The Office and Authority of a Justice of the Peace* (Williamsburg, VA: William Parks, 1736), 135; Hale, *Historia Placitorum Cornonæ*, 279; *Conductor Generalis: or, The office, duty, and authority of justices of the peace* (Philadelphia: B. Franklin & D. Hall, 1750), 67. In seventeenth-century Connecticut, in what appears to have been a distinctive regional practice, wives could testify for their husbands in civil suits. By the eighteenth century, however, this was no longer the case. See Dayton, *Women Before the Bar*, 80.

38. Matthew Hale enumerated a constellation of attributes that contributed to witnesses' credibility, including their "Quality, Carriage, Age, Condition, Education, and Place of Commorance," but he did not specifically reference gender. See Matthew Hale, *History of the Common Law of England* (London: E. & R. Nutt, & R. Gosling, 1739), 253–57 (quotations ["weigh," "credibility"], 257); Gilbert, *Law of Evidence*, 147–61 (quotation ["reasons and Accounts"], 158); Matthew Hale, *The Primitive Origination of Mankind, Considered and Examined According to the Light of Nature* (London: William Godbid, 1677), 129. On the relationship between the Enlightenment and standards for legal evidence, see Barbara J. Shapiro, *Probability and Certainty in Seventeenth-Century England: A Study of the Relationships between Natural Science, Religion, History, Law, and Literature* (Princeton, NJ: Princeton University Press, 1983); Barbara J. Shapiro, *A Culture of Fact: England, 1550–1720* (Ithaca, NY: Cornell University Press, 2000); Andrea Frisch, *The Invention of the Eyewitness: Witnessing and Testimony in Early Modern France* (Chapel Hill: University of North Carolina Press, 2004); Brewer, *By Birth or Consent*, 161–80. On the anglicization of New England courts, see especially John M. Murrin, "The Legal Transformation: The Bench and the Bar of Eighteenth-Century Massachusetts," in *Colonial America: Essays in Politics and Social Development*, 3rd ed., ed. Stanley N. Katz

and John M. Murrin (New York: Alfred A. Knopf, 1983), 540–71; Mann, *Neighbors and Strangers*; Dayton, *Women Before the Bar.*

39. John Hill, *The Young Secretary's Guide, or, a Speedy Help to Learning* (Boston: Thomas Fleet, 1750), 93; George Fisher, *The American Instructor, or Young Man's Best Companion*, 9th ed. (Philadelphia: B. Franklin & D. Hall, 1748), 166; William Bradford, comp., *The Secretary's Guide, or Young Man's Companion* (Philadelphia: Andrew Bradford, 1737), 167.

40. For forms with witnesses' initials, see *The Attorney's Compleat Pocket-Book* (London: Henry Lintot, 1756); Fisher, *American Instructor.* For forms without witnesses' names, see *Attorney's Compleat Pocket-Book*; Fisher, *American Instructor*; Hill, *Young Secretary's Guide*; Bradford, *Secretary's Guide.*

41. On manuals' roles in standardizing commercial and legal activity, see Konstantin Dierks, *In My Power: Letter Writing and Communications in Early America* (Philadelphia: University of Pennsylvania Press, 2009), 52–99; Eve Tavor Bannet, *Empire of Letters: Letter Manuals and Transatlantic Correspondence, 1688–1810* (Cambridge: Cambridge University Press, 2005).

42. Unlike the affidavit in *The Attorney's Compleat Pocket-Book*, New Englanders' petitions did not identify the genders or occupations of absent witnesses and instead referred generally to "material witnesses." For instance, see Petition of John Hulet (1751), RI Petitions, vol. 8, 13, RISA. For additional examples, see Petition of Francis Bowman (1747), MA Archives, vol. 42, 505–7, MSA; Petition of Joseph Arnold (1747), RI Petitions, vol. 5, 128, RISA; Petition of James Allen (1748), MA Archives, vol. 42, 634–38, MSA.

43. *Attorney's Compleat Pocket-Book*, 16.

44. Deposition of Patricia Cornell, *Lawton v. Langworthy*, Newport CCP, May 1736, #103, RIJRC; Deposition of Freelove Tweedy, *Bowers v. Bagnall*, Newport SCJ, 1755, RIJRC.

45. On handbooks and financial education, see Daniel Defoe, *The complete English Tradesman, in familiar letters; directing him in the several parts and progressions of the trade*, vol. 1 (London: Charles Rivington, 1725); *The Secretary's Guide, or Young Man's Companion* (quotation, 169); Bannet, *Empire of Letters*, 140–49; A Lady, "A New Method" ("all the arts"), *Boston Gazette*, Mar. 24, 1740, [1]. On differences between women's and men's education, see Laurel Thatcher Ulrich, *Good Wives: Image and Reality in the Lives of Women in Northern New England, 1650–1750* (New York: Alfred A. Knopf, 1980), 43–44; Mary Beth Norton, *Liberty's Daughters: The Revolutionary Experience of American Women, 1750–1800* (Boston: Little, Brown, 1980), 256–63; Linda Kerber, *Women of the Republic: Intellect and Ideology in Revolutionary America* (Chapel Hill: University of North Carolina Press, 1980), 191–193; Patricia Cline Cohen, *A Calculating People: The Spread of Numeracy in Early America* (Chicago: University of Chicago Press, 1982); Patricia Cleary, "'Who shall say we have not equal abilitys with the Men when Girls of 18 years of age discover such great capacitys?' Women of Commerce in Boston, 1750–1776," in *Entrepreneurs: The Boston Business Community, 1700–1850*, ed. Conrad Edick Wright and Katheryn P. Viens, (Boston: Northeastern University Press, 1997), 39–62; Cleary, *Elizabeth Murray*, 96, 125; Mary Kelly, *Learning to Stand and Speak: Women, Education, and Public Life in America's Republic* (Chapel Hill: University of North Carolina Press, 2006), 34–47.

46. Deposition of Ruth Besse, *Burge v. Leonard* (Apr. 1760), Suffolk Files, 80,630, MSA.

47. Depositions of Elizabeth Kimball and Sarah and Dorcas Fowler (Aug. 7, 1730), *Hayward v. Fowler*, Suffolk Files, 29,918, MSA.

48. Deposition of Livine Love (Feb. 22, 1762), RI Petitions, vol. 11.2, 19, RISA. An alternate reading of the episode would suggest that Tree was the rightful creditor but initially lacked written records.

49. Depositions of Samuel, Miriam, and Nicholas Watson (Oct. 16, 1750), RI Petitions, vol. 7, 98, RISA; Petition of Edward Slocum (1750), RI Petitions, vol. 7, 98, RISA.

50. Colonists often referred to both bills obligatory and promissory notes as "notes," and the two kinds of instruments indeed functioned similarly at law, even though only bills obligatory required witnesses. Mann, *Neighbors and Strangers*, 29.

51. Among witnesses' vital legal functions was ensuring that documents were legitimate and unaltered. When financial instruments contained obvious insertions or cancelled text, parties noted that witnesses had signed *after* such changes were made. See, for instance, *Almy v. Gardner and Hammond*, Newport CCP, May 1776, #218, RIJRC.

52. Depositions of William Thomas, David Sears, Abigail Thayer, and Hezekiah Bilding (1753), MA Archives, vol. 43, 776–83, MSA.

53. Deposition of Elizabeth Phillips, *Brayton v. McQuellen*, Newport SCJ, 1766, RIJRC.

54. For instance, see Deposition of Mary Asten, *Sheffield v. Weast*, Newport SCJ, 1733, RIJRC.

55. Deposition of Abigail Thayer (1753), MA Archives, vol. 43, 781–82, MSA.

56. Deposition of Elizabeth Phillips and Deposition of Michael Phillips, *Brayton v. McQuellen*, Newport SCJ, 1766, RIJRC.

57. *Hooper v. Johnston*, Newport CCP, May 1761, unnumbered, RIJRC; *Grant v. Michener*, Newport CCP, May 1761, #53, RIJRC.

58. See, for instance, Zara Anishanslin, *Portrait of a Woman in Silk: Hidden Histories of the British Atlantic World* (New Haven, CT: Yale University Press, 2016), 176–77, 185–87. On colonists' active building of family connections, see also Karin Wulf, "Bible, King, and Common Law: Genealogical Literacies and Family History Practices in British America," *Early American Studies* 10, no. 3 (Fall 2012): 467–502.

59. *Smith v. Coggeshall*, Newport CCP, May 1751, #24, RIJRC; *Tillinghast v. Buliod*, Newport CCP, May 1751, #38, RIJRC; *Holmes v. Easton*, Newport CCP, May 1751, #227, RIJRC; *Rogers v. Baley*, Newport CCP, May 1751, #238, RIJRC; *Clark v. Carr*, Newport CCP, May 1751, #322, RIJRC. Mary Lyndon's signing of bonds is part of a larger story of literacy and numeracy possessed by Josias Lyndon's dependents. Cesar Lyndon, an enslaved man within the Lyndon household, was also literate and kept a journal in which he recorded financial transactions and assorted memoranda. See Tara Bynum, "Cesar Lyndon's Lists, Letters, and a Pig Roast: *A Sundry Account Book*," *Early American Literature* 53, no. 3 (Fall 2018): 839–49.

60. For a lease bearing the signatures of Joseph and Susannah Fox, see *Stoneman v. Stoddard*, Newport CCP, Nov. 1767, #85, RIJRC. For bonds bearing the signatures of Joseph and Abigail Fox, see, for instance, *Brown and Gidley v. Hill*, Newport CCP, May 1746, #99, RIJRC; *Almy v. Gardner*, Newport CCP, May 1766, #218, RIJRC; *Nichols v. Haszard*, Newport CCP, May 1766, #225, RIJRC. For Joseph Fox's work as a scrivener, see *Fox v. Phillips*, Newport CCP, May 1756, #143, RIJRC; *Robinson v. Trip and Spencer*,

Newport CCP, Nov. 1761, #239, RIJRC; *Polock v. Elizer*, Newport SCJ, March 1766, RIJRC.

61. Julie Hardwick, *The Practice of Patriarchy: Gender and the Politics of Household Authority in Early Modern France* (Philadelphia: University of Pennsylvania Press, 1998) (quotation, 18). See also Donna Merwick, *Death of a Notary: Conquest and Change in Colonial New York* (Ithaca, NY: Cornell University Press, 2002).

62. For a similar argument that testifying in early modern France was a "public and neighborhood matter," see Hardwick, *Family Business*, 72.

63. Witness summonses are present in many case files. These were legal forms that used the same language to regardless of the gender of the witnesses summoned. For representative summonses of female and male witnesses, respectively, see *Dyre v. Bill*, Newport CCP, May 1741, #187, RIJRC; *Spencer v. Nixon*, Newport CCP, May 1741, #247, RIJRC.

64. "An Act for Taking Depositions Out of Court" (1718), *Acts and Laws of His Majesties Colony of Rhode-Island, and Providence-Plantations in America* (Boston: John Allen, 1719), 98–99; "An Act for Taking Affadavits out of Court" (1695), *Acts and Laws of His Majesty's Province of the Massachusetts-Bay in New-England* (Boston: Samuel Kneeland, 1759), 64. This move to accept depositions given outside of court was a departure from common law preference for oral testimonies, which supposedly permitted a fuller evaluation of witnesses' statements than did written depositions. See Hale, *History of the Common Law*, 254–55; Gilbert, *Law of Evidence*, 60.

65. Nelson, *Office and Authority*, 500.

66. Witness depositions noted the name of the justice of the peace who had recorded the testimony and the time and place where he had done so. For an example of several witnesses testifying at the home of a justice of the peace with the opposing party present, see *Burt v. Potter*, Newport CCP, May 1731, #21, RIJRC. For outlines of this process, see, for instance, *Abridgement of Burn's Justice*, 127–29; *Conductor Generalis*, 162–73; William Simpson, *The Practical Justice of the Peace and Parish-Officer of His Majesty's Province of South Carolina* (Charleston, SC: Robert Wells, 1761), 100–101; Webb, *Office and Authority*, 137.

67. Sarah and Ann Bars to James Otis, Apr. 16, 1762, Otis Family Papers, MHS.

68. "An Act Establishing and Regulating Fees" (1767), *Acts and Laws of the English Colony of Rhode-Island, and Providence-Plantations in New-England, in America* (Newport, RI: Samuel Hall, 1767), 98; "An Act for Regulating Trials of Civil Causes" (1701), *Acts and Laws of His Majesty's Province of the Massachusetts-Bay in New-England* (Boston: Samuel Kneeland, 1759), 133. Both Rhode Island and Massachusetts adjusted witnesses' fees repeatedly during the eighteenth century.

69. Sharon V. Salinger, *"To serve well and faithfully": Labor and Indentured Servants in Pennsylvania, 1682–1800* (Cambridge: Cambridge University Press, 1987), 151; Billy G. Smith, *The "Lower Sort": Philadelphia's Laboring People, 1750–1800* (Ithaca, NY: Cornell University Press, 1990), 92–93, 108–24, 233. Witnesses were consistently compensated less per diem than leading appointees, such as an attorney general. For instance, see "An Act Establishing and Regulating Fees" (1767), 96–98; "An Act for the Establishing and Regulating of Fees" (1666), *Acts and Laws of His Majesties Colony of Rhode-Island, and Providence-Plantations in America* (Boston: John Allen, 1719), 21.

70. *Abridgement of Burn's Justice*, 127. Manuals condemning the lack of compensation for witnesses were specifically referring to procedures for criminal cases. Another line of

argument maintained that legal fees deterred colonists from initiating lawsuits unnecessarily. Fees for witnesses were part of this system, and fees for each additional witness discouraged parties from summoning unnecessary ones. See "An Act for Discouraging Vexatious and Unjust Suits in Law" (1718), *Acts and Laws of His Majesty's Colony of Rhode-Island and Providence-Plantations, in New England, in America* (Newport: Ann Franklin, 1745), 75–76.

71. On women's and men's wages, see Crane, *Ebb Tide*, 106–8; Smith, *The "Lower Sort,"* 112; Karin Wulf, *Not All Wives: Women of Colonial Philadelphia* (Ithaca, NY: Cornell University Press, 2000), 141. On fees for witnesses, see also Hardwick, *Practice of Patriarchy*, 102–3.

72. Deposition of Eunice Hill, *Ingraham v. Cook*, Suffolk SCJ (Feb.1762), Suffolk Files, 82,635, MSA; Deposition of Patience Macomber, *Peckham v. Crandall*, Newport CCP, May 1791, #66, RIJRC.

73. The boardinghouse was located on Milk Street, one block away from Boston's main thoroughfare. See *Brown v. Bowdoin*, Suffolk SCJ (Feb. 1750/1751, and Mar. 1750/1751), Suffolk Files, 67,695, 67,704, 67,755, MSA.

74. My strategies for reading witness depositions build on other historians' methods for analyzing legal sources, particularly Natalie Zemon Davis's interpretations of pardon petitions in early modern France. See Natalie Zemon Davis, *Fiction in the Archives: Pardon Tales and Their Tellers in Sixteenth-Century France* (Stanford, CA: Stanford University Press, 1987). For a first-person deposition, see *Grant v. Bennet*, Newport CCP, May 1741, #134, RIJRC. For third-person depositions, see *Huxham v. Gould*, Newport CCP, May 1741, #104, RIJRC. For depositions switching between the first and third persons, see *Burt v. Potter*, Newport CCP, May 1731, #21, RIJRC.

75. My analysis is based on 311 witness depositions (69 by women, 242 by men). My sample of witness depositions includes depositions from all years included in my systematic sampling (see note 7), as well as other witness testimonies that I came across during my research in the records of the Newport and Suffolk county courts and the Massachusetts and Rhode Island legislatures between 1730 and 1776.

76. Gilbert, *Law of Evidence*, 158.

77. Gilbert, *Law of Evidence*, 150–51.

78. Gilbert, *Law of Evidence*, 152–53. See also Elaine Forman Crane, *Killed Strangely: The Death of Rebecca Cornell* (Ithaca, NY: Cornell University Press, 2002), 50.

79. Shapin, *Social History of Truth*; Mary Poovey, *A History of the Modern Fact: Problems of Knowledge in the Sciences of Wealth and Society* (Chicago: University of Chicago Press, 1998); Parrish, *American Curiosity*; Shapin and Shaffer, *Leviathan and the Air Pump*; James Delbourgo, *A Most Amazing Scene of Wonders* (Cambridge, MA: Harvard University Press, 2006).

80. Deposition of Ann Aston, *Card v. Freeborn*, May 1741, unnumbered case file, RIJRC; Deposition of Seth Adams (Jul. 26, 1747), Suffolk Files, 63,764; Deposition of Samuel Carr, *Burt v. Potter*, Newport CCP, May 1731, #21, RIJRC.

81. Deposition of Jonathan Foster, Ruth Freeman, and Alexander Clayton (1747/1748), MA Archives, vol. 42, 623–24, MSA; Deposition of Joseph and Benjamin Sheffield, *Havens v. Sheffield*, Newport CCP, May 1761, #231, RIJRC.

82. Deposition of Abigail Thayer (1753), MA Archives, vol. 43, 781–82, MSA; Deposition of Solomon Hicks, *Wilcox v. Wanton*, Newport CCP, May 1761, #15, RIJRC;

Deposition of George Gardner, *Havens v. Sheffield*, Newport CCP, May 1761, #231, RIJRC.

83. Deposition of Thaddeus Wilmouth (1756), RI Petitions, vol. 9.2, 108, RISA; Deposition of Asa Miner (1766), RI Petitions, vol. 12, 60, RISA; Deposition of David Daniels (1750), MA Archives, vol. 43, 261–62, MSA; Deposition of Sarah and Dorcas Fowler (1730), Suffolk Files, 29,855, MSA; Deposition of Eunice Hill (1762), Suffolk Files, 82,635, MSA.

84. Depositions of William Thomas, David Sears, and Abigail Thayer (1753), MA Archives, vol. 43, 776, 779–82, MSA.

85. Depositions of Mehitable Downs, Thomas Brenton, and Elisha Norton (1767), *Stoddard v. Stoneman*, Newport CCP, Nov. 1767, #185, RIJRC.

86. Deposition of Benjamin Whipple (n.d. [1767?]), RI Petitions, vol. 13.2, 181, RISA; Deposition of Peleg Spencer, *Grant v. Bennet*, Newport CCP, May 1741, #134, RIJRC.

87. Deposition of Margaret Curtelo, *Burt v. Potter*, Newport CCP, May 1731, #21, RIJRC; Deposition of Sarah Cook (1762), Suffolk Files, 82,635, MSA.

88. For instance, see Deposition of Enoch and Lucy Kinyon (1766), *Jeffers v. Issacks*, Newport SCJ, Sept. 1769, RIJRC. I have located eleven cases in which both a wife and her husband testify. In seven such instances, the wife simply swore to the accuracy of her husband's testimony. While this sample is not large enough to be statistically significant, it indicates that recording only husbands' testimonies in full was a widespread but not universal practice.

89. Deposition of Thankfull Thompson, *Champlin v. Babcock*, Newport SCJ, 1755, RIJRC.

90. Witnesses occasionally noted small points of divergence when otherwise swearing to the truth of other witnesses' testimonies, indicating that they listened carefully throughout the proceedings. For instance, see Deposition of Mary Smith, *Fuller v. Hows*, Newport SCJ, 1730, RIJRC; Deposition of Alice Weast, *Sheffield v. Weast*, Newport SCJ, 1733, RIJRC.

Chapter 5 · The Problem of Debt and Vocabularies of Grievance

1. Margaret Ellen Newell, *From Dependency to Independence: Economic Revolution in Colonial New England* (Ithaca, NY: Cornell University Press, 1998); Gary B. Nash, *The Urban Crucible: Social Change, Political Consciousness, and the Origins of the American Revolution* (Cambridge, MA: Harvard University Press, 1979); Bruce H. Mann, *Republic of Debtors: Bankruptcy in the Age of American Independence* (Cambridge, MA: Harvard University Press, 2002).

2. For Rhode Island petitions, see RI Petitions, vols. 2–16 and 25.2, RISA. For Massachusetts petitions, see MA Archives, vols. 17–19B, 41–44, 105, 303, MSA.

3. On understandings of widowhood, see Vivian Bruce Conger, *The Widow's Might: Widowhood and Gender in Early British America* (New York: New York University Press, 2009), 23–42, 116–18; Sandra Cavallo and Lyndan Warner, eds., *Widowhood in Medieval and Early Modern Europe* (New York: Routledge, 2014).

4. On petitioning in the British Atlantic World, see Raymond C. Bailey, *Popular Influence on Public Policy: Petitioning in Eighteenth-Century Virginia* (Westport, CT: Greenwood Press, 1979); Alison G. Olson, "Eighteenth-Century Colonial Legislatures and Their Constituents," *Journal of American History* 79, no. 2 (Sept. 1992): 543–67; David

Zaret, *Origins of Democratic Culture: Printing, Petitions, and the Public Sphere in Early-Modern England* (Princeton, NJ: Princeton University Press, 2000). For recent examples of the flourishing scholarship on petitions by blacks and indigenous peoples, see José Carlos de la Puente Luna, *Andean Cosmopolitans: Seeking Justice and Reward at the Spanish Royal Court* (Austin: University of Texas Press, 2018); Brian P. Owensby and Richard J. Ross, eds., *Justice in a New World: Negotiating Legal Intelligibility in British, Iberian, and Indigenous America* (New York: New York University Press, 2018); Bradley J. Dixon, "'His one Netev ples': The Chowans and the Politics of Native Petitions in the Colonial South," *WMQ* 76, no. 1 (Jan. 2019): 41–74; Norah L. A. Gharala, *Taxing Blackness: Free Afromexican Tribute in Bourbon New Spain* (Tuscaloosa: University of Alabama Press, 2019). On women's petitions, see Mary Beth Norton "Eighteenth-Century American Women in Peace and War: The Case of the Loyalists," *WMQ* 33, no. 3 (July 1976): 386–409; Linda K. Kerber, *Women of the Republic: Intellect and Ideology in Revolutionary America* (Chapel Hill: University of North Carolina Press, 1980), 85–99; Cynthia A. Kierner, *Southern Women in Revolution, 1776–1800: Personal and Political Narratives* (Columbia: University of South Carolina Press, 1998); Susan Zaeske, *Signatures of Citizenship: Petitioning, Antislavery, and Women's Political Identity* (Chapel Hill: University of North Carolina Press, 2003).

5. Ann Maylem, "All persons that have any Demands," *Boston Post-Boy*, May 24, 1742, [4]; Ann Maylem, "All persons that have any Demands," *Boston Post-Boy*, May 31, 1742, [4].

6. Ann Maylem, née Low, was the eldest of the three children of Samuel Low, a wealthy Barrington landholder. No record of her birth survives, but the Lows' second child was born on March 19, 1701. See Maylem Family Bible, NHS; Samuel Low File Papers, Bristol County Probate Records, vol. 6, 171–72, MSA; *Sibley's Harvard Graduates: Biographical Sketches of Those Who Attended Harvard College*, vol. 6, *1713–1721* (Boston: Massachusetts Historical Society, 1942), 96–98; Suffolk County Probate Records, vol. 31, 279–81, MSA.

7. Lawrence C. Wroth, "John Maylem: Poet and Warrior," *Publications of the Colonial Society of Massachusetts* 32 (Boston: The Society, 1937), 92n3; Maylem Family Bible, NHS.

8. For letters drafted by Maylem and bearing her signature, see Ann Maylem to James Otis, Aug. 8, 1746, Sept. 6, 1746, Sept. 8, 1746, and Sept. 9, 1746, Otis Family Papers, MHS. For letters drafted by others but bearing Maylem's signature, see Ann Maylem to James Otis, Oct. 23, 1745, and July 31, 1746, Otis Family Papers, MHS. For the same signature on financial documents and Maylem's August 1744 petition, see Suffolk Files, 169,641, MSA.

9. Lease, John Maylem to Thomas Paine, Oct. 17, 1739, Robert Treat Paine Papers, MHS; Ann Maylem, *A Short Narrative of the Unjust Proceedings [. . .]* (Newport: Ann Franklin, 1742); *Read v. Maylem*, Newport CCP, May 1743, #280, RIJRC. On rum distilling, see Elaine Forman Crane, *A Dependent People: Newport, Rhode Island in the Revolutionary Era* (New York: Fordham University Press, 1985), 9–15, 39; Jordan B. Smith, "The Invention of Rum" (PhD diss., Georgetown University, 2018).

10. For John Maylem's death, see "New-Port, March 19," *Boston Post-Boy*, Mar. 22, 1742, [3]. For Ann Maylem's announcements of her appointment as administrator, see Ann Maylem, "All persons that have any Demands," *Boston Post-Boy*, May 24, 1742, [4]; Ann Maylem, "All persons that have any Demands," *Boston Post-Boy*, May 31, 1742, [4]; Ann Maylem, "All persons that have any Demands," *Boston Post-Boy*, June 21, 1742, [4]. For the births of the Maylems' children, see Maylem Family Bible, NHS.

11. John Maylem's estate appeared to be solvent, according to the account that Ann Maylem submitted in 1743, which listed debts totaling £521. Later suits by John's creditors, however, indicated that several of them had received only partial payments from Ann. See Inventory and Account of Administration, included in *Read v. Maylem*, Newport CCP, May 1743, #280, RIJRC; *Draper v. Maylem*, Newport CCP, May 1743, #402, RIJRC; *Ellery v. Maylem*, Record Book, Newport CCP, vol. B, 416, RIJRC; *Ingraham v. Maylem*, Newport CCP, May 1744, #220, RIJRC.

12. Marylynn Salmon, *Women and the Law of Property in Early America* (Chapel Hill: University of North Carolina Press, 1986), 140.

13. Rhode Island's 1718 statute only remained in effect until 1728, but its repeal did not significantly change the colony's legal practices surrounding estate administration. See Elaine Forman Crane, *Ebb Tide in New England: Women, Seaports, and Social Change, 1630–1800* (Boston: Northeastern University Press, 1998), 157–64. On trends throughout British North America, see Salmon, *Women and the Law of Property*, 141–68.

14. Mann, *Republic of Debtors*, 36–53.

15. Mann, *Republic of Debtors*, 53–60; Peter J. Coleman, "The Insolvent Debtor in Rhode Island, 1745–1828," *WMQ* 22, no. 3 (July 1965): 413–34; "An Act of the Equal Distribution of Insolvent Estates" (June 1758), *Acts and Laws of the English Colony of Rhode-Island, and Providence-Plantations in New-England, in America* (Newport: Samuel Hall, 1767), 154–57.

16. Ann Maylem stated that she alone had employed Gardner to distill the molasses. Other witnesses claimed that Maylem and her late husband's partner, Jonathan Diman, had jointly hired Gardner. See Maylem, *Short Narrative*; Depositions of Jacob Dehane (Sept. 20, 1744) and Nathaniel Coggeshall (Mar. 12, 1745), Suffolk Files, 169,641, MSA.

17. Smith, "Invention of Rum," 184–207.

18. Ann Maylem later explained in print that John Maylem had first obtained a bond of defeasance from George Gardner in 1739 and that, because Gardner was indebted to George Goulding, the bond was assigned to Goulding in 1740. Other documents suggested that the bond of defeasance was the product of a new agreement between John Maylem, Jonathan Diman, and Goulding in 1740. See Maylem, *Short Narrative*; *Maylem v. Diman*, Newport CCP, Nov. 1744, #198, RIJRC; Petition of Ann Maylem (Sept. 1744), RI Petitions, vol. 6, 13, RISA; Petition of Ann Maylem (Aug. 1748), RI Petitions, vol. 6, 149, RISA.

19. Ann Maylem stated that Jonathan Diman obtained the bond of defeasance from her on March 16, 1742, whereas Nathaniel Coggeshall and Jacob Dehane noted that they had helped settle accounts between Maylem and Diman "a short time" after John Maylem's death. See *Maylem v. Diman*, Newport CCP, Nov. 1744, #198, RIJRC; Depositions of Jacob Dehane (Sept. 20, 1744) and Nathaniel Coggeshall (Mar. 12, 1745), Suffolk Files, 169,641, MSA.

20. Maylem, *Short Narrative*; Depositions of Ezekiel Burroughs and George Gardner (n.d.), Suffolk Files, 169,641, MSA.

21. Maylem, *Short Narrative*; *Maylem v. Diman*, Newport CCP, Nov. 1744, #198, RIJRC; Depositions of Nathaniel Coggeshall and Joseph Tillinghast (Sept. 20, 1744), Suffolk Files, 169,336, MSA; Depositions of Ezekiel Burroughs and George Gardner (n.d.), Suffolk Files, 169,641, MSA.

22. Maylem, *Short Narrative*; Deposition of Ezekiel Burroughs and Deposition of George Gardner (n.d.), Suffolk Files, 169,641, MSA.

23. Maylem, *Short Narrative*; *Maylem v. Diman*, Newport CCP, Nov. 1744, #198, RIJRC; *Maylem v. Gardner*, listed in Docket Book, Newport CCP, Nov. 1743, RIJRC; *Maylem v. Gardner*, Newport CCP, May 1744, #207, RIJRC; *Maylem v. Gardner*, Newport CCP, Nov. 1745, #1, RIJRC; Petition of Ann Maylem (Sept. 1744), RI Petitions, vol. 6, 13, RISA; Petition of Ann Maylem (Aug. 1748), RI Petitions, vol. 6, 149, RISA; Petitions of Ann Maylem (Aug. 20, 1744, and Feb. 1745), Suffolk Files, 169,641, MSA; Town Council Minutes, Feb. 6, 1743, Newport TC, vol. 9, 14, NHS.

24. Account of Administration, included in *Read v. Maylem*, Newport CCP, May 1743, #280, RIJRC. On widows' right to retain necessities, see Crane, *Ebb Tide*, 159.

25. Promise of Benjamin Ellery (Oct. 18, 174?), *Maylem v. Ellery*, Sept, 1743, Cases in Equity, vol. 6, Part II, 49–51, RISA.

26. For the initial lawsuits, see *Read v. Maylem*, Newport CCP, May 1743, #280, RIJRC; *Draper v. Maylem*, Newport CCP, May 1743, #402, RIJRC; *Ellery v. Maylem*, Record Book, Newport CCP, vol. B, 416, RIJRC; *Ingraham v. Maylem*, Newport CCP, May 1744, #220, RIJRC. For Maylem's appeals, see *Maylem v. Read*, Sept. 1743, Cases in Equity, vol. 6, Part II, 44–46, RISA; *Maylem v. Draper*, Sept. 1743, Cases in Equity, vol. 6, Part II, 47–48, RISA; *Maylem v. Ellery*, Sept. 1743, Cases in Equity, vol. 6, Part II, 49–51, RISA.

27. By 1745, Ann Maylem simultaneously pursued other sources of revenue, including seeking payments from Massachusetts debtors and claiming additional land from her late father's estate. This latter strategy was advantageous, because Ann Maylem would have been the sole owner of any property she acquired from her late father's estate; John Maylem's creditors could not claim property owned by Ann alone. See Ann Maylem to James Otis, Oct. 23, 1745, Otis Family Papers, MHS; Petition of Ann Maylem to Nathaniel Hubbard (n.d.), Samuel Low File Papers, Bristol County Probate Court File Papers, vol. 6, 171–72, MSA.

28. On Ann Franklin, see Margaret Lane Ford, "A Widow's Work: Ann Franklin of Newport, RI," *Printing History* 12 (1990): 15–26. On female printers and broadsides as job printing, see also Joseph M. Adelman, *Revolutionary Networks: The Business and Politics of Printing the News, 1763–1789* (Baltimore: Johns Hopkins University Press, 2019), 25–26, 32–33.

29. Town Council Minutes, Feb. 6, 1743, Newport TC, vol. 9, 14, NHS; Ann Maylem to James Otis, July 31, 1746 and Samuel Low to James Otis, Aug. 8, 1746, Otis Family Papers, MHS.

30. On female-authored publications, see Catherine A. Brekus, *Sarah Osborn's World: The Rise of Evangelical Christianity in Early America* (New Haven, CT: Yale University Press, 2013), 171–73, 175–80, 184. For Sarah Osborn's publication, see [Sarah Osborn], *The Nature, Certainty, and Evidence of True Christianity* (Boston: Samuel Kneeland, 1755). See also Karen A. Weyler, *Empowering Words: Outsiders and Authorship in Early America* (Athens: University of Georgia Press, 2013).

31. Maylem, *Short Narrative*. For examples of men's use of print in disputes, see William Fletcher, *The State of Action Brought by William Fletcher against William Vassall, for Defaming Him: Tried In the Superior Court At Boston, August Term, A.D. 1752 and now Pending by Appeal to His Majesty in Council* (Boston, 1753); "Boston, July 10," *Boston Gazette*, July 14, 1755, [1]; John Hunt, "Watertown, July 22d 1755," *Boston Gazette*, July 18, 1755, [1]; Thomas Forsey, "To the Public," *Newport Mercury*, Aug. 29, 1763, [3]; Thomas Forsey, "To the Public," *Newport Mercury*, Sept. 19, 1763, [1]; Waddell Cunningham, "From the New-York Gazette of September 1," *Newport Mercury*, Sept. 19, 1763, [1]. On

male merchants' use of print in disputes, see also Toby L. Ditz, "Formative Ventures: Eighteenth-Century Commercial Letters and the Articulation of Experience," in *Epistolary Selves: Letters and Letter-Writers, 1600–1945*, ed. Rebecca Earle (Aldershot, UK: Ashgate, 1999), 70–73.

32. Maylem, *Short Narrative*; Patricia Cline Cohen, *A Calculating People: The Spread of Numeracy in Early America* (Chicago: University of Chicago Press, 1982); Mary Poovey, *A History of the Modern Fact: Problems of Knowledge in the Sciences of Wealth and Society* (Chicago: University of Chicago Press, 1998); Miles Ogborn, *India Ink: Script and Print in the Making of the English East India Company* (Chicago: University of Chicago Press, 2007).

33. Maylem, *Short Narrative*.

34. On detinue, see William Blackstone, *Commentaries on the Laws of England*, vol. 3 (Oxford, UK: Clarendon Press, 1768), 146, 151.

35. *Maylem v. Diman*, Newport CCP, Nov. 1744, #198, RIJRC.

36. *Maylem v. Gardner*, listed in Docket Book, Newport CCP, Nov. 1743, RIJRC; *Maylem v. Gardner*, Newport CCP, May 1744, #207, RIJRC; *Maylem v. Gardner*, Newport CCP, Nov. 1745, #1, RIJRC. On actions of account, see Giles Jacob, *The Common Law Common-Plac'd* (London: E. & R. Nutt, & R. Gosling, 1733), 4–5.

37. Legislative records contain the original signed copies of some petitions and clerks' copies of others. Clerks' copies include all of a petition's text, including the petitioner's signature, in a single hand. For Maylem's signature on petitions, see Petition of Ann Maylem (Aug. 20, 1744), Suffolk Files, 169,641, MSA; Petition of Ann Maylem (Sept. 1744), RI Petitions, vol. 6, 13, RISA. For copied petitions lacking Maylem's signature, see Petition of Ann Maylem (Feb. 1745), Suffolk Files, 169,641, MSA; Petition of Ann Maylem (Aug. 1748), RI Petitions, vol. 6, 149, RISA.

38. Petition of Ann Maylem ("distressed, "ruin") (Aug. 20, 1744), Suffolk Files, 169,641, MSA; Petition of Ann Maylem ("distressed," "ruin'd") (Sept. 1744), RI Petitions, vol. 6, 13, RISA; Petition of Ann Maylem ("accomplice," "wicked," "fraud & craft") (Feb. 1745), Suffolk Files, 169,641, MSA; Petition of Ann Maylem ("distressed," "wickedly") (Aug. 1748), RI Petitions, vol. 6, 149, RISA.

39. Petition of Ann Maylem (Sept. 1744), RI Petitions, vol. 6, 13, RISA.

40. Petition of Ann Maylem (Aug. 1748), RI Petitions, vol. 6, 149, RISA.

41. Ann Maylem to James Otis, Oct. 23, 1745, and July 31, 1746, Otis Family Papers, MHS.

42. Ann Maylem to James Otis, Aug. 8, 1746, Sept. 6, 1746, Sept. 8, 1746 [two letters], and Sept. 9, 1746, Otis Family Papers, MHS.

43. Ann Maylem to James Otis, July 31, 1746, Otis Family Papers, MHS.

44. Ann Maylem to James Otis, Aug. 8, 1746 ("the case," "greatest Disadvantages"), Sept. 6, 1746 ("speedy comming"), Sept. 8, 1746 ("in grat hast," "unesy distres"), Sept. 8, 1746 ("I cannot tack"), and Sept. 9, 1746, Otis Family Papers, MHS. Maylem wrote two letters to Otis on September 8.

45. Ann Maylem to James Otis, Oct. 23, 1745, Aug. 8, 1746, Sept. 6, 1746 ("went into court," "my life"), Sept. 8, 1746, and Sept. 9, 1746, Otis Family Papers, MHS.

46. Maylem, *Short Narrative*.

47. Petition of Ann Maylem (Aug. 20, 1744), Suffolk Files, 169,641, MSA; Petition of Ann Maylem (Sept. 1744), RI Petitions, vol. 6, 13, RISA; Petition of Ann Maylem (Aug. 1748), vol. 6, 149, RISA.

48. Maylem, *Short Narrative*; *Maylem v. Diman*, Newport CCP, Nov. 1744, #198, RIJRC; *Maylem v. Gardner*, listed in Docket Book, Newport CCP, Nov. 1743, RIJRC; *Maylem v. Gardner*, Newport CCP, May 1744, #207, RIJRC; *Maylem v. Gardner*, Newport CCP, Nov. 1745, #1, RIJRC; Petition of Ann Maylem (Sept. 1744), RI Petitions, vol. 6, 13, RISA; Petition of Ann Maylem (Aug. 1748), RI Petitions, vol. 6, 149, RISA; Petitions of Ann Maylem (Aug. 20, 1744, and February 1745), Suffolk Files, 169,641, MSA; Town Council Minutes, Feb. 6, 1743, Newport TC, vol. 9, 14, NHS.

49. On petitions as sources for historical research, see especially Natalie Zemon Davis, *Fiction in the Archives: Pardon Tales and Their Tellers in Sixteenth-Century France* (Stanford, CA: Stanford University Press, 1987); Lex Heerma van Voss, ed., *Petitions in Social History* (Cambridge: Press Syndicate of the University of Cambridge, 2002).

50. This percentage is based on all extant petitions for re-hearings of debt cases that were submitted the Rhode Island ($N = 386$) and Massachusetts ($N = 134$) legislatures between 1730 and 1776. Rhode Island petitions are extant for this entire period, while those for Massachusetts are only extant for 1730–1757. For Rhode Island petitions, see RI Petitions, vols. 2–16 and 25.2, RISA. For Massachusetts petitions, see MA Archives, vols. 17–19B, 41–44, 105, 303, MSA.

51. This figure is based on all extant petitions for re-hearings of debt cases that were submitted the Rhode Island ($N = 386$) and Massachusetts ($N = 134$) legislatures between 1730 and 1776. Rhode Island petitions are extant for this entire period, while those for Massachusetts are only extant for 1730–1757.

52. Petition of Susannah Hood and Answer of James Allen (1748), MA Archives, vol. 42, 647–53, MSA; Petition of Elizabeth Tiffany (1748), RI Petitions, vol. 7, 8, RISA.

53. Mary Sarah Bilder, "The Origin of the Appeal in America," *Hastings Law Journal* 48 (July 1997): 913–68; Blackstone, *Commentaries*, vol. 3, 317, 382–391, 422–23.

54. Petition of Peter Luce ("no laches") (1740), MA Archives, vol. 303, 24, MSA; Answer of Samuel Lamphear ("take advantage") (1755), MA Archives, vol. 44, 193, MSA; Answer of Bartholomew Cheever ("laches and faults") (1749), MA Archives, vol. 18, 402, MSA.

55. Answer of Benjamin Trott to Petition of Jacob Sheafe (1739), MA Archives, vol. 41, 267, MSA.

56. Petition of Silas Tallman (Aug. 18, 1746), RI Petitions, vol. 5, 113, RISA; Petition of Bethiah Hedge (Feb. 19, 1738), RI Petitions, vol. 3, 136, RISA.

57. Petition of Deborah Johnson (1743), RI Petitions, vol. 5, 47, RISA.

58. Petition of Mary Carr ("neglected") (June 1742), RI Petitions, vol. 4, 150, RISA; Petition of Ann Carr ("neglected") (May 1750), RI Petitions, vol. 7, 129, RISA; Petition of Mary Whipple ("mistook") (Aug. 1785), RI Petitions, vol. 22, 46, RISA; Petition of Susannah Waldo ("obliged") (Nov. 21, 1742), MA Archives, vol. 18, 84, MSA; Petition of Patience Spencer ("sick") (Oct. 1747), RI Petitions, vol. 6, 132, RISA; Petition of Martha Hart ("difficulty of the season") (June 1750), RI Petitions, vol. 7, 164, RISA; Petition of Martha Hart ("distance") (Aug. 1748), RI Petitions, vol. 7, 16, RISA.

59. Petition of Samuel Boone ("weather") (1768), RI Petitions, vol. 13, 69, RISA; Petition of Ebenezer How ("sick," "could not possibly") (1742), MA Archives, vol. 42, 115, MSA; Petition of Peter Wanton ("out of the government") (Aug. 1758), RI Petitions, vol. 10, 67, RISA; Petition of William Coles ("same day") (Apr. 1751), MA Archives, vol. 43, 297, MSA; Petition of Joseph Green and Nicholas Boylston ("oversight") (Sept. 1756), MA

Archives, vol. 44, 306, MSA; Petition of John Sullivan ("multiplicity") (1750), MA Archives, vol. 42, 241, MSA.

60. Petition of Mary Carr (June 1742), RI Petitions, vol. 4, 150, RISA; Petition of John Congdon (Oct. 1762), RI Petitions, vol. 11, 61, RISA.

61. Petition of Susannah Waldo and Answer of Samuel Waldo (1742), MA Archives, vol. 41, 267, MSA.

62. For petitions drafted by the same lawyers who had neglected their clients' cases, see Petition of Jane Stevens (1743), MA Archives, vol. 42, 245, MSA; Petition of William Coles (1751), MA Archives, vol. 43, 297, MSA; Petition of Isaac Polock (1745), RI Petitions, vol. 6, 58, RISA; Petition of Isaac Hobhouse (1743), MA Archives, vol. 42, 204, MSA; Petition of Joseph Green and Nicholas Boylston (1756), MA Archives, vol. 44, 306, MSA.

63. Petition of John Bannister (June 1747), RI Petitions, vol. 6, 142, RISA.

64. Petition of James Mumford (June 1768), RI Petitions, vol. 13, 33, RISA.

65. Petition of Samuel Gardiner ("urgent business") (June 1767), RI Petitions, vol. 12, 94, RISA; Petition of Edward Slocum ("fishing") (Feb. 1756), RI Petitions, vol. 9, 59, RISA; Petition of Nathaniel Richardson ("service") (June 1749), MA Archives, vol. 42, 840, MSA; Petition of Andrew Hall Jr. ("sea") (Apr. 1750), MA Archives, vol. 43, 161, MSA. For additional references to men's "business," see Petition of Isaac Hobhouse (Apr. 1743), MA Archives, vol. 42, 204, MSA; Petition of Robert Crook (Feb. 1759), RI Petitions, vol. 10, 63, RISA; Petition of Benjamin Belknap (Oct. 1765), RI Petitions, vol. 11.2, 158, RISA; Petition of John Bannister (June 1769), RI Petitions, vol. 13.2, 148, RISA.

66. Petition of Jane Stevens ("obliged") (May 1743), MA Archives, vol. 42, 247, MSA; Petition of Sarah Harris ("bound") (Mar. 1756), RI Petitions, vol. 9.2, 2, RISA.

67. Petition of Jane Stevens (May 1743), MA Archives, vol. 42, 247, MSA; Petition of Sarah Harris (Mar. 1756), RI Petitions, vol. 9.2, 2, RISA.

68. Petition of Lydia Manchester (Oct. 1769), RI Petitions, vol. 13.2, 166, RISA. See also Petitions of Ann Carr (Feb. 1749 and May 1750), RI Petitions, vol. 7, 129, RISA; Petition of Sarah Hopkins (May 1746), RI Petitions, vol. 5, 103, RISA.

69. Petition of Lydia Manchester (Oct. 1769), RI Petitions, vol. 13.2, 166, RISA; Petition of Jane Stevens (May 1743), MA Archives, vol. 42, 247, MSA.

70. For men settling with creditors prior to departing, see Petition of Sarah Harris (Mar. 1756), RI Petitions, vol. 9.2, 2, RISA; Petition of Jeremiah Hawkins (Oct. 1761), RI Petitions, vol. 10, 166, RISA; Petition of Samuel Gardiner (June 1767), RI Petitions, vol. 12, 94, RISA. For men's hiring of attorneys prior to departing, see Petition of Jane Stevens (May 1743), MA Archives, vol. 42, 247, MSA; Petition of Josiah Hatch (June 1743), MA Archives, vol. 42, 269, MSA; Petition of Andrew Hall Jr. (Apr. 1750), MA Archives, vol. 43, 161, MSA.

71. Petition of Hope Brown and Joseph Brown ("appeared") (1743), RI Petitions, vol. 5, 35, RISA; Petition of Darius Sessions ("discovered") (1767), RI Petitions, vol. 12, 110, RISA. On witnesses' absences from court, see also Petition of Isaac Eveleth (1742), MA Archives, vol. 42, 136, MSA; Petition of Sarah Hopkins (1746), RI Petitions, vol. 5, 103, RISA; Petition of Samuel Belknap (1750), MA Archives, vol. 43, 285, MSA; Petition of Ebenezer Crossman (1769), RI petitions, vol. 13, 86, RISA. On evidence omitted from case files, see also Petition of Harrison Gray (1743), MA Archives, vol. 42, 272, MSA; Petition of Benjamin Tripp and John Martin (1763), RI Petitions, vol. 11, 109, RISA;

Petition of Sarah Crossing (1780), RI Petitions, vol. 18, 43, RISA. On new witnesses, see also Petition of Hope Brown et al. (1742), RI Petitions, vol. 5, 15, RISA; Petition of Elisha Greene (1771), RI Petitions, vol. 14, 97, RISA. On new evidence, see also Petition of Martin Blake (1747), RI Petitions, vol. 5, 132, RISA; Petition of Joseph Abbe (1755), MA Archives, vol. 44, 140, MSA; Petition of Margaret Gifford (1765), RI Petitions, vol. 11.2, 115, RISA; Petition of Hayward Smith and James Sabin (1768), RI Petitions, vol. 13, 107, RISA; Petition of Lydia Manchester (1769), RI Petitions, vol. 13.2, 166, RISA.

72. Petition of Samuel Boone (Aug. 1752), RI Petitions, vol. 8, 94, RISA.

73. Petitions of Martha Hart (Aug. 1748, May 1749, and June 1750 [two petitions]), RI Petitions, vol. 7, 16, 74, 164, RISA.

74. Petition of Sarah Staniford, MA Archives, vol. 19A, 53–55, MSA. John Staniford's estate was declared insolvent in 1754 and some of his possessions were sold at auction. Sarah Staniford's petition in 1753 was probably part of her effort to avoid such proceedings. See "These serve to notify," *Boston Gazette*, Feb. 12, 1754, [3], "To be sold by publick Vendue," *Boston Evening Post*, Apr. 8, 1754, [2].

75. Petitions of Martha Hart (Aug. 1748, May 1749, and June 1750 [two petitions]), RI Petitions, vol. 7, 16, 74, 164, RISA; Petition of Sarah Staniford, MA Archives, vol. 19A, 53–55, MSA. See also Petition of Hannah Norton (1750), RI Petitions, vol. 7, 79, RISA; Petition of Margaret Giffords (1765), RI Petitions, vol. 11.2, 115, RISA.

76. *Battey v. Wanton*, Newport SCJ, Aug. 1754, RIJRC.

77. Petitions of Martha Hart (Aug. 1748, May 1749, and June 1750 [two petitions]), RI Petitions, vol. 7, 16, 74, 164, RISA; Petition of Sarah Staniford, MA Archives, vol. 19A, 53–55, MSA.

78. Of petitions concerning unfamiliarity with the law and on which legislators issued decisions ($N = 33$), 73% were granted. For information on the petitions consulted, see table 5.1.

79. Petitions of Anne Clarke (1755 and 1756), RI Petitions, vol. 9, 76, 173, RISA; Petition of Ann Carr (1750), RI Petitions, vol. 7, 129, RISA; Petition of Hannah Curtis (1754), RI Petitions, vol. 8, 159, RISA. For petitions from the 1780s containing similar language, see Petition of Lydia Durfee (1785), RI Petitions, vol. 22, 34, RISA; Petition of Elizabeth Potter (1788), RI Petitions, vol. 24, 60, RISA.

80. Of those consulted, 33 petitions by men concerned their unfamiliarity with the law. See Petition of Christopher Almy ("ignorant") (1745), RI Petitions, vol. 6, 56, RISA; Petition of Zachariah Matthewson ("not knowing") (1747), RI Petitions, vol. 5, 125, RISA; Petition of William Brown ("so long") (1743), MA Archives, vol. 42, 350, MSA; Petition of George Dunbar ("residing," "stranger") (1730), MA Archives, vol. 41, 94, MSA.

81. Petition of Caleb Gardner ("ignorant mulatto") (1767), RI Petitions, vol. 13.2, 94, RISA; Petition of Robert Binney ("sailor") (1761), RI Petitions, vol. 10, 161, RISA; Petition of Daniel Spencer ("infant") (1757), RI Petitions, vol. 9, 191, RISA.

82. Petition of John Colman (1747), Answer of James Fairservice, and Committee Report, MA Archives, vol. 42, 468, 471, 472, MSA. See also Petition of John Slack and Answer of Thomas Speakman, (1756), MA Archives, vol. 19A, 278, 282, MSA.

83. Petition of Ann Maylem, (Aug. 20, 1744), Suffolk Files, 169,641, MSA.

84. Petition of Ann Maylem (Sept. 1744), RI Petitions, vol. 6, 13, RISA.

85. Petition of Ann Maylem (Feb. 1745), Suffolk Files, 169,641, MSA; Petition of Ann Maylem (Aug. 1748), RI Petitions, vol. 6, 149, RISA.

86. John Maylem's son wrote occasionally about his limited means. See Wroth, "John Maylem," 94, 107. One of Maylem's daughters, Frances, married mariner William Gubbins, whose estate was valued at only £3 when he died. See Maylem Family Bible, NHS, and Inventory of Estate of William Gubbins (Dec. 1766), Newport TC, vol. 15, 91, NHS. Another of Maylem's daughters, Mary, turned to retailing as a source of income. See Mary Maylem, "Just Imported," *Newport Mercury*, May 4, 1767, [4].

87. *Maylem v. Eli*, Newport CCP, May 1765, #343, RIJRC; *Low v. Maylem*, Kent CCP, Jan. 1767, #113, RIJRC; Town Council Minutes, June 1743, Newport TC, vol. 10, 3, 6, NHS; Town Council Minutes, July 1766, Newport TC, vol. 15, 37, NHS.

88. *Maylem v. Low*, Newport CCP, May 1765, #197, RIJRC; Petition of Hooker Low (1768), RI Petitions, vol. 13, 80, RISA.

Chapter 6 · Redefining Financial Work in the Late Eighteenth Century

1. Gary B. Nash, *The Urban Crucible: Social Change, Political Consciousness, and the Origins of the American Revolution* (Cambridge, MA: Harvard University Press, 1986); Benjamin Carp, *Rebels Rising: Cities and the American Revolution* (New York: Oxford University Press, 2007).

2. Linda K. Kerber, *Women of the Republic: Intellect and Ideology in Revolutionary America* (Chapel Hill: University of North Carolina Press, 1980); Mary Beth Norton, *Liberty's Daughters: The Revolutionary Experience of American Women, 1750–1800* (Boston: Little, Brown, 1980); Joan R. Gunderson, *To Be Useful to the World: Women in Revolutionary America, 1740–1790* (New York: Twayne, 1996); Carol Berkin, *Revolutionary Mothers: Women in the Struggle for America's Independence* (New York: Alfred A. Knopf, 2005).

3. Kerber, *Women of the Republic*; Norton, *Liberty's Daughters*; Jeanne Boydston, *Home and Work: Housework, Wages, and the Ideology of Labor in the Early Republic* (Oxford, UK: Oxford University Press, 1990); Rosemarie Zagarri, *Revolutionary Backlash: Women and Politics in the Early American Republic* (Philadelphia: University of Pennsylvania Press, 2007); Ellen Hartigan-O'Connor, *The Ties that Buy: Women and Commerce in Revolutionary America* (Philadelphia: University of Pennsylvania Press, 2009), 181–83, 188–91. The literature on the republican court, however, counters that some elite women maintained robust civic roles as they facilitated political and social alliances during the Early Republic. See Catherine Allgor, *Parlor Politics: In Which the Ladies of Washington Help Build a City and a Government* (Charlottesville: University Press of Virginia, 2000); Susan Branson, *These Fiery Frenchified Dames: Women and Political Culture in Early National Philadelphia* (Philadelphia: University of Pennsylvania Press, 2001); "Re-reintroducing the Republican Court," Forum, *Journal of the Early Republic* 35, no. 2 (Summer 2015): 165–301.

4. For the argument that elite women withdrew from finance and law, see Mary Beth Norton, "Eighteenth-Century American Women in Peace and War: The Case of the Loyalists," *WMQ* 33, no. 3 (July 1976): 386–409; Cornelia Hughes Dayton, *Women Before the Bar: Gender, Law, and Society in Connecticut, 1639–1789* (Chapel Hill: University of North Carolina Press, 1995), esp. 102–3.

5. Elaine Forman Crane, *A Dependent People: Newport, Rhode Island in the Revolutionary Era* (New York: Fordham University Press, 1985); Nash, *Urban Crucible*; Carp, *Rebels Rising*; Donald F. Johnson, "Occupied America: Everyday Experience and the Failure of Imperial Authority in Revolutionary Cities under British Rule, 1775–1783" (PhD diss., Northwestern University, 2015).

6. On the dispersal of families, see especially Sarah M. S. Pearsall, *Atlantic Families: Lives and Letters in the Later Eighteenth Century* (Oxford, UK: Oxford University Press, 2008); Maya Jasanoff, *Liberty's Exiles: American Loyalists in the Revolutionary World* (New York: Alfred A. Knopf, 2011). For overviews of women's experiences during the imperial crisis and Revolution, see Berkin, *Revolutionary Mothers*; Alfred F. Young, *Liberty Tree: Ordinary People and the Making of the American Revolution* (New York: New York University Press, 2005), 100–143; Kerber, *Women of the Republic*; Norton, *Liberty's Daughters*.

7. Allan Kulikoff, "The Progress of Inequality in Revolutionary Boston," *WMQ*, vol. 38, no. 3 (July 1971): 393; Catherine A. Brekus, *Sarah Osborn's World: The Rise of Evangelical Christianity in Early America* (New Haven, CT: Yale University Press, 2013), 293, 295.

8. Brekus, *Sarah Osborn's World*, 306.

9. Johnson, "Occupied America"; Donald F. Johnson, "Ambiguous Allegiances: Urban Loyalties during the American Revolution," *Journal of American History* 104, no. 3 (Dec. 2017): 610–31; Serena R. Zabin, *The Boston Massacre: A Family History* (New York: Houghton Mifflin Harcourt, 2020). For comparisons with a southern port, see Lauren Duval, "Mastering Charleston: Property and Patriarchy in British-Occupied Charleston," *WMQ*, vol. 75, no. 4 (Oct. 2018): 589–622.

10. Brekus, *Sarah Osborn's World*, 294, 297, 334.

11. Jill Lepore, *The Book of Ages: The Life and Opinions of Jane Franklin* (New York: Alfred A. Knopf, 2013), 145–47; Jane Franklin Mecom to Benjamin Franklin, Dec. 1, 1767, American Philosophical Society, Philadelphia, as quoted in Lepore, *Book of Ages*, 146.

12. In 1776, the Cuming sisters relocated to Halifax, Nova Scotia, where they continued their business. See "A List of the Names," *Boston Gazette*, Dec. 11, 1769, [2]; Young, *Liberty Tree*, 115–16; Patricia Cleary, *Elizabeth Murray: A Woman's Pursuit of Independence in Eighteenth-Century America* (Amherst: University of Massachusetts Press, 2000), 132–44, 188–92, 194–95.

13. Jane Mecom was later among those who permanently fled Boston in April 1775, following the battles of Lexington and Concord. See Lepore, *Book of Ages*, 152, 169–72. On urban women providing food and lodging to British soldiers, see Johnson, "Occupied America," 84. On female entrepreneurs during the imperial crisis and Revolution, see also Susan Hanket Brandt, "Marketing Medicine: Apothecary Elizabeth Weed's Economic Independence during the American Revolution," in *Women and the American Revolution: Gender, Politics, and the Domestic World*, ed. Barbara B. Oberg (Charlottesville: University of Virginia Press, 2019), 60–79; Kaylan M Stevenson, "'Until Liberty of Importation is Allowed': Milliners and Mantuamakers in the Chesapeake on the Eve of Revolution," in *Women and the American Revolution*, ed. Oberg, 39–59; Susan Brandt, "'Getting into a Little Business': Margaret Hill Morris and Women's Medical Entrepreneurship during the American Revolution," *Early American Studies* 13, no. 4 (Fall 2015): 774–807; Hartigan-O'Connor, *Ties that Buy*, 56, 179.

14. Mary Gould Almy, "Journal of the Siege of Rhode Island," Aug. 8, 1778, and Aug. 12, 1778, in Elizabeth Evans, ed., *Weathering the Storm: Women of the American Revolution* (New York: Scribner's, 1975), 257, 259.

15. John Gorham Palfrey, "Life of William Palfrey: Paymaster-General in the Army of the Revolution," in *Library of American Biography*, vol. 7, conducted by Jared Sparks

(New York: Harper & Brothers, 1848): 335–448. For a fuller discussion of husband-wife collaborations during the Revolution, see Sara T. Damiano, "Writing Women's History through the Revolution: Family Finances, Letter-Writing, and Conceptions of Marriage," *WMQ* vol. 74, no. 4 (Oct. 2017): 697–728. See also Norton, *Liberty's Daughters*, 198–227.

16. For purchases of provisions by Susannah Palfrey, see "Col. Palfrey to Jabez Rice," account, Sept. 22, 1778, to Mar. 13, 1779, Palfrey Family Papers, MS Am1704.18, Houghton. On Susannah's activities as an intermediary who collected debts, see William Palfrey to Susannah Palfrey, Sept. 23 and Sept. 29, 1779, Palfrey Family Papers, MS Am1704.4, Houghton. On privateering investments, see William Palfrey to Susannah Palfrey, May 23, June 20, July 18, Aug. 15, and Aug. 18, 1780, Palfrey Family Papers, MS Am1704.4, Houghton; Martin Brimmer to William Palfrey, May 4, 1780, Palfrey Family Papers, MS Am1704.3, Houghton; John Livingston to Susannah Palfrey, receipt, May 15, 1780, Palfrey Family Papers, MS Am1704.18, Houghton; William Palfrey to Martin Brimmer, May 23, 1780, and William Palfrey to John Rand, June 12, 1780, William Palfrey Letter Book, Palfrey Family Papers, MS Am1704.18, Houghton; John Livingston to Mrs. Palfrey, n.d., Palfrey Family Papers, MS Am1704.18, Houghton.

17. William Palfrey to Susannah Palfrey, Aug. 8, 1780, and Sept. 10, 1780, Palfrey Family Papers, MS Am1704.4, Houghton.

18. William Palfrey to Susannah Palfrey, n.d. [1776?], Apr. 4, 1776 ("send"), and June 1, 1779, Palfrey Family Papers, MS Am1704.4, Houghton. For an additional discussion of wives' handling documents during their husbands' absences, see Damiano, "Writing Women's History," 713–15.

19. Erwin C. Surrency, "The Lawyer and the Revolution," *American Journal of Legal History* 8, no. 2 (Apr. 1964): 127–33; Charles Robert McKirdy, "Lawyers in Crisis: The Massachusetts Legal Profession, 1760–1790" (PhD diss., Northwestern University, 1969), 52–71. For laypeople waiting to finalize a legal contract, because doing so would require using stamped paper, see *Palmer v. Brownell*, Newport CCP, May 1766, #346, RIJRC. On closures of Virginia's county courts during the Stamp Act, see A. G. Roeber, *Faithful Magistrates and Republican Lawyers: The Creation of Virginia Legal Culture, 1680–1810* (Chapel Hill: University of North Carolina Press, 1981), 161.

20. Record Books, Suffolk CCP, 1774–1780, MSA; Record Books, Newport CCP, 1777–1780, RIJRC.

21. Dudley Colman to Mary Colman, June 12, 1776, Dudley Colman Papers, 1771–1849, box 1, fol. 2, [2], MHS.

22. Abigail Adams to John Adams, July 16, 1775, Adams Family Papers [electronic edition], MHS; Sally Paine to Robert Treat Paine, Jan. 21, 1776, *Papers of Robert Treat Paine*, vol. 3, 132.

23. William B. Norton, "Paper Currency in Massachusetts during the Revolution," *New England Quarterly* 7, no. 1 (Mar. 1934): 43–69; Ralph Harlow, "Economic Conditions in Massachusetts during the American Revolution," *Publications of the Colonial Society of Massachusetts* 20 (1917): 166–67; Oscar Handlin and Mary F. Handlin, "Revolutionary Economic Policy in Massachusetts," *WMQ* 4, no. 1 (Jan. 1947): 7–8; James Henretta, "The War for Independence and American Economic Development," in *The Economy of Early America: The Revolutionary Period, 1763–1790*, ed. Ronald Hoffman, John McCusker, Russell Menard, and Peter J. Albert (Charlottesville: University Press of Virginia, 1988), 79;

Margaret Ellen Newell, *From Dependency to Independence: Economic Revolution in Colonial New England* (Ithaca, NY: Cornell University Press, 1998), 308–11.

24. Woody Holton, "Abigail Adams, Bond Speculator," *WMQ* 64, no. 4 (Oct. 2007): 821–38.

25. Statement of Rebecca Baldwin, *Cleuley v. Baldwin*, Suffolk CCP, Apr. 1786, #C80, MSA. On similar complications within Philadelphia voluntary associations that doubled as lending agencies, see Jessica C. Roney, *Governed by a Spirit of Opposition: The Origins of American Political Practice in Colonial Philadelphia* (Baltimore: Johns Hopkins University Press, 2014), 120–21.

26. Sally Cobb Paine to Robert Treat Paine, Nov. 3, 1776, *Papers of Robert Treat Paine*, vol. 3, 315; Dudley Colman to Mary Colman, May 22, 1776, and Aug. 1, 1777, Dudley Colman Papers, MHS. See also Abigail Adams to John Adams, June 8, 1779, Adams Family Papers, [1], MHS; William Palfrey to Susannah Palfrey, Aug. 1, 1780, Aug 8, 1780, Aug. 26, 1780, Sept. 10, 1780, and Sept. 26, 1780, Palfrey Family Papers, MS Am1704.4, Houghton.

27. Mark Peterson, *The City-State of Boston: The Rise and Fall of an Atlantic Power, 1630–1865* (Princeton, NJ: Princeton University Press, 2019), 381; Jacqueline Barbara Carr, *After the Siege: A Social History of Boston, 1775–1800* (Boston: Northeastern University Press, 2005), 151; Lynne Withey, *Urban Growth in Colonial Rhode Island: Newport and Providence in the Eighteenth Century* (Albany: State University of New York Press, 1984), 115.

28. For a postwar lawsuit between men in which a debtor argued that his creditor's lawsuit should be dismissed because the transaction occurred beyond the statute of limitations, see *Ferguson v. Clark*, Newport CCP, May 1786, #99, RIJRC.

29. *Mumford v. Banister*, Newport CCP, Nov. 1790, #169, RIJRC; *Miller v. Champlin*, Newport CCP, May 1796, #72, RIJRC. For advertisements for Miller's shop, see "Elizabeth Miller," *Newport Mercury*, Aug. 13, 1792, [4]; "Fresh Raisins," *Newport Mercury*, Sept. 13, 1796, [4].

30. Receipts, July 28, 1789, and Aug. 28, 1789, *Edes v. Lobb*, Suffolk CCP, April 1791, #C41, MSA. For additional examples of women renting property or running boardinghouses, see *Troutbeck v. Parker*, Suffolk CCP, Apr. 1786, #C81, MSA; *Cowley v. Stevenson*, Newport CCP, Nov. 1790, #12, RIJRC.

31. *Baley v. Shaw*, Newport SCJ, Aug. 1791, RIJRC; *Gould v. Banks*, Newport SCJ, 1785, RIJRC; *Flagg v. Franklin*, Newport CCP, May 1786, #41, RIJRC; *Barker v. Durfee*, Newport SC, Mar. 1792 (filed with *Barker v. Durfee*, Newport SC, Aug. 1794), RIJRC; *Cook v. Updike*, Newport CCP, May 1795, #133, RIJRC; *Bannister v. Potter*, Newport CCP, Mar. 1796, RIJRC.

32. Depositions of Elizabeth Dunham and Daniel Watts, *Hoxie v. Clark*, Newport SCJ, Sept. 1784, RIJRC. For an additional example in which a husband and wife ran a boardinghouse and the wife kept the accounts, see *Ballard v. Thurston*, Newport CCP, May 1791, #99, RIJRC. On shipbuilding, see Steven J. J. Pitt, "Building and Outfitting Ships in Colonial Boston," *Early American Studies* 13, no. 4 (Fall 2015): 881–907.

33. For a detailed discussion of these statistics, see the appendix.

34. Petition of Mary Whipple (1785), RI Petitions, vol. 22, 46, RISA. See also Petition of Sarah Crossing (1780), RI Petitions, vol. 18, 43, RISA; Petitions of Lydia Durfee (1785), RI Petitions, vol. 22, 34, 107, RISA; Petition of Elizabeth Porter (1788), RI Petitions, vol. 24, 60, RISA; Petition of Mary Dennison (1789), RI Petitions, vol. 24, 151, RISA.

35. Deposition of Elizabeth Dunham, *Hoxie v. Clark*, Newport SCJ, Sept. 1784, RIJRC.

36. In Suffolk County, women composed 7% of the witnesses who signed bonds and promissory notes, and 8% of those who testified in court. In Newport County, women made up 11% of the witnesses who signed bonds and promissory notes, and 4% of those who testified in court. Suffolk figures are based on samples consisting of all witness signatures present on financial documents submitted to the Court of Common Pleas ($N = 175$) and all witnesses who testified in cases before that body ($N = 12$) during the April terms of 1781, 1786, 1791, and 1796. Newport figures are based on samples consisting of all witness signatures present on financial documents submitted to the Court of Common Pleas ($N = 119$) and all witnesses who testified in cases before that body ($N = 25$) during the May terms of 1781, 1786, 1791, and 1796. Because officials recorded the depositions of witnesses who testified in front of justices of the peace but not those who testified in court, extant depositions provide an incomplete portrait of who served as witnesses. I used depositions, summons, and accounts of court fees to identify male and female witnesses.

37. Boydston, *Home and Work*; Jeanne Boydston, "The Woman Who Wasn't There: Women's Market Labor and the Transition to Capitalism in the United States," *Journal of the Early Republic* 16, no. 2 (Summer 1996): 183–206. Older but still influential works include Mary P. Ryan, *Cradle of the Middle Class: The Family in Oneida County, New York, 1790–1865* (New York: Cambridge University Press, 1981); Nancy F. Cott, *The Bonds of Womanhood: "Woman's Sphere" in New England, 1780–1835* (New Haven, CT: Yale University Press, 1973); Barbara Welter, "The Cult of True Womanhood: 1820–1860," *American Quarterly* 18, no. 2 (Summer 1966): 151–74. For a microhistory of two women who violated these nineteenth-century norms, see Susan Branson, *Dangerous to Know: Women, Crime, and Notoriety in the Early Republic* (Philadelphia: University of Pennsylvania Press, 2008). For a parallel emergence of gendered divisions of labor among Britain's middle class, see Leonore Davidoff and Catherine Hall, *Family Fortunes: Men and Women of the English Middle Class, 1780–1850* (Chicago: University of Chicago Press, 1987).

38. Toby L. Ditz, "Shipwrecked; or, Masculinity Imperiled: Mercantile Representations of Failure and the Gendered Self in Eighteenth-Century Philadelphia," *Journal of American History* 81, no. 1 (June 1994): 51–80; Toby L. Ditz, "Formative Ventures: Eighteenth-Century Commercial Letters and the Articulation of Experience," in *Epistolary Selves: Letters and Letter-Writers, 1600–1945*, ed. Rebecca Earle (Aldershot, UK: Ashgate, 1999), 59–78; Toby L. Ditz, "Secret Selves, Credible Personas: The Problematics of Trust and Public Display in the Writing of Eighteenth-Century Philadelphia Merchants," in *Possible Pasts: Becoming Colonial in Early America*, ed. Robert Blair St. George (Ithaca, NY: Cornell University Press, 2000), 219–43; Pearsall, *Atlantic Families*; Konstantin Dierks, *In My Power: Letter Writing and Communications in Early America* (Philadelphia: University of Pennsylvania Press, 2009); Lindsay O'Neill, *The Opened Letter: Networking in the Early Modern British Atlantic World* (Philadelphia: University of Pennsylvania Press, 2015).

39. Pearsall, *Atlantic Families*; Dierks, *In My Power*. For an earlier period, see Ian K. Steele, *The English Atlantic: An Exploration of Communication and Community* (New York: Oxford University Press, 1986).

40. For useful overviews, see Bruce H. Mann, "The Transformation of Law and Economy in Early America," in *The Cambridge History of Law in America*, vol. 1, *Early America (1580–1815)*, ed. Michael Grossberg and Christopher Tomlins (Cambridge:

Cambridge University Press, 2005), 391–98; Clare Priest, "Law and Commerce, 1580–1815," in *The Cambridge History of Law in America*, vol. 1, ed. Grossberg and Tomlins, 430–45.

41. Gerald W. Gawalt, *The Promise of Power: The Emergence of the Legal Profession in Massachusetts, 1760–1840* (Westport, CT: Greenwood Press, 1979); Martha G. McNamara, *From Tavern to Courthouse: Architecture and Ritual in American Law, 1658–1860* (Baltimore: Johns Hopkins University Press, 2004); D. Kurt Graham, *To Bring Law Home: The Federal Judiciary in Early National Rhode Island* (DeKalb: Northern Illinois University Press, 2010). For a southern law firm's efforts to build its business, see Sally E. Hadden, "DeSaussure and Ford: A Charleston Law Firm of the 1790s," in *Transformations in Legal History: Essays in Honor of Professor Morton J. Horwitz*, ed. Daniel W. Hamilton and Alfred L. Brophy (Cambridge, MA: Harvard Law School, 2009). On early nineteenth-century mercantile elites, see Naomi Lamoreaux, *Insider Lending: Banks, Personal Connections, and Economic Development in Industrial New England* (New York: Cambridge University Press, 1994); Conrad Edick Wright and Katheryn P. Viens, eds., *Entrepreneurs: The Boston Business Community, 1700–1850* (Boston: Northeastern University Press, 1997).

42. On the familiar letter, see Keith Stewart, "Toward Defining an Aesthetic for the Familiar Letter in Eighteenth-Century England," *Prose Studies* 5, no. 2 (1982): 184–89; Ditz, "Formative Ventures"; Eve Tavor Bannet, *Empire of Letters: Letter Manuals and Transatlantic Correspondence, 1688–1820* (Cambridge: Cambridge University Press, 2005), 43; Pearsall, *Atlantic Families*, 56–80. On the complex meanings of "friend," see Ditz, "Shipwrecked," 70. On heterosocial friendships, see also Cassandra A. Good, *Founding Friendships: Friendships between Men and Women in the Early American Republic* (Oxford, UK: Oxford University Press, 2015).

43. On William Fletcher, see George A. Washburne, *Imperial Control of the Administration of Justice in the Thirteen American Colonies, 1684–1776* (New York: Columbia University, 1923), 137. On economic depression and increasing rates of failure, see Nash, *Urban Crucible*; Bruce H. Mann, *Republic of Debtors: Bankruptcy in the Age of American Independence* (Cambridge, MA: Harvard University Press, 2003), 53–61. For a more detailed discussion of William and Elizabeth Fletcher's affairs, see Sara T. Damiano, "Agents at Home: Wives, Lawyers, and Financial Competence in Eighteenth-Century New England Port Cities," *Early American Studies* 13, no. 4 (Fall 2015): 808–35.

44. In the lawsuit, William Fletcher sued William Vassall, another Boston merchant engaged in the Caribbean trade, for repeatedly insulting him before audiences of merchants. The case advanced through Boston's courts and finally reached the British Privy Council in London. In the course of the dispute, Fletcher published a pamphlet to rally support for his cause and repair his reputation. See William Fletcher, *The State of Action Brought by William Fletcher against William Vassall, for Defaming Him: Tried In the Superior Court At Boston, August Term, A.D. 1752 and now Pending by Appeal to His Majesty in Council* (Boston, 1753); Washburne, *Imperial Control*, 134–38; John Tudor, Agreement with William and Elizabeth Fletcher, Mar. 13, 1761, Dana Family Papers, MHS.

45. William Fletcher to Trowbridge, Feb. 16, 1756, Dana Family Papers, MHS. See also William Fletcher to Trowbridge, Feb. 20, 1759, Dana Family Papers, MHS. On economic opportunities in St. Eustatius, see Wim Klooster, *Illicit Riches: Dutch Trade in the Caribbean, 1648–1795* (Leiden, Neth.: KITLV Press, 1998), 95–97; Andrew Jackson O'Shaughnessy, *An Empire Divided: The American Revolution and the British Caribbean* (Philadelphia: University of Pennsylvania Press, 2000), 213–37; Wim Klooster, "Inter-

Imperial Smuggling in the Americas, 1600–1800," in *Soundings in Atlantic History: Latent Structures and Intellectual Currents, 1500–1830*, ed. Bernard Bailyn and Patricia L. Denault (Cambridge, MA: Harvard University Press, 2009), 171–73.

46. William Fletcher, Powers of Attorney, Jan. 6, 1755, and Jan. 10, 1755, Dana Family Papers, MHS; Marylynn Salmon, *Women and the Law of Property in Early America* (Chapel Hill: University of North Carolina Press, 1986), 14–18.

47. Edmund Trowbridge, described by historians as "one of the wealthiest and best-connected lawyers of the pre-Revolutionary era," attended Harvard College and began his legal practice in 1732 as a part of the first generation of the Massachusetts bar. See Sally Hadden and Patricia Minter, "A Legal Tourist Visits Eighteenth-Century Britain: Henry Marchant's Observations on the British Courts, 1771–1772," *Law and History Review* 29, no. 1 (2011): 132. See also Clifford K. Shipton, *Sibley's Harvard Graduates*, vol. 8 (Boston: Massachusetts Historical Society, 1951), 507–20; Charles McKirdy, "Massachusetts Lawyers on the Eve of the American Revolution: The State of the Profession," in *Law in Colonial Massachusetts, 1630–1800*, ed. Daniel R. Coquiellette (Boston: Colonial Society of Massachusetts, 1984), 355. On John Cushing, see L. Kinvin Wroth and Hiller B. Zobel, eds., *Legal Papers of John Adams*, vol. 1 (Cambridge, MA: Belknap Press of Harvard University Press, 1965), xcvii–xcviii.

48. For instance, see William Fletcher to Trowbridge, Feb. 16, 1756, and June 1756, Dana Family Papers, MHS.

49. John Tudor, Receipt to Elizabeth and William Fletcher, June 13, 1757, Dana Family Papers, MHS; John Tudor, Agreements with William and Elizabeth Fletcher, June 13, 1757, and Mar. 13, 1761, Dana Family Papers, MHS.

50. For Edmund Trowbridge's and John Cushing's involvement, see William Fletcher to Trowbridge, Feb. 16, 1756, n.d. [1759?], and June 1, 1760, Dana Family Papers, MHS; William Fletcher to John Cushing, Aug. 1758, William Cushing Papers, MHS. For Elizabeth Fletcher's involvement, see William Fletcher to Trowbridge, Feb. 16, 1756, and June 1, 1760, Dana Family Papers, MHS; William Fletcher to John Tudor, Feb. 22, 1757, Tudor Family Papers, Houghton; William Fletcher to unspecified [John Tudor], June 1, 1760, Dana Family Papers, MHS; John Tudor, Receipt to Elizabeth and William Fletcher, June 13, 1757, Dana Family Papers, MHS; John Tudor, Agreement with William and Elizabeth Fletcher, June 13, 1757, Dana Family Papers, MHS; John Tudor, Agreement with William and Elizabeth Fletcher, Mar. 13, 1761, Dana Family Papers, MHS.

51. Steele, *English Atlantic*, 2; William Fletcher to Trowbridge, Aug. 1755, Mar. 20, 1758, Aug. 22, 1758, June 1760, and Aug. 26, 1760, Dana Family Papers, MHS.

52. William Fletcher to Trowbridge, Aug. 1755, Dana Family Papers, MHS.

53. William Fletcher to Trowbridge, Feb. 16, 1756, Dana Family Papers, MHS; William Fletcher to Trowbridge, June 1756, Dana Family Papers, MHS.

54. William Fletcher to Trowbridge, Aug. 1755 and June 1756, Dana Family Papers, MHS; William Fletcher to John Cushing, Aug. 1758, William Cushing Papers, MHS; Ditz, "Shipwrecked," 58–59.

55. William Fletcher to Trowbridge, Feb. 16, 1756, Dana Family Papers, MHS; Ditz, "Shipwrecked," 71–3. See also Pearsall, *Atlantic Families*, 80–144, 149–78.

56. For Elizabeth Fletcher's first letter from St. Eustatius, see Elizabeth Fletcher to Edmund Trowbridge, Sept. 7, 1764, Dana Family Papers, MHS. The first letter sent from St. Martin is William Fletcher to Edmund Trowbridge, Jan. 22, 1770, Dana Family

Papers, MHS. On sons John and Harry accompanying Elizabeth to the Caribbean, see Elizabeth Fletcher to Edmund Trowbridge, July 22, [1783?], Dana Family Papers, MHS.

57. William Fletcher to Trowbridge, May 25, 1783, Nov. 20, 1783, and Aug. 1, 1784, Dana Family Papers, MHS; William Fletcher to [Trowbridge?], July 6, 1789, Dana Family Papers, MHS; Elizabeth Fletcher to Trowbridge, July 22, [1783?], Dana Family Papers, MHS. Elizabeth Fletcher's apologies for her poor spelling resemble those found in some other women's letters. See Lepore, *Book of Ages*, 103–14.

58. Elizabeth Fletcher to Trowbridge, July 22, [1783?], Dana Family Papers, MHS.

59. Elizabeth Fletcher to Trowbridge, Sept. 7, 1764, and July 22, [1783?], Dana Family Papers, MHS.

60. William Fletcher to Trowbridge, Feb. 16, 1756, and Aug. 1755, Dana Family Papers, MHS.

61. Elizabeth Fletcher to Trowbridge, Sept. 7, 1764, and July 22, [1783?], Dana Family Papers, MHS.

62. Trowbridge to William Fletcher, Sept. 17, 1783, Dana Family Papers, MHS; Edmund Trowbridge to John Fletcher, Oct. 1, 1783, Dana Family Papers, MHS.

63. William Fletcher to Trowbridge, May 25, 1784, Dana Family Papers, MHS; Elizabeth Fletcher to Trowbridge, Sept. 7, 1764, and July 22, [1783?], Dana Family Papers, MHS.

64. For biblical references to God as the protector of widows, see Isaiah 54:4–5 ("[Thou] shalt not remember the reproach of thy widowhood any more. For thy Maker is thine husband") and Psalm 68:5 ("A father of the fatherless, and a judge of the widows, is God in his holy habitation"). Eighteenth-century prescriptive and religious texts routinely referenced this interpretation of the Bible's stance on widowhood. See, for instance, John Edwards, *The Whole Concern of man. Or, what he ought to know and do, in order to eternal salvation* (Boston: S. Kneeland, 1725), 183; "A Letter to a Widow on the Death of Her Husband," in William Bradford, *The Secretary's Guide, or, Young Man's Companion*, 4th ed., (New York: William Bradford, 1729), 113. On understandings of widowhood, see Vivian Bruce Conger, *The Widow's Might: Widowhood and Gender in Early British America* (New York: New York University Press, 2009), 23–42, 116–18; Sandra Cavallo and Lyndan Warner, eds., *Widowhood in Medieval and Early Modern Europe* (New York: Routledge, 2014).

65. Robert Parker to Thomas and Samuel Wharton, Apr. 5, 1768, and Hannah Laycock to Thomas and Samuel Wharton, Apr. 6, 1768, Wharton Family Papers, HSP. The Philadelphia merchants first enlisted Henry Marchant in person, then continued their collaboration through letters. See Henry Marchant to Thomas Wharton and William Pollard, May 16, 1769, Henry Marchant Letter Book, 1769–1772, 9–11, Henry Marchant Papers, RIHS. On affluent women in eighteenth-century Britain, see Amanda Vickery, *The Gentleman's Daughter: Women's Lives in Georgian England* (New Haven, CT: Yale University Press, 1998).

66. Hadden and Minter, "Legal Tourist," 137–39.

67. Robert Parker to Thomas and Samuel Wharton, Apr. 5, 1768, and Hannah Laycock to Thomas and Samuel Wharton, Apr. 6, 1768, Wharton Family Papers, HSP.

68. Hannah Laycock to Thomas and Samuel Wharton and William Pollard, Oct. 19, 1768, Wharton Family Papers, HSP. See also Hannah Laycock to Thomas Wharton and William Pollard, Jan. 31, 1769, June 3, 1769, July 5, 1769, Sept. 6, 1769, and Feb. 7, 1770, Wharton Family Papers, HSP.

69. Hannah Laycock to Thomas and Samuel Wharton and William Pollard ("deprive"), Jan. 1, 1769, Hannah Laycock to Thomas Wharton and William Pollard, Jan. 4, 1778 ("perplexing"), and July 4, 1769 ("altogether incapable"), Wharton Family Papers, HSP. See also Hannah Laycock to Thomas Wharton and William Pollard, July 5, 1769, and Sept. 6, 1769, Wharton Family Papers, HSP.

70. Hannah Laycock to Thomas Wharton, Feb. 24, 1775, Wharton Family Papers, HSP. See also Hannah Laycock to Thomas and Samuel Wharton, Apr. 6, 1768, Wharton Family Papers, HSP.

71. Hannah Laycock noted in one her letters that she was "near 70" and wished in her advanced age to "have a few moments respitt from the cares of a fluctuating world." See Hannah Laycock to Thomas Wharton, Jan. 4, 1773, Wharton Family Papers, HSP.

72. William Pollard to Thomas Wharton, Apr. 1, 1769, Wharton Family Papers, HSP; Henry Marchant to Thomas Wharton and William Pollard, Oct. 23, 1769, Henry Marchant Letter Book, 1769–1772, 52, Henry Marchant Papers, RIHS.

73. Henry Marchant to Thomas Wharton and William Pollard, Jan. 8, 1771, Henry Marchant Letter Book, 1769–1772, 190, Henry Marchant Papers, RIHS. See also Henry Marchant to Thomas Wharton and William Pollard, June 8, 1770, Henry Marchant Letter Book, 1769–1772, 106, Henry Marchant Papers, RIHS; Henry Marchant to Thomas Wharton and William Pollard, Apr. 29, 1771, Henry Marchant Letter Book, 1769–1772, 262, Henry Marchant Papers, RIHS.

74. Ditz, "Shipwrecked."

75. Samuel Allyne Otis to James Otis, Mar. 26, 1772 ("fond"), Otis Family Papers, MHS; Thomas Marshall to James Otis, Feb. 14, 1763 ("trifling"), Otis Family Papers, MHS; Henry Marchant to John Murray, Aug. 7, 1770 ("Providence"), Henry Marchant Letter Book, 1769–1772, 128, Henry Marchant Papers, RIHS. Marchant followed up with Murray and reminded him that the affair was of "much consequence" to the widow. See Henry Marchant to John Murray, Sept. 7, 1770, Henry Marchant Letter Book, 1769–1772, 139, Henry Marchant Papers, RIHS. Male merchants also used similar tactics when urging one another to pay debts to women. For example, see John Hoskins to Russell and Stoley, Dec. 20, 1797, Lowell Family Papers, Houghton. Hoskins remarked that "it is one of the first pleasures of this life to be serviceable and render justice to the unfortunate" and asked Russell and Stoley to pay the "poor widow" so that she "may be enabled speedily to feel the good effects of this small sum to you but large to her."

76. Hannah Laycock to Thomas Wharton and William Pollard, Apr. 3, 1769, Wharton Family Papers, HSP.

77. Hannah Laycock to Thomas Wharton and William Pollard, June 3, 1769, Wharton Family Papers, HSP.

78. For example, see the records and correspondence of Martha Saunders Salisbury, Salisbury Family Papers, AAS. See also Woody Holton, *Abigail Adams: A Life* (New York: Atria Books, 2010); Michael A. Blaakman, "Martha Bradstreet and the 'Epithet of Woman': A Story of Land, Libel, Litigation, and Legitimating 'Unwomanly' Behavior in the Early Republic," *Early American Studies* 13, no. 3 (Summer 2015): 544–85.

79. Martha Stevens, Administration Bond, Sept. 30, 1776, Ebenezer Byles to Martha Stephens, Aug. 31, 1780, and Feb. 14, 1781, and Account of Lands Unsold, Dec. 5, 1785, David Stoddard Greenough Family Papers, MHS.

80. Charles Church Chandler was of roughly similar age and background to Hannah Laycock's attorney, Henry Marchant. Like Marchant, Chandler established his elite pedigree by attending college (at Harvard) and then returning home, where he established himself as a leading lawyer and held a variety of political offices. See Clifford Shipton, *Sibley's Harvard Graduates: Biographical Sketches of Those Who Attended Harvard College*, vol. 15, *1761–1763* (Boston: Massachusetts Historical Society, 1970), 373–74.

81. The extensive correspondence between Martha Stevens and Ebenezer Byles is contained in the David Stoddard Greenough Family Papers, MHS. Occasional references to Byles as "resigning [his] trust" suggest that he may have been acting as the trustee of Stevens's land, but the collection does not contain the legal documents establishing such a trust. See, for instance Martha Stevens to Ebenezer Byles, Jan. 21, 1782, David Stoddard Greenough Family Papers, MHS.

82. Byles to Stevens, Feb. 14, 1781, David Stoddard Greenough Family Papers, MHS. For overviews of post-Revolutionary economic turmoil, see Jonathan M. Chu, "Debt and Taxes: Public Finance and Private Economic Behavior in Postrevolutionary Massachusetts," in *Entrepreneurs: The Boston Business Community*, ed. Wright and Viens, 121–49; Terry Bouton, *Taming Democracy: 'The People,' the Founders, and the Troubled Ending of the American Revolution* (Oxford, UK: Oxford University Press, 2007); Woody Holton, *Unruly Americans and the Origin of the Constitution* (New York: Hill & Wang, 2007).

83. Honor Sachs, *Home Rule: Households, Manhood, and National Expansion on the Eighteenth-Century Kentucky Frontier* (New Haven, CT: Yale University Press, 2015); Toby L. Ditz, "Manhood and the US Republican Empire," in *The Oxford Handbook of American Women's and Gender History*, ed. Ellen Hartigan-O'Connor and Lisa G. Materson (Oxford, UK: Oxford University Press, 2018), 43–70.

84. Byles to Stevens, Feb. 14, 1781 ("many people"), and Mar. 29, 1782 ("continuall trespass"), David Stoddard Greenough Family Papers, MHS. For additional discussion of trespassers, see, for example, Byles to Stevens, Apr. 14, 1779, Apr. 17, 1779, and June 4, 1782, David Stoddard Greenough Family Papers, MHS; Stevens to Byles, Feb. 28, 1782, and Mar. 4, 1784, David Stoddard Greenough Family Papers, MHS.

85. Byles to Stevens, Aug. 31, 1780, David Stoddard Greenough Family Papers, MHS. See also Byles to Stevens, July 5, 1780, David Stoddard Greenough Family Papers, MHS.

86. Byles to Stevens, Dec. 6, 1779, David Stoddard Greenough Family Papers, MHS.

87. Stevens drafted at least some of her letters with assistance from Belcher Noyes, an agent and advisor in Boston. It is reasonable to assume, however, that Stevens, like other literate women who enlisted help with their correspondence, played a significant role in their composition. For evidence of Noyes's role in drafting letters, see Martha Stevens to Ebenezer Byles, Nov. 17, 1780, and Account of Martha Stevens with Belcher Noyes, July 1785, David Stoddard Greenough Family Papers, MHS.

88. For instance, see Stevens to Byles, Aug. 5, 1779, May 7, 1781, Feb. 28, 1782, Apr. 22, 1783, and May 25, 1784, David Stoddard Greenough Family Papers, MHS.

89. For instance, see Byles to Stevens, May 7, 1781, May 27, 1783, and Sept. 13, 1784, David Stoddard Greenough Family Papers, MHS.

90. Stevens to Byles, Apr. 9, 1781 ("judge"), and Stevens to John Worthington, Jan. 15, 1782 ("perhaps"), David Stoddard Greenough Family Papers, MHS.

91. On the language of friendship, see Ditz, "Shipwrecked." On the legal profession, see Gawalt, *Promise of Power*; McNamara, *Tavern to Courthouse*. During the late eighteenth and

early nineteenth centuries, wages and outright compensation also became increasingly common for other white collar and administrative workers, including clerks, overseers, and managers. See Boydston, *Home and Work*, esp. 66–70; Brian P. Luskey, *On the Make: Clerks and the Quest for Capital in Nineteenth-Century America* (New York: New York University Press, 2010).

92. Stevens to Byles, Aug. 31, 1782, and May 25, 1782, David Stoddard Greenough Family Papers, MHS.

93. Account, Ebenezer Byles to Martha Stevens, Sept. 6, 1782, and Byles to Stevens, July 5, 1782 ("friend"), and Apr. 2, 1784 ("thankfully"), David Stoddard Greenough Family Papers, MHS.

94. Stevens to Byles, June 11, 1782 ("many articles"), and Feb. 28, 1782 ("ample"), David Stoddard Greenough Family Papers, MHS.

95. Byles to Stevens, Feb. 19, 1778 ("more capable"), Nov. 4, 1779, Feb. 14, 1781, and Apr. 3, 1781, David Stoddard Greenough Family Papers, MHS.

96. Stevens to Byles, Jan. 21, 1782 ("'will not allow," "think of"), Mar. 3, 1781 ("mention"), and Dec. 24, 1781 ("very dilatory," "scarce thinks"), David Stoddard Greenough Family Papers, MHS. For additional examples of Stevens's complaints about Chandler, see Stevens to Byles, Dec. 1, 1781, Apr. 5, 1782, Dec. 27, 1783, Mar. 4, 1784, and June 20, 1785, David Stoddard Greenough Family Papers, MHS.

97. Stevens to Byles, Mar. 3, 1781, David Stoddard Greenough Family Papers, MHS.

98. For Byles's involvement as late as 1792, see Byles to Increase Sumner, Dec. 29, 1792, David Stoddard Greenough Family Papers, MHS.

99. For instance, see Account, Ebenezer Byles to Martha Stevens, Sept. 6, 1782, David Stoddard Greenough Family Papers, MHS; Byles to Stevens, Mar. 21, 1778, Apr. 1, 1778, Mar. 17, 1779, June 4, 1780, and Feb. 14, 1781, David Stoddard Greenough Family Papers, MHS.

100. Wastebook, Martha Stevens Estate, 1785–1801, David Stoddard Greenough Family Papers, MHS.

101. On the relationship between emerging class divisions and understandings of gender and sex in the Early Republic, see especially Clare A. Lyons, *Sex among the Rabble: An Intimate History of Gender & Power in the Age of Revolution, Philadelphia, 1730–1830* (Chapel Hill: University of North Carolina Press, 2006); Kathleen M. Brown, *Foul Bodies: Cleanliness in Early America* (New Haven, CT: Yale University Press, 2009). On elite women's changing attitudes toward the law, see Dayton, *Women Before the Bar*, esp. 102–3.

102. Boydston, *Home and Work*; Boydston, "Woman Who Wasn't There"; Ruth H. Bloch, "The American Revolution, Wife Beating, and the Emergent Value of Privacy," *Early American Studies* 5, no. 4 (Fall 2007): 223–51; Hartigan-O'Connor, *Ties that Buy*, 181–83, 188–91.

103. Scott Sandage, *Born Losers: A History of Failure in America* (Cambridge, MA: Harvard University Press, 2005); Jane Kamensky, *The Exchange Artist: A Tale of High-Flying Speculation and America's First Banking Collapse* (New York: Viking, 2008); Stephen Mihm, *A Nation of Counterfeiters: Capitalists, Con Men, and the Making of the United States* (Cambridge, MA: Harvard University Press, 2007); Graham, *To Bring Law Home*; Sharon Ann Murphy, *Investing in Life: Insurance in Antebellum America* (Baltimore: Johns Hopkins University Press, 2010); Jessica Lepler, *The Many Panics of 1837: People, Politics, and the Creation of a Transatlantic Financial Crisis* (New York: Cambridge University

Press, 2013); Jonathan Levy, *Freaks of Fortune: The Emerging World of Capitalism and Risk in America* (Cambridge, MA: Harvard University Press, 2012); Hannah Atlee Farber, "Underwritten States: Marine Insurance and the Making of Bodies Politic in America, 1622–1815" (PhD diss., University of California, Berkeley, 2014); Gautham Rao, *National Duties: Customs Houses and the Making of the American State* (Chicago: University of Chicago Press, 2016); Sharon Ann Murphy, *Other People's Money: How Banking Worked in the Early American Republic* (Baltimore: Johns Hopkins University Press, 2017).

104. Lamoreaux, *Insider Lending*, 2; Rachel Tamar Van, "Free Trade and Family Values: Kinship Networks and the Culture of Early American Capitalism" (PhD diss., Columbia University, 2011), 193.

105. Boydston, *Home and Work*; Lamoreaux, *Insider Lending*; Robert E. Wright, "Women and Finance in the Early National U.S.," *Essays in History* [University of Virginia] 42 (2000), http://www.essaysinhistory.com/women-and-finance-in-the-early-national -u-s/; Ellen Hartigan-O'Connor, "The Personal Is Political Economy," *Journal of the Early Republic* 36, no. 2 (Summer 2016): 335–41.

Conclusion

1. Carole Shammas, "Re-Assessing the Married Women's Property Acts," *Journal of Women's History* 6, no. 1 (Spring 1994): 9–30; Nancy F. Cott, *Public Vows: A History of Marriage and the Nation* (Cambridge MA: Harvard University Press, 2000), 52–54; Nancy Marie Robertson and Susan M. Yohn, "Women and Money: The United States," in *Women and Their Money 1700–1950: Essays on Women and Finance*, ed. Anne Laurence, Josephine Maltby, and Janette Rutherford (New York: Routledge, 2009), 218–20. See also Norma Basch, *In the Eyes of the Law: Women, Marriage and Property in Nineteenth-Century New York* (Ithaca, NY: Cornell University Press, 1982); Hendrik Hartog, *Man and Wife in America: A History* (Cambridge, MA: Harvard University Press, 2000).

2. Lois Beachy Underhill, *The Woman Who Ran for President: The Many Lives of Victoria Woodhull* (Bridgehampton, NY: Bridgeworks, 1995), 61–70 (quotation, 63); Susan M. Yohn, "Crippled Capitalists: The Inscription of Economic Dependence and the Challenge of Female Entrepreneurship in Nineteenth-Century America," *Feminist Economics* 12, no. 1-2 (Jan./Apr. 2006): 85–97; Amanda Frisken, *Victoria Woodhull's Sexual Revolution: Political Theater and the Popular Press in Nineteenth-Century America* (Philadelphia: University of Pennsylvania Press, 2004), 1–8.

3. On the Equal Credit Opportunity Act, see especially Louis Hyman, "Ending Discrimination, Legitimating Debt: The Political Economy of Race, Gender, and Credit Access in the 1960s and 1970s," *Enterprise & Society* 12, no. 1 (Mar. 2012): 200–232. On the financial sector, see World Economic Forum, *Gender Gap Global Report: 2017* (Geneva, Switzerland: World Economic Forum, 2017), 33, http://www3.weforum.org/docs/WEF_GGGR_2017.pdf; Marianne Bertrand, Claudia Goldin, and Lawrence F. Katz, "Dynamics of the Gender Gap for Young Professionals in the Corporate and Financial Sectors," *American Economic Journal: Applied Economics* 2, no. 3 (July 2010): 228–55. On women in finance and in entrepreneurship during the late nineteenth and early twentieth centuries, see Yohn, "Crippled Capitalists"; Nancy Marie Robertson, "'The principles of sound banking and financial *noblesse oblige*': Women's Departments in US Banks at the Turn of the Twentieth Century," in *Women and Their Money*, ed. Laurence, Maltby, and Rutherford, 243–53; Susan M. Yohn, "'Men seem to

take delight in cheating women': Legal Challenges Faced by Businesswomen in the United States, 1880–1920," in *Women and Their Money*, ed. Laurence, Maltby, and Rutherford, 226–42. For a synthetic overview, see Angel Kwolek-Folland, *Incorporating Women: A History of Women in the United States* (New York: Palgrave, 2002).

4. On change and continuity in gender history, see especially Judith Bennett, *History Matters: Patriarchy and the Challenge of Feminism* (Philadelphia: University of Pennsylvania Press, 2006), 54–81.

5. On William Blackstone's influence, see Hugh MacGill and R. Newmeyer, "Legal Education and Legal Thought, 1790–1920," in *The Cambridge History of Law in America*, vol. 2, *The Long Nineteenth Century*, ed. Michael Grossberg and Christopher Tomlins (Cambridge: Cambridge University Press, 2008), 68–105; Holly Brewer, "The Transformation of Domestic Law," in *The Cambridge History of Law in America*, vol. 1, *Early America*, ed. Michael Grossberg and Christopher Tomlins (Cambridge: Cambridge University Press, 2008), 288–323; Ellen Holmes Pearson, *Remaking Custom: Law and Identity in the Early Republic* (Charlottesville: University of Virginia Press, 2011).

6. For an overview of such debates, see Mary Beth Norton, *Liberty's Daughters: The Revolutionary Experience of American Women* (Boston: Little, Brown, 1980), xviii.

Primary Sources

Eighteenth-century New Englanders relied heavily on legal institutions to enforce relationships of personal credit and debt. The vast archives generated by the courts and other municipal and provincial bodies therefore offer an invaluable entry point into the region's gendered political economy and its dependence on women's financial and legal labor. Analyzed in the aggregate, legal records shed light on the overall workings of the credit economy and the courts. Individual cases, meanwhile, offer revealing windows into everyday practices that men and women otherwise had little occasion to document.

County-based Courts of Common Pleas possessed original jurisdiction for all civil matters concerning more than forty shillings, and disgruntled litigants could appeal in a county's Superior Court of Judicature. For the colonial period, researchers must consult manuscript and microfilm records of these institutions. (Pre-Revolutionary newspapers reported on only a fraction of civil suits, and jurists did not yet publish law reports.) Records of the upper and lower courts include docket books (listing each case's plaintiffs and defendants) and record books (consisting of paragraph-long case summaries). Case files hold all documents filed with the court during lawsuits, and those for debt cases generally include three documents, at a minimum: the writs summoning defendants to court, the declarations in which plaintiffs stated their complaints, and the financial records documenting the debts at issue. Case files may also contain other highly revelatory items, including answers filed to rebut plaintiffs' claims and witness summonses and depositions. While docket books and record books offer useful entry points for identifying female litigants and tracking lawsuits through the courts, the rich details in case files reward researchers in ways that often cannot be predicted from the content of docket or record book entries. This is particularly the situation when searching for evidence of women's financial and legal activities, since clerks reproduced systems of patriarchy and coverture within dockets and record books by attributing legal actions to male heads of household.

Records for the Newport County Courts exist only in manuscript form and are held at the Rhode Island Supreme Court Judicial Records Center in Pawtucket, Rhode Island. The collection is unusually complete in comparison with other troves of county-based colonial legal sources. Records for the Suffolk County Courts are located at the Massachusetts State Archives in Boston, Massachusetts. Researchers interested in that county's Court of Common Pleas case files must consult the original records, and most other Suffolk court records are on microfilm. The Suffolk Files collection contains Superior Court case files and assorted other legal records. Record books for the Suffolk County Court of Common Pleas are not extant for 1756 through 1776, but the court has constructed an index based on surviving case files. The New England Historic Genealogical Society has made this index available online at americanancestors .org.

A wide range of individuals petitioned the Massachusetts and Rhode Island legislatures. Such petitioners included litigants requesting re-hearings of debt cases, and women desiring dispensations from the strictures of coverture or inheritance law. I consulted the petitions to the Rhode Island General Assembly at the Rhode Island State Archives in Providence, Rhode Island, and the petitions to the Massachusetts General Court, which are held within the Massachusetts Archives Collection at the Massachusetts State Archives. Both the Rhode Island and Massachusetts petitions are available in their original form and on microfilm. The Rhode Island State Archives also houses the records of the colony's Equity Court, which only existed from 1741 to 1744.

Probate records offer snapshots of individuals' estates at the time of death, including any outstanding financial obligations. The manuscript records of colonial Newport's Town Council, which doubled as a probate court, are held at the Newport Historical Society in Rhode Island. The records of the Suffolk County Probate Court are in manuscript form and on microfilm at the Massachusetts State Archives. The Church of Jesus Christ of the Latter-day Saints has also digitized and posted (on familysearch.org) the microfilm editions of many key collections of Massachusetts legal records, including the Suffolk Files, Massachusetts Archives Collection, and Suffolk County Probate Court records.

Most libraries and archives hold collections of family papers, and these documents offer an in-depth look at the financial practices of middling and elite families. Evidence of women's economic activities appears in virtually all of these collections, although it is sometimes omitted from their catalog entries and finding aids. Families' correspondence and financial records capture credit ties, the sharing of financial responsibilities, women's use of credit as laborers and consumers, and, in some instances, their sustained management of businesses. At the Massachusetts Historical Society in Boston, collections containing particularly rich evidence of women's financial activities included the Amory Family

Papers, the Dana Family Papers, the David Stoddard Greenough Family Papers, the James Murray Papers, the James Murray Robbins Family Papers, and the Murray-Robbins Family Papers. Other especially valuable collections included the Green Family Papers and the Salisbury Family Papers at the American Antiquarian Society in Worcester, Massachusetts, and the Palfrey Family Papers at Harvard University's Houghton Library in Cambridge, Massachusetts.

Lawyers' papers, including correspondence with clients and financial records documenting services rendered, allowed me to investigate the evolution of the attorney-client relationship and its gendered dimensions. Archives holding the papers of Massachusetts and Rhode Island attorneys include the American Antiquarian Society (Worcester, MA), Baker Library (Cambridge, MA), Houghton Library (Cambridge, MA), Massachusetts Historical Society (Boston), Newport Historical Society (Newport, RI), and Rhode Island Historical Society (Providence). Manuscript collections that were especially valuable to my research included the Otis Family Papers at the Massachusetts Historical Society, the papers of William Channing and William Ellery at the Newport Historical Society, and the Henry Marchant Papers at the Rhode Island Historical Society. Published collections of lawyers' papers include *The Papers of Robert Treat Paine*, 5 vols. (University of Virginia Press, 2005–2020), and the diaries, correspondence, and legal papers of John Adams, published through the Adams Papers Editorial Project. In addition to documenting the practices of leading Massachusetts attorneys, these collections contain extensive and valuable material concerning Robert Treat Paine's marriage to Sally Cobb Paine and John Adams's union with Abigail Smith Adams. The Massachusetts Histoical Society has also produced digital editions; these are available online at masshist.org.

Finally, printed materials shed light both on individuals' financial activities and the gendered prescriptions surrounding them. Newspapers—including the *Boston Evening Post, Boston Gazette, Boston Post-Boy, Boston Weekly Newsletter,* and *Newport Mercury*—devoted up to half of every issue to advertisements and notices, and many of these concerned the workings of the credit economy. I also consulted legal treatises, letter-writing manuals, and commercial handbooks to understand the ways in which they both reflected and attempted to standardize gendered financial and legal practices. Such texts circulated widely throughout the British Atlantic world and were readily available in cosmopolitan port cities, including Boston and Newport—that is, places with numerous booksellers and subscription libraries. While many eighteenth-century newspapers and books are available online, I was fortunate to examine many of these texts at the Library Company of Philadelphia, whose extensive holdings facilitate consideration of these sources' paratextual elements and materiality.

Secondary Sources

This book's examination of gendered financial labor in eighteenth-century Boston and Newport bridges the histories of economic culture, law, and gender. Scholarship on the economic development of British North America and the Atlantic World offers a useful starting point. Key overviews include John J. McCusker and Russell R. Menard, *The Economy of British America, 1607–1789* (Chapel Hill: University of North Carolina Press, 1985); Stephen Innes, ed., *Work and Labor in Early America* (Chapel Hill: University of North Carolina Press, 1988); Cathy Matson, ed., *The Economy of Early America: Historical Perspectives and New Directions* (University Park: Pennsylvania State University Press, 2006); and Emma Hart, *Trading Spaces: The Colonial Marketplace and the Foundations of American Capitalism* (Chicago: University of Chicago Press, 2019). Works emphasizing the centrality of merchants to economic development include Thomas Doerflinger, *A Vigorous Spirit of Enterprise: Merchants and Economic Development in Revolutionary Philadelphia* (Chapel Hill: University of North Carolina Press, 1986); David Hancock, *Citizens of the World: London Merchants and the Integration of the British Atlantic Community, 1735–1785* (Cambridge: Cambridge University Press, 1995); and Cathy Matson, *Merchants & Empire: Trading in Colonial New York* (Baltimore: Johns Hopkins University Press, 1998). On changing consumer practices, see especially Richard Bushman, *The Refinement of America: Persons, Houses, Cities* (New York: Knopf, 1992); T. H. Breen, *The Marketplace of Revolution: How Consumer Politics Shaped American Independence* (New York: Oxford University Press, 2004); and Jan de Vries, *The Industrious Revolution: Consumer Behavior and the Household Economy, 1650 to the Present* (Cambridge: Cambridge University Press, 2008).

Colonial New England has long been a vibrant site of scholarly inquiry. Studies investigating the social and economic development of New England include Bernard Bailyn, *New England Merchants in the Seventeenth Century* (Cambridge, MA: Harvard University Press, 1955); Daniel Vickers, *Farmers & Fishermen: Two Centuries of Work in Essex County, Massachusetts, 1630–1850* (Chapel Hill: University of North Carolina Press, 1994); Stephen Innes, *Creating the Commonwealth: The Economic Culture of Puritan New England* (New York: W. W. Norton, 1995); Margaret Ellen Newell, *From Dependency to Independence: Economic Revolution in Colonial New England* (Ithaca, NY: Cornell University Press, 1998); Daniel Vickers, with Vince Walsh, *Young Men and the Sea: Yankee Seafarers in the Age of Sail* (New Haven, CT: Yale University Press, 2005); and Barry Levy, *Town Born: The Political Economy of New England from its Founding to the Revolution* (Philadelphia: University of Pennsylvania Press, 2009). On Boston and Newport, see Elaine Forman Crane, *A Dependent People: Newport, Rhode Island in the Revolutionary Era* (New York: Fordham University Press, 1985); Gary B. Nash, *The Urban Crucible: Social Change, Political Con-*

sciousness, and the Origins of the American Revolution (Cambridge, MA: Harvard University Press, 1979); Benjamin Carp, *Rebels Rising: Cities and the American Revolution* (Oxford, UK: Oxford University Press, 2007); and Mark Peterson, *The City-State of Boston: The Rise and Fall of an Atlantic Power, 1630–1865* (Princeton, NJ: Princeton University Press, 2019).

Increased reliance on credit and debt undergirded the economic development of British North America and spurred a concomitant rise in debt litigation. The key work on these interrelated legal and economic changes in New England remains Bruce Mann, *Neighbors and Strangers: Law and Community in Early Connecticut* (Chapel Hill: University of North Carolina Press, 1987). Parallel transformations occurred in Britain one century earlier, and these are helpfully analyzed by Craig Muldrew, *The Economy of Obligation: The Culture of Credit and Social Relations in Early Modern England* (New York: St. Martin's, 1998). On credit, debt, and litigation in the British Atlantic World, also see Mary M. Schweitzer, *Custom and Contract: Household, Government, and the Economy in Colonial Pennsylvania* (New York: Columbia University Press, 1987); Toby L. Ditz, "Shipwrecked; or, Masculinity Imperiled: Mercantile Representations of Failure and the Gendered Self in Eighteenth-Century Philadelphia," *Journal of American History* 81, no. 1 (June 1994): 51–80; Simon Middleton, "Private Credit in Eighteenth-Century New York City: The Mayor's Court Papers, 1681–1776," *Journal of Early American History* 2, no. 2 (2012): 150–77; Daniel Vickers, "Errors Excepted: The Culture of Credit in Rural New England, 1750–1800," *Economic History Review* 63, no. 4 (Nov. 2010): 1032–57; and Tawny Paul, *The Poverty of Disaster: Debt and Insecurity in Eighteenth-Century Britain* (Cambridge: Cambridge University Press, 2019).

On transformations in New England's legal system and the development of the legal profession, see Gerald W. Gawalt, *The Promise of Power: The Emergence of the Legal Profession in Massachusetts, 1760–1840* (Westport, CT: Greenwood Press, 1979); John M. Murrin, "The Legal Transformation: The Bench and Bar of Eighteenth-Century Massachusetts" in *Colonial America: Essays in Politics and Social Development*, 3rd edition, ed. Stanley N. Katz and John M. Murrin (New York: Alfred A. Knopf, 1983), 540–71; Mary Sarah Bilder, *The Transatlantic Constitution: Colonial Legal Culture and the Empire* (Cambridge, MA: Harvard University Press, 2004); and Martha G. McNamara, *From Tavern to Courthouse: Architecture and Ritual in American Law, 1658–1860* (Baltimore: Johns Hopkins University Press, 2004). The flourishing scholarship on law and society in the nineteenth-century United States also provides a model for earlier periods. See Areila J. Gross, *Double Character: Slavery and Mastery in the Antebellum Southern Courtroom* (Princeton, NJ: Princeton University Press, 2000); Laura F. Edwards, *The People and Their Peace: Legal Culture and the Transformation of Inequality in the Post-Revolutionary South* (Chapel Hill: University of North

Carolina Press, 2009); and Martha Jones, *Birthright Citizens: A History of Race and Rights in Antebellum America* (New York: Cambridge University Press, 2018).

Although conventional histories of legal and economic development often omit women, gender historians have done important work to highlight gendered labor patterns and legal systems. On white women, see especially Laurel Thatcher Ulrich, *Good Wives: Image and Reality in the Lives of Women in Northern New England, 1650–1750* (New York: Alfred A. Knopf, 1982); Marylynn Salmon, *Women and the Law of Property in Early America* (Chapel Hill: University of North Carolina Press, 1986); Jeanne Boydston, *Home and Work: Housework, Wages, and the Ideology of Labor in the Early Republic* (Oxford, UK: Oxford University Press, 1990); Laurel Thatcher Ulrich, *A Midwife's Tale: The Life of Martha Ballard, Based on her Diary, 1785–1812* (New York: Random House, 1990); Mary Beth Norton, *Founding Mothers & Fathers: Gendered Power and the Forming of an American Society* (New York: Alfred A. Knopf, 1996); and Marla R. Miller, *Entangled Lives: Labor, Livelihood, and Landscapes of Change in Rural Massachusetts* (Baltimore: Johns Hopkins University Press, 2019). Works emphasizing the distinctive positions of never-married women, sailors' wives, and widows include Lisa Norling, *Captain Ahab Had a Wife: New England Women and the Whalefishery, 1720–1870* (Chapel Hill: University of North Carolina Press, 2000); Karin Wulf, *Not All Wives: Women of Colonial Philadelphia* (Ithaca, NY: Cornell University Press, 2000); Linda L. Sturtz, *Within Her Power: Propertied Women in Colonial America* (New York: Routledge, 2002); and Vivian Bruce Conger, *The Widow's Might: Widowhood and Gender in Early British America* (New York: New York University Press, 2009).

Recent studies engaged in important intersectional analyses of black women's market activities include Marisa J. Fuentes, *Dispossessed Lives: Enslaved Women, Violence, and the Archive* (Philadelphia: University of Pennsylvania Press, 2016); Justene Hill, "Felonious Transactions: Legal Culture and Business Practices of Slave Economies in South Carolina, 1787–1860," *Enterprise and Society* 18, no. 4 (December 2017): 772–83; Shauna J. Sweeney, "Market Marronage: Fugitive Women and the Internal Marketing System in Jamaica, 1781–1834," *William and Mary Quarterly*, 3rd series, 76, no. 2 (April 2019): 197–222; Erin Trahey, "Among Her Kinswomen: Legacies of Free Women of Color in Jamaica," *William and Mary Quarterly*, 3rd series, 76, no. 2 (April 2019): 257–88; and Jessica Marie Johnson, *Wicked Flesh: Black Women, Intimacy, and Freedom in the Atlantic World* (Philadelphia: University of Pennsylvania Press, 2020).

For scholars of British North America, studies of other Atlantic sites offer fruitful points of comparison and conceptual frameworks. Stressing that households and families constituted early modern businesses and commercial networks, such works argue that women's labor, capital, and connections were essential to the functioning of early modern gendered economies. See Margaret R. Hunt, *The Middling Sort: Commerce, Gender, and the Family in England, 1680–1780* (Berkeley: University of California Press, 1996); Julie Hardwick, *The Practice of Patriarchy: Gender and the Politics of Household Authority in Early Modern France* (Philadelphia: University of Pennsylvania Press, 1998); Jane E. Mangan, *Trading Roles: Gender, Ethnicity, and the Urban Economy in Colonial Potosi* (Durham, NC: Duke University Press, 2005); Julie Hardwick, *Family Business: Litigation and the Political Economies of Daily Life in Early Modern France* (Oxford, UK: Oxford University Press, 2009); Susanah Shaw Romney, *New Netherland Connections: Intimate Networks and Atlantic Ties in Seventeenth-Century America* (Chapel Hill: University of North Carolina Press, 2014); Alexandra Shepard, *Accounting for Oneself: Worth, Status, and the Social Order in Early Modern England* (Oxford, UK: Oxford University Press, 2015); Maria Ågren, ed., *Making a Living, Making a Difference: Gender and Work in Early Modern European Society* (Oxford, UK: Oxford University Press, 2016); and Amy M. Froide, *Silent Partners: Women as Public Investors during Britain's Financial Revolution, 1690–1750* (Oxford, UK: Oxford University Press, 2016).

Finally, this volume builds most directly on studies of women's involvement in the intertwined realms of law and economic life in early America. Such works offered important orientations and remained touchstones throughout my research. For the influential argument that women's economic and legal authority diminished between the seventeenth and eighteenth centuries, see Cornelia Hughes Dayton, *Women Before the Bar: Gender, Law, and Society in Connecticut, 1639–1789* (Chapel Hill: University of North Carolina Press, 1995); and Elaine Forman Crane, *Ebb Tide in New England: Women, Seaports, and Social Change, 1630–1800* (Boston: Northeastern University Press, 1998). Works emphasizing women's extensive contributions to eighteenth-century port economies include Patricia Cleary, *Elizabeth Murray: A Woman's Pursuit of Independence in Eighteenth-Century America* (Amherst: University of Massachusetts Press, 2000); Ellen Hartigan-O'Connor, *The Ties that Buy: Women and Commerce in Revolutionary America* (Philadelphia: University of Pennsylvania Press, 2009); and Serena R. Zabin, *Dangerous Economies: Status and Commerce in Imperial New York* (Philadelphia: University of Pennsylvania Press, 2009).

Page numbers followed by *f* indicate a figure; page numbers followed by *t* indicate a table.